THE VIKINGS READER

THE

VIKINGS

REASER

ARMAND PETERSON, EDITOR

University of Minnesota Press
Minneapolis

Previous publication information for material in this book can be found in the Publication History on pages 363–70.

Published by the University of Minnesota Press
111 Third Avenue South, Suite 290
Minneapolis, MN 55401-2520
http://www.upress.umn.edu

Library of Congress Cataloging-in-Publication Data

Peterson, Armand.
    The Vikings reader / Armand Peterson.
        p.   cm.
    Includes bibliographical references.
    ISBN 978-0-8166-5337-9 (hc : alk. paper)—ISBN 978-0-8166-5338-6 (pb : alk. paper)
    1. Minnesota Vikings (Football team)—History. I. Title.
    GV956.M5P48 2009
    796.332'6409776579—dc22

                                                                    2009011106

Design and production by Mighty Media, Inc.
Text design by Chris Long

Printed in the United States of America on acid-free paper

The University of Minnesota is an equal-opportunity educator and employer.

16 15 14 13 12 11 10 09   10 9 8 7 6 5 4 3 2 1

CONTENTS

PREFACE

I WAS LUCKY ENOUGH TO SIT IN THE STANDS FOR THE VIKINGS' FIRST regular-season game at Metropolitan Stadium against the Chicago Bears on September 17, 1961. I watched in awe as the quarterbacks from both teams warmed up, throwing the ball 50 yards with apparent ease, and I was amazed by the speed of the pass receivers and defensive backs. I had seen the West Coast glamour boy, running back Hugh "the King" McElhenny (an expansion draft choice from the San Francisco 49ers), a few times on our grainy black-and-white TV, and I couldn't wait to see him in person. He didn't disappoint me. Neither did the other Vikings castoffs and rookies who surprised the so-called NFL experts by winning three games in that inaugural season . . . compared to the expansion Dallas Cowboys, who did not win a game in their first season in 1960.

Professional football had been a footnote as the movers and shakers of the Twin Cities pursued a Major League Baseball franchise in the 1950s. The Twins and Vikings both debuted in 1961, but the Twins were Minnesota's favorite team throughout most of the 1960s. National polls showed that professional football surpassed baseball as the country's favorite sport in 1965. No polls could be found specifically for Minnesota, but the Vikings finally passed the University of Minnesota football Gophers in attendance in 1967. By 1969, thanks to the colorful "40 for 60" gang, the Vikings were clearly Minnesota's favorite team.

They have remained our favorites in good times and bad—throughout the dominating years of the 1970s, when the Vikings won division titles eight of ten seasons, and in the 1980s, when they won only two division titles but still managed five playoff appearances. The 1990s were turbulent times, filled with controversies on and off the field, but the team continued to win our hearts with three division titles and seven playoff appearances. The first decade of the twenty-first century has so far been bracketed by two division titles, in 2000 and 2008, and Vikings fans dare to hope that the team is poised to make successful playoff runs in the future.

The Vikings have given us much to cheer about during their 48-year history. They rank fifth in winning percentage over this span, trailing only Dallas, Miami, Oakland, and Pittsburgh. The team has won 17 division championships and made the postseason playoffs 25 times. There have been a lot of great memories. Yet when some fans look back they tend to remember only the four Super Bowl losses, or Staubach's Hail Mary pass in 1975, or the conference championship losses in 1987, 1998, and 2000. Sometimes we all forget how fun it was in 1969 when the Vikings dominated opponents on the way to Super Bowl IV, or in 1998 when they set an NFL record for points scored, or in 2007 when rookie running back Adrian Peterson torched the San Diego Chargers for an NFL-record 296 yards rushing. During those wonderful times, the weekend's game dominated our Monday morning conversations around the kitchen table, on Main Street, and in our factories and offices.

The stories in *The Vikings Reader* were compiled to transport us back to the times when the games were played. These are from a range of contemporary sources: newspaper and magazine articles, book excerpts, and a radio transcription. The stories were written as the events unfolded and represent what we were feeling and talking about at the time. You will read about the unforgettable moments in Vikings history but also about the great players, unconventional characters, and rogues whose escapades were documented in our newspapers, magazines, and books. There are features about television blackouts, accidental hot-air balloon ascensions, tailgaters, roller-skating cheerleaders, ownership controversies, and stadium debates . . . in other words, the entire Vikings experience.

Most of the stories are by local writers, and you will enjoy articles by the Vikings' early scribes and beat writers—men like Jim Klobuchar, Dick Gordon, Halsey Hall, Don Riley, Ralph Reeve, Sid Hartman, and Roger Rosenblum, as well as a story by former *Tribune* women's pages editor Barbara Flanagan. Sportswriters in the 1960s and 1970s were not as critical of coaches and players as they are today, and you will notice a definite change in tone as you move through the book, reading stories by current writers such as Patrick Reusse, Jim Souhan, Kevin Seifert, Jay Weiner, Bill Williamson, Bob Sansevere, Tom Powers, and Jeff Seidel.

Perspective has been provided by a selection of stories from national magazines, including *Sports Illustrated*, *Newsweek*, *Pro Football Weekly*, *Sporting News*, and newspapers from around the country. There are stories by Pulitzer Prize–winner Jim Murray and acclaimed writers Wells Twombly, Thomas Gifford, Frank Deford, Mickey Herskowitz, Ted Maule, Dave Kindred, and Peter King.

I wrote material to introduce the articles and provide background information, but I made no attempt to analyze, interpret, alibi, or critique, as is often the case in biographies or retrospective books. *The Vikings Reader* is neither a muckraking exercise nor a shameless whitewash: the stories are left to speak for themselves. I hope reading them captures for you the same thrill I had on that September day in 1961 when I saw my first Vikings game.

The Dutchman and 36 Stiffs

THE BIRTH OF THE VIKINGS

THE DREAM THAT WAS TO BECOME THE MINNESOTA NFL FRANCHISE can trace its origin to a lunch meeting at the venerable Minneapolis Athletic Club in July 1952, for it was there that Charlie Johnson, executive sports editor of the *Minneapolis Star* and *Morning Tribune*, Norm McGrew, promotions coordinator for the Minneapolis Chamber of Commerce, and Jerry Moore, an up-and-coming businessman who was active in the Chamber, agreed to work together to promote the building of a stadium to attract a Major League Baseball franchise. They believed that the rapidly growing and economically powerful Minneapolis–St. Paul metro area deserved more national recognition, but felt it would not come until the cities obtained a major league franchise.

And in 1952 "major league" meant baseball.

The Minneapolis Lakers had just won their fourth professional basketball "World Championship" over the New York Knickerbockers, but the National Basketball Association was considered a minor attraction, with franchises forced to compete with college sports, boxing, circuses, and other exhibitions for dates in their "home" arenas. For example, the first three Lakers home games against the Knicks were played in the St. Paul Auditorium because the Minneapolis Auditorium was booked for the Northwest Sportsmen's Show.

In March 1953 the Minneapolis Chamber of Commerce formed the

Twin Cities Boosters to plan the major league effort. This might have seemed like a pipe dream, since the major leagues had consisted of the same 16 teams, representing only 10 cities, since 1903. However, big changes were coming. The National League's Boston Braves had moved to Milwaukee for the 1953 season and two changes in the American League were approved—in 1954 the St. Louis Browns would move to Baltimore, and in 1955 the Philadelphia Athletics would move to Kansas City.

The common denominator for these three new major league cities was that they had city-financed stadiums ready to go, and in August 1954 the Metropolitan Sports Area Commission was formed. Jerry Moore was named chairman, and shortly a 160-man "Minute Man" organization was formed to sell bonds to build a stadium in Bloomington. In typical fashion, the Twin Cities area could not come up with a coordinated effort. St. Paul passed a referendum to build a competing stadium in the Midway district. The existing baseball fields—Nicollet Park for the Minneapolis Millers and Lexington Park for the St. Paul Saints—were judged inadequate for remodeling. The Millers played their first game at Metropolitan Stadium in Bloomington on April 24, 1956 and the Saints played their first game at Midway Stadium on April 25, 1957.

The Minneapolis interests courted New York Giants owner Horace Stoneham, who at the time owned the Millers, but these hopes were dashed by a blockbuster announcement in May 1957—the Giants were moving to San Francisco and the Brooklyn Dodgers to Los Angeles in 1958. When subsequent efforts to woo the Cleveland Indians or Washington Senators seemed to be coming up empty, Minneapolis became involved in plans for the Continental League, a third major league proposed by New York City lawyer William Shea and New York mayor Robert Wagner, both angered by the loss of the Dodgers and Giants. Respected baseball executive Branch Rickey joined the effort, lending it instant credibility. Minneapolis businessman Wheelock Whitney led the Minnesota effort. Ultimately, the Continental League threat forced Major League Baseball to make expansion plans.

The push for a National Football League team began a little later than the one for baseball, and most of the work was out of the public eye. Pro football was no stranger to Minnesota, as several teams had conducted training camps in the state, and NFL games were televised on CBS's local affiliate, WCCO channel 4. WCCO radio 830 also carried broadcasts of NFL games. The annual Catholic Welfare Charities exhibition games at Parade Stadium in late August or early September regularly drew big crowds. On August 22, 1953, the Green Bay Packers (training in Grand Rapids) defeated the New York Giants (training in St. Peter) 31–7 before a crowd of 20,560.

But in his "Lowdown on Sports" column in the *Minneapolis Sunday Tribune* the following day, Charlie Johnson made no claim that the successful promotion proved the Twin Cities was ready for an NFL franchise. Instead, he used the occasion to discuss the potential salary inflation in the NFL caused by the rise of the Canadian Football League, and then in the second half of the column switched gears to talk about Major League Baseball expansion. Baseball was obviously foremost in his mind.

University of Minnesota Golden Gopher football ruled Minnesota sports in the 1950s. The team had an average attendance of 57,533 at Memorial Stadium in the decade. A whopping 64,629 attended a game against Purdue in 1957. The *Minneapolis Tribune*'s Peach Sports Section—printed, appropriately, on peach-colored paper—had been a fall staple for many years, and featured daily stories about Gophers football. Three or four reporters covered most home games and one or two were often sent to cover other important Big Ten games. People all over the state leaned over radios on Saturday afternoons to listen to broadcasts of Gophers games.

When asked to identify the national pastime, however, most Minnesotans would have answered, "baseball." A comparison between local newspaper coverage of the 1958 World Series and the 1958 National Football League championship game demonstrates the relative standing of the two sports at the time. The Baltimore Colts–New York Giants overtime game on December 28, 1958, has acquired mythic status. At the time, a cover story by *Sports Illustrated* writer Tex Maule called it "The Best Football Game Ever Played." Today there is practically a cottage publishing industry devoted to books about the game. Watched by a television audience of 45 million—a record at the time for football—the game has been credited with launching the modern NFL.

None of the St. Paul or Minneapolis daily newspapers sent reporters to the game, however. The *Minneapolis Tribune* had two sports writers on travel to cover college football games—Dick Cullum in California to cover the East–West Shrine Game and the Rose Bowl, and Sid Hartman in Florida to cover the North–South Game and the Orange Bowl. *St. Paul Pioneer Press* executive sports editor George Edmond was in Pasadena to cover the Rose Bowl. Game reports for the Colts–Giants game were from Associated Press wires. The *Tribune* and *Pioneer Press* printed short page-one stories about the Colts–Giants game. The small *Pioneer Press* one-column story—below the fold, in newspaper parlance—was trumped by a two-column UPI story from West Covina, California, three columns to the left, "Driver Gets 54 Tags After 4-Mile Chase."

Contrast that to coverage of the World Series that year, pitting the Milwaukee Braves against the New York Yankees in a rematch of the 1957

Series, won by the Braves. Small dailies all over the state, which had carried short wire stories of the Colts–Giants game, but no front page stories, printed almost daily stories about the Series on their front pages, with continuation and other stories in the sports sections. The top left story of the October 1 front page of the *Fergus Falls Daily Journal*, for example, read "Clear, Cool Day for Opening of Series," and contained the starting lineups and batting averages for game one of the Series in Milwaukee. On October 9, printed the day game seven was played, the *New Ulm Daily Journal* carried a full-page banner headline above the newspaper logo on page one, "Worried Milwaukee Calls on Burdette."

The Twin Cities dailies had extensive World Series coverage as well. The *Minneapolis Tribune* sent Sid Hartman to Milwaukee for the first two games of the Series, and Tom Briere to the last two games there. *St. Paul Pioneer Press* sports editor Joe Hennessy also reported the first two games from Milwaukee, and the *Press* and evening *St. Paul Dispatch* carried stories throughout the Series by Pulitzer Prize–winner Red Smith and noted United Press International sportswriter Oscar Fraley, author of 31 books, including *The Untouchables*. On most days you could find a story or photo from the Series on the front pages, with multiple stories and photos in the sports sections. For games in New York that finished before the late edition print deadlines, the *Dispatch* carried a line score on page one, complete with play-by-play summaries for the whole game.

Thus, it is not difficult to understand why the movers and shakers originally looked to baseball in their quest to lift the Twin Cities up to major league status. In later years, Max Winter, a Minneapolis businessman who owned the 620 Club restaurant, promoted various entertainment acts as well as some tours for the Harlem Globetrotters, and was general manger and part owner of the Minneapolis Lakers, said he became interested in NFL football after seeing a game in Chicago in 1955. Three years later, no longer involved with the Lakers, he formed Minnesota Sports, Inc., with E. W. Boyer, H. P. Skoglund, and Ole Haugsrud to pursue an NFL franchise.

Haugsrud had owned an NFL team, the Duluth Eskimos, from 1925 to 1929. The league was just in its infancy, with irregular schedules and frequent franchise collapses. Haugsrud made a splash in 1926 when he signed Stanford All American Ernie Nevers, a Willow River, Minnesota, native who had attended Superior Central High School. The team was billed as "Ernie Nevers' Eskimos," and played 28 of its 29 games on the road all across the country. The Eskimos were 6–5–2 in league games to finish in eighth place among 22 NFL teams. The team was idle in 1928 and Haugsrud sold the team to Orange, New Jersey, in 1929, but terms of the sale gave him first ownership rights for the next NFL franchise to be established in Minnesota.

Throughout the 1950s the Chicago Cardinals drew only around 20,000 fans per game—about half the crowds drawn by the Chicago Bears—and were frequently rumored to be moving to a new city. In August 1956, *Minneapolis Morning Tribune* columnist Sid Hartman reported that an "informed source" told him the Cardinals would move in 1957 and that Minneapolis or Buffalo, New York, might get the franchise. Many potential new owners around the country either talked to NFL commissioner Bert Bell or Cardinals owner Walther Wolfner about the franchise, but none could get past the talking stage. Many also talked to Bell about expansion of the 12-team league. However, at the time the league rules called for a unanimous vote of all 12 owners to approve expansion, and it was clear that at least two owners—Wolfner and Washington's George Preston Marshall—were strongly opposed. Wolfner, obviously, wanted to keep his options open to ensure he was first in line to benefit from expansion.

One of the Cardinals' many suitors was Lamar Hunt, the 26-year-old son of billionaire Texas oilman H. L. Hunt, who had inquired about an expansion franchise in early 1958. Commissioner Bell told him to talk to Wolfner, as the Cardinals' situation had to be solved before any expansion talk could be considered. Hunt did talk to Wolfner several times, but without success. After one more fruitless meeting with Wolfner in Miami in February 1959, Hunt started to work on a plan for a new league. He touched base with Bell a couple more times, but it was obvious that NFL owners would not be approving expansion in the near future. Minnesota interests received the same reply from the NFL in April, when Bell told Ole Haugsrud that there was no chance of expansion into Minneapolis.

Hunt began to contact prospective owners who had also been talking to the NFL and Cardinals owner Wolfner, and quickly secured six teams as nucleus of a new league, including Minnesota. (New York, Los Angeles, Houston, Dallas, and Denver were the others.) The first meeting of the new American Football League was held on August 14, 1959, in Chicago. The NFL ratcheted things up on August 29 during a press conference prior to a Bears–Pittsburgh Steelers exhibition game. Bears owner George Halas and Steelers owner Art Rooney, two focal points of an expansion committee appointed by commissioner Bert Bell a year earlier, suddenly declared that the NFL was expanding, beginning in 1961. This was a big surprise, since the full committee had never met. Houston and Dallas were mentioned as likely candidates—two cities already on the AFL roster. Lamar Hunt resisted suggestions that the AFL should now disband, and forged ahead. Buffalo and Boston were added to bring the league roster up to

Max Winter, Minneapolis promoter, restaurateur, and former Minneapolis Lakers part owner and general manager, joined other prospective owners at a strategy session for the new American Football League in New York City on October 28, 1959. Front row, left to right: Robert Howsam, Denver; Winter; 27-year-old league founder Lamar Hunt, Dallas (with ball); K. S. Adams Jr., Houston. Back row: Barron Hilton, Los Angeles; Ralph Wilson, Buffalo, New York; Harry Wismer, New York City.
AP PHOTOGRAPH COURTESY OF AP IMAGES.

eight and the AFL college draft was scheduled for November 21–22 at the Pick-Nicollet Hotel in Minneapolis.

Meanwhile, Charlie Johnson was now openly partial to the NFL over the AFL, and he and columnist Sid Hartman had frequent conversations with George Halas. They believed that Halas was supportive of an NFL expansion franchise in Minneapolis. An interesting sideline to the AFL meetings was that a regular-season NFL game between the New York Giants and the Chicago Cardinals was played on November 22 at Metropolitan Stadium, before a capacity crowd of 26,625. An earlier game between the Philadelphia Eagles and the Cardinals had been played at the Met on October 25, drawing 20,112. Cardinals owner Wolfner had been guaranteed $240,000 for the two games, in the hopes that the games would impress NFL owners on the readiness of the Twin Cities for a franchise.

Chaos reigned at the Pick-Nicollet when rumors began circulating that the NFL was going to vote to approve an expansion franchise in Minneapolis–St. Paul.

St. Paul Pioneer Press, November 23, 1959

PRO GRID LOOPS BATTLE OVER TWIN CITIES BERTH
STADIUM LEASE IS ISSUE

Reidar Lund

Utter confusion filled the corridors, conference rooms and even the telephone booths on the second floor of the Pick-Nicollet hotel late Sunday night as a tug-of-war developed between the fledgling American Football League and the National Football League for the lease of Bloomington stadium.

At 12:35 A.M. today the conference broke up and Lamar Hunt of Dallas, said:

"The American Football League definitely will play in the Twin Cities in 1960. Reports of the Minneapolis–St. Paul interests pulling out of the AFL were unfounded."

Asked if the National Football League would have a franchise in the Twin Cities in 1960, Hunt replied:

"I can't speak for the National League but the American League will be here. H. P. Skoglund will be the spokesman for the Twin Cities AFL group, and you will have to ask him."

Skoglund, however, left the meeting 20 minutes early and was not available. Hunt said he was on his way to talk with Bill Boyer of the stadium committee.

Asked what the situation was on Max Winter and the American League, Hunt replied:

"The situation on Mr. Winter is not within the jurisdiction of the AFL for comment. You will have to ask Mr. Skoglund."

Asked if he had any assurance of a stadium for the AFL team in the Twin Cities for 1960, Hunt answered, "Yes."

Two groups were reported seeking the National Football League franchise, which is expected to come with the proposed expansion of the NFL.

One is headed by Ole Haugsrud of Duluth and the other reportedly by Louis Gross of Minneapolis.

The Twin Cities American Football League owners apparently had sought a release from the AFL Sunday night. But Hunt, one of the charter member owners in the league pointed to a clause in the AFL which finds each of the charter members committed to field a team. If one does not meet this commitment, he faces the possibility of a $650,000 damage suit. This is what may face the Twin Cities AFL group if it fails to get a release from the new league.

The Twin Cities group apparently was seeking a new lease because it was not certain it would have a stadium since rumors were current the NFL had the stadium lease. Haugsrud, according to a contract when he sold the Duluth Eskimos in 1929 to National League interests, has first call on a National League franchise in Minnesota. He said Sunday night he would head a group for such a franchise and expected his agreement of 30 years ago to be respected.

The Twin Cities AFL group is headed by Winter, Skoglund and Bill Boyer. At 11:15 P.M. Winter stalked out of the conference rooms indicating there might be a breach in the Twin Cities organization but Boyer remained in the session.

The question of the Twin Cities fielding a team in the AFL apparently rested with what decision the stadium committee would make on the lease. Members of the stadium committee include Gerald Moore, Boyer, Fred Paul and Walter Kramer.

Reports circulating the lobby and the corridors were that the stadium committee definitely would favor a lease to the National Football League.

Among those in the conference room was Frank Leahy. All AFL cities were represented.

Informed of reports that 10 of the NFL's 12 clubs have voted in a poll in favor of admitting Minneapolis–St. Paul, [interim] Commissioner Austin H. Gunsel said the matter was being handled by George Halas, head of the league's expansion committee. He said he was aware that such a poll was being conducted but did not know the result. He quoted article four of the league's constitution, which deals with expansion as saying:

"The National Football League shall be limited to 12 teams unless it be enlarged or changed by unanimous approval of all members of the league."

Philadelphia and Washington were believed opposed to the Minneapolis–St. Paul proposition.

Gunsel said he talked to Halas last Thursday about the Twin Cities' approach and that he assumed the owner-coach of the Chicago Bears was going to ask the pleasure of other league members.

Gunsel emphasized: "We did not seek them out. They took the initiative. We do not wish the new league any hard luck."

The former FBI agent, appointed to fill in for the late Commissioner Bert Bell, said he did not understand why the Minneapolis–St. Paul group made overtures to the NFL at this time.

"I don't know what happened in the other league for them to come to us," he asserted.

The NFL has played two games in Minneapolis this year—"home" games of the Chicago Cardinals—to see how the area reacted to professional football. The Cards played the Philadelphia Eagles there about a month ago and drew a disappointing crowd.

However, Sunday with the Cards facing the eastern conference–leading New York Giants a sell-out crowd of 26,625 turned out. Gunsel said the NFL had agreed to try the Minneapolis–St. Paul area because of handsome financial guarantees to the competing teams.

Halas, as head of the expansion committee, has been working on the problem for more than a year. He has said the league should expand now, naming Houston and Dallas as possible NFL cities. However, George Preston Marshall, owner of the Washington Redskins, opposes the Halas expansion idea.

Halas's Bears played in Detroit Sunday and he left before being reached on the Minneapolis–St. Paul development. Halas said earlier that it was unlikely any new teams would participate in the NFL draft scheduled for November 30 in Philadelphia. If any new clubs are admitted to the league, Halas said, they will operate with veteran players from other franchises.

"They must be able to compete on equal or near equal footing," the Bears' owner said.

It appears unlikely, although always possible, that the NFL will expand before its annual league meeting in January. Without the balancing hand of Bell to guide them the owners could be heading for a knock-down, drag-out battle on many subjects, including expansion, appointment of a new commissioner, and schedule making.

◆

The Minneapolis–St. Paul AFL partners participated in the league's college draft on November 23, but sentiment was switching towards obtaining an NFL expansion franchise. Boosters anxiously awaited the results of expansion talks at the NFL Winter Meetings in Miami Beach. The proceedings were initially preoccupied with choosing a successor for commissioner Bert Bell, who had died of a heart attack on October 11. After Los Angeles Rams general manager Pete Rozelle finally won enough support to garner the appointment, the owners began to seriously work on the expansion issue. On January 28, 1960, Rozelle announced that the NFL would add Dallas in 1960 and Minneapolis–St. Paul in 1961. It had been a long wait for Max Winter, who frequented the lobby of the Hotel Kenilworth for 10 days, hoping for good news.

Minneapolis Tribune, January 29, 1960

MARSHALL, BROWN HELPED NFL BID

"Sid Hartman's Roundup" column

Leo D'Orsey, attorney for the Washington Redskins, left the National Football league meeting at noon Thursday [January 28] and told a Miami sports writer:

"The Twin Cities are dead. They are going to vote Dallas into the league and let Minneapolis–St. Paul wait until a decision is made at a future meeting."

Max Winter, Minneapolis–St. Paul delegate at the NFL meetings, overheard D'Orsey. Winter was convinced that hope was gone for the Twin Cities to be included in NFL expansion plans. Several hours later, Pete Rozelle, NFL commissioner, walked out of the meeting and called newsmen together in the lobby.

"Gentlemen, I have an announcement to make," Rozelle said as Winter stood by patiently and studied Rozelle's apparent stone face.

"Dallas has been voted into the NFL for 1960." Winter reported that Rozelle paused after mentioning Dallas "and I had to sit down."

Rozelle continued: "And the Twin Cities of Minneapolis–St. Paul will be activated in 1961."

Winter said he heard the words—but he couldn't believe that a dream had come true.

BROWN FIGHTS

Winter credited Paul Brown and Dave Jones of Cleveland and George Marshall of Washington for the most important help in the afternoon session.

"I was told that Brown made it known that, unless Minneapolis–St. Paul received a definite commitment at this meeting, Cleveland wouldn't vote for Dallas.

"Marshall did the same thing, according to the word out of the meeting.

"This was contrary to what was expected of Marshall since he had indicated he was against expansion in 1960.

"But Marshall told me in the afternoon there wouldn't be any expansion unless it included the Twin Cities. And he kept his word.

"George Halas of the Chicago Bears and Art Rooney of Pittsburgh also fought our case. Without their help, we would not have been admitted."

HALAS HAPPY

Halas, who guaranteed the Twin Cities a franchise, said he never would have allowed postponement of the vote to expand.

"Nothing can keep the Twin Cities from having pro football in 1961 if they sell 25,000 season tickets and have a stadium to seat 35,000 to 40,000," said Halas from Miami, Florida.

"I think the Twin Cities are in a better position than Dallas. Give Minneapolis–St. Paul a year to prepare and they will have as good or better a team than Dallas.

"The Twin Cities will get 36 players like Dallas. In addition Minneapolis–St. Paul will get a first draft choice, something Dallas didn't get this year.

"I was happy to see Marshall join me in the fight for expansion. I am glad the old pro joined when the chips were down."

●

Popular columnist and radio personality Halsey Hall was among the celebrants. He pointed out that the new NFL franchise was made possible by the willingness of Minneapolis and St. Paul supporters and officials to finally work together. There had always been athletic rivalries between the two cities, ranging from the baseball Minneapolis Millers and St. Paul Saints in the American Association to the hockey Millers and Saints of various minor leagues, and continuing down to high school and adult amateur sports. The annual Twin Cities high school championship football game between the champions from St. Paul and Minneapolis, for example, was an eagerly awaited match-up that gave the winning conference bragging rights for the next year.

While these might be dismissed simply as friendly contests, a deep-seated enmity existed between the two cities, dating back to their infancy. Established first, St. Paul was originally a transportation hub, but became overshadowed by Minneapolis, with its lumber and flour milling industrial base. In the twentieth century Minneapolis grew more powerful, fueled by companies that had a national and international focus, while St. Paul's economy became more dependent on local and regional consumers. The two cities were bitter competitors in the political and cultural arenas, as well as in business.

The rancor between the two was real. St. Cloud State University Professor Mary Lethert Wingerd, author of *Claiming the City: Politics, Faith, and the Power of Place in St. Paul* and a fifth-generation St. Paulite, has written that "the first commandment [St. Paul] children learned at their parent's knee was never to spend their money in Minneapolis!" Similarly, she said, "most Minneapolitans would never consider relocating to St. Paul."

The sibling rivalry threatened to derail efforts to lure a major league franchise when the two cities built competing baseball stadiums in 1956 and 1957, but Wheelock Whitney recruited some St. Paul business interests for his Continental League effort and the intercity cooperation continued in the quest for a pro football franchise.

Sporting News, February 10, 1960

TWIN CITIES UNITE IN NFL ENTRY

Halsey Hall

The blending of the Twins has been accomplished at long last.

Now that Big-Time hopes in the Twin Cities of St. Paul and Minneapolis have been realized through acquisition of a National Football League franchise, the Major League Baseball outlook has received a tremendous shot in the arm.

Technically, the Twin Cities are in the majors now, the Continental loop. Oddly enough, the target date here is 1961, the same year set for the Twins [Cities] baptism in the National Football League.

Max Winter, president of the new gridiron entry, was on the verge of giving up many times before he was granted an NFL franchise at Miami Beach.

Under formal organization the new setup is known as Minnesota Pro Football, Inc., with Winter as president and managing director. Dan Williams of St. Paul is vice-president and Ole Haugsrud of Duluth chairman of the board.

Capital of one million dollars will be raised with Minneapolis furnishing $600,000, St. Paul $300,000, Duluth and the rest of the state $100,000.

It is emphasized that the first order of business will be the hiring of a general manager. Then a coach. But the 1961 start, as against the 1960 debut of Dallas in the league, is seen as a blessing.

"We can use the time," said Winter. "This way we have plenty of time to organize.

NICKNAME WILL BE PICKED LATER

The Twin Cities—an official name still has to be selected—will be permitted players from a National League pool of current players and a liberal choice in the drafting process after next season.

Two civic leaders, W. W. (Bill) Boyer and H. P. Skoglund, will be invited to join the new organization. They were two of the ringleaders in the move for an American Football League franchise here, which was an actuality until permission was asked of the AFL to withdraw when it became fairly certain that National League expansion would take place in this territory.

For Minneapolis, this is not strictly a new venture. The old Minneapolis Marines were in the National Football League when George Halas and Guy Chamberlain formed the Decatur (Illinois) Staleys, forerunners of the Bears. The Marines played their games at Nicollet Park, famous home-run plaza of the baseball Millers.

After they broke up, largely because of old age, the Redjackets took over for a couple of years starting in 1929. Herb Joesting, twice an All American for Minnesota's Gophers, led this team, which had many fine players but not enough balance to keep up with the Bears, Cardinals, Giants, Packers and Portsmouth.

Duluth, of course, is another league veteran and there is personal history in the current Minnesota pro organization. Ole Haugsrud was one of the founders of pro football at the Head of the Lakes about 1930 [1925—ED.] with the Kelley-Duluth 11. Haugsrud then signed Ernie Nevers, Stanford's all-time great and a resident of Superior, Wisconsin, across the Duluth harbor, and formed the Ernie Nevers Duluth Eskimos.

On that team was a tremendous guard, Dan Williams. He's the same man who is vice-president of the new outfit and who has been a civic leader in St. Paul for many years.

Meanwhile, Twin Cities officialdom hails the burying of the imaginary hatchet that was supposed to be cutting any chances the Twins had of getting together.

Mayors Dillon of St. Paul and Peterson of Minneapolis both proudly announced, in effect, that this proves what can be done when enmities are forgotten.

Games will be played at Metropolitan Stadium in suburban Bloomington, home of the baseball Millers. For football, it had a crowd of 26,000 last fall for a Giants–Cardinals match. The Minneapolis city council has meetings scheduled in the near future looking forward [to] an okay for seating enlargement to 35,000 or 40,000.

•

Bert Rose, who had been public relations director for Pete Rozelle with the Los Angeles Rams, was hired as the team's first general manager. At Rose's suggestion, the board of directors selected "Vikings" as the team nickname, a perfect designation for a region with a strong Nordic population and tradition. The Vikings participated in the college draft on December 27, 1960, and for coach hired 12-year veteran quarterback Norm Van Brocklin of the Philadelphia Eagles, who retired after playing in the Pro Bowl on January 15, 1961. The 34-year-old Van Brocklin was selected for nine pro bowls in his career, and won two NFL championships. He was also a star punter, compiling a 42.9-yard career average. In 1951 he split quarterback duties with Bob Waterfield, but his 73-yard touchdown pass to Tom Fears in the fourth quarter beat the Cleveland Browns 24–17 in the NFL championship game. In 1960 he had quarterbacked the Philadelphia Eagles to a 10–2 season and beat the Green Bay Packers 17–13 in the championship game. Van Brocklin was named the NFL Most Valuable Player as well as the Player of the Year.

Van Brocklin didn't have much time to bask in his glory, as the expansion draft was held on January 17 in New York.

Sporting News, February 1, 1961
VIKINGS SIT DOWN AT NFL'S TABLE—MUNCH LEFTOVERS
EACH OLD-LINE CLUB OFFERS 8 NAMES ON AVAILABLE LIST;
NUMBER INCLUDES FRINGE PLAYERS SCHEDULED FOR RELEASE
Joe King

Manufacturing big league teams is all the craze these days, and the National Football League took a second whack at it during the annual meeting here, in outfitting the Minnesota Vikings.

The consensus among observers was that the fourteenth club in the pioneer football league was no nearer a pennant than the brand-new Angels and Senators of the American League of baseball, and possibly more remote from glory in its inaugural year than the non-winning NFL Dallas Cowboys of '60.

Bert Rose, general manager of the Vikings, conceded that he didn't expect to better the Dallas record, and that "four or five years of hard work" would be necessary to fashion a contender. "I don't mean a title winner, either," he added.

The 12 old-line clubs, with Dallas exempt, each put eight names from a roster of 38 on the available list for Rose and his new coach, Norm Van Brocklin.

This was pretty nearly equivalent to offering nothing at all. First, the league reduced the player limit from 38 to 36 effective next fall, so that two of the availables would have been cut anyway. Second, inasmuch as a normal turnover in personnel is six or more, to accommodate topmost rookies, hardly anything at all was sacrificed.

The Vikings were allowed, for their $550,000, to pick three men from each club, for a total of 36 from the pool of 96. However, it is likely that they may be able to pick from 75 or 80 of the 96 in all, because most of these fringe athletes will go on waivers in camp.

The league allowed Dallas a year ago to select three men from among 11 of a roster strength of 36. This enabled the Cowboys to nab a good number of top substitutes and a few excellent players. The deal for Minnesota, with 30 exempted, did not come nearly so close to the upper quality level.

VIKINGS DRAFTED COLLEGE STARS

However, the owners decided that Minneapolis had the benefit of partic-ipating in the draft of 20 rookies, a privilege Dallas did not enjoy, and that the pool of veterans should not be so liberal.

The Vikings were lucky in being able to obtain an experienced quarter-back in George Shaw, whom the Giants surrendered in exchange for the number one Minnesota draft pick for '62. However, Dallas also got a break in nabbing the flashy Eddie LeBaron from the Redskins, but he could not win.

The Vikings are said to have several star rookies, including Tommy Mason of Tulane, Fran Tarkenton of Georgia and Ed Sharockman of Pitt, but rookies cannot carry a team if the veteran backbone is not present.

There are, of course, two theories on shaping up new franchises. The so-far popular idea is that the newcomer must make his own way, just as the older members had to do in the past. The practice has been followed in the NFL and A. L. [American League baseball] expansion. The N. L. [National League baseball] will have the last chance for the immediate future in equipping the New York and Houston teams, and may, off present indica-tions, adopt the opposite theory that a weak newcomer hurts everybody and is to be avoided.

The NFL, for example, might have struck down the middle by allowing the Vikings to take one man per team from players No. 20 to 32, to provide a genuine old pro nucleus of 12.

Of course, all these experiments have to be proved out in action, but the result of the first, with Dallas, has not been reassuring.

The football people contend that there are two deep differences between their sport and baseball. First, you can't judge a football club until its sec-ond season, because the main, time-taking job is creating teamwork among men who have not played together. Granted the talent is there, that is.

A second baseman, they say, either can or can't make the double play, and that won't change. However, an offensive tackle with the wrong moves in the first six games may be a good man when he fits into a pattern with the rest. A line is a unit. So is a platoon, while a second baseman remains an individual.

Vikings candidates arrive by bus at Bemidji State College in July 1961. Training camps were informal in the early days, compared to the media circus that they became later. PHOTOGRAPHS FROM *STAR TRIBUNE*. COURTESY OF THE MINNESOTA HISTORICAL SOCIETY.

Second, the means to upgrade the product is available, in the steady annual supply of college heroes.

●

Van Brocklin would have agreed with Joe King. As training camp began, he took to calling the expansion draftees "my 36 stiffs." The Vikings picked Bemidji State College as the site for the training camp after visiting many possible locations, including the St. Olaf, St. John's, Minnesota–Duluth, Concordia (Moorhead), and Grand Rapids college campuses, and Breezy Point Lodge near Brainerd. Some sportswriters complained about the distance from the Twin Cities, but the team said the relatively cool weather in July, and the game and practice fields at Bemidji were ideal. Van Brocklin, who had accompanied general manager Bert Rose on the fact-finding trips, said the facility was better than any he had experienced with the Los Angeles Rams and Philadelphia Eagles. "I like the dormitory setup, the closeness of dining, medical, dental, and other housekeeping facilities, and I think the weather's going to be just what we need to get ready."

"A DUTCHMAN AND 36 STIFFS," FROM *PURPLE HEARTS AND GOLDEN MEMORIES: 35 YEARS WITH THE MINNESOTA VIKINGS* (1995)

Jim Klobuchar

Standing in the shade of the nearest available maple tree on the sidelines in Bemidji, Minnesota, The King of the Halfbacks, Hugh McElhenny, looked tanned and vaguely appalled.

No one yet had been able to identify what kink of destiny had put him on the roster of the newly-fabricated Minnesota Vikings after nine years in San Francisco. He had freshly arrived in Bemidji on his way to eventual immortality. He wore a stylish black polo shirt and the obligatory California shades. Spectators who were clumped around the Viking practice field failed to recognize him, a dereliction that didn't wound The King's vanity. At the moment he preferred concealment to adoration.

With resourceful planning, The King had arrived in the early afternoon, in time to miss the day's second two-hour, full-pads scrimmage under the late July sun. That was another thing that mystified him in this abrupt career change that uprooted him from the Pacific surf, where he was loved and pampered, to the jackpine wilderness of northern Minnesota, where in 1961 they knew walleyes better than National Football League running backs. A letter in McElhenny's mail from the Minnesota Vikings' general manager, Bert Rose, designated the start of practice as the third week of

July. Hugh McElhenny was one of those venerable running backs who liked football in sensible doses. What was the big rush to get yourself killed, starting practice a few weeks after Memorial Day?

He stood watching 80 armored nonentities sweat and pound on each other trying to look like a football team. No progress seemed imminent. The scruffy ensemble was redeemed by a few faces McElhenny recognized or knew by reputation. He couldn't possibly overlook Don Joyce, the old defensive end from the Baltimore Colts, looking very squat and globular at 300 pounds. He recognized Bill Bishop, an exile from the Chicago Bears, one of the most ornery defensive tackles ever created. Doc Middleton, the former Lions receiver, was familiar. He knew George Shaw, the quarterback who had been smothered by injuries and a glum future playing first behind John Unitas in Baltimore and then Charley Conerly in New York. Alternating snaps with Shaw he recognized the saucy rookie from Georgia, Francis Tarkenton. Clancy Osborne and Karle Rubke he'd played with in San Francisco.

And he couldn't mistake the figure advancing toward him out of the mélange of crunching bodies. The whistle was new. The coach's cap was new. The conspiratorial giggle was familiar. It was something Norm Van Brocklin always did when he was sharing a private joke or having a hell of a time. The Dutchman walked up to McElhenny with the exuberance of an island outcast greeting the first mate of a rescue ship. He draped an arm around the polo shirt, playfully removed the shades to be sure he had the right man, and welcomed Hugh McElhenny to the Minnesota Vikings.

"King," he said, "you're a beautiful sight. Come on out on the field. I want to introduce you to your new teammates. You're a start for us. We've got a start on a football team. You're going to be an inspiration to these guys."

McElhenny smiled warily. It had been several years since he'd been compared to Moses. Maybe he'd better get used to it. The Vikings were going to pay him $21,500 for the first year. Everybody else on the team, including its high draft choices, got hamburger money alongside that. The Dutchman was positively eloquent. "Before we can be a football team we've got to look like a football team. With you in there, Mac, that'll start tomorrow."

The King mentally fumbled through a calendar.

"Tomorrow?"

"Right," the Dutchman said.

"Isn't tomorrow Sunday?"

"Right. We work out full go with pads."

McElhenny looked to the trees for solace. He rolled his eyes prayerfully. "Jesus," he said.

Van Brocklin always defended the Vikings' choice of Bemidji as their

Norm Van Brocklin was just 35 years old when he became the first head coach of the Vikings in 1961. He quarterbacked the Philadelphia Eagles to the NFL championship in 1960 and was voted the league's Most Valuable Player. From left to right: Mick Tingelhoff, Van Brocklin, unidentified player, and John Kirby. PHOTOGRAPH COURTESY OF THE MINNESOTA HISTORICAL SOCIETY.

first training outpost. Critics clamored for a site closer than the 250 miles separating Minneapolis and St. Paul from the scene of the team's post-incubation crawls and pratfalls. They wailed about the drive time from the Twin Cities, five hours. The Dutchman thought that was wonderful. The Dutchman had a minimal admiration for what he always called "the 36 stiffs" the NFL bestowed on the Vikings in the first-year player pool. Practicing in the sight of wild rice bogs on the fringe of the wilderness gave his team exactly what it needed, he contended, obscurity.

The Vikings' first game was a 38–13 exhibition loss to the Dallas Cowboys in Sioux Falls, South Dakota, on September 10, 1961.

Major League Baseball had voted to expand in the fall of 1960—the National League to New York and Houston in 1962 and the American League to Los Angeles and Washington, D.C., in 1961—and approved the move of the existing Washington Senators to Minneapolis–St. Paul. Thus, the Minnesota Twins played the area's first major league regular-season game at Metropolitan Stadium when they lost to the expansion Washington Senators 5–3 on April 21, 1961.

Minnesota's fledgling professional football fans—all 32,236 of them—were not expecting much as they walked through the turnstiles at Metropolitan Stadium for the franchise's first league game against the Chicago Bears on September 17, 1961. The NFL's 1960 expansion team, the Dallas Cowboys, after all, had managed only one tie and 11 losses in their inaugural season. The Vikings, furthermore, had gone 0–5 in exhibition play, including a 31–7 drubbing by the Bears on September 1.

The playing field would have looked familiar to fans who had never seen an NFL game in person, but who had watched the grainy black-and-white NFL telecasts available at the time. The field was chalked over the dirt portions of the baseball infield and the leveled pitching mound, since the Minnesota Twins still had a two-week home stand remaining on their schedule. (Ten of the 14 NFL teams played in stadiums also used for Major League Baseball, and an eleventh, the Green Bay Packers, played three of their seven home games in Milwaukee County Stadium, home of the National League Milwaukee Braves.) The goal posts were on the goal line rather than on the end line, as in college football.

Whether he liked it or not, Coach Van Brocklin needed his "stiffs." Fifteen of the Vikings' first-game starters came from the expansion draft, while five came from trades and one was a free agent. Linebacker Rip Hawkins, a second-round draft choice from North Carolina, was the only rookie in the starting lineup.

Minneapolis Tribune, September 18, 1961
VIKINGS BLAST BEARS 37–13 IN DEBUT
TARKENTON HURLS FOUR TD PASSES

Jim Klobuchar

Rookie Fran Tarkenton, a pass-throwing prodigy from Georgia, stirred Minnesota's Vikings into a touchdown frenzy that struck down the Chicago Bears 37–13 and rocked pro football Sunday.

The 21-year-old rebel fired four touchdown passes and scored once himself to startle a Metropolitan stadium crowd of 32,236 and leave the heavily favored Bears distraught.

It was a National Football League bombshell—a runaway victory by a first-year team making its league debut with a squad of alleged misfits and callow rookies.

Tarkenton, hurling passes with glacial calm and exploiting nearly every Bears bungle, completed 17 of 23 passes for 250 yards in one of the extraordinary first-game performances by an NFL rookie quarterback.

He entered late in the first period with the Vikings holding a 3–0 lead but demonstrating continued failures to click in touchdown territory.

Within two minutes after the second quarter opened he whipped a 14-yard pass to Bob Schnelker for a 10–0 Viking lead.

The Bumbling Bears recouped momentarily, escaped their errors long enough to lunge 66 yards in 13 plays and sent Rick Casares over from the three to cut their halftime deficit to 10–6. They seemed to have momentum here. But the Vikings reversed it with one chilling tackle that permitted Tarkenton to deliver the touchdown that set off the stampede. It came early in the third period.

Rookie Rip Hawkins smashed Willie Galimore on the Bears' 27 and the Chicago speedster fumbled, Rich Mostardi recovering. Three plays later, from the 29, Tarkenton arched a pass to Jerry Reichow, who out-stepped defensive back Dave Whitsell and made the catch gliding into the corner of the zone.

Moments later Tarkenton writhed away from the Bears' pass rush and shot a 47-yarder to Reichow on the Bears' two. The Vikings fumbled twice in three plays on the goal line. But it was their day—everything came up roses. On fourth down Tarkenton rolled out and passed to Hugh McElhenny for two yards and a touchdown.

Charlie Sumner's interception sent the Vikings galloping again late in the third period and Tarkenton went over from the two, dragging a frustrated Joe Fortunato and Rich Petitbon with him.

The top-off was Tarkenton's fourth-down pitch to Dave Middleton from the two that boomed the Viking advantage to 37–6. The Bears got back on

Metropolitan Stadium filled for an early Vikings game. Prior to the construction of permanent stands in left field in 1965, temporary bleachers were moved in close to the football field sidelines. Fresh sod was planted on the mound and baseline areas after the completion of the Twins' baseball season. PHOTOGRAPH COURTESY OF THE MINNESOTA VIKINGS.

the board in the late minutes when Billy Wade passed 10 yards to Galimore.

Rookie Mike Mercer, whose 12-yard field goal in the first period shoved the Vikings into a 3–0 lead, kicked four extra points.

The Chicagoans' misfortunes came close to chaos.

Bears quarterback Ed Brown hit two of seven passes, and had two intercepted. His relief, Billy Wade, also threw two interceptions. They fumbled four times and made the day of technical misdeeds complete by having center Ken Kirk's pass from center on a punt sail over John Adams' head at a time when the game was up for grabs.

The Bears went 22 minutes before completing a pass.

Smoldering over their 30–7 exhibition shellacking by the Bears two weeks ago—one of five Minnesota losses in a winless exhibition campaign—the Vikings made a physical showdown out of it yesterday.

Don Joyce, Jim Marshall, Jim Prestel and Bill Bishop hit savagely up front. The rookie linebacker, Rip Hawkins, raided the Bears' backfield constantly. Galimore, dangerous through the first 35 minutes, lost effectiveness after a violent encounter with the 270-pound Joyce.

Still, the Bears were troublesome on the ground until their mistakes forced them to shift offensive tactics.

The Bears' own blitzing game ran afoul of Tarkenton's heady signal changes on the line of scrimmage. Trap plays that got fullback Mel Triplett loose for important gains, and screen passes to McElhenny, Tom Mason and Triplett scored repeatedly.

Viking veteran George Shaw, struggling to hold his no. 1 job, moved the club smartly in the first minutes. After the Bears' J. C. Caroline was called for interference at midfield, Shaw passed 14 yards to Middleton and then eight to McElhenny, whose running had all the elements of the old McElhenny craft.

But the Bears held on the five and Mercer kicked his field goal.

Kirk's wild pass from center put the Vikings on the 19 later in the first period. Minnesota flubbed that chance, however, and Mercer's kick from the 19 was no good.

A few plays later the Vikings were back on the 20 after Clancy Osborne intercepted a partially deflected pass.

Tarkenton entered to push the Vikings to the one but Tarkenton's fourth-down thrust from the one fell short.

That was the last time the Vikings failed, however.

The victory left the National League in the unlikely situation of matching Minnesota and Dallas at Dallas next week with both unbeaten after their first games. Dallas defeated Pittsburgh yesterday.

●

The euphoria was short-lived, as the team went on a seven-game losing streak, but they beat the Baltimore Colts (who would finish 8–6 for the year) 28–20 in game nine and pummeled the Los Angeles Rams (who finished 4–10) 42–21 in game 12. The Vikings' 3–11 record was a significant improvement on the expansion Dallas Cowboys' 1960 record. Although the Vikings defense finished dead last in the league in points and yards

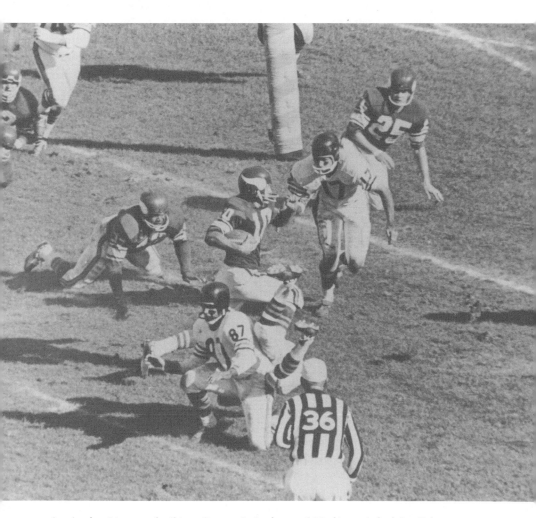

Opening day victory over the Chicago Bears on September 17, 1961! Rookie quarterback Fran Tarkenton scores on a fourth-quarter scramble to secure a 37–13 win as Bears defensive back Richie Petitbon (17) arrives too late to make the stop. PHOTOGRAPH FROM *STAR TRIBUNE*. COURTESY OF THE MINNESOTA HISTORICAL SOCIETY.

allowed, the offense, led by the resourceful Fran Tarkenton, was entertaining and showed promise for the future.

The team was happy to sell a little over 26,000 season tickets for that first season, but professional football played second fiddle to the University of Minnesota Golden Gophers, who still had a huge following. The Gophers had an 8–2 overall record in 1960, and their 6–1 Big Ten record tied for first and earned them an invitation to the Rose Bowl, which they lost to the University of Washington 17–7. The team had an identical record in 1961, but their 6–1 conference record was second to Ohio State. The Gophers were invited back to the Rose Bowl when the Ohio State administration turned down the invitation. The school—hard to believe in today's environment—was concerned that postseason football games detracted from the educational purpose of the institution. The Gophers redeemed themselves with a 21–3 victory over UCLA.

Playing on campus in Memorial Stadium, which had a listed capacity of 63,555, the Gophers drew an average of 60,322 to six home games in 1961. The all-time record of 66,284 was set at a game with Purdue on November 18. In contrast, the Vikings, playing at Metropolitan Stadium with a capacity of just over 40,000, averaged 33,872 for their seven home games in 1961. The Green Bay game on October 22 drew 42,007 fans, the only crowd over 40,000 during the season.

On the field the Vikings were a disappointing 2–11–1 in 1962, but improved to 5–8–1 in 1963. The 34–31 victory over the Detroit Lions on November 24 was played under the most strange and trying circumstances. It was played just two days after the assassination of President John F. Kennedy. The AFL postponed its weekend games, as did many colleges. The University of Minnesota's game against Wisconsin was moved to Thanksgiving Day, but not before the Badgers had arrived in Minneapolis. NFL commissioner Pete Rozelle made the decision to play NFL games after talking to Kennedy's press secretary, Pierre Salinger, a friend dating back to his college days. Salinger told him that the President, a great sports fan, would have wanted the games to go on.

Out of respect for the President and his family, however, Rozelle decided that the NFL games would not be televised. At Metropolitan Stadium, there were no cheerleaders and no music. The mood was somber, and the stadium eerily quiet during the game. The only halftime activity was a ceremony to honor three of the 17 men in the inaugural class of the NFL Hall of Fame—Bronko Nagurski (International Falls, University of Minnesota, and the Chicago Bears); Ernie Nevers (born in Willow River, Minnesota, played at Stanford and with the Duluth Eskimos and Chicago Cardinals); and Johnny "Blood" McNally (St. John's College, Duluth Eskimos, Green Bay, and Pittsburgh).

The Vikings drew 28,763 for the game, 4,200 below their season average, but 196 more than attended the San Francisco game on September 29. Attendance around the rest of the NFL was above average except for Cleveland. Nevertheless, the league was criticized for lacking respect for the President. Rozelle in later years said he regretted his decision.

The Spartan conditions at the training camp in Bemidji gave the team a scare in 1964 when defensive back Tom Franckhauser injured his head in a violent collision. Trainer Fred Zamberletti took one look at the player and loaded him in a van and rushed him to a hospital. (There were no doctors or medical facilities on the field.) His quick work saved Franckhauser's life. This was probably the first time most Vikings fans had heard Zamberletti's name, but they would come to know him much better over the years—as of 2008 he is the only person to have been with the team for every one of its games.

The flag flew at half-staff during the Vikings' 34–31 victory over the Detroit Lions on Sunday, November 24, 1963, just two days after the assassination of President John F. Kennedy. PHOTOGRAPH FROM *STAR TRIBUNE*. COURTESY OF THE MINNESOTA HISTORICAL SOCIETY.

St. Paul Pioneer Press, August 2, 1964

ZAMBERLETTI STRONG AFTER 40-HOUR VIGIL

Roger Rosenblum

His name was Fred Zamberletti. He was stretched out on his dormitory bed, fully clothed, eyes glistening with apparent satisfaction and seemingly not a bit tired.

This was surprising, because Fred Zamberletti had not closed his eyes for 40 hours and the prospect of immediate sleep was not in sight.

Zamberletti, tall, cherub-faced and stocky, is the Minnesota Vikings' trainer—has been since the team was activated in 1961. And he was one of the key figures in a fast-paced teamwork operation credited with saving the life of Viking halfback Tom Franckhauser earlier this week.

It was Fred and backfield coach Tom McCormick who sped Franckhauser first to the Bemidji clinic, and then to the hospital for emergency surgery for a brain hemorrhage.

Zamberletti never left the hospital until it was time to report directly to the training room for ankle taping after breakfast the next morning. What did he do during those long, quiet hours while Franckhauser hovered between life and death?

"Well," Fred replied, "they had another emergency case on the floor and the nurses were kept pretty busy. I helped the nurses turn him in bed. Then Beverly (Mrs. Franckhauser) came in about 2 A.M. and I tried to calm her down. We chatted until nearly four before she thought she could catch some sleep."

The news was brighter the next morning, and Franckhauser was taken off the critical list, from where he has continued to make steady progress toward eventual recovery.

Later that day, on the field, Zamberletti was the recipient of numerous congratulations—including ones by coach Norm Van Brocklin—for his alert and vital performance.

"I'll tell you something," Fred said, the trace of a normally present smile disappearing, "All the congratulations I need are to see Tom walk out of that hospital one of these days, come back on the field—whether as a player or friend—and be himself again. I want to see him back in his home as a husband and father. When that happens I'll be repaid for anything I might have done."

Accurate diagnosis of Franckhauser's condition was a must. How did Zamberletti recognize the signs?

"Well, to start with, Franckhauser is the type of boy who never comes around with nuisance injuries, and he never complains. Therefore I realized he must have been in trouble.

"I figured it must have been his head when I saw his legs in outward rotation and he complained of numbness in the ankles. He had uneven dilation and constrictions in the pupils of his eyes. It all added up," he said.

Fred, 32 years old, is a native of Melcher, Iowa, and a graduate of the University of Iowa, from which he holds a master's degree in physical therapy. Zamberletti has worked at Hibbing hospital and came to the Vikings from the University of Toledo, where he was the trainer.

Zamberletti and his wife, Val, are parents of two daughters, Lisa, four, and Lori, two and a half, and one son, Thomas, one. They recently purchased a home in St. Paul, where Fred works as a physical therapist at Midway Hospital during the off-season. He's earned the nickname of "mother" from Van Brocklin.

●

The Vikings improved significantly in 1964. They beat the Baltimore Colts, the eventual Western Conference champs, 34–24 in the 1964 season opener, and won their last three games to finish at 8–5–1 and finish in a second-place tie with Green Bay. The team was fourth in the NFL in points scored, and the defense, while it gave up a lot of yards, ranked sixth in points allowed. Quarterback Fran Tarkenton was driving opponents' defensive coordinators crazy with his scrambling.

FROM CHAPTER 10, *TRUE HEARTS AND PURPLE HEADS: AN UNAUTHORIZED BIOGRAPHY OF A FOOTBALL TEAM* (1970)

Jim Klobuchar

Van Brocklin himself was baffled at times by the apparent madness of Tarkenton's death-defying loops and pirouettes, in which he would very often fake one rusher into the very jaws of another to escape almost certain catastrophe.

"What are you thinking," a solicitous minister once asked, "when you have a man like Roger Brown chasing you from one direction and Alex Karras from another?"

"I'm thinking, Reverend," Tarkenton replied, "how bad it would be for me if they ever caught up."

Yet Francis eventually developed an ad lib artistry that convinced opposing players Van Brocklin actually had drawn up plays to exploit it. In other words, "The Scrambling Series—Right or Left, on Two."

This attitude overtook Grady Alderman on his first appearance in the Pro Bowl [1963—ED.] when the Packers' Forrest Gregg asked him flat out:

"What blocking does Van Brocklin give you when Tarkenton lights out on one of those scrambles?"

Teammates had to help Alderman to his feet five minutes later. He was still limp and powerless from the effects of uncontrollable laughter.

"Listen," Alderman explained, "the only way you can keep your sanity when Tarkenton starts to scramble, let alone your job, is to approach the whole thing like a World War I fighter pilot. You have to look for targets of opportunity.

"You never know which way to block a guy because you never know where Tarkenton is running by now. Blocking for Tarkenton is like trying to stand still in the school hall when somebody rings the recess bell. There's a big rush of humanity in many directions. When we played the Colts I spent more time blocking Mick Tingelhoff, our center, than Ordell Braase, the Colts' end.

"In other words, it was every man for himself, and that included the rushers. I've seen guys collapse in front of me when they did nothing but trip over a blade of grass, they were so bushed.

"If you were still on your feet—and you always had time to get up several times on Tarkenton's best days—you just looked for any guy in an opposing uniform who looked a little more tired than you were, and you tried to cream him.

"I did that once to a tackle from the Rams, and he fell on top of me and said, 'Why did you put the knock on me? I was just standing there wondering whether Tarkenton had the guts to come back this way the fourth time on the same play.'

"And you know, sometimes he did exactly that. I remember one play with the Bears when I had already hit somebody, maybe it was Doug Atkins, two or three times, and we were lying on the ground figuring the play was over or was way downfield by now, and Tingelhoff yells, 'Look out, here he comes again,' and we all stomped to our feet and started hitting again, except for Atkins. As I recall, he just walked off the field in disgust."

Tarkenton's defense of his freelancing was pretty tautly reasoned: "I just couldn't see standing in there in the pocket and 'eating the ball' the way you were supposed to, by the book. What for? If there was a chance I could salvage something out of a play by scrambling, what was so wrong about that? I think the guys I played with will agree that I never rapped our offensive line the way others did. I never rapped it at all. They knew they weren't All Pros. I can't remember them objecting very much when we tried to wing it. And, really, I didn't scramble all that much. I got a big reputation for it, and I suppose two or three times a game I'd give it that round-the-world business way back there. Believe me, I didn't have the faintest idea how it was going to come out, whether I'd keep running or find a way to get rid of the ball."

"I'd be the first to admit," he said some time after leaving the Vikings, "that there were times when I shouldn't have gone off on those wild scrambles. Van Brocklin's beef was that I could have gotten rid of the ball quicker, and a lot of the times he was right. As the years went on, I worked on that. But he was wrong when he said I was doing it for selfish reasons. He gave people the idea I was trying to put on a show to make myself bigger box office, and that I was sacrificing the good of the team. That was a lot of bull. Football players are a blunt bunch, sometimes brutally. They would have been the first ones to let me know. I know there were a few guys on the Vikings who didn't exactly love the way I quarterbacked the team, but I can't remember any of the players accusing me of being selfish."

Tarkenton started those gyrations as a condition of life in his first year of quarterbacking. Gradually he refined what enemy linemen swore was a form of football ESP. He learned the best escape routes, what decoy moves worked on one kind of rusher but didn't on another. Above all, he made an art out of locating friendly ends and backs far downfield, while dashing in several directions at once.

"The Vikings," observed one of their winded pursuers, "had the only unrehearsed, unlisted offense in football."

This was a fact, not only out of necessity but because of the renegade temperament the team acquired after a couple of years under Van Brocklin. The Vikings answered the snickers of the pedigreed teams with an unbuttoned defiance that was the essence of Van Brocklin.

It didn't win many games for them in those first few years. But from the time they played their first exhibition game, nobody laughed at them. The Mets, Astros, Senators, Cowboys, Expos, San Diego—all of the first-termers in the expansion years went through the pimply embarrassments of being everybody's rubes.

But not Van Brocklin's team. Whatever his future in the trade, he may have been the perfect expansion coach. He had a nails-hard scholarship as a football man and an indomitability that transmitted itself to the struggling kids and sulking outcasts who made up his first team.

They developed an offbeat spirit of the corps, the pooled fervor of the banished and the impetuous novices.

Tarkenton was the natural fulcrum for these diverse passions. He played a zany potato-patch kind of football, and it infected the others. There were days Van Brocklin would swear Tarkenton called his plays not in the conventional cryptology of the blackboard, e.g., "Open 2 right, 29—GO," but: "Reichow, you run as far as you can; Mason, you head for Row 25 and then cut for the air blowers; Brown, hang around me because they're a gonna be comin' like bulls."

Actually, there was precedent for it. No football training camp has ever been spared the one about how Sammy Baugh used to call his pass plays in the wartime days when they never had the same team on consecutive weekends. "Right end," Baugh would drawl, "you go down 15 yards and angle for the middle; right half, you follow him out and look for fumbles; left end, just fug around awhile to keep the rest of them confused."

Before many games the Vikings with Tarkenton quarterbacking had acquired a reckless élan that sometimes made them look like the Beaver Boys playing their season opener. Everybody watched for laterals, especially after the Viking–San Francisco game in 1962 when the play went Tarkenton to Reichow to Brown to Mason to Reichow to Alderman to Tingelhoff and collapse.

"I damned near called a double dribble," one of the harassed officials admitted afterward.

●

The prototype quarterback of the 1950s and 1960s dropped straight back into the pocket, and when pressured would throw the ball away, or duck and take the sack. Tarkenton became the model for the new generation of mobile quarterbacks, but Coach Van Brocklin, who was a classic drop-back passer, often felt his quarterback missed opportunities when he took off too soon on a scramble. During training camp in one of those early seasons, when Tarkenton had completed one of his back-and-forth scrambles, Van Brocklin asked him if had been planning to throw the ball or was merely on his way to swim in the nearby lake.

The highlight of the 1964 season was the last-minute, come-from-behind 24–23 victory over Green Bay on October 4 at Lambeau Field, when Tarkenton used all of his scrambling talents to thwart the Packers' pass rush and drive Coach Lombardi crazy.

St. Paul Pioneer Press, October 5, 1964
TARK PLANNED SCRAMBLE ON CRUCIAL PASS PLAY
Staff writer

Francis Tarkenton was not guessing, he was thinking, when he tossed a 44-yard pass to Gordy Smith here Sunday on the play which set up the Minnesota Vikings' winning field goal against the Green Bay Packers.

It was fourth down with 22 long yards to go for a first down and only 46 seconds showing on the clock when Tarkenton eluded a horde of Packers defensive linemen, scrambled and then fired the bullseye.

The Packers, obviously, were in their "victory defense" to guard against just such a pass as Tarkenton completed.

"I knew the only way to get the yardage we needed was to scramble," a happy Tarkenton said in the dressing room. "I sent both running backs into the flat to keep the linebackers with them. Gordy was supposed to run a shallow pattern and (Tom) Hall was the intended receiver."

Smith said that when he saw Tarkenton scrambling he simply headed downfield and hoped for the best. Hall, in the meantime, had run a deep comeback pattern and Tarkenton spotted him about 40 yards downfield.

"When I saw Gordy go for the ball I almost dropped dead of fright," Tarkenton admitted later. "I thought he was going to break up the pass unintentionally."

Rookie center Mick Tingelhoff, signed as an undrafted free agent from the University of Nebraska, works on a primitive blocking dummy at the Vikings training camp in 1962. He started 240 consecutive games—every game of his 17-year career—plus 21 playoff games, played in six Pro Bowls, and was selected as an All Pro five times. PHOTOGRAPH COURTESY OF THE MINNESOTA VIKINGS.

Hall, who received the game ball from his teammates, said he had his eyes on the ball, and that "all of a sudden someone darted in front of me. I was certain it was an interception, but I looked around and there was Gordy."

Smith said he was in position to get his hands on the pass and figured it was his duty to go after it. "Tell Francis I'm sorry I spoiled his play," Smith said with a wry grin. Tarkenton, however, couldn't be induced into an argument at that point.

Coach Norm Van Brocklin, who finally saw the tide turn on the close finishes, admitted:

"This is my biggest thrill as a coach. I thought our offensive line played tremendous football. That Tarkenton is something, isn't he? He does just as well either scrambling or staying in the pocket. His ability to run is a big plus because he's so quick."

Defensive halfback George Rose claimed he had clear possession of the ball for what looked like an interception of a Bart Starr pass just before Paul Hornung kicked a field goal in the fourth quarter. The officials, however, ruled it an incomplete pass.

The Vikings suffered a 15-yard penalty on the kickoff following Fred Cox's winning field goal, but Van Brocklin was at a loss on the interpretation. "The officials called a double foul, and then walked off 15 against us. I've never seen that one before."

Cox, whose kick was true to its mark, admitted, "I was pretty nervous until the ball left my foot. Then I knew it would be good."

●

Milwaukee Sentinel, October 6, 1964

PACKER-VIKING TILT WAS LAST WORD IN CUSTOMER FOOTBALL

Lloyd Larson

"Everybody in the joint knows he's going to pass, so how could he get away with it?" one of thousands of dejected Packer fans was heard muttering as he elbowed his way out of the Green Bay stadium Sunday after the hard to take 24–23 loss to the Vikings.

That's right. Everybody in the joint, including the Packers, knew it had to be a pass. With less than a minute to play, fourth down and 22 to go from his own 36, Fran Tarkenton had to go for it in a big way. The only big way was through the air.

The other part of the muttering brings to mind the time a leading pro golfer was asked a similar how come question after taking 13 assorted swipes at the ball on one hole. "It was simple," concluded the star suddenly turned duffer after giving a blow-by-blow account of his nightmarish experience that knocked him out of the running for top money.

In the case of the Packers, the explanation is equally simple—just as simple as the memory of it is painful. He, meaning Tarkenton, took the snap from center and kept on running around behind the line until he found a teammate open. Said teammate, Gordon Smith, fielded the long pitch cleanly for the big gainer, an absolute must, and the Packers had their heads in a noose from which there was no escape.

EVERYBODY HAD TO IMPROVISE

They talk of customer golf. Well, Sunday's thriller was the ultimate in customer football, that is for those who were able to look at the game objectively. It may not have been the greatest game ever played in total. But for excitement and nail-biting suspense, it must rank with the best.

Every time the Vikings had the ball, especially when Tarkenton chose to pass instead of handing off to Bill Brown or Tom Michel, it reminded me a little of a kids' pickup game. Organized confusion set in the moment the elusive quarterback went into his scampering act and eligible receivers fanned out in all directions.

Defenders and receivers had to follow suit as Tarkenton improvised. Secondary assignments and pass patterns went down the drain. That was a sight to behold.

Now and then, it even looked like Tarkenton was training for the Olympics. He was sprinter, hurdler, and steeplechaser rolled into one. But he refused to stay on course. And that presented the Packers with a problem they could not solve.

●

A more infamous highlight of that 1964 season occurred on October 25 in San Francisco. The Vikings had taken a 27–17 lead in the fourth quarter when defensive end Jim Marshall jumped over a fallen player and picked up a fumble by 49ers receiver Billy Killmer. Marshall had been trailing the pass play, but instead of reversing field he continued running towards the 49ers' goal line. By the time his teammates realized he was running the wrong way it was too late to stop him. Several Vikings on the sidelines attempted to get his attention by shouting and waving their arms, but Marshall didn't break stride. When he crossed the goal line he threw the ball out of the end zone, resulting in a safety.

Although the Vikings ultimately won the game 27–22, and although he had otherwise played one of his greatest games, Marshall would forever be associated with this one play. The warm embrace of his teammates and Vikings fans ultimately helped Marshall to recover emotionally from his embarrassment. He became good-natured enough about the play to accept an invitation to travel to Dallas in January to accept the Dallas Bonehead Club's "Bonehead of the Year" trophy. Unfortunately, Marshall was an hour late for the event because he boarded a plane bound for Chicago instead of Dallas.

St. Paul Pioneer Press, October 27, 1964

MARSHALL LOSES SLEEP BUT NOT FRIENDS

Roger Rosenblum

Jim Marshall was a man without sleep early Monday. Later in the day he suddenly discovered he was a man with an awful lot of friends.

In case word or picture has not filtered through, Jim Marshall is a defensive end for the Minnesota Vikings. He is the same Jim Marshall who made National Football League history Sunday when he scooped up a San Francisco fumble and raced 60 yards into the end zone—in the wrong direction.

This bit of footwork was recorded as a safety for the 49ers, but this misguided generosity did not affect the outcome as the Vikings recorded a 27–22 victory.

Marshall basically is a fun-loving, prank-playing 239-pounder with a constant twinkle in his eye. But the twinkle disappeared, along with his sense of humor, when he realized what had occurred.

Marshall, along with his planeload of teammates, arrived home in the Twin Cities in the wee hours of Monday morning. Jim went home and tried to sleep.

"I didn't get one minute of rest," he said later in the day. "I was real concerned about what I'd done and what would happen to me.

"I had promised to attend a football lunch, and I kept debating whether I should go. I didn't want people laughing at me. I made a mistake and believe me, I paid for it plenty just in my own mind.

"Then I decided I'd better keep my word, so I showed up. And do you know what? They gave me a standing ovation. I think it was just about the nicest thing that's ever happened to me. The people around here are just great—I don't know what else to say."

The most famous case of a "Wrong-Way-Corrigan" on the gridiron was Roy Riegels's Rose Bowl run (California vs. Georgia Tech) in 1929.

Riegels, now a resident of Woodland, California, consoled Marshall Monday.

"I feel just as sorry for the boy now as I did for myself back in 1929," he commented. "He's going to have to live with this for a long, long time. About the only thing I can say is that I hope he doesn't let it get him down. He's just going to have to get used to the teasing."

Marshall figures he can adjust to that. "I won't mind the teasing now that I know the fans here are in back of me. I was so down in the dumps I didn't know where to turn. But going to that lunch was the wisest decision I've made in some time."

Through it all the words of his coach, Norm Van Brocklin, may turn out to be even more consolation. Said Stormin' Norman: "Marshall played a whale of a ball game, as he always does. We're with him all the way."

There were not many dull moments around Coach Van Brocklin. He had a stormy relationship with the sporting press, most of whom he thought were incompetent to judge his football team. But he could be very charming, as he was in the following story that appeared in the *Minneapolis Sunday Tribune*'s Women and Society section. In that politically-incorrect era, when it was assumed that information of interest to women was really "soft" news and best confined to special women's sections of newspapers, Barbara Flanagan's "A Woman's Guide to the Vikings" story demonstrated that the Vikings were beginning to move out of the sports pages and into our social lives.

Tailgaters at Metropolitan Stadium at a game in 1964. Parties ranged from simple affairs to catered functions with tablecloths and formal dinnerware. PHOTOGRAPH COURTESY OF THE MINNESOTA HISTORICAL SOCIETY.

Minneapolis Tribune, August 15, 1965

A WOMAN'S GUIDE TO THE VIKINGS

Barbara Flanagan

Some men might think women and football go together like lollipops and pickles. Some men!

Well, girls, NOT Norman Van Brocklin. He's stubborn-Dutch about it. And besides he has Delft-blue eyes, a dollop of dash, and a kind of knightly delight in the fact that his own wife has a finely-honed knowledge of pro football.

Need another reason to listen to Van Brocklin on football (or on anything)? He's a smash on the ladies' luncheon circuit. Of course, that may be because he's the only man who looks good chewing gum in a poncho and stocking cap.

The coach of the Minnesota Vikings simply believes that women like football because men like football. He even believes that women can understand the pro game as well as the men—or even a little better.

Getting down to the basics, Van Brocklin believes that most women like football "subconsciously," he said, "because it has something to do with sex."

Well, doesn't everything?

"The football hero . . . you know," he said, "The fact that he's wearing a uniform just leaves something to the imagination."

The coach liked that idea. Then, with a beguiling smile he would rarely waste on a recalcitrant rookie, he said:

"Nothing changes. It hasn't changed since the days of Adam and Eve in the Garden of Eden." He apparently wasn't referring to football.

"Actually," said Van Brocklin, "women welcome pro football because it gets them out of the house on Sunday afternoons. And their husbands don't resent their company at the game because it makes it easier for them to go.

"Always remember . . . if the little woman doesn't like football, he has to stay home and rake the leaves."

The coach thinks football games on Sunday afternoon are a new form of social life. "Pro football is big all over the country today because the silk stocking set, the country clubbers, have discovered it," he said.

Discovering pro football just isn't enough. There are even some male fans—although only the honest will admit it—who don't know the difference between "red dog" and a bloody "blitz."

And when it comes to "cornerbacks" and "flankerbacks" and "split ends" and "tight ends"—and you're still working on the old single wing formation—pro football can be puzzling.

"Some of that jargon is comparable to barbershop poolroom talk," said Van Brocklin. "We use red dog, but not blue dog or super dog. Those words are television's contribution to pro football."

The coach advises ignoring it and starting at the beginning.

At this point his wife Gloria Van Brocklin, a slim, tanned mother of three with a model figure and brains enough to know when to give up pre-medical studies to concentrate on her husband, spoke up.

"A woman fan who really wants to get something out of the game," she said, "has first of all to learn to keep the chit-chat to the time outs. There is plenty of time for talking then and if you talk all the time and don't watch the action, you lose continuity."

Van Brocklin couldn't have said it better.

One idea he has for easy understanding is to pick a favorite player and watch him.

"Billy Brown is the masculine image," he said. "Tommy Mason is the suave smoothie. He appeals to the girls. And then there's Francis Tarkenton."

Francis is the all-American little boy grown up. Everybody loves Francis.

Tarkenton is the quarterback, the guy who runs the team. He is a "scrambler." What is scrambling?

In pro football talk, a scrambler is a quarterback who squirms out of the pocket of protecting blockers, runs around until he's surrounded and then throws the ball or runs with it.

Tarkenton is so talented at scrambling that in some of his split-second choreography on the field he performs like a baller in a cliff-hanger. (A baller is simply someone who participates in a ball or a dance—and that's Francis, every Sunday afternoon).

This shouldn't give the impression that Tarkenton scrambles willy-nilly. He does it with care that looks casual, but he always sets his feet before he throws.

"The important job," said Van Brocklin, "is to teach the quarterback to see and react. Recognize the defense and react. Call audibles if necessary.

"Probably one reason Francis scrambles so much is that he doesn't have the height and sometimes can't see his receivers down field." Tarkenton is only a whirling 5 feet, 11 inches tall.

And what, pray, are audibles? Audibles are signals called orally at the line of scrimmage and are used to change the play after a quarterback has had a look at the defenses.

What of "red dog" and "blitz"? It helps to watch Tarkenton again. Van Brocklin explained that red dog is just one way to designate different linebackers going after the quarterback. It's one combination of men. The blitz is another.

If the blitz is on, you see a bunch of burly linemen on the other team breaking through—or blitzing—to get at Tarkenton.

Worrying about whether or not they'll get through and fracture Francis's collarbone is one way to get involved in pro football.

Van Brocklin also suggests that a woman might spend some time in the stands watching Paul Flatley running pass patterns. Flatley, an end who may be The End because of his off-field sartorial elegance and eye for pretty girls, is obviously something special.

Sportswriters describe him as "foxy" and "having all the moves." What the pretty girls say about him hasn't been recorded, but there is no doubt that Flatley can look mighty heroic grabbing that ball.

Flatley has a built-in shift that apparently allows him to switch from low to high to reverse on the double gallop.

Watching him do it is another way to get excited.

Van Brocklin knows that line play is the most difficult for the unschooled football fan to watch. Not to watch it, however, is missing a lot of the fun.

"Concentrate on tackle Grady Alderman in the line," Van Brocklin said. "And on defense, watch the Ripper—Rip Hawkins—at work."

Hawkins does nice work. When you see him, you understand why he weighs 230 pounds.

Van Brocklin also has all sorts of other suggestions for the woman who wants to learn pro football by looking:

The split end (also called the spread end) is always to the weak side of the line. That means he's out there looking kind of lonely.

The flanker is always lined up to the other team's tight end. He's on the flank—a bit off to one side and hovering hawk-like.

The tight end and the flanker are always on the strong side—where the boys are.

There are all sorts of pass patterns and different ends run the different patterns differently. Make sense? It's up to the quarterback to see, react and time himself to each one of the ends—whoever is in the game at that time—and know their differences and still get the ball there.

Van Brocklin pointed out that the Vikings have to learn about 100 plays on offense and can execute nine defenses—plus the audibles. No wonder they're in bed at 10 P.M. in their Bemidji, Minnesota, training camp.

Now none of this explains why Ed Sharockman has had his nose broken 12 times or why Tommy Mason is so adept at razzle-dazzle running. Or even why fullback Bill Brown is called "The Coach" by his teammates.

"A woman can learn much more about football if she can watch the practice at Bemidji," Mrs. Van Brocklin said. She pointed out that Vikings-watching is great sport for entire families on vacation in the area. Practice sessions are free, open to the public and usually fascinating.

Mrs. Van Brocklin, who has been watching her husband with a football in his hands for 19 seasons, 17 in the National Football League where he was a physical spellbinder at quarterback, also has some other ideas for the woman fan.

"It's embarrassing to a man if a woman makes idiotic remarks," she said, "but the man shouldn't object to an honest question."

Some other suggestions from Gloria Van Brocklin:

When you can't watch the game in person, watch it on TV. By careful TV watching, you can pick up football terminology.

Buy a game program—get one ahead if you can—and read the information in it about the players and the plays.

Try not to watch the ball all the time. You learn so much more about the game if you don't.

Watch the different phases of play—the passing attack or its defense, the running attack or its defense.

And when you don't understand, ask the man next to you to explain it.

The Van Brocklins—and their three daughters, Karen, 15, Lynne, 14, and Judy, 13—will all be on hand next Friday night at Metropolitan Stadium when the Vikings play their only home exhibition game of the season.

The girls are as fanatic about football as their parents. At least one, young Judy, has her heart set on marrying a football player.

"She's got the sweets for Tommy Mason," said Van Brocklin. "And as to marrying a pro football player . . . well, they could do worse."

Mrs. Van Brocklin looked at Coach Van Brocklin and just smiled.

"You see," said Van Brocklin, "I believe the Lord looked out for me when he didn't give me a son. I'd be so darn demanding, I'd ruin the kid.

"Some of the kids I coach even cringe when I just raise my voice. But they're bright. If they aren't when they come in, they are when they leave. They know that I know enough to know that everybody's human."

At this point Van Brocklin made a sighing sound—something like a tornado blowing through the Grand Tetons.

"You know what I really am? I'm just too soft-hearted."

Van Brocklin stunned even his closest friends when he resigned after a 41–21 loss to the Baltimore Colts in 1965. The team had lost its first two games of the season, but entered the Baltimore game 5–3, with a three-game winning streak, including a 27–17 win over the eventual Eastern

Conference champion Cleveland Browns. The game was in Minnesota and Colts starter Johnny Unitas was injured and would not play. Van Brocklin felt it was a pivotal game for the franchise, and was crushed by the loss. He announced the resignation at a press conference on Monday morning, but got a visit from Gophers coach Murray Warmath and calls from Joe Stydahar, his old coach at the Los Angeles Rams, and other friends. By late Monday he called general manager Jim Finks and said he had made a mistake and wanted his job back, and Finks obliged. The team lost the next three games, but rallied to win the last two to finish 7–7, but it appeared that the coach had lost control of the team.

The Vikings were an uninspired 4–9–1 in 1966 and tensions between Van Brocklin and Fran Tarkenton, which had once been kept in the locker room, became more public. They had often clashed over the quarterback's scrambling, but the coach now felt that Tarkenton was a divisive influence in the clubhouse. Trade rumors began circulating as the season wound down when Van Brocklin benched Tarkenton for the last home game of the season against the Atlanta Falcons. This was a bitter blow to Tarkenton, since the game was televised throughout Georgia, his native state. Tarkenton appeared in the game only to hold for extra-point tries.

The bitterness lingered after the season, and in early February Tarkenton said it was impossible for him to return to the Vikings. He sent a letter to general manager Jim Finks, Coach Van Brocklin, and the team's five directors, asking to be traded.

One day later Van Brocklin verbally submitted his resignation . . . his second in 16 months. The five Vikings owners voted unanimously to accept this one.

Tarkenton was traded to the New York Giants in return for two first round draft choices: running back Clint Jones (1967), and offensive tackle Ron Yary (1968), a future Hall of Famer; and two second round choices: receiver Bob Grim (1968), who appeared in one Pro Bowl, and offensive guard Ed White (1969), a four-time Pro Bowler. These players were to have significant roles in the championship run that began in 1968.

40 for 60

BUD GRANT BUILDS A POWERHOUSE

VIKINGS GENERAL MANAGER JIM FINKS WASTED NO TIME HIRING
Bud Grant to replace Van Brocklin as head coach. Finks knew Grant well
from their days in the Canadian Football League. Together they instilled
discipline in the organization and moved the team into the elite ranks of
the NFL. Both were eventually voted into the NFL Hall of Fame.

Harold Peter "Bud" Grant Jr., arguably the greatest all-around athlete
in University of Minnesota history, was a popular choice. He had enlisted
in the U.S. Navy after graduating high school in Superior, Wisconsin, in
1945. He played football at the Great Lakes Naval Training Station under
legendary coach Paul Brown, and then enrolled at the University of Minnesota after his discharge, where he earned eight varsity letters—one in
baseball, three in basketball, and four in football. He had attracted Major
League Baseball scouts as a teenager, and played semi-pro baseball in Minnesota and Wisconsin until the late 1950s. Grant gave up his final year
of basketball eligibility to sign with the NBA Minneapolis Lakers for the
1949–1950 season. He played with them for two years and then signed
with the Philadelphia Eagles, who had drafted him in the first round in
1950. Grant played defensive end in 1951, and then moved to offensive end
in 1952, where he finished second in the league in receiving.

Grant refused to sign a new contract for the 1953 season and bolted
the NFL for the Winnipeg Blue Bombers of the Canadian Football League.
In "playing out his option" he was at least 30 years ahead of his time. He

played four years for the Blue Bombers and then became their head coach in 1957. In ten years under Grant, 1957–1966, Winnipeg won the Grey Cup—the CFL's Super Bowl—four times.

He had declined an offer to become the Vikings' first head coach. "In 1959 and 1960, Winnipeg was the league champion," explained Grant. "We were a young team at Winnipeg then, and I felt it would be a winner for some time. But the Vikings were just starting. They were an expansion club that would suffer growing pains."

Jim Finks was quarterback for the Pittsburgh Steelers from 1949 to 1955. He played in the Pro Bowl in 1952 and was the league leader in pass attempts, completions, and yards in 1955. He retired after that season, spent one year as assistant coach at Notre Dame, and then signed as an assistant coach with the Calgary Stampeders in 1957, eventually working his way up to general manager. The Minnesota Vikings signed him to be their general manager in 1964.

"BUILDING A VIKING POWERHOUSE," FROM *BUD: THE OTHER SIDE OF THE GLACIER* (1986)
Bill McGrane

Bud Grant arrived in Minnesota in the late winter of 1967 and promptly defused suggestions that he would rebuild the Vikings.

"We want to grow," he said. "We want to build on what is already here. But we aren't rebuilding . . . the foundation of this team is already in place."

Odd . . . the Vikings, at least to the casual observer, seemed to have spent the first six years of their professional existence windsurfing from one emotional pole to the other, with far more time spent in the troughs than on the crests.

In the middle of the 1966 season, for example, when the Packers were at their zenith, the Vikings played like demons to win 20–17 at Green Bay, only to lose at home the next week to a mediocre Detroit team in a wave of pratfalls and blown assignments.

From 1961 through 1966, the Vikings were coached by Van Brocklin, a Hall of Fame quarterback with a house of mirrors personality.

Funny, combative, brilliant, brooding, gifted, mercurial . . . a lot of that last quality, mercurial. The toughest opponent the Dutchman ever faced was himself.

His team had rushed to early bloom in 1964, posting an 8–5–1 record and narrowly missing the playoffs. But they fell back after that. The 1966 team distinguished itself by leading the league in penalties en route to the 4–9–1 finish. The bottom fell out as Van Brocklin benched Tarkenton in December when the infant Atlanta team came to Minnesota. Tarkenton was from

Atlanta, and the demotion mortified him. To complete the equation, Atlanta won the game.

Indeed, the casual observer might be forgiven for failing to notice that the foundation for progress was in place when Grant came back over the border in 1967.

But darned if he wasn't right.

Underneath all of the inconsistency and the hell-for-leather mindset of Van Brocklin's team, there was talent on this football team.

Grant's Vikings teams would win more than 150 games, and a lot of the winning would be done by people from those early years . . . Tingelhoff, Alderman, Sunde, Bowie, Cox, Brown, Osborn, Marshall, Eller, Larsen, Winston, Sharockman, and Kassulke.

And Grant got more help almost immediately.

Tarkenton was gone, traded to New York, but his price had been draft choices, and Jim Finks . . . operating from a hospital bed after gallbladder surgery . . . pumped new talent into the roster. Clint Jones and Gene Washington were first-rounders from Michigan State . . . Bob Grim and Bob Bryant came in the second round. Then Finks sent two veterans, Hal Bedsole and Tommy Mason, to the Los Angeles Rams for their first-round choice, and the move brought into focus the defense that would become the game's finest. The Vikings drafted Alan Page.

Bud Grant and Alan Page are not friendly, and Grant prefers to let matters rest at that. But their differences have done nothing to dilute Grant's respect for Page's awesome ability.

"He was the best defensive player I've ever seen," said Grant. "Alan was a great competitor . . . as much as he protested so many things about football, when the whistle blew, he couldn't overcome the fact that he was a great competitor.

"Very few people truly utilize their abilities," Grant went on. "Most people take their talents for granted . . . they come to depend upon them without ever thinking of trying to improve them. Alan worked at his ability, he made a great effort to improve himself. That effort made him a remarkable football player."

Actually, Grant knew a good deal about the Vikings . . . he read the Minnesota papers and talked to people and kept current over the years in Canada.

"I used to go to their office in the off-season and look at game films," he said. "The first few times I did it, Norm couldn't have been nicer . . . he told me to look at as much film as I wanted. Then, I went there one time when he saw me and said, 'What in the hell are you doing here? We can't have you hanging around here all the time!'

The NFL draft was simpler in the days before Mel Kiper and ESPN. Here general manager Jim Finks and Bud Grant discuss strategy, with potential names listed on a makeshift blackboard leaning against the wall. Note the candles burning on Grant's desk and on the shelf next to the black-board: Grant hated cigarette smoke, and this was his defense against the chain-smoking Finks.
PHOTOGRAPH COURTESY OF THE MINNESOTA VIKINGS.

"That was the last time I went to their office."

One thing that Grant knew that troubled him was the league-leading penalty total the club had drawn in 1966 . . . penalties aren't a ready mix with Grant's football philosophy.

Dave Osborn, the running back, recalled Grant's first year in Minnesota.

"Nothing upset Bud more than mental mistakes, and penalties are mental mistakes. He told us we couldn't afford to play dumb football, and penalties were dumb. He told us, too, that we would go from being the most-penalized team to being the least-penalized team . . . and we did. We still weren't good enough, but we quit doing dumb things," said Osborn.

The theory has been advanced that football teams are like families and that the head coach . . . ready or not . . . provides the father image for his players to mirror.

"The players were on Norm's wavelength when I got here," said Grant. "Looking at where they were and where I wanted them to be . . . there couldn't have been a much sharper contrast."

And where was it that Grant wanted them to be?

"Playing with discipline."

Which probably explains the bogus plea he made in 1967 training camp for a rule that didn't even exist.

At a team meeting, Grant told the players that the groundkeeper had asked their cooperation in avoiding an area of the field that had been newly sodded.

Of course, the groundkeeper hadn't said a word about the new sod.

"But I made a real point of it," Grant explained. "I sort of went overboard, explaining. I identified the area clearly, I said it was important for all of us to stay off it, and I said I didn't want anybody to forget about it."

Why did he do it?

"It's possible to make up a rule," Grant answered, "and learn about people by how they react to it.

"After I told the players about staying off the new sod, I went out on the field and watched.

"There were players who would come running up to the sodded area, recognize it, and go around it.

"There were players who would run onto it and then stop . . . you knew they'd forgotten and then remembered what I said after they started across. Those fellows would back up and go around.

"There were some who could come running out and go across the sodded area without even realizing it.

"Finally, there was one fellow who just roared on across the sodded area, in defiance to what I had said."

And the moral of the story?

"It's important to learn things like that about people," said Grant. "You learn who the players are who will forget what you tell them, you learn who will remember what you tell them, and you learn who just won't buy what you tell them. The same thing will happen in a game.

"That's why soldiers march in the army . . . nobody ever won a war by marching, you march to learn how to take orders as a group."

If it is possible for defensive linemen to have a good disposition, the Viking defensive tackle Gary Larsen fit that image. A big, sunny-faced blond, Lars was a nice guy.

But August two-a-days can try the patience of even the best disposition.

Gary Larsen gave in to one of those moments of tempest on the practice field at Mankato, and Grant, the new coach, was quick to seize his opportunity.

Larsen got into a fight.

"I don't even remember who the other player was," said Bud, "and the thing I knew, for sure, was that Larsen hadn't started it. But he fought . . . it was a brawl, and the two of them were flailing away at each other."

And then Grant flailed Larsen.

"It wasn't his fault that it started," said Bud, "but I needed to make a point. I really ripped into him. I had to . . . if it happened on the practice field it could happen in a game. Being undisciplined wasn't going to help us . . . you can't play football in a rage."

That first training camp had some sharp curves for the Viking veterans . . . they were the Grant rules. As it had been in Canada, his list of player rules was short, but very sturdy.

"If you're going to have a rule, have a reason for it," he said.

Smoking, for instance.

Bud Grant detests smoking. One secret ambition he harbors to this day is to have his football team, en masse, come out publicly against the use of tobacco in any form.

His father died with a cigarette smoldering in his fingers . . . and as these pages were being written, Grant was serving as pallbearer at the funeral of his closest boyhood chum, a former smoker.

"I told them at that first camp that they could smoke if they insisted, but only in their rooms or in the john. They couldn't smoke in the meetings or in the locker room or the dining hall or walking around the campus. I didn't make a big deal out of it . . . I just told them that was the way it would be. I knew they had smoked wherever they pleased when Norm was there . . . Norm was a smoker. Well, Norm wasn't there anymore, and I don't smoke."

He isn't keen on beer drinking in dorm rooms, either.

"I watched them lug those little refrigerators into the dorm when we moved in," he said. "I knew they had kept beer in their rooms in the past, although they were not supposed to, but I didn't say anything right away . . . I wanted to have a reason."

He had it several nights into camp.

During a team meeting, Grant prowled the player rooms in the dorm.

"Paul Flatley and Paul Dickson roomed together. I opened their fridge. There was a row of pop cans right across the front, but behind the pop, there was beer . . . they must have had a case of it. I mean, my kids could have done a better job of disguising it. I went back to the meeting and told them to have the refrigerators out of the rooms by the weekend."

If the veterans fretted that Van Brocklin had been replaced by a Boy Scout leader . . . and more than a few of them did, early on . . . their concern deepened when, before the first preseason game, Grant held National Anthem practice.

Athletes, in the main, seem to feel an obligation to fuss and fidget during the playing of the National Anthem.

They stand with hands on hips or twirling their headgear, and paw the grass or roll tight neck muscles, all the while chewing mightily at a wad of gum. If you haven't seen a hockey goalie whanging his pads into place over the "rockets' red glare," then you've probably noticed a linebacker repositioning his athletic supporter and its contents with "bombs bursting in air."

The one thing very few of them do is stand still.

Grant did away with "antsy anthems" in short order.

"I suppose this sounds corny today," he said, "but I believe in the National Anthem. I feel good about it. I know that attitude is passé for many people, but my feeling for my country has a high priority. I grew up during a war, and I spent my youth preparing to go to war. About the only thing left today out of all that is respect for the flag . . . it's really our last demonstration of patriotism.

"There are a lot of times when I still get misty-eyed at the playing of the National Anthem."

If not misty-eyed, Grant's charges would at least hear the playing of the anthem in an orderly fashion.

Several days before the first 1967 preseason game, Bud looked over his squad for someone who was big and had had military training of some sort.

He settled promptly on Carl Eller, a vast defensive end called Moose. Eller had been in the National Guard. He also enlisted John Kirby, a linebacker and another Guardsman.

"I said, 'Moose, if you stand up there tall during the playing of the anthem, people are going to respect you for it.'

"He bought it," said Grant. "We went over how the players should stand . . . every man on a yard line, heels together, eyes front, left arm at your side, helmet in your right hand. Then I asked Eller to take the rookies aside and teach them. He not only did it, he was enthusiastic about it, he was proud to be chosen as the model. When you want to set a new thing into motion, you have to pick the right people to lead for you."

Carl Eller played defensive end for the Minnesota Vikings for 15 years . . . expertly, but the end of his playing career was bittersweet. Eller retired from football with drug and alcohol problems.

But he didn't stay that way.

Through treatment, through the support of others, and through his own belief and courage, Moose is recovering today. More than that, he has visited NFL teams across the country, working in the effort to educate athletes to the truth of alcohol and drug use.

"One of my biggest regrets," said Eller, "is that I didn't get closer to Bud as a player. I really learned from him after my playing days were finished. I wish now that I could have modeled myself after him."

The Vikings practiced standing at attention for the National Anthem . . . they even practiced singing.

They went to Tulsa, Oklahoma, that weekend to play the Philadelphia Eagles . . . the irony was not wasted on Grant . . . and won 34–0. And their anthem formation was letter-perfect.

"People can only keep their eyes on the flag for so long during the playing of the anthem," Grant explained. "After that, they look at other things. What is the most logical thing to look at a football game? The players. And not just the fans . . . the players on opposite sides of the field are looking at each other.

"It's a form of discipline . . . if the player across the field sees you chewing gum or scratching your butt, that's one thing. But if he sees you standing tall, taking pride in the way you look, he'll notice. He might not want to, but he's going to respect you for it."

Admirable as the new-wave discipline might be, the Vikings had hired Grant for more simplistic reasons . . .

To win, for instance.

Shortly before Grant went to Minnesota, Jim Finks, the man who had hired him, talked about Bud.

"There will be things about him that you don't understand," said Finks. "He won't always communicate why he does something the way he does, and even when he does, it might not make sense to you.

"But he knows how to win, and, more important, he knows how to live with winning."

Grant was asked what Finks's words meant to him.

"It's harder to live with winning than it is to live with losing," he said.

"Green Bay did a good job of it, back when they were having their run. Lombardi got a lot of credit, and I'm sure he played an important role in their success, but I think a lot of it had to do with being in Green Bay. Achieving and holding on to success is more attainable in a small city like Green Bay than it is in a big city. There just are fewer distractions in Green Bay than there are in Los Angeles or New York.

"The difficulty comes in remembering what it took to get you there, to be successful in the first place," said Grant.

"When you're winning, everybody wants a piece of you. Suddenly, there are opportunities for distraction, the notoriety that goes with winning. We all want to be recognized for our accomplishments, but that recognition, unless you guard against it, can carry you further and further away from the attitude that permitted you to become a winner.

"Players can become so involved in the things surrounding the game . . . the distractions . . . that they have to fight to be on time for practice, instead of hanging around the locker room, waiting for practice to start. I guess you can call that coping," said Grant, "the need to be able to deal with success and the price you must pay for it."

Minnesota . . . relatively isolated in the geographic sense and solid in its Scandinavian heritage . . . struck Grant as a promising site for long-term success.

Fair enough . . . Grant knew how to live with winning, but the Vikings still needed to learn how to win.

The 1967 season didn't appear to be a step forward—the team, at 3–8–3, had one less win than in 1966. However, Jim Finks brought in another CFL veteran in 1967—quarterback Joe Kapp, whom he had signed for Calgary in 1959. Kapp, who had quarterbacked the University of California into the 1959 Rose Bowl, was a versatile athlete who had also won two letters in basketball, but because he wasn't a classic drop-back passer he didn't attract much attention from NFL teams. After two injury-plagued seasons, Finks traded Kapp to the British Columbia Lions, where he led the CFL in passing four years in a row, from 1962 to 1965, and captured the Grey Cup in 1964. Kapp, of mixed German and Mexican heritage, impressed his teammates with his bravura and hard-nosed play. He and linebacker Lonnie Warwick got into a brawl requiring a trip to Midway Hospital for both of them after a 30–27 loss to Green Bay late in the season—Kapp argued he was responsible for the loss, while Warwick blamed it on the defense!

The Vikings won three out of four to start the 1968 season, but were 3–4 at the halfway mark. From there they went 5–2 to take the Central Division crown. The Baltimore Colts—who would go on to lose to the New York Jets in Super Bowl III—dominated the Vikings 24–14 in a steady rain to win the Western Conference championship. Kapp completed 26 of 44 passes (both new Vikings records) and ran for 52 yards in 10 carries, but was given a beating by the Colts' defense. Caked with mud and blood, and hardly able to walk or speak, Kapp had to be helped off the field. "I never saw a tougher man in all my life than Joe Kapp in Baltimore," equipment manager Jimmy Eason said.

The season wasn't over, however. The loss to the Colts earned the Vikings a berth in the little-remembered Bert Bell Benefit Bowl, most often just called "The Playoff Bowl." The game, named to honor Bell, who had been the NFL Commissioner from 1946 to 1959, was for third place in the NFL (the AFL did not play a similar game) and was played at the Orange

Bowl in Miami for all 10 years of its existence. It wasn't that popular a game. Vince Lombardi, the legendary coach of the Green Bay Packers, who played in the game following the 1963 and 1964 seasons, had no time for it. "He called it the 'Shit Bowl,'" Bob Skoronski, Packers offensive lineman, told author David Maraniss for his biography of Vince Lombardi, *When Pride Still Mattered: A Life of Vince Lombardi*. "That's the word he used. He said it was a losers' bowl for losers." The Vikings lost to the Dallas Cowboys 17–13 on January 5, 1969, before a crowd of only 22,961.

The game was played one more time, after the conclusion of the 1969 season. There was discussion about continuing to have some sort of runner-up game after the NFL and AFL merged in 1970, but the new alignment in the leagues already called for seven playoff games—three in each conference plus the Super Bowl—and in the end there was no appetite to continue the "Losers' Bowl."

The Vikings started the 1969 season with a 24–23 loss to the New York Giants on two fourth-quarter touchdown passes by ex-Viking Fran Tarkenton. Joe Kapp threw seven touchdown passes (an NFL record shared with four others) the next week to beat the Colts 52–14 in the home opener, and exact some revenge for the 1968 playoff loss. The team rallied around Kapp's slogan, "40 for 60"—all 40 men on the roster playing hard for the full 60 minutes—and went on a 12-game winning streak before losing an inconsequential game 10–3 at Atlanta on the last day of the season.

Scheduling conflicts with a possible Twins playoff game against the Baltimore Orioles forced the move of the Vikings' October 5 game with the Green Bay Packers to Memorial Stadium on the University of Minnesota campus. The Vikings beat the Packers 19–7 in a tough defensive battle, and many football fans played defense, as well—the Memorial Stadium seats were obviously laid out for college-age physiques, forcing middle-aged Vikings fans to wedge themselves into their designated spaces. The 60,740 attendance total was 13,000 more than could be seated at Metropolitan Stadium, and stood as a Vikings home record until 1983, the second year in the Hubert H. Humphrey Metrodome.

St. Paul Dispatch writer Bill Boni used the occasion to propose that the Vikings move to Memorial Stadium and leave Metropolitan Stadium for baseball. It was perhaps one of the earlier stadium proposals/suggestions in what has become a 40-year saga. This early debate led to the building of the multi-purpose Metrodome to house the Vikings, Twins, and Gophers, beginning in 1982. The concrete was hardly dry on the Dome when new debates began, leading to the push for single-purpose facilities in the 1990s and the construction of new Twins and Gophers stadiums in the early 2000s.

St. Paul Dispatch, October 6, 1969
"WRITING OUT LOUD" COLUMN
Bill Boni

HOW ABOUT KEEPING VIKES AT UM?

The biggest impact the entire weekend made here was in the satisfactory mechanics surrounding the emergency transfer of the Viking–Green Bay game from the Met to Memorial Stadium. If I had my druthers (and I'm only sorry to have to acknowledge that I won't have), the Vikings would play all their home games at Memorial Stadium and then, after this season, would join with the University of Minnesota in refurbishing the place to make it a more up-to-date arena.

This could be done, too, and without any extravagant outlay.

Not that the idea wouldn't meet some opposition. Just as an example (and it's hard to understand why this should be so), Channel 5 in its dinnertime news report Sunday tried very hard to give the impression that the switch of sites made things miserable for the customers. What they showed was a variety of shots of people trudging or sloshing down tree-lined streets in the direction of Memorial Stadium.

If it's raining, what's so different between sloshing down a tree-lined street or sloshing through a puddle-specked parking lot? Scenically, the tree-lined street even might be preferable.

THREATENED TRAFFIC SNARL? IT DIDN'T

But consider this.

The doom-forespellers had been saying, right from the moment when the chance first arose that the Viking game might be moved, that there would be the world's worst traffic tangle around Memorial Stadium that day. This observer, as a minority of one, refused to believe it. I've been to Gopher games that drew full houses of 63,000 plus and I've not been in a traffic tangle yet.

There was none, or none of major consequence, on my route Sunday, even though this included detouring off I-94 to avoid the gasoline tank truck which had spilled its guts about an hour before kickoff.

Sure, people walked a lot of streets to get to the stadium. They always have. It is testimonial to the fact that there are more parking spaces around Memorial Stadium than show up on official charts. Each man has his favorite hideaway, and on Sundays (as opposed to Saturdays, when the Gophers play) there probably are more open spaces, inasmuch as none are taken up by students attending classes and there is virtually no business or truck traffic in the area then.

Viking games at the Met? That's the worst thing I can face on a Sunday, the idea of getting sewed up in another of those inevitable freeway–

Cedar Avenue crushes. You either have to leave far too early, or leave late enough to miss the opening kickoff.

MODERN KNOW-HOW CAN SPRUCE IT UP

Okay, so Memorial Stadium is an architectural antique and its aisles are so crowded and its concession and restroom facilities so poor they'd hardly serve a proper high school stadium.

But modern-day construction procedures and architectural innovations have saved buildings in far worse shape. Los Angeles had a miserable facility in its huge Coliseum where USC, UCLA and the Rams play. Did Los Angeles abandon the place? It did not. It discarded some 20,000 seats as being too far from the scene of the action, put backs and arm rests on some 50,000 others which had been bare benches before, and thus emerged with a stadium which nowadays attracts capacity audiences, whereas customers had been getting into the habit of staying home.

Memorial Stadium is a better fan-suited structure to begin with because its seats rise more rapidly and don't run up as far. It could be made even better for football by discarding the running track and dropping the football field some 10 feet lower. It could be made better still if the Vikings and the University of Minnesota collaborated in buying an all-weather playing surface (all right, Tartan Turf; but Astroturf probably would want to bid on it).

TWINS WOULDN'T HAVE TO BUY TARTAN

There's been some talk about domed stadiums. A dome would be nice. It's not essential. Smart engineers might be able to devise a cantilevered roof that would put at least a share of the seats on each side under cover. Smart engineers also ought to be able to figure out a way to provide a new press box without rebuilding the whole stadium.

I know, I know—the Vikings have another six seasons to go on their rental agreement at the Met, and they sank all that money into that double-decked left field stand. But think of what it would mean to both the Vikings and the Twins to have the Met clear only for baseball. No conflicts, for one thing, and for another, nobody would be pushing the Twins to install Tartan Turf at the Met, which they don't really want.

Back to sports? Okay, back to sports. Cruelest crack of all on Sunday, probably, came from the Viking fan who hollered as Joe Kapp called for another unproductive Viking shot into the Green Bay line:

"Just because you're playing in Warmath's park, you don't have to play like him."

It wasn't just cruel, it wasn't unfair. The Vikings beat Green Bay on defense. Defense is what Warmath hasn't got.

This team captured the imagination of Minnesota fans. Hometown crowds got more raucous than in prior years; fans began sporting Vikings jerseys and caps to games—even Vikings "stadium bags" (short sleeping bags to keep legs and feet warm at cold games). A big increase in pregame tailgating parties helped create a party atmosphere at the games. (Many tailgaters picked up the parties again after the game to celebrate and to wait out the interminable postgame traffic jams.) Local TV and radio stations scrambled to feature Vikings highlights and to produce player interviews and feature stories. At many businesses that fall, Monday mornings could just as well have been paid holidays, as fans hashed and rehashed Sunday's game.

Folks had a lot to talk about. The offense led the NFL in scoring, while the defense ranked first in fewest points and yards allowed. In contrast to 1966, when center Mick Tingelhoff was the only Viking selected to the All NFL team, in 1969 there were six Vikings selected—offensive linemen Tingelhoff and Grady Alderman, flanker Gene Washington, defensive linemen Carl Eller and Alan Page, and place kicker Fred Cox.

There were some quirky things to talk about in the week following the Vikings' 10–7 win over the 49ers in a snowstorm in their last home game on December 14. At halftime, a hot air balloon had risen through the snow and out of sight. Fans at the time thought the spectacular takeoff was part of the act, but on Monday they were surprised to learn that the balloon was supposed to have remained tethered to the ground.

They were even more surprised to learn that the balloon pilot was 11-year-old Rick Snyder of St. Paul. Rick had been in the gondola with his mother, Audrey, a licensed balloonist. She jumped out of the gondola because their combined weight was preventing the balloon from rising off the field. Unfortunately, the tether rope broke and the balloon rose before Mrs. Snyder could get back into the gondola. The balloon barely cleared the right field light standards. Dakota County sheriff's officials were alerted and tried to find the balloon. Rick, who knew some flying techniques from watching his parents, started bringing the balloon down by shutting down the heat and pulling a cord that opened an air-flap at the top of the balloon.

Unfortunately, the descent brought him down to the Minnesota River. He tried to bring the balloon up by adding heat, but it crashed into the cold water, about 30 feet from shore. Rick managed to swim ashore while still wearing his boots, helmet, and heavy jacket. A passing motorist picked him up and drove him back to the stadium, where he was warmed up, apparently none the worse for his unplanned adventure. Rick's father found the balloon washed ashore near the Black Dog power plant in Burnsville.

Joe Kapp added to the bizarre news week two days later when he refused to accept the team MVP trophy at the annual WCCO Awards Banquet.

Eleven-year-old Rick Snyder went on an unscheduled hot-air balloon ride during the halftime show at the game between the Vikings and 49ers on December 14, 1969. The balloon rose into the snowy sky and out of sight after its tether lines accidentally broke. Fans figured it was just part of the show, but Rick was later rescued after crashing into the Minnesota River and swimming to shore. PHOTOGRAPH FROM *DISPATCH–PIONEER PRESS*. COURTESY OF THE MINNESOTA HISTORICAL SOCIETY.

St. Paul Pioneer Press, December 18, 1969

'69 VIKINGS HAVE NO MVP SINCE KAPP REFUSES TROPHY

Ralph Reeve

They tried to give Joe Kapp the Viking MVP trophy Wednesday night, but the ruggedly handsome quarterback turned it down.

"There is no most valuable Viking," said Kapp, his voice charged with emotion.

"There are 40 most valuable Vikings. We have four games left to go. We have '40 for 60' . . . I just can't accept this."

With that, Kapp walked off the platform at the Prom Center to the gaping astonishment of an awestruck crowd of 1,000 persons, and left emcee Paul Giel stranded at the microphone with the MVP trophy like a bride waiting at the altar with some wilted lilies.

"Anybody want a trophy?" asked Giel.

Hal Scott, co-emcee, grabbed the microphone and quipped:

"We will now take up a collection to make up 40 of these."

Kapp earlier had been named and accepted the award for the Viking best offensive player of 1969.

Defensive captain Jim Marshall was named the best defensive player and punter Bob Lee was named the best rookie.

Later, while waiting for photographers to take pictures of the award winners, Kapp was asked why he turned down the MVP trophy.

Kapp grinned, a little embarrassed, and then assumed a fierce expression. He leaned over and snarled in the questioner's ear:

"There ain't no Most Valuable Player.

"There ain't no Santa Claus.

"And there ain't no red-nosed reindeer, either!"

Viking offensive captain Grady Alderman, asked for his feelings on Kapp's surprising actions, shrugged and said, "That's Joe . . .

"I'm sure it was a sincere feeling. He truly deserved it."

Mick Tingelhoff said:

"Joe's got a lot of strong feelings. He's a team man. He's the first man to come up with the '40 for 60' slogan."

The slogan, adopted by the Vikings for 1969, means 40 players for 60 minutes.

If Kapp was bashful about accepting two trophies, he wasn't about being the source of the Viking slogan.

"Damn right. I coined that '40 for 60' slogan," he said. "Up in Canada it was 30 for 60."

Earlier, the fans at the annual WCCO Awards Night dinner heard assistant coach Bus Mertes make this presentation of the best offensive player:

"He's good-looking, courageous, respected by all who know him and a man who demands that respect. And he's not like Virgil Carter; he believes in the coaches."

When Mertes announced Kapp was the "best offensive player," big Joe strode up to the microphone, obviously thrilled, and said:

"This has gotta be the finest award I've ever received. I'm very proud. It's just a pleasure being the quarterback of this team, and I accept this for the quarterbacks."

Later, they called on Bill Brown, the 1968 MVP, to make the presentation of the 1969 MVP.

"Well, at least I didn't have to worry," said Brown. "If I was giving it out (the MVP award), I wasn't getting it."

Brown described the player chosen for the 1969 MVP trophy:

Joe Kapp throws a jump pass against the Cleveland Browns. He was a throwback, leading by virtue of his physical courage and intensity rather than by his passing skills. PHOTOGRAPH COURTESY OF THE MINNESOTA VIKINGS.

"He's a fine football player; he's a leader, a team man; he's 40 for 60 . . . the MVP this year is . . . Joe Kapp."

Kapp strode up to the microphone while the band played "Jingle Bells" and 1,000 fans stood and clapped, cheered and whistled.

It was too much for the toughest quarterback in pro football.

●

The Vikings were behind 17–7 at the half in the Western Conference championship game against the Los Angeles Rams on December 27, but were buoyed by a long and loud standing ovation by bundled fans as they took the field for the second half. The defense, which had been having trouble with the Rams in the first half, stiffened and Dave Osborn scored on a one-yard run to drop the deficit to 17–14 at the end of the third quarter. The Rams scored a field goal, but Kapp directed a 65-yard drive—scoring on a scramble from the two—and the Vikings had their first lead of the game, 21–20. The Vikings smothered Rams return man Ron Smith at the 12 on the subsequent kickoff and then sacked quarterback Roman Gabriel at the two. On the next play Carl Eller tackled Gabriel in the end zone for a safety and a 23–20 victory.

Fans were in a frenzy anticipating the NFL championship game against the Cleveland Browns, whom they had trounced 51–3 on November 9. About 300 showed up for an interdenominational worship service prior to the game at the Metropolitan Sports Center, home of the hockey North Stars and an easy walk to the Met. The service was the brainstorm of *Minneapolis Star* columnist Jim Klobuchar, who suggested that the noon kickoff time "might force some churchgoers to choose between God and mammon." Four Bloomington ministers presided over the service at center ice: Rev. Robert Cash of Bloomington Church of Christ, Rev. Ralph Shoemaker of Portland Av. United Methodist Church, Rev. John Propert of Westwood Community Baptist Church, and Rev. Richard Keene Smith of St. Patrick's Episcopal Church.

The scripture lesson was "Straight Towards the Goal."

Although it might have come straight out of Bud Grant's playbook, it actually was taken from Philippians 3:14—"So I run straight towards the goal, in order to win the prize, which is God's call to Christ Jesus."

The Vikings completely dominated the Cleveland Browns on an icy Metropolitan Stadium field, 27–7, to win their first of four NFL championships. The Vikings scored on their first two possessions on some freak plays that set the tone for the day. Gene Washington caught a crucial 33-yard pass when Browns cornerback Walt Sumner slipped and fell down on the icy field. From the Browns' seven, Kapp scored despite a botched handoff.

Famous sportswriter Wells Twombly could hardly believe the play. (Twombly also talked about the local TV blackout, foreshadowing a subject that would soon become a national debate. NFL rules at the time prohibited the televising of home games, even when a game was sold out.)

Sporting News, January 17, 1970

THE WORSE THEY LOOK, THE BETTER VIKES ARE

Wells Twombly

His feet slipping slightly on the frozen tundra beneath his cleats, the fullback moved toward a hole that filled suddenly with unfriendly flesh. Altering his course desperately, he managed to gain nine yards on a horrible shattered draw play that will never appear in a football instruction film, except perhaps as a wretched example.

A few breathless seconds later, the quarterback cut loose with a 33-yard pass that resembled, ever so grotesquely, a water fowl that had been grazed by buckshot. His best receiver had to backtrack up the field in order to catch it.

Finally, this $16 million professional football club, allegedly composed of the best athletes in captivity, herked and jerked its way down to its opponents' seven-yard line. At this moment in the National Football League's 50-year history, it managed one of the ugliest touchdowns ever witnessed by 47,900 frost-smeared eyeballs.

Quarterback Joe Kapp, whose artlessness badgers the imagination, tried to hand off to fullback Bill Brown, who wasn't there. In his desperation, he backed up, bumping into halfback Dave Osborn. Now the Minnesota Vikings had the Cleveland Browns just where they wanted them in the NFL's championship game.

The worse the Vikings look, the better they are. There's never been a club quite like them. They utterly offend people who think that football is nothing more than sweaty ballet. They do the darndest things.

THOSE VIKINGS ARE BRUTAL

So there was Kapp down there, slamming into his friends and colleagues on the Browns' seven-yard line in the very first period. And what did he do? He scored. Son-of-a-gun, if that crass, crude German-Mexican from California didn't charge straight ahead, drag some Browns along with him and put his snub nose into Cleveland's end zone.

When it was over, the Browns had a 27–7 defeat that didn't seem, by the score, anyway, as brutal as it really was. The Vikings take no prisoners. They aren't a football team, they're a gang war. They do everything awkwardly. They're a piece of camp art.

Kapp throws terrible passes. He doesn't even grip the ball properly. They flutter and roll. The two Minnesota running backs seem to wear cement overshoes. Even the field-goal kicker, Fred Cox, one of the best, slams line drives above the opposition's finger tips.

The humorous thing is that the Vikings don't know how bad they look. They're winning. They're awesomely powerful. They totally disarm another ball club, taking its offense away completely. Funny thing is, they think they're pretty, too.

"You guys say I have a weak arm and a fluttery arm," said Kapp. "But I'll tell you what kind of arm I have—it's an arm that's good enough to win."

And that is the Vikings' whole lovely secret. That's why they survived the National League's long, long season and classier-looking outfits like the Dallas Cowboys and Los Angeles Rams failed. The Vikings aren't pretty, but they're good enough to win.

More than anything else, they reflect the personality of Kapp, who never will make the advertising people forget Joe Namath. He is large, a late-model Neanderthal with short stubby fingers and hulking shoulders.

But late in that last NFL game of the year, in that nine-degree weather at Minneapolis' Metropolitan Stadium, he charged 13 yards around right end and found Cleveland's malevolent left linebacker, Jim Houston (240 pounds), standing between him and weak sunlight.

Slam. Bang. There was Houston lying face down on the frosty turf. He slept fully 20 minutes. In the dressing room, his vision returned. His brain stopped spinning.

"I just woke up from a terrible dream," he said.

So did the rest of the National Football League. The Vikings are large enough, mean enough to keep winning for years. In fact, it appears that coach Bud Grant's building program is just starting.

"This team has togetherness . . . togetherness. Call it love or something corny like team spirit," said fullback Brown.

"A fellow the other day was asking me if this team has any racial problem," said Minnesota's white tackle Grady Alderman. "I had to stop and try and think who was white and who was black on this club. Those faces aren't brown or pink. Those are the faces of friends of mine who wear purple uniforms. That sounds cornball, but it's true."

FREEZEOUT IS SENSELESS

One thing that professional football has to start thinking about is getting out of the frozen north with these postseason games. There's no logical reason to play football in Minneapolis–St. Paul on the fourth day of January.

It used to be said that any club that won a championship owed it to its fans to have the game in the same stadium where the people bought tickets all season. That is a lovely sentiment, meant chiefly for baseball teams who play their games in the spring-summer-early autumn.

To hold a championship game so far north in the dead of winter is actually a disservice to the folks in Minneapolis, St. Paul, Bloomington, Bemidji, etc. Even though the Vikings' management spent $18,000 struggling to keep the field mildly playable, the 47,900 Arctic explorers who showed up didn't see football at its best.

The question remains: Is it better to dress in thermal underwear and a parka made out of wolf's fur and watch a game through binoculars in temperatures you wouldn't put a dog outdoors in—or is it better to take the whole thing to Miami and watch it in a warm living room on television?

There are three million souls in the Minneapolis–St. Paul area. But only 47,900 saw the game. If the thing had been held in the south, everyone who owned a television set could have tuned in.

This frostbitten thinking is just that. The television camera has made an interesting change in our society, and the NFL, which gets so much of its revenue from it, ought to pay closer attention.

●

The Vikings' luck ran out in Super Bowl IV, however. Most experts thought the AFL New York Jets' victory over the NFL Baltimore Colts in Super Bowl III had been a fluke, and the Vikings were two-touchdown favorites over the Kansas City Chiefs, who had finished second in the AFL Western Division. In the AFL, with just 10 teams, the first-round playoffs matched the second-place team of one division against the first-place team of the other. The 16-team NFL was split into four equal divisions.

Super Bowl IV—it was officially called the "AFL-NFL World Championship Game" at the time—was the last championship contest between the separate leagues. By terms of the June 1966 merger agreement, the two leagues began to conduct a joint college draft in 1967 and in 1970 they became the American and National Football Conferences of the NFL. Baltimore, Cleveland, and Pittsburgh moved from the NFC to the AFC to form two 13-team conferences.

Sports Illustrated, January 19, 1970
WHAM, BAM, STRAM!
Tex Maule

In the Super Bowl the ingenious boss of the Kansas City Chiefs aimed a devastating machine at Minnesota, and engineer Len Dawson used it to outmaneuver and eventually destroy the Vikings.

An unlikely-looking little man who favors red vests, checked trousers and infinite variety last Sunday put the art of invention back into football. Hank Stram, coach of the Kansas City Chiefs, threw some of his fanciest formations at the Minnesota Vikings in the Super Bowl and beat them for the championship of the football world by a humbling margin, 23–7.

Of course, Stram did not do this all by himself. His strategy was implemented by what must be recognized now as the finest team in pro football; that is what the winner of the Super Bowl is. The Chiefs' lines—on both offense and defense—gave the Purple People Eaters a world-champion case of indigestion. Len Dawson, who before this game was considered a rather namby-pamby type of quarterback, given to collapsing in a heap before any kind of rush, faced the famous charge of Minnesota's Four Norsemen coolly and threw with marvelous aim, completing 12 of 17 passes for 142 yards and a touchdown. And he threw only one interception. He sorted through the multiple options of the vastly complicated Stram offense as deftly as a computer and came up with the right call on almost every occasion.

Before the more than 80,000 spectators assembled in New Orleans under cloudy skies—there was a threat of a tornado—Stram explained a bit of his philosophy of football.

"This game will match the offense of the future against the offense of the past," he said. "The decade of the '60s was the decade of simplicity. During the '60s the good teams—the Green Bay Packers, for example—came out almost all the time in the same set and ran the play. In effect, what they said was here we come, see if you can stop us.

"Well, the '70s will be the decade of difference—different offensive sets, different defensive formations. What we try to do is to create a moment of hesitation, a moment of doubt in the defense.

"It will be a decade of experiment. I think football teams reflect the personality of coaches, and I like to think my personality is reflected in the variety of the Chiefs' attack and defense. I like to see Hank Stram in the stacked defense and the 18 different offensive sets we use and the 300 and something plays we can run off those sets."

There are only so many places you can run on a football field against any pro defense, and only so many ways you can run there, but Stram strives mightily to mask where his team will go and how it will arrive at the point of attack.

As the third quarter began, the Vikings woke up briefly and managed a 69-yard drive, Dave Osborn lunging acrobatically for four yards and a touchdown in typical Osborn fashion. With the score 16–7 Minnesota needed a touchdown and a field goal to go ahead—and had time to achieve them. But time ran out on the Vikings when Kansas City scored its second touchdown. With the ball on the Vikings' 46, Dawson dropped back and fired short to

Kansas City head coach Hank Stram was carried off the field after the Chiefs' 23–7 win over the Vikings in Super Bowl IV on January 11, 1970. Stram wore a microphone during the game, and in a feature produced by NFL films he could be heard describing the Vikings defense as a "Chinese fire drill." He said the game matched the offense of the future (the Chiefs, naturally) against the offense of the past. AP PHOTOGRAPH COURTESY OF AP IMAGES.

Otis Taylor, who ran long—all the way in for the score. Taylor went into the end zone standing up, and the Chiefs were Superchiefs.

A key play in the scoring move was another of those end-arounds, for it got Dawson off a tough third-down spot at his own 32. It looked like a play that had been resurrected from the early 1920s, when quarterbacks in desperate straits now and then called the Statue of Liberty. In those days the quarterback dropped back, posed like Miss Liberty and an end circling behind him took the ball from his hand and lost 10 or 11 yards.

That is not quite the way the Chiefs run it. The first time Dawson called the "52 Go Reverse," as the Chiefs term it, Pitts swept right for those 19 yards. The second time, late in the second quarter, Pitts gained 11 yards and helped the Chiefs run the clock down just before the half.

The Chiefs had used the end-around only a couple of times during the AFL season, and without notable success. "One time we ran it for no gain," Pitts said. "Then we tried it against the Jets and it gained five yards. But we look at different coverage in the AFL. Our cornerbacks play bump and run with the wide receivers. They stay up close and hit the receiver as he crosses the line, then go with him. So they are playing up close to the line. You try the 52 Go on them and they are right there. And another thing, the fact that the Viking defensive ends—Carl Eller and Jim Marshall—were pinching, gave me running room outside."

On Sunday each of the plays was outside Eller's end. "Taylor got some great crack-back blocks on Eller," Pitts said.

Dawson asked Pitts to do the end-around for the third time, and his seven-yard carry gave the Chiefs a first down and the momentum to continue their last scoring thrust.

Earsell Mackbee, the Viking cornerback, hit Taylor as he caught Dawson's pass—and hurt his own shoulder. That's the kind of day it was for the Vikings. "I pinched a nerve," said Mackbee. "The arm went dead and I couldn't grab him; that's how he got away."

Taylor got away down the sideline and Karl Kassulke came across to try to block him out of bounds. Taylor gave him an inside fake, broke free, and that was that.

Jack Patera, who coaches the Viking defense, said after the game, "We were aware of all their sets. All we could do was try to help the defense recognize them and hope for the best. I don't know how much Kansas City hurt us and how much we hurt ourselves. I know we didn't play our game. We were more cautious, but that can come from their offense. The defense sets and adjusts mentally, then they reset and you have to figure which one they are in. We got into the Super Bowl playing aggressive defense, but we couldn't—or wouldn't—be aggressive in this game."

He had a sheaf of play cards underneath his arm and he held them up.

"Let's put it this way," he said. "It's always the same face, but with different makeup. And I'm a good makeup man with a complete set of tools." Between Stram and Dawson, the Chiefs showed Minnesota everything but mercy in this performance.

As much of the country saw for itself, the Vikings were never in the game. Kansas City began the scoring, ominously enough for Minnesota, with a record 48-yard field goal by Jan Stenerud. When he added another, from 32 yards out, and yet another, from the 25, the Vikings resembled anything but two-touchdown favorites. And when Frank Pitts picked up 19 yards to help set up the third goal on the kind of play nobody but Stram uses anymore—the old familiar end-around with some new KC quirks—Minnesota was bewitched, bothered and beginning to panic.

The Vikings fumbled Stenerud's kick-off after that third field goal, and the Chiefs struck quickly for a touchdown, little Mike Garrett carrying for the last five yards on a pretty piece of deceit by the KC line, which had the Viking defenders looking for a sweep as Garrett knifed through the left side of the line.

"Against the teams we play in the NFL Sunday after Sunday we have a file that tells us their preferences and what they do best," he said. "Here's the Kansas City file. I can't tell you what they do best, because they do so many things and do all of them well. They hit the same hole but they hit it in different ways. The blocking may be basically the same, but the blocks come from a different angle."

On defense the Chiefs may not have been as esoteric, but they were equally effective. The Vikings had hoped they would be able to run the middle of the Chiefs' defense because they thought Mick Tingelhoff, their All Pro center, could handle the Chiefs' middle linebacker, Willie Lanier, man to man. On running plays through the heart of a defensive line, the center usually cuts off the middle backer, sealing him away from the thrust of the run.

Tingelhoff never had a chance to block Lanier. The Chiefs had decided that if they were to win they would have to keep Quarterback Joe Kapp from rolling outside their flank on runs or passes—plays like the one in the NFL championship game in which he ran over Cleveland Linebacker Jim Houston and left him senseless—and force Kapp to remain in his pocket and throw the ball.

To keep Kapp confined, they played in what the pros call an odd line—a formation with a tackle nose to nose with the center. With either 6'7", 275-pound Buck Buchanan or 6'1", 265-pound Curly Culp eyeing him from inches away, Tingelhoff, who weighs 237, found himself totally occupied trying to keep either of them from destroying him. One or the other of the Viking guards had to search for the elusive Lanier, and neither found him often.

The Chiefs' odd line not only contained Kapp and kept him from drifting to either side, it shut off much of the violent Viking running game. Dave Osborn, who ran for 108 yards against the Browns, managed only 15 against the Chiefs. Kapp, who had 57 against Cleveland, got just nine on Sunday—and ultimately a bad case of the Aaron Browns. The Chiefs' huge end got to him in the fourth quarter and crunched him to the field. Exit the heretofore unbreakable Kapp, in pain, to be replaced by Gary Cuozzo.

Brown's opposite number, Jerry Mays, tormented Kapp, too, and later told how.

"It was a funny day on defense. We were in the stack over 90 percent of the time—with the linebackers stacked behind the line—and we never played it that much before. Minnesota's recognition was destroyed. Kapp would roll to the strong side when we were overshifted that way. We got the message the third or fourth time the Vikings got the ball and couldn't get a first down. We felt stronger and the pace quickened."

He turned to Lanier. "Honey Bear," he said, "how many times did we storm?"

"One time," Lanier said, grinning. "And they scored a touchdown on that one."

The fact that the Chiefs felt it necessary to blitz only once reflects the deep faith Stram and his assistants have in the efficacy of the big, mobile and tough Chiefs' defensive line.

They got to Kapp early in the game for a six-yard loss, and that inspired them. "We hadn't seen anyone get to him and we did it, bingo," Mays said.

"Kapp's a tough being," Mays continued. "Once I got in on him and he hit me on the helmet with his follow-through." Mays lifted up his helmet, which was cracked just over the ear-hole. "He didn't even feel it."

Kapp tried a few of the long passes that had been so successful against Cleveland, but with no success at all. James Marsalis, the extraordinarily competent rookie cornerback for the Chiefs, shut off a couple of them. "We knew they were long-ball conscious," Marsalis said. "The movies showed they like to go for the quick six, so our main concern was to cut that off. We played a lot of zone to do it. Gene Washington is smooth and he has a lot of speed and John Henderson isn't slow, either, but we have a lot of fast receivers in our league who have great moves, too. Guys like Don Maynard, George Sauer, Lance Alworth, Fred Biletnikoff."

He didn't say it, but you felt that he meant the AFL receivers had all of Henderson and Washington's speed with more polish.

"We got great pressure from the front four," Marsalis added, "which made the quarterback look for the short pass and get rid of it too soon. That always helps on interceptions."

Yes. The Chiefs intercepted Kapp twice and Cuozzo once, and there was a fine irony at one point in the fourth quarter in the contrasting fortunes of Kapp, the redoubtable runner, and Dawson, who never runs. Kapp began his disastrous encounter with Aaron Brown by rolling out desperately to his left in an effort to avoid him. Brown caught Kapp, pounced on him and then scrambled to his feet. Kapp struggled, rolling from his face to his back and lying still for a moment before getting up. He was obviously in severe pain; when he walked off the field—he would not return—he was hunched over, grimacing and holding his damaged left arm.

Later, when the Chiefs had the ball, Dawson, who moves gingerly on a knee that was hurt badly enough to keep him out of six games during the regular season, dropped back to pass. He found no one open, then, à la Kapp, ran to his left and gained 11 yards and a first down.

And so, in agony for the Vikings and delirium for the Chiefs, the old order changes. Next season both leagues will be realigned under the NFL umbrella and the Super Bowl will be a less emotional confrontation. You will recall that in the first Super Bowl the Packers beat the Chiefs 35–10.

Stram used almost the same game plan for that game as he did for Sunday's.

"I was criticized then," said Stram. "Our defense wasn't that good then. But I don't have time to gloat now. I will just hold to my philosophy, and that includes winning with grace and style.

"On that long bus ride from Long Beach to Los Angeles for the first Super Bowl, the team was quiet and preoccupied. They were afraid of the game, of coming into the presence of greatness—the Green Bay Packers. They still respect the Packers, but today they were relaxed and easy and laughing on the way to the stadium."

The Packers had laughed at what they saw in some of the 1966 AFL game films—not at the Chiefs, but at some of the opposition. This time Stram and the Chiefs may have had a few chuckles themselves.

●

Vikings fans soon got over the disappointment, and looked forward to the 1970 season and the chance to get back to the Super Bowl. The team had easily eclipsed both the University of Minnesota Gophers and the Minnesota Twins in popularity, and Vikings players were in constant demand for personal appearances and autographs. The Vikings average attendance eclipsed the Gophers for the first time in 1967, despite having 15,000 fewer seats. On a national scale, the Harris Poll reported that professional football had passed baseball as the nation's favorite sport in 1965.

The only bad news during the off-season came when it was reported that Joe Kapp was holding out for a huge salary increase. Kapp was represented by San Francisco lawyer John Elliott Cook, who was among the first of a new breed of agents working for NFL players. He had gained notoriety by negotiating a near-million-dollar contract for San Francisco 49ers quarterback John Brodie by threatening to have his client jump to the AFL (not possible in 1970 because of the NFL-AFL merger).

Cook was demanding a multiyear, million-dollar contract for his client, reportedly a total of $1,250,000—$200,000 annually for five years, plus a $250,000 signing bonus. By comparison, the 1969 NFL MVP, quarterback Roman Gabriel of the Los Angeles Rams, was being paid $125,000 per year, and legendary quarterback Johnny Unitas of the Baltimore Colts had a three-year, $375,000 contract.

Vikings general manager Jim Finks couldn't hide his distaste for Cook and other player agents. What really galled him was the fact that Kapp directed the Vikings to talk exclusively to Cook. He refused to take any calls from the team.

Kapp became a free agent on May 1, but Vikings fans hoped that the impasse was just part of the negotiation process. *Sports Illustrated* ran a three-part story on Kapp, entitled "A Man of Machismo," beginning with its July 20, 1970, issue. A cover photo on that issue was labeled "The Toughest Chicano." In this series of articles, Kapp expressed admiration for coach Bud Grant and his Vikings teammates and talked about coming back to the Super Bowl. Nothing was said about his holdout.

But no progress was made in negotiations and things got especially tense when Kapp didn't report to training camp. In an August 5 press conference Finks said the Vikings were prepared to play the 1970 season without Kapp.

Minneapolis Tribune, August 6, 1970

VIKINGS REFUSE TO MEET KAPP DEMANDS

Merrill Swanson

The Minnesota Vikings said Wednesday they refuse to give in to Joe Kapp's salary demands and are prepared to play the 1970 season without the man who quarterbacked them to the National Football League championship in 1969.

Judging by the reaction of Kapp's agent, the Vikings may have to—and be 39 for 60 in '70.

Kapp, who became a free agent May 1, reportedly is asking for a five-year contract of more than $1 million. General manager Jim Finks would not confirm that figure, but made it plain that the Vikings would not pay what Kapp is asking through his agent, John Elliott Cook.

Finks sent a terse telegram to Cook explaining his position and added at a press conference, "we are so far apart it is not worth the time for us to meet."

The telegram advised Cook that Finks had decided against a meeting that had been planned earlier for Nevada and that "our offer made to Joe Kapp is outstanding and we would expect Joe to accept and report immediately."

"We have been advised of the telegram," Cook said by telephone, "and our position is virtually 100 percent determined. Beyond that, I have no comment."

Finks said he has not talked with Cook for 10 days although he tried to telephone him at Lake Tahoe, Nevada, twice yesterday. Finks added he has not talked with Kapp since April and tried unsuccessfully to telephone him two days ago.

When Kapp failed to appear for the veterans' first day of practice yesterday—although he cannot work out with the team until he signs a contract—Finks sent the telegram.

"It's up to Joe to come to us and show us he wants to play football with the Vikings," Finks said. "We are not going to meet his demands. If there is a middle ground, something we can talk about, fine.

"We respect Joe, but we're not going to give in to any demands that would be totally out of line with the principles we have used in the past for signing players."

Finks said the Vikings' stand was "in the best interest of all concerned, players, coaches, fans and management," and was arrived at "after we finally realized that all the players were here in camp, working hard, in good condition and ready to play football."

He also said the Vikings have not received any inquiries, "either directly or indirectly" from another NFL team about Kapp.

Finks said the decision to send the telegram had "nothing to do with the position of quarterback, whether there is a strength or weakness at the position."

The Vikings have a veteran quarterback in Gary Cuozzo, plus second-year man Bob Lee and rookie Bill Cappleman.

Finks was asked if the Vikings could have won the NFL championship without Kapp.

"I could turn that question around," Finks responded, "and ask if we could have won the championship without Cuozzo.

"This club is not built around one man. It took a total effort in 1969 to win the NFL championship and it will take a total effort in 1970, with or without Joe Kapp."

Kapp has minimized his efforts in the past, saying at one point, while refusing the team's most valuable player award, "there is no most valuable player. There are 40 of them."

There seemed to be some sentiment among Kapp's teammates, however, that he would be missed if he does not play for the Vikings this season.

"He has that certain something—charisma," one veteran said. "He gave us a lift. I think Kapp could help this team even if he was sitting on the bench."

●

On October 2 Kapp was traded to the Boston Patriots, who had split their first two games. His former teammates wished him well, glad to see him playing somewhere, but Kapp had a tough year in Boston—he started 10 of the remaining 12 games, but the team finished with a 2–12 record. On a snowy field in Boston on December 13, the Vikings thrashed the Patriots 35–14, holding Kapp to 128 passing yards, and intercepting him three times. It was to be Kapp's last season in the NFL.

Undaunted by the loss of their gonzo quarterback, the Vikings finished with a 12–2 record again in 1970. Gary Cuozzo, who had been obtained in a trade with New Orleans in 1968 and had backed up Kapp for two years, took the reins. (He had played in 28 games from 1963 to 1966 at Baltimore as Johnny Unitas's backup.)

All home games had been sellouts, forcing loyal Twin Cities fans who couldn't get tickets to drive to locations where they could pick up television broadcasts—as the NFL, since 1951, prohibited local TV broadcasts of home games within a 75-mile radius. But some enterprising local hotels, bars and country clubs (like Hazeltine, Southview, and Wayzata) installed special antennas that permitted them to receive signals from KGLO in Mason City, Iowa.

The NFL finally lifted the blackout of televised home games in 1973, thanks in no small part to pressure from President Nixon, an ardent Washington Redskins fan who had been pushing for the NFL to repeal the rule for almost 10 years. In 1972 the U.S. Senate held hearings on the blackout policy, threatening to withdraw the antitrust exemption for the NFL that President Kennedy had signed in 1961. A trial period for lifting the ban was rushed through the House in 1972, and a permanent bill was passed in 1973, approving blackouts of telecasts of home games only if the game is not sold out 48 hours prior to the start of the game.

Minneapolis Tribune, November 23, 1970

VIKING SPECTATORS FELT THE COLD, BUT TV VIEWERS SAW THE SNOW

Brian Anderson

Football fans who watched the Vikings defeat Green Bay from the cozy confines of local bars Sunday succeeded in avoiding the frigid weather, but they didn't escape the snow—on their TV screens.

"As far as we know, we could be watching a rerun of the UCLA game," said a frustrated viewer at the Leamington Hotel.

Almost all the Twin Cities bars that have installed special antennas to pick up the Vikings' game signal from KGLO-TV in Mason City, Iowa, reported below average reception yesterday. (The National Football League "blacks out" local reception of home games.)

The snow-filled screens apparently resulted because KGLO-TV telecast the game at only 80 percent of its normal power.

Station Manager Lloyd Loers said yesterday he had been told by the CBS sports department that if he did not reduce power 20 percent for the game he would not be allowed to carry it.

He said CBS originally told him on Friday that it was going to substitute another game for the Vikings–Green Bay game. "I told them that wasn't fair to the people in our area, so they said we could carry it if we only went 80 percent," he said.

The station normally telecasts at 100,000 watts. Loers said the cut to 80,000 watts likely would result in fuzzy reception in outlying areas. He said this was the first time his station had been forced to reduce power for a football game.

Loers said the station's Federal Communications Commission license allows it to operate at a 20 percent power reduction.

Some fans complained about the reception, but most bars reported large crowds.

Ralph Meyer, building superintendent at the Leamington, estimated that 400 persons were squinting at the 10 television sets in the ballroom. George T. Namie, assistant manager at George's-in-the-Park, estimated nearly 700

Officials use a broom to try to find sideline markers in a Vikings 10–7 win over San Francisco in a snowstorm at Metropolitan Stadium on December 14, 1969. OPPOSITE: Snow-covered Vikings fans seemed to enjoy the game—and the weather—that day. PHOTOGRAPHS FROM *DISPATCH–PIONEER PRESS.* COURTESY OF THE MINNESOTA HISTORICAL SOCIETY.

watched the game there, and Cal Olson, manager of the Hopkins House, figured he had "a couple thousand."

A crowd of 1,100 was reported at the Stagecoach Inn, near Shakopee, where manager Reggie Collihan estimated only about 10 percent of the game was not received.

Winds gusting up to 39 miles per hour also raised havoc with antennas, causing rolling pictures in many locations.

Jim Fiala, the head of Microwave Heating Division, E.A.S. Inc., the firm that has installed about 15 of these special antennas in the area, conceded yesterday that the reception wasn't very good.

"These football people are nuts," he said, as the Leamington crowd roared over some imperceivable motion on the screens. They can't even see the numbers, and still they're cheering away. Personally, I wouldn't give football the time of day."

●

The Vikings offense fell off only a bit in 1970—three fewer points per game—but seemed lackluster without the charismatic Kapp. However, the team reveled in its image as Nordic warriors, impervious to the weather. The public image of the team was coach Bud Grant, whose icy stare defied the weather. He banned sideline heaters for the Vikings, but gladly had them installed for the visiting team.

It was a lesson Grant said he learned in Canada. "I don't mean that our players don't get cold . . . Our job is to play football whether it is warm or cold or wet or dry. It just so happens, we often play when it's cold." The image of Vikings players standing at the sidelines to cheer for their team-mates while opponents huddled around their heaters was not lost on the press and broadcasting corps.

Minneapolis Star, December 7, 1970

COLD? NOT VIKINGS

PLAY BEST IN CHILL; BUT BEARS NEED HEAT

Dick Gordon

"Cold," says Bud Grant, "is a state of mind."

From one who was there on the Metropolitan Stadium sidelines Saturday and is only now thawing out, I might dispute the Spartanish Viking's claim.

At the same time there is no arguing that cool Grant discipline was the prevailing Viking mood in the cold. It was never more evident than in the contrasting styles of the Chicago Bear–style heater and the team that "generates its own heat" while winning a third straight Central Division football championship.

"I don't like the cold," said Louisiana-born Roy Winston afterward. "But I noticed one thing. At the end of the game, when the Bears had a chance to win, they were huddled around their heaters. They weren't even watching the game."

Every Viking was watching every single minute of the game, from as close to the sidelines as he could get.

"The coach has got to be right about it (the no heater, no glove policy)," said quarterback Bob Lee. "We always win in real cold weather."

Saturday's 16–13 victory over the Bears stretched the two-year Viking mark in Minnesota freezefests to 5–0. The other ice victories came against Green Bay two weeks ago, San Francisco last December plus Los Angeles and Cleveland in the postseason playoffs.

There was no raucous sideline cheerleading during the team's sixteenth consecutive home triumph, all weather included, Saturday: Just the more commonplace "Good stick, Moose," when Carl Eller nailed Chicago quarterback Jack Concannon behind the line.

And "smart play, Charlie," from Gary Cuozzo when Charlie West let a tricky high punt bound clear into the end zone in the third quarter.

There was no swearing or yelling at George Seals after the bad Bear nailed Fred Cox's nose with a well-aimed elbow on a first-quarter kickoff. Only one shout, "Let's watch that 69" (Seals's number).

Dr. Don Lannin, team physician, treated Cox, with his head tilted back on the bench, with the same lack of excitement; and Freddy the Foot, of course, continued play.

Once Lee, the no longer inexperienced quarterback, ignored Grant on the sidelines, he was so interested in encouraging the defense.

"There are enough people doing that," said the coach. And Grant and Lee discussed offensive strategy more than has been done since Appomattox.

The closest thing to a crisis developed when the field became frozen and equipment manager Jim (Stubby) Eason needed a few extra seconds to find size 12 tennies for Ron Yary. But he found 'em.

"Come on, let's run with it," said Grady Alderman when Cecil Turner's kickoff runback made Viking ball control a must. That touchdown changed everything except Viking expressions. They remained grimly intent with no grins.

Shortly afterward the Bears were on the Vikings' 34. A tying field goal or a winning touchdown beckoned.

The Vikings still were standing and watching every play, with their hoarse "come ons" and "how to gos." Grant's only ear protection against the 8-degree temperature (-33 windchill) was the press box phone.

Down at the other end of the field, Bears boss Jim Dooley was unrecognizable with a hood over his head. Half a dozen of his players were warming their hands on the gas heaters, their backs turned to combat.

"The cold didn't bother me," said Viking Dale Hackbart after the final second had ticked off the championship. "Maybe I'm getting used to it. You have to play in it so you grin and bear it. And naturally you pay attention to what's going on. If you didn't you'd freeze to death."

●

The defensive unit—who led the league again in fewest points scored and yards against—became wildly popular. Fans reveled in the deeds of their fabulous front four. Eventually dubbed the "Purple People Eaters," they were the successors to the NFL's earlier marquee "Fearsome Foursomes" of the San Diego Chargers and Los Angeles Rams.

Sports Illustrated, December 14, 1970
MESSAGE FROM MINNESOTA: THREE DOTS AND A DASH
Pat Putnam

That's the front four—three blacks and a white—and last week Chicago was on the receiving end as the Vikings clinched the title.

Okay, fellows, said coach Bud Grant to his Minnesota Vikings, our quarterback this week against Chicago will be Bob Lee. Bob Lee? The punter? No, that was last year. This year, after Joe Kapp went off to seek his fortune in Boston, Lee, a seventeenth-round draft choice from University of the Pacific, became Gary Cuozzo's backup. Two weeks ago, when Cuozzo severely sprained an ankle against the Jets, Lee went in and threw four interceptions. The Vikings couldn't have cared less. With Kapp, Cuozzo, Lee or, if Grant so chose, with pudgy Fred Zamberletti, the trainer, at quarterback, they knew they could beat Chicago just as they had beaten almost everybody else—with their crushing defense. And, of course, last Saturday in Bloomington, Minnesota, they did, 16–13.

Frozen by Viking weather and savaged by the Vikings' superb front four, Chicago managed only two field goals against the best defense in football but made the game typically Viking close by scoring on an 88-yard kick-off return by Cecil Turner. The win was Minnesota's tenth in 12 games and enabled it to become the first NFL team to clinch a division title. Lee matched Turner's run with a 33-yard scoring pass to John Henderson, and Fred Cox more than matched Chicago's field goals with kicks of 21, 23 and 10 yards. But enough about points.

The day of the game broke clear and cruelly cold, with a wind gusting up to 40 mph turning 9-degree weather into a 33-below windchill factor and the lawn at Metropolitan Stadium into solid green concrete. The Bears came out gloved and with giant heaters set up behind their bench. The Vikings came out bare-handed and heater-less. "We're out there to play football, not to keep warm," said Grant. "We'll be cold, but we'll survive. I want our play-ers' full attention on the game every minute, not on keeping their back-sides warm."

It's all part of the Grant master plan that in four years has turned the Vikings from a gang of violent individuals into a tightly disciplined foot-ball team. "Take our game with Green Bay last year," Grant said. "It's in the fourth quarter and it can go either way. Then their Donny Anderson gets hurt. They send in a substitute. Now he's got to be the warmest man on the field. He should have been, he was standing next to the heater all day. He comes in and—pop!—he fumbles, we recover and that was the ball game. And we didn't fumble once the whole game. As long as we live in this coun-try, we must have the discipline of learning to play in it."

"If Grant says we'll win by freezing, then, by God, we'll freeze and win," said one Viking. "But I sure wish he'd tell my toes they weren't so cold."

And so last Saturday the Vikings huddled on the sideline, huge men hunched over and stamping their feet for warmth, preparing to attack Chi-cago with their defense. Other coaches talk about getting good field posi-tion for their offense. Grant talks about good field position for his defense. "The defense wins, the offense sells tickets," he preaches. He took the role of quarterback and made it a bit part. "Kapp didn't win for us last year," he says. "He was just one-fortieth of the team. That's all Cuozzo is. That's all Lee is."

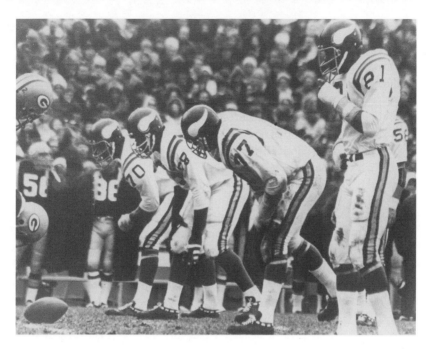

The Purple People Eaters—Jim Marshall (70), Alan Page (88), Gary Larsen (77), and Carl Eller (81)—terrorized opposing quarterbacks. They started every game together as a unit for six seasons (1968–73), winning five divisional championships. During this streak, the Vikings led the NFL in fewest points allowed three times and were second once. They led the NFL in passing defense three times and were second twice. PHOTOGRAPH COURTESY OF THE MINNESOTA VIKINGS.

But then Grant has the front four, the Purple Gang or, as they sometimes call themselves, the Three Dots and a Dash, an allusion to the three blacks— Jim Marshall, Alan Page and Carl Eller—and the one white, Gary Larsen. Eller is the bachelor and free spirit; Larsen, the gentle family man; Marshall, the happy adventurer, making the most of every one of life's minutes; Page, at 25, the youngest, a little bit of each but in sum like none.

"Alan is still dealing in his potential self," says Eller, the 6'6" defensive end. "It would be hard right now to describe him, except to say he's truly a great person. Marshall is a guy who deals in the fantastic. Gary is a quiet person, a guy who enjoys being with his family, and he has a beautiful family. I think this makes him a beautiful person."

"Clothes are a passion with Carl," says Larsen. "Everybody kind of wonders what he's going to wear next. Last year he had a Cadillac limousine and he'd sit in the back and let a friend of his named Blue drive him around. Anybody else would have felt self-conscious, but not Carl. Then one day he just got tired of that and sold the car."

At a recent gathering, Eller appeared in a wolfskin coat, black leather bells and a cap of wolf heads. "That coat took a pack of wolves to make," says Page. "It decimated the wolf population of Canada. It's unbelievable—but then so is Carl." Another recent Eller acquisition is a Charles Addams-type house which he shares with his mother. "Because I live with my mother, you know why I bought a big house," Eller says with a grin. "She has her privacy and I have mine. That house is my proudest possession. It represents a cornerstone of me. I think it's the only thing about me that is really solid."

Off-season, Eller studies acting in Los Angeles at the Phillip Browning Workshop. "They teach realism in acting," he says, "the actual portrayal of a character as you see him. Ideally, I see myself playing a more sophisticated type of role. One where you would portray a more defined character. One with great definition. Something like a Lee Marvin or a Tony Quinn. The role I most identify with is Laurence Harvey in *Butterfield 8*."

Watching Eller swoop down on enemy quarterbacks, it is hard to equate him with Laurence Harvey or the aesthete who sat in a motel room last week and recited poetry, his own: "What am I? Bird, tulip, grass or green? Whatever."

"I think the poet can be seen in the football player," says Eller. "Football is a great medium of expression, a performance that is more total because it is completely spontaneous. If you knew all about Carl Eller, then you could see Carl Eller in my playing, and from it you'd probably understand me even better."

The other poet of the front four is Marshall, who views life as a series of challenges and rushes forward to meet them all. At the moment his passion is skydiving. Before that there was fencing, skiing, water skiing, scuba diving, hunting, fishing, archery and . . .

"And oil painting, and licenses in real estate and as a stockbroker, and nine million other things," says Anita Marshall, his beautiful wife. "Nothing he does surprises me anymore."

But skydiving? A professional athlete?

"Hey, it's ten times safer than football," says Marshall, who has jumped out of a plane 200 times. "I just woke up at seven one morning and decided I wanted to try it." At nine he was at an airfield. At 10 he was at 2,800 feet and stepping out of a plane. "And it was great," he says. "For the first time I felt completely free, completely detached from earth. It was a feeling I've never been able to recapture."

"Now he wants to climb a mountain," says Anita.

"I've got one all picked out. It's in British Columbia. We got to within 60 miles of it last year, but that was as close as we could get. I've got to climb that mountain."

"We climbed one," says Anita.

"Aw, that wasn't a mountain," Marshall says. "Besides, you were with me and you made me stop halfway up."

Most of Marshall's poetry was written for Anita. Like: "I love your lips while they are red with wine, and red with the wildest desire. . . ."

"Oh, he had some real heavy lines," says Anita.

Marshall smiles at her. "They worked, didn't they?"

Marshall learned to ski the same way he learned to skydive. Eller took him to the top of the highest hill he could find and said, "Jim, follow me." And Eller took off with Marshall a few seconds behind.

"Carl thought it was funny," Marshall recalls. "He was laughing and yelling all the way down—until he fell and I went past him. Then I stopped with one of those great swooshing slides. Swoosh! I damn near made it, too."

"Carl and Jim, I don't think I've ever seen them in a bad mood," Gary Larsen says. "They're always laughing, having a good time."

"They're out of their minds," says Page, trying not to smile. "When I first met Jim I thought he was stone crazy. Now that I know him a lot better. . . ."

It was Marshall who led the rookie party in 1967, Page's first year. The veterans ordered the rooks to drink beer. Page said no, he didn't smoke or drink. Okay, they said, then you have to drink hot Coke or get out. Page got up and walked out.

"I have to admit I was kind of worried," he says. "I had heard all the stories about how the veterans treat the rookies, and at the time I thought a lot of those guys were crazy. I didn't know what they'd do, but except for some needling, they didn't do anything. The Vikings don't ride rookies. About all they have to do is sing for their dinner at training camp. And every day during the season they have to buy five dozen doughnuts and bring them to the locker room."

When the doughnuts arrive, it's every man for himself. If you get there first, you get all you can grab. If you get there last, there won't be anything but empty sacks.

●

Unfortunately, the Vikings didn't make it back to the Super Bowl. They lost at home to the NFC West champion San Francisco 49ers in the first round of the playoffs, 17–14, in weather—it was only 9 degrees at game time—that should have favored the Vikings. They scored first on a 22-yard fumble return by Paul Krause, but the offense, doomed by two lost fumbles and two interceptions, didn't score a touchdown until the final seconds of the game, when the 49ers were content to let the clock run out.

The Vikings finished 11–3 to win the Central Division again in 1971, no thanks to the offense, who ranked twenty-fifth out of 26 in passing and seventeenth in rushing. The defense ranked number one again, giving up only 139 points. For the second straight year, offensive mistakes—four interceptions and a lost fumble—led to a first-round home playoff defeat, this time to Dallas, the Eastern Division champions, 20–12. The Cowboys went on the win the Super Bowl.

Individual players continued to earn accolades. Tackle Alan Page was voted the NFL's Most Valuable Player. He is the only lineman ever to win the award. In fact, only two other defensive players have ever been honored—Detroit Lions linebacker Joe Schmidt shared the award with Philadelphia Eagles quarterback Norm Van Brocklin in 1960, and New York Giants linebacker Lawrence Taylor won the award outright in 1986. Carl Eller won the Newspaper Enterprise Association George S. Halas Trophy in 1971, given to their choice as the NFL's outstanding defensive player. Four future Hall of Famers became perennial All Pro and Pro Bowl selections. Page was an All Pro selection six times, 1969–1971 and 1973–1975. Eller made the team five times, 1968–1971 and 1973, while offensive tackle Ron Yary began a streak in 1971 that extended through 1976. Free safety Paul Krause made the All Pro team only once—in 1975—after joining the Vikings in 1968, but six of his eight Pro Bowl appearances were as a Viking, and he is the NFL's career leader in interceptions.

The 1971 playoff loss was the first-ever NFL game played on Christmas Day. In the old days, with a 12-game schedule and a single championship playoff game, Christmas usually wasn't a problem. The championship game in 1955 between the Cleveland Browns and Los Angeles Rams, however, was moved to Monday, December 26, to avoid Christmas. Similarly, the 1960 game between the Green Bay Packers and Philadelphia Eagles was also moved to Monday.

The AFL used a 14-game schedule in its first season in 1960, and the NFL followed suit in 1961. In 1971 the regular season ended on Sunday, December 19, and the NFL decided to schedule two playoff games on Christmas Day and two on December 26—to insure that all four games could be seen on nationwide television. This caused a national uproar, and a Missouri legislator threatened to introduce a bill to prohibit Christmas games in the future. The Vikings game began at noon. Despite some threatened protests, the game was a sellout.

All regular-season home games had been sellouts again in 1971, and tailgating was turning the Metropolitan Stadium parking lot into a gigantic party place, even in cold weather.

The first Christmas Day game in NFL history was played at Metropolitan Stadium in 1971. There were protests throughout the country and some legislators threatened to introduce bills to ban games on Christmas Day, but most fans, like these at the Met, took the game in stride and with a sense of humor. It was a sellout. PHOTOGRAPH FROM *DISPATCH–PIONEER PRESS.* COURTESY OF THE MINNESOTA HISTORICAL SOCIETY.

Sports Illustrated, December 6, 1971

PIGSKINS PRECEDED BY PÂTÉ ON ASPHALT

Jerry Kirshenbaum

Minnesota Viking fans are a hardy, chest-beating lot. They like to eat and booze it up a lot. They do it in the Metropolitan Stadium parking lot. Frozen noses and toeses is their lot.

Snow flurries swirled across the pavement, the temperature stalled at 9 degrees and those hardy Minnesota Viking fans were arriving for last season's game with the Chicago Bears. The kickoff was still three hours off, but Minnesotans, remember, are positively mad about fresh air. Not content to simply cheer their team on, they accordingly celebrate every home game, whatever the weather, with a bacchanalian feast in the Metropolitan Stadium parking lot. In this smorgasbord on asphalt, the football is part of a hero sandwich: the festivities start in the morning and end well past dark, with the game buried in the middle.

An exercise in that old football-going custom known as tailgating, only done on a Paul Bunyan scale, the party in the parking lot is an occasion for some Viking fans to play cards on picnic tables, others to break out portable TV sets and watch football games being played elsewhere and everybody to fill up on great quantities of food and drink. Of the 48,000-plus who attend Minnesota games, as many as 10,000 have tailgated at a time, a phenomenon that prompts St. Paul radio station KSTP to conduct its pregame grandstand quarterback interviews not in the grandstand, but in the parking lot. "There just isn't anybody in the stands until kickoff," Jim Ramsburg, KSTP's programming manager, explains. Adds another radioman, "Everybody's outside getting boozed up."

Encircling the stadium like covered wagons around a campfire, the crowds arrive not just in the usual cars and station wagons, but in every kind of mobile home and camper, plus a couple of buses painted in Viking purple. Cold as it was at the Bears game, small knots of celebrants abandoned the warmth of their vehicles, the better to attend to their barbecue grills and portable stoves. And when the weather is balmier, as during the tropical 26 degrees of last month's game with San Francisco, the crush of tailgaters gives Metropolitan Stadium, looming on the horizon in the Minneapolis suburb of Bloomington, an epic *War and Peace* quality.

Everybody is dressed for warmth, but there is room for such fashion flourishes as silver-lame facemasks and Viking snowmobiling suits advertised in Twin Cities stores as "purple people warmers." Dressed in all their quilted and thermally insulated glory, people move stiffly about like so many windup toys, their drinks (or "antifreeze," as somebody in every group insists on putting it) clinking in mittened hands and their faces frozen in a beatific glow no doubt caused in part by the sublime satisfaction of not having to worry about the ice cubes melting.

If the affair has the atmosphere of an Arctic street fair, the food is prepared with a care worthy of a Pillsbury bake-off. For the 49ers game, the Elks Club of Hopkins, Minnesota, bused 200 delegates to a state Elks conference into the parking lot for a pregame snack. Instead of chicken-salad sandwiches, they devoured 250 pounds of buffalo roasted on a spit by a white-capped chef. Not far away, 150 tailgaters in leis stood around consuming pineapples, salmon in aspic, coconuts and rum punch, everything going down the hatch to the sounds of Tahitian drum chants issuing from a loudspeaker. As palm fronds, part of the decorations, rustled in the raw air, cohost John Ebin, an officer in a Minneapolis brokerage firm, allowed, "I guess there's getting to be a lot of one-upmanship involved in all this."

Without doubt the most ambitious of the tailgaters to date is a group of 26 fans who call themselves the Guzzling Gourmets. Before this season's Chicago game, they dressed their womenfolk in mink stoles, set their table with candelabra, Limoges china and mum centerpieces, then sat down for an eight-course dinner. The mushrooms stuffed with pâté de foie gras were exquisite, the breast of chicken in ham Newburg sauce divine, the peaches in champagne scrumptious and the after-dinner cigars just right for putting gentlemen in the proper frame of mind for football. That may seem like a difficult act to follow, but the Guzzling Gourmets topped it when two of their number got the bright idea of getting married in the Met Stadium parking lot before the 49ers game.

"Anybody can get married in a church or justice of the peace's office," the bride, a 27-year-old bond underwriter named Caryl Meyer, enthused on her wedding day as exhaust fumes mingled with the odors of food. With the stadium as backdrop and a Minneapolis judge performing the double-ring ceremony, Caryl stepped out of a Winnebago camper and into holy wedlock with Bill Caughfey, a 37-year-old bartender. Following a wedding feast of steamed lobster and three varieties of oysters, Caryl shed her coat and white-knit bridal minidress, put on long underwear and heavy sweaters and hurried into the stadium to watch the Vikings lose 13–9.

That left the bridegroom in the company of the many happy tailgaters who simply don't make the opening kickoff. Caughfey relaxed in the camper, sipping Scotch and listening to the game on radio. "I don't like to sit out in the cold the way Caryl does," he said. Nonetheless, he finally made it to his seat.

Although Viking fans obviously need no inducements, tailgating has been actively encouraged by promotion-minded Twin City Federal, a savings-and-loan firm that is offering a prize of two expenses-paid Super Bowl trips to whoever prepares the most mouth-watering meal in the parking lot this season. In the same spirit, the *Minneapolis Star* prints weekly tailgating recipes for such delicacies as avocado soup and then dispatches a couple of staffers to the stadium to ladle out free samples. So far the paper has avoided the fate of a group of car dealers who, or so legend has it, used the parking lot a few years ago to entertain their salesmen and simultaneously show off their new station wagons. Everything went as planned until the salesmen got into a spirited game of football on the pavement—tackle, not touch—that ended with one of them suffering a broken jaw and another being hauled away by Bloomington police.

All this has enabled Minnesota to supplant Green Bay as the undisputed tailgating champion of the NFL. Until four years ago, Minnesota law prohibited bars and restaurants from serving liquor on Sunday—which made the parking lot as good a place as any to whoop it up. Some fans also found tailgating a way to interest their wives in attending the games. Another explanation was offered by a suburban St. Paul cattle salesman named Connie

Olson as he relaxed with friends in his camper long after the final gun had sounded at one game.

Olson and his guests had just finished a huge steak dinner and, in the gathering darkness, dying embers from the charcoal grill glowed on the pavement outside. "When you leave late like this, you beat the traffic," Olson said as Bing Crosby's "White Christmas" sounded over a portable radio. Of course, if Olson and others like him stay much later to avoid traffic following Sunday-afternoon games, they'll have to start worrying about the Monday-morning rush hour.

Its usefulness in easing traffic is one reason Bloomington police give for tolerating tailgating, although it remains a matter of interpretation whether the drinking that goes on is legal or not. The stadium—and the parking lot—come under the jurisdiction of a commission representing the cities of Minneapolis, Richfield and Bloomington, and the drinking question all but unravels the stadium manager, an ex-FBI man named William H. Williams. Approached by a reporter awhile back, Williams refused to discuss tailgating unless his visitor promised not to write anything to suggest that anybody touches a drop. "We don't want the WCTU or somebody on our backs," he said.

As a consequence the official attitude is decidedly ambivalent. On the one hand, when the Viking management offered earlier this season to provide portable toilets in the parking lot, something that would have pleased many fans, Williams flatly refused. On the other hand, he and everybody else in Bloomington recognize only too well that Metropolitan Stadium, the home of the Minnesota Twins, is not really suited for football, and that tailgating is helping to keep the Vikings there.

There has been talk of a new domed stadium in downtown Minneapolis to house the Vikings, and the University of Minnesota would love to land the pro team as a tenant in its 56,652-seat football stadium. But neither the automobile ramps contemplated for the downtown stadium nor the university's widely scattered parking areas would be nearly as suitable for partying as Metropolitan Stadium's sprawling lot. Admitting that this is an important consideration in any move the club might take, Viking general manager Jim Finks says, "Tailgating is half the fun these people get from going to the games."

For many of the fans the fun seems to increase the colder the weather gets, something no doubt explained by the same chest-beating instincts that have moved Bud Grant, the Viking coach, to prohibit his players from using hand warmers or wearing gloves on the sidelines. One expression of northwoods machismo was the party that Ching Johnson, a Minneapolis contractor who attends games in Norseman headgear, threw last year on the back of a 60-foot semitrailer, with music provided by a country-western band. Green Bay was the opponent, and it was so cold during the game that a number of fans tried to warm up by sneaking into the stadium beer cooler. Instead of going home afterward, 350 people swarmed aboard Johnson's truck, including Jim Klobuchar, a Minneapolis columnist, who reported breathlessly: "I got kissed five times and ate three passing corned-beef sandwiches without taking my hands out of my pockets."

With the phenomenon showing no signs of subsiding, the parking lot has become a meeting place for everybody but the Viking front four—who meet at the quarterback. The effect tailgating has had on the life of Keith Hopper, a Minnesota State College Board aide, sounds like something that Ann Landers might want to pass along to the lonely hearts in her audience. It seems that Hopper, an Oklahoman who moved to Minnesota five years ago, had difficulty meeting people until he took up tailgating. "It's been quite a social outlet," Hopper says. He moves today in a wide circle of friends that includes a retired grocer, a chemist, a mattress salesman and a cattleman. He met them all in the Metropolitan Stadium parking lot.

●

The team's Viking mascot was perfect for its cold-weather identity, although the team could not claim to have created it. Hub Meeds, a White Bear Lake truck driver, rented costumes and beards with his brother to wear to Super Bowl IV in New Orleans. Super Bowl officials, thinking the pair were official Vikings mascots, ushered them down to the sidelines. Meeds got sideline passes from the Vikings the next season and eventually was hired as the team's official mascot.

Minnesota Truck Merchandiser, Fall 1978
TRUCKING KEEPS FANS IN HIGH GEAR
Staff writer

Although he is most often seen waving a sword, Hub Meeds is more comfortable with a 10-speed Road-ranger in his hand. On fall Sundays he works the sidelines at Metropolitan Stadium.but during the week he works I-35W between the Twin Cities and Northfield, Minnesota, in a Cummins powered white cab-over. Hub Meeds is the Minnesota Vikings' mascot and a trucker for World Wide, Inc.

The bearded White Bear Lake, Minnesota, driver gets nothing but recognition and a sideline pass as the team's mascot. For a man who is alone in a cab between 3:00 A.M. and noon hauling groceries, Meeds is no introvert when he trades shifter for sword and steps on stage in front of 46,000 fans at a Vikings game.

Truck driver Hub Meeds rented a Viking costume to wear to Super Bowl IV, but he found himself being escorted onto the playing field by Super Bowl security personnel, who assumed he must have been a team mascot. He eventually signed a contract to become the Vikings' "official" mas-cot. PHOTOGRAPH BY RICK A. KOLODZIEJ. COURTESY OF THE MINNESOTA VIKINGS.

Meeds's career as the Vikings' mascot began in 1970 when he rented a costume and beard for the Super Bowl in New Orleans. Aided by his appearance, Meeds managed to get on the field and never used his ticket. A call to the Vikings' office, the following season, produced a sideline pass for home games. Meeds replaced the fake beard and rented costume with real facial hair and a homemade outfit and became the Vikings' mascot.

Meeds enjoys the attention he has received since becoming The Viking. His picture has appeared in newspapers around the country and he was invited to be on the television program *To Tell The Truth*. When the Vikes are in contention for the Super Bowl, Meeds receives many requests for interviews.

Hub Meeds, the trucker, puts about 1,200 miles behind him every week. Hub Meeds, The Viking, has covered a few miles in his seven-year career. The mascot travels with the team to one away game each season and the playoffs. Meeds has appeared at games in New York, New Orleans, Dallas, Houston, San Francisco, St. Louis and Green Bay.

Away games can be tough on the mascot since fans tend to take their frustrations out on The Viking. Meeds says the amount of projectiles thrown at him varies from city to city and the crowd reaction is always worse when the home team is losing.

Dodging flak is nothing new for Meeds since he picked up his basic truck driving experience through Uncle Sam. After the service he worked for Indianhead Truck Line, Inc., Roseville, until he purchased his own rig, which he eventually sold to World Wide.

Truck driving is Meeds's year-round employment and surprisingly his role as The Viking is not limited to football season. Meeds is invited to appear in numerous parades throughout the summer and he is constantly keeping up with requests for autographed pictures.

Meeds has considered retiring his beard and sword for the past two seasons but his five children won't hear of it. They enjoy having a mascot in the family. After seeing Meeds's enthusiasm on the field you wonder if he could ever settle for a seat in the stands again.

●

Despite having the best record in the NFC in 1970 and 1971, the two first-round playoff losses made Vikings fans wonder if the team had peaked. The defense was still strong, but the offense simply could not find a way to score against tough teams.

Super Losers

CHAMPIONSHIP SEASONS AND BIG GAME DISAPPOINTMENTS

VIKINGS GENERAL MANAGER JIM FINKS DROPPED A BOMBSHELL ON January 27, 1972, when he announced that the team had sent three players and two future draft choices to the New York Giants to bring quarterback Fran Tarkenton back to Minnesota. Vikings fans were ecstatic, figuring this was their ticket back to the Super Bowl. Most veteran players welcomed him back, but Alan Page, who joined the Vikings after Tarkenton left for New York, had some reservations. "I don't think much of the trade," he told *Sports Illustrated* writer Tex Maule. "Tarkenton is a good quarterback, but I don't think anybody's that good."

Tarkenton had several television and print endorsements in hand almost as soon as he stepped off the plane in Minnesota. Perhaps some of Page's resentment could be traced to the feeling that he had been virtually ignored after winning the 1971 MVP award—he thought Vikings management could have done more to help market his services. Tarkenton and Page came to an uneasy truce over the next few years, respecting each other's abilities, but never becoming close friends.

Although Tarkenton had a good year in 1972, the team slipped backwards with a 7–7 record, missing the playoffs for the first time since 1967. The team passing offense rose to fourth in the league, up from 1971's miserable twenty-fifth. Touchdown passes went from nine to 19, while interceptions fell from 18 to 13, and Tarkenton finished in the top three in all

Defensive tackle Alan Page (88) was so quick off the ball that he often ran right through attempted double-teams. He was a Pro Bowl selection nine consecutive seasons and All Pro six times with the Vikings, and he was NFL MVP in 1971. He was inducted into the NFL Hall of Fame—appropriately—in 1988. PHOTOGRAPH COURTESY OF THE MINNESOTA VIKINGS.

major passing categories. The defense had also slipped from first in the league in points allowed to eleventh.

In retrospect, the team was probably overconfident in 1972. Many players admitted they had thought they were a cinch for the Super Bowl with Tarkenton at quarterback. But Tarkenton did not look for excuses for the team's mediocre performance.

"TWO STARS, TWO ORBITS," FROM *TARKENTON* (1976)

Jim Klobuchar and Fran Tarkenton

The departure of the rollicking Chicano, Joe Kapp, did not lessen the Vikings' September-to-December dominance of the National Football Conference in 1970 and 1971. But where they had crashed the Super Bowl in 1969 with Kapp at quarterback, they failed in their first playoff games the following two years. Grant privately assigned much of the blame the second time to instability at quarterback. He opened the season with three—Gary Cuozzo, Norm Snead, and Bobby Lee. Nobody ever really seized the job, or was allowed to, depending on your perception of the weekly rotation. The unsettled conditions did not bother the Viking defensive front four of Page, Marshall, Eller, and Larsen, who controlled most of the action in the years when they were supreme. It also did not seem to bother Grant. He maintained that the quarterback is not necessarily the most important man in the offense and that a team could win with a journeyman performance at the position as long as the man was competent, erred only rarely, and stood properly at attention for the national anthem.

But in the 1971 playoff game against Dallas, what may have been the strongest of all Viking teams defeated itself with an interception and other second-half futilities. The defeat recast Grant's thinking. The one regret in his acceptance of the Viking job in 1967 was the exit a few months earlier of Francis Tarkenton. When the Vikings learned he was available five years later, Grant told Jim Finks, "He is the one quarterback in football I want for this team."

Tarkenton came back to the Vikings with no pronouncements. It was a winning team. There was no reason to believe it was going to stop winning because of or in spite of his presence. He met that proposition with the usual Tarkenton throwaway line. "My object," he said, "is just to be around when the Vikings win another title. I'll try not to be an obstruction."

So there were no marching bands to drum him to the Viking training camp, shifted to Mankato, Minnesota, in the mid-1960s, and nobody called a sensitivity meeting to decide how his old playmates ought to react. He slipped into his old hard hat and purple decor without MacArthuresque stances. He came back like the grateful and wiser politician who may have campaigned in bigger wards but was more relaxed with his first constituents. At 32 his face was fuller, his hair more profuse. But with the unspoken prudence of any immigrant entering a Bud Grant training camp, he had restyled it to accommodate both his helmet and the coach. There were seams in Tarkenton's face now. His expressions, although as spontaneous and droll as they were 11 years before, reflected a mature and distinguished athlete still in quest of a higher satisfaction.

He was wealthier by some very stunning numbers. But the locker room of a pro football team is no resort for returning maharajas. Jim Marshall flung some appropriate shafts, and the welcoming ceremonies were quickly done. The momentary awkwardness vanished, replaced by the trust and assurance generated by people Tarkenton knew and believed in—Alderman, Marshall, Brown, Tingelhoff, Eller, and others. His popularity with his old teammates was not unanimous. Page had his reservations. So did Lonnie Warwick, the middle linebacker who was an old hunting companion of Van Brocklin's, and Ed Sharockman, the defensive back. They weren't necessarily antagonistic. They did wonder about Tarkenton's deeper loyalties and his flair for finding new employers. First it was Minnesota to Broadway, then back to a championship contender when Broadway might have lost some of its allure and did not produce All Pro offensive linemen.

Tarkenton sensed some of that, but it was never very serious and nothing that could not be resolved by day-to-day fraternity. That and winning. His acceptance was warm. Grant himself did not try to hide his high regard for his new quarterback. And to the rookies in camp the quarterback might have been a lofty figure with all of his experience and remarkable football mind, except that Tarkenton had no interest in playing that role. Whatever the raps against him, Tarkenton was never a protocol man on the football field or in the locker room. His runabout style as a young professional was as much a product of his temperament as it was a response to the inadequacies of his offensive line. That style, of course, had modified by the time he returned to the Vikings. He had once played the game like a gnome liberated from the workshop. It was a form of behavior that concealed an important quality most of the discerning professionals knew was there: his ability to move a team consistently and conventionally, if it was the kind of team that allowed such virtues. The Vikings of 1972 were such a team. He would still scramble now and then. Did Fred Astaire ever give up dancing? Only now he didn't run around the chicken coop. When he did roam from the pocket, Grant had an explanation for it that was so startling in its clarity it ended for all time any lingering complaint about scrambling.

"He's buying time," Grant would say. "The more time he buys, the better chance he has of completing the pass."

The computers proved it, although every once in a while you could buy so much time a Jethro Pugh or a Cedric Hardman would stop the sale with a thud.

As the self-designated new boy in camp, Tarkenton made most of the required sounds, and he meant them. "There are a lot of good things to say about the organization the way it is set up now," he said, "especially about the coach, his staff, and the stability here. But I don't really want to labor that. All of it was true before I got here. My saying it now isn't going to make it any more true than when other people said it before me."

Yet it wasn't as stable as the surface readings suggested.

Three of the Super Bowl veterans—Gene Washington, Charley West, and Clint Jones—had negotiated their contracts jointly. Finks was troubled by that, and bitterness developed. None of the three was filled with brother-hood for the Viking organization when the dispute was finally settled. Page injured his leg. There were other hurts involving important players. And in the opening game of the season the Vikings had Washington beaten, only to let it grease through their hands in the fourth quarter. In defiance of the laws of probability, they did it again the next week against Miami, when the Dolphins needed a fourth-quarter touchdown and Garo Yepre-nian's 51-yard field goal to win. The Vikings won some, lost some. They fumbled and blew audibles in ways Grant teams rarely did. In Chicago they scored an apparent winning touchdown in the fourth quarter but lost it, and the game, because Ed White was allegedly downfield when the pass was thrown. St. Louis beat them in the fourth quarter on a pass from the Viking castaway, Gary Cuozzo. They were blown down by Pittsburgh and Green Bay, and committed the capstone futility by losing the last game to two 49er touchdowns in the last five minutes.

The Vikings finished the season at 7–7, as Van Brocklin undoubtedly pre-dicted. With a Super Bowl contender and one of the most expensive quarter-backs in football, they bombed.

Nobody with knowledge faulted Tarkenton. Even his critics credited him with a superb season. So did the fans. With a week remaining, they voted him the team's Most Valuable Player Award. He stood at a microphone and spoke of his chagrin.

"I've done a lot for this team," he said in a self-rebuke that was intended as a piece of pained buffoonery but got heavier as it went. "It was 11–3 last year, and now we're 7–6. I'm the quarterback who was supposed to pro-vide leadership, help this team win the Super Bowl. I don't want to belittle the award, but the only award that's meaningful is the one they give after the Super Bowl. This has to be my biggest disappointment of a lot of disap-pointments."

The defeats, the wrangle over the commercials, and the re-emergence of all the old derisions of Tarkenton as a 7–7 quarterback made 1972 the most stifling kind of personal defeat for him. He took some of it home with him and found himself being remote and sometimes uncivil where he had never been before.

"I just don't think, though," recalls John Beasley, "that anybody could see how Tarkenton himself could have handled the season any better." Beasley was one of the unbuttoned elves on the team, a Californian who played an acceptable tight end and spread much merriment and unsolicited wisdom on his confederates.

"With Tarkenton coming back we all had this unconscious feeling that we were just going to walk onto the field and everybody was going to concede us into the Super Bowl. We really looked on ourselves as world-beaters. As the season wore on, it was 'Migawd, what's happening?' After that some of them were saying, 'Christ, let's get it over with.'

"I remember walking into the steam room in the middle of the season, when we were still in the running, and hearing one of the best linemen in football say, 'I wish this goddamned season was over.' And there were still seven games to go!

"I was pretty shocked and a little teed off, because I thought at that point he was living off his All Pro reputation. It was that kind of season with us.

"But the big guy for us then, and in the seasons that followed, was Tarkenton. When he first rejoined the Vikings I was ready not to like him. Football players gossip a lot. Sometimes they get pretty sloppy with the truth. I heard from guys with the Giants that Tarkenton was a pretty hard guy to talk to, he was kind of selfish and just wanted to run the show.

"I matured in pro football at the time when Joe Kapp was the Viking quarterback, and I unconsciously compared every quarterback's style with Kapp's. He was a piece of work. Big, blustery, fearless old Chicano Joe. I'll never forget him coming back to the motel the week we played in the Runner-up Bowl in Miami in 1968. He rolled in about two or three hours after curfew, beating on my door. He looked like he had run off-tackle against a hurricane. His shirt was ripped off, and his pants were mangled. 'Somebody on the highway,' he said, 'called me a goddamned Mexican.' He figured that was explanation enough for his unusual appearance, and I guess it was.

"Tarkenton obviously was a different kind of guy. But I liked him almost from the first day. He was in a bind, coming back to his old team. It wasn't going anywhere when he left, but while he was gone it became one of the best, year in and out, and they were giving him the ball and saying, 'This is a winning football team. Everybody knows it. How about 13–1 this year?'

"He never let on, but he had to feel the pressure of that. He came across very friendly and content, like he meant it when he said this was his football home. There weren't any real problems in camp. He had leadership, all right. He was just a terrific head. You had confidence that one way or another the play he called was going to work. It was also reassuring to have him in the huddle. Most of the time he seemed to be enjoying it. In the huddle Tarkenton gives you a funny little look sometimes. He'd call a play and wink at me and say, 'And we got Beazer over the middle.' It sounded like something a kid would say in the playground huddle, and Tarkenton seemed to be spoofing all of the technical jargon he's been spouting all these years. You had the idea he was totally in command of the offense because there wasn't any situation in football he hadn't faced."

When they added up all of the figures for 1972, they showed that Francis Tarkenton had completed nearly 57 percent of his passes, led an offense that outscored the 1971 Vikings by 56 points, and had reduced the Vikings interceptions from the previous year by eight—and the team still finished 7–7.

There was the same baleful symmetry to that figure. It hovered over Tarkenton's head like a biblical judgment or a slogan dreamed up by some braying critic: 50–50 with Francis.

He had managed his career as carefully and independently as the rules allowed. He was willing to walk a lonely road in his dealing with football management, trusting to his instincts and nerve to head him in the right direction. But 1972 was his walk in the graveyard. They opened the gates to a football team that had won more than 80 percent of its games for five years, and it didn't matter who played quarterback, Joe Kapp, Gary Cuozzo, Bobby Lee, or Norm Snead. So here was Francis Tarkenton, the sophisticated head who had called and run every football play imaginable in his 11 years in the business. Join the club, Francis, they said. On this team everybody who plays quarterback is a winner.

Considering the heraldry, what happened had the general impact of Neil Armstrong taking one giant step for mankind and landing on his head.

Tarkenton graded his own performance as sound. He realized that the point was inconsequential. One of the truths of leadership it had taken time for him to learn was that football teams are not built for the glorification of quarterbacks. Moreover, Grant had it in perspective. The quarterback calls the plays and handles the ball and throws the pass, but there is no particular reason why the game necessarily rises or falls on the performance of the quarterback. More so than any other player, he is in position to shape the outcome of a game, positively or negatively. But he doesn't always influence it that way, or even in a majority of the games. His position, like anybody else's, assumes a certain level of competence. If he fulfills it, he is meeting the requirements of the job. If he doesn't, the game and his job are in jeopardy. But the quarterback is the triggerman of a football offense, the ful-crum of all the action. He is the most visible of all players and therefore the one who is likely to receive disproportionate acclaim when his team wins, and unwarranted scorn when it loses.

He is also usually highly paid and profits externally. So Tarkenton never asked the fans or the writers or his teammates to spend their vesper hours mourning his fate.

"Grady," Tarkenton asked his friend on the return flight from San Francisco the night of the last game, "do you really suppose somewhere the Lord decided: 'Tark, you will have a number of good things in your life and you will meet many wondrous people and sights, but it is just not going to be your lot to play on a championship professional football team'?"

Alderman pondered this harsh proposition. "I don't know what your brethren think," he said, "but Catholics don't figure the Lord would do such a thing to a Methodist."

Tarkenton brightened. He told Alderman he could certainly understand now how the Catholic Church, with that kind of faith, had lasted two thousand years.

●

The Vikings rebounded in 1973, winning their first nine games and finishing with a 12–2 record, the beginning of a remarkable four-year stretch in which they played in three Super Bowls and probably should have played in the fourth. The defense also rebounded, finishing second in fewest points allowed, while the offense, spurred by NFL Offensive Rookie of the Year Chuck Foreman, became more diverse. It ranked sixth in rushing, compared to twentieth in 1972.

Foreman rushed for 801 yards, the most for a Vikings back since Bill Brown's 805 yards in 1968. He also caught 37 passes, joining with second-year running back Ed Marinaro, who had 26 receptions, to form a dangerous combination coming out of the backfield.

Although he had set NCAA rushing records at Cornell and was runner-up in the Heisman Trophy voting in 1971, Marinaro was a surprise second-round draft choice by the Vikings in 1972. Most experts downplayed the competition he had faced in college. Marinaro never became the running threat he had been in the Ivy League, but became an accomplished pass receiver.

Philadelphia Inquirer, October 19, 1973

FROM WORLDS APART, THEY JOINED TOGETHER

Skip Myslenski

Chuck Foreman is a ghetto kid who's found instant stardom; Ed Marinaro is an Ivy Leaguer whose success is more modest. As teammates, they're helping the Vikings back to glory.

Walter Eugene Foreman grew up in a ghetto in Frederick, Maryland, played defensive tackle in high school; running back, cornerback, running back and wide receiver in four successive years at the University of Miami, reaped little publicity until he shaked, rattled and rolled through a plethora of postseason bowl games, and was the Minnesota Vikings' number one selection in the 1973 draft. While his mother was pregnant with him, she regularly listened to a soap opera called *The Guiding Light* and was so moved by the death of the heroine's child that she decided to call her next son by the deceased youngster's name. Thus Chuck Foreman, though some of the players still call him Walter.

Edward Francis Marinaro was born in New York City, grew up in northern New Jersey, played running back from his football start at the age of 12 in the Pop Warner League, set 17 NCAA rushing records while starring at Cornell, prompted tomes which either praised his accomplishments or derided them as mere Ivy League whimsy, and was the Minnesota Vikings' number two selection in the 1972 draft. Thus Eddie Marinaro, though some veterans still call him Rookie.

Chuck Foreman, a shy, quiet man, hoped to be selected by a contender and was perforce pleased when he learned he would be joining the Vikings though he then fretted and still frets over the approaching bitter Minnesota winter. Eddie Marinaro, a loquacious city kid, thought Minneapolis was the end of the world when he realized he would be moving there, but has since developed an appreciation for both the people and the area, though he still misses the opportunity to buy a New York hot pastrami sandwich at moment's notice.

After signing his contract, Chuck Foreman bought his parents a new house and moved them out of the Frederick ghetto; indeed, he dislikes even visiting the old neighborhood, and when he does stays no longer than a day. Eddie Marinaro often returns to where he was born, stopping by Errico's Deli (owned by an uncle) on Amsterdam Avenue and sometimes working behind the counter when customers overrun it; though the area is questionable and crime is commonplace, he can park with impunity, no one ever thinking to rip off the neighborhood boy turned celebrity.

Chuck Foreman drives a Dodge Charger, the car he won as the Most Valuable Player in last year's Senior Bowl, and is thinking of buying an under-

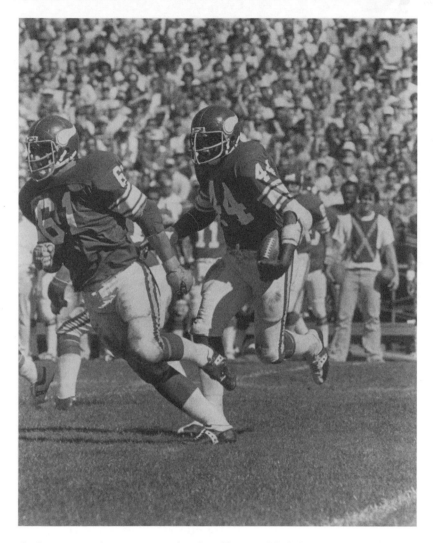

Chuck Foreman on the move. He was the Vikings' first-round draft choice in 1973 out of the University of Miami. He rushed over 1,000 yards three seasons, led the NFL in pass receptions in 1975, and was a Pro Bowl selection five consecutive years (1973–77). Injuries shortened his career, and he retired at age 30. PHOTOGRAPH COURTESY OF THE MINNESOTA VIKINGS.

stated, distinguished black Toronado. Eddie Marinaro arrived for his first season in a Viking-purple Porsche, for his second in Viking-gold Porsche, and is planning on purchasing a Mercedes-Benz before his third season.

Chuck Foreman's performance—79 carries for 416 yards, 18 receptions for 191 yards—have made him a leading candidate for this year's Rookie of the

Year award. Eddie Marinaro's performance—51 carries for 153 yards, 11 receptions for 73 yards—have begun to fulfill the promise he showed at Cornell.

They are good friends, and together they form the starting backfield for the undefeated Minnesota Vikings.

* * *

MARINARO "I had something to prove not only to my detractors, but to myself as well. You know, you start hearing stuff enough times and you can start believing it. I never claimed I could come into the pros and do what I did in college. That's ridiculous. But I just wanted to be part of the team. I just wanted to justify myself. All the time in college I kept hearing that stuff well, hey, what could I say? I was out there busting my ass and no one would recognize it.

"Last year, being from the Ivy League, I got kidded pretty good. I mean, guys here on their off-days they go hunting. I've never been hunting in my life. If I went, I'd probably shoot myself. Or get shot. And because of the Ivy League, they called me Avis. Later some of them even said, 'Hell, you're not even Avis. You're Budget Rent-A-Car.'

"Had I come as just another Ivy Leaguer, say as a free agent, I probably wouldn't have taken so much. But since I'd had so much publicity, since I had a reputation as a pop-off, which really wasn't true, well a lot of players on this team came up the hard way you might say. Fred Cox, a free agent. Mick Tingelhoff, a free agent who is starting. They kidded me pretty good.

"But I was ready for them. I knew what to expect. They saw me on television, a long-haired loudmouth. But I came to camp with my hair so short, so short, man, it was almost a crew cut. And when they told me to sing I sang. They told me to sing again, I sang again. I never opened my mouth.

"And on the field I pulled out all the stops. I did things I never did before. Like in college, I went through the normal hitting in scrimmages. But I never had the reputation as a hitter. In camp though I was always in there and, man, did I have some lumps. In fact I read in one of the papers, 'Marinaro Relishes Hitting . . . '

"Being drafted so late kinda put me in my place all by itself. It was the best thing that could have happened to me. Getting drafted in the second round shattered my ego, no, not shattered, but it cut it down to size. People had been putting me down so much and naturally I had to overreact, I had to build myself up again. But after the late draft, I was off the hook, people didn't expect me to be an immediate star. I was just another ball player again, not a big bonus baby. I had to start from the bottom all over again. I had to make the team. And that summer I worked hard, I was filled with anticipation, wondering 'Am I good enough?' Then I found out."

FOREMAN "Every rookie is under some pressure, you know, wondering whether you'll make it or not, worrying how the veterans will accept you, or whether you'll be accepted at all. But the attitude I took was not to think of myself as a rookie, to think of myself as a first year man. If you think of yourself as a rookie, you'll always be a step behind.

"See, I never doubted my abilities. I had shown I had ability; if I wasn't any good at all, I wouldn't have been drafted. So the only thing I had to do was satisfy myself. I knew what I could do and what I couldn't do. I felt the only thing the other people had over me was experience. So I didn't let myself have any pressure. I didn't think that way. I blocked it out of my mind.

"I can relate my strong mind to my childhood, to how my parents raised me. I was exposed to a lot. I didn't want to go that way. My parents didn't want me to go that way. And in high school I realized the only way out was through football. So I worked hard. Man, I didn't drink a beer until I was in college. My friends, yeah, some of them are in jail, or dead, or hooked on heroin."

MARINARO I've always felt that the people who show off the biggest egos, who have to talk about themselves, they're working to get confidence, overcompensating for a lack of confidence in themselves. I remember as a grammar school kid, I was very conceited, I always talked about what I did in competition. But as I got more successful that grew into a self-confidence. By that I mean I became more confident within myself, I didn't have to let everyone know about it anymore.

There are a lot of people who don't say anything, but that doesn't mean they're any less confident than, say, a Namath. They're just different personalities. See, if you didn't feel you could do the job, you wouldn't. If you had any doubts at all, there's no way you'd get it done.

Do I feel vindicated? Yes and no. Yes, because I made the team, I'm starting, whatever. But I'm really not satisfied with how I'm playing. I have personal, private goals for myself. When I reach them, then I'll feel fully satisfied.

FOREMAN I came here with the attitude that I'd be a starter. But the success I've had, man, I never thought in those terms. Still, I'm the same old me. You know, most professional football players have had publicity of some kind in college and I think the way they handled it there will be the same way they handle it here. Now, man, I like enjoy being in the limelight. But I don't let it go to my head, I don't walk around saying, "Hey, look at me. I'm a star."

It's my personality. I really am shy. I don't like people to come up to me and say, "Hey, you'll be Rookie of the Year." Or, "Hey, you're great." I don't know what to do. What do you say, "Yeah, I know?" Man, I blush. Sometimes I go hide . . .

Man, I'm lucky. I guess every other night I just sit down and say to myself, "Do you know just how lucky you really are?" Some guys may not appreciate it. But I think of all the other things I could have been. I could have been one of the really bad ones. Yeah, I've been lucky. And every night, every night I thank God for it.

MARINARO I was pretty loose after I made the team last year. In training camp, when there was a lot of pressure on me to make it, I was as serious as anyone. But as my role changed, as I settled in as a third-string running back, there was no pressure on me. I knew if I played, it would only be for a little bit, a short while. But this year, as a starter, I'm concentrating more.

Before a game, man, I feel like you do in high school, when you get a note telling you that you have to go see the principal on the next day. You spend the rest of the time wondering about all the things he might want to talk with you about, the good things and the bad, but mostly the bad, all those things he could yell at you about. All that stuff's going through your mind.

Of course you always try and think positive, think only of the good things that can possibly happen to you during the game. But I don't care what anyone says, you have a fear of what you can do wrong. As a young player I worry about fumbles, dropped passes, missed blocks. Maybe if I was someone like O. J. Simpson or Larry Brown, then I might not worry about them. Someday I may reach that point. But now, it's important for me not to make mistakes.

FOREMAN Before a game I'm very quiet, concentrating on my assignments. But very cool. I never get nervous or anything like that. Even before my first game, opening day, I wasn't nervous. The only thought I had was how good are these other guys and how good will I do against them. Maybe on Friday, then I'm psyched up so to speak. But by Sunday I'm cooled out. I don't have any pregame jitters, I've already been through that.

Man, it's funny, during the week I listen to rock 'n' roll and soul, but sometime around Friday night, I start putting on jazz. It's an unconscious thing, but I just start listening to jazz, listening and cooling out.

MARINARO In college, if you have pro aspirations, you have to think of yourself, especially if you're in the situation I was in. We weren't going to challenge for the national championship. We could have been Ivy League champions and I really wanted that. But deep down I realized I had to do certain things to become a professional football player. A lot of guys I played with really wanted to win the Ivy League. But the next year they were going to go out and become lawyers or doctors or accountants.

But now that I am a professional football player, well, I regard it as my profession, my job, which means you think of money too. So I'd sacrifice being an All Pro, for example, to have the Vikings get a shot at the Super Bowl. It'd be better for me financially.

I mean, look at last Sunday. If I was only thinking of myself, I'd be upset about that game. I ran six times for 12 yards, caught one pass for 12 more. Now if I did that on another team, a poor team, I might be more annoyed. You know, that's not going to get me into the Pro Football Hall of Fame. But it was for the Vikings, and to just be playing on this team is to be respected. And most importantly we won, and that's what counts now.

FOREMAN You know what I like best about a game, to do the plays and watch the fans go crazy. We're entertainers. I don't want them to sit there with their heads in their hands, 'Ho-hum, here we go again.' I want them back the next week. It's something like an Alfred Hitchcock movie. They know the final score. But I want them to leave in suspense, wondering what you'll do the next week, wanting to come back and see.

They call us football players. But we are entertainers. We're not close to the audience like Marvin Gaye or Isaac Hayes. But we're entertainers just the same . . . And artists, running's an art. Like a writer does a great book, or Isaac Hayes writes and produces a good song. Running's an art in the same way.

That's why it's so good in slow motion, people can see all the moves, the cuts, all the tricks. Man, when you're out there, it's just like being in a dream world, especially on a good run. You just put those moves on and, say, have you ever been chased by a dog? Well, that's how I feel when I carry the ball. I gotta get away, I gotta get away. It's not fear. But for me, it gets my adrenalin going, not letting those big guys get me, not letting them get a good shot at me. It's like being tied up and having to get free. It's a matter of life and death.

And after a spectacular run I feel really good inside. I don't bust the ball. Man, I want to bust it, that's what I feel inside. But I'm cool about it. I just flip the ball to the man. But inside, man, inside it's like 1,000 little kids jumping up and down on Christmas morning.

●

In the 1973 NFC divisional playoff game, the Vikings trailed the Washington Redskins at halftime, 7–3, but a locker room tirade by Carl Eller inspired the team to make a comeback, and they won 27–20 on two fourth-quarter touchdown passes by Tarkenton to John Gilliam.

The Vikings controlled the football and forced six turnovers in the NFC championship game against Dallas the next week, and won going away, 27–10.

But the Vikings were completely dominated by the Miami Dolphins in Super Bowl VIII, 24–7. It was Miami's second consecutive Super Bowl victory, coming on the heels of their perfect, 17–0, 1972 season. It was also their third consecutive Super Bowl appearance. They had lost to Dallas 24–3 in Super Bowl VI.

Dolphins quarterback Bob Griese only threw seven passes, completing six, as fullback Larry Csonka pounded the ball 33 times for 145 yards and two touchdowns. Tarkenton was 18 for 28 passing, for 182 yards, but the team could only net 72 yards on 24 rushes—and 18 of those yards came on Tarkenton scrambles.

St. Paul Pioneer Press, January 14, 1974
"EYE OPENER" COLUMN
Don Riley

The only other disaster that could have befallen the Vikes would have been for them to be locked in the dressing room. And that, peons, would have been the biggest break they got. Hell, the game was over when Buoniconti won the toss—the only damn thing I predicted all day. Now let's not make excuses. Don't blame a bad call on Kingsriter; don't blame a stupid call on the five-yard line; don't blame Voigt's clip . . . Let's lay it on the line: The Vikes were crucified by the best football team in the history of the game . . . Now you know what they mean by execution. The Vikes couldn't have been executed with more dispatch if Miami marched them into the gas chamber, tossing cyanide capsules at their heels . . .

They talk about Miami equaling the Green Bushers dynasty. Rubbish. This outfit'd eat up the old Bushers like a caveman tearing into a flank of venison after an all-day hunt . . . Jim Taylor couldn't have got past the line of scrimmage. Paul Hornung's shoulder pads would have been dissolved. Bart Starr couldn't have found Carroll Dale with a spyglass and a pack of bloodhounds . . . This outfit isn't big and at time looks soft. But it's so much smarter and disciplined than the other outfits, it has to win you over . . . The defense will give here and there and suddenly the Dolphins have more people on you than a morals squad raid . . . The Vikes were never in this game; they'd had a better chance starting the Little Sisters of the Poor. At least they'd have had a prayer . . . Never has one championship club outclassed another so badly since the early rinky-dink KC and Oakland teams were trying to put a man on the moon—or get a Super Bowl first down . . .

And don't blame Tarkenton. Or the blocking backs or the line sweepers. The Vike defense, rigid and immobile, must have been a joke in the Miami huddle. Certainly it did little to confuse a simple Dolphin attack which called its shots all day. They could have sent a Western Union messenger boy to the Vikes with their next play and still made 10 yards . . . And let's not hear that we were robbed by the Ma Barker gang disguised as officials. The

Dolphins don't make foolish mechanical or mental errors. The Vikes, who used to pride themselves in perfection, pulled more booboos than a two-year-old in a sandbox . . .

Now everyone looks to the future. The only reason that would keep Miami out of the Super Bowl next year would be the Fat Head disease which has afflicted the KC Chiefs, Dallas and NY Jets over the years. But there is Shula, a man who opens every day in church at 6 A.M.; and Griese who is no showboat and doesn't chase Johnny Walker Red or dames in the wee hours; and Csonka who is young and still a little hungry; and Morris who'd like to change the name to Morris-Csonka and Co. But most of it is an intangible: Character. Csonka calls it undercurrent; Griese calls it something innate; Shula calls it work and sweat and pride. Whatever it is, it borders on a mystique—the kind that for so many years carried the Yankees, the Boston Celtics, the Montreal Canadiens . . . You couldn't describe it but it's there . . .

So, Miami looks powerful for perhaps another two or three years. What about the Vikes . . . Well, they've got some heads that are older than the pyramids. Nobody can tell if Eller, Marshall, Winston, Tinglehoff and Larsen can generate enough youthful enthusiasm to rally for another giant stand. Tarkenton can fire for another three or four years. But the Vikes are a four- or five-man rebuilding job. The biggest break they get, and I never thought I'd say it, is to be playing in the Central's Black and Blue division. The Bushers are wobbly. The Bears are two years away from a threat. And the Vikes could beat Detroit with a powderpuff and wearing high heels.

Oh, yes, the Black and Blue Division. Maybe we need an injection of a little of that Miami finesse. The Dolphins don't need hard noses or hard heads. They've got something far more important: A belief in themselves. That's something damn difficult to trade for.

●

The Vikings had another solid year in 1974, winning the Central Division of the NFC with a 10–4 record. Tarkenton again ranked with league leaders in all positive passing statistics, and halfback Chuck Foreman was the team leader in both rushing and pass receptions, as the team went against conventional pro football wisdom and continued to develop a ball-control passing offense, designed to set up the running game, instead of the other way around. New star players began to replace some of the stalwarts of the late 1960s. On offense, strongman Ed White became a fixture at guard. He was a Pro Bowl selection four times, in 1975–1977 with the Vikings and in 1979 with San Diego. Fullback Ed Marinaro was a rushing and receiving threat out of the backfield. Receiver John Gilliam, obtained in a trade with St. Louis, was the team's deep threat, and made the Pro Bowl four consecutive years, 1972–1975. On defense Doug Sutherland replaced

Happy fans run on the field to congratulate the Vikings after their 14–10 victory over the Los Angeles Rams in the NFC championship game on December 29, 1974. PHOTOGRAPH FROM *STAR TRIBUNE*. COURTESY OF THE MINNESOTA HISTORICAL SOCIETY.

Gary Larsen on the front four, and the unit continued to be effective. Jeff Siemon took over as middle linebacker as a rookie in 1972, and made the Pro Bowl four times in his 11-year career, in 1973 and 1975–1977, while Matt Blair started to work his way into the linebacking corps. He would have a six-year Pro Bowl run, 1977–1982.

In the divisional playoffs, a 16-point third quarter broke open a 7–7 halftime tie with the St. Louis Cardinals, and the Vikings won easily, 30–14. The NFC championship game was a tough defensive battle. Trailing 7–3 in the third quarter, the Rams had the ball on the Vikings two, but were stopped when a deflected pass was intercepted by Wally Hilgenberg in the end zone. The Vikings drove 80 yards in 15 plays to take the lead, 14–3, and they held on to win 14–10. The defense held Lawrence McCutcheon, the NFC's leading rusher, to 32 yards.

The Vikings were favorites— again—in Super Bowl IX, but they were completely manhandled by the Pittsburgh Steelers, 16–6. The Vikings' defense held its own—the only score in the first half was a safety scored when Tarkenton fumbled a handoff to Dave Osborn and recovered in the Steelers' end zone. The Vikings only managed 17 yards rushing and 102 net yards passing, and their only score came in the fourth quarter on a recovery of a blocked punt. Tarkenton, hounded all day by the Steelers' front four—dubbed the "Steel Curtain" and now the heirs in public attention to the "Purple People Eaters"—threw three interceptions and had four other passes deflected. The Steelers only had 84 passing yards, but gained 249 on the ground, led by Franco Harris, who had 158 yards in 34 carries—eclipsing the record set by Csonka against the Vikings in Super Bowl VIII.

The loss was devastating to Vikings fans, who alternated between despair and anger. It was also hard on former Vikings like Karl Kassulke, who had been on the losing side in Super Bowl IV. Kassulke, one of the hardest-hitting safeties in the league, played for the Vikings from 1963 to 1972. His career was cut short by a motorcycle accident just prior to training camp in 1973. He was paralyzed and spent the rest of his life in a wheelchair.

Minneapolis Star, January 13, 1975
AN AFTERNOON OF DISAPPOINTMENT
FORMER VIKING KARL KASSULKE
Dick Gordon

"Three times and out," Karl Kassulke said. "A very sad feeling."

It wasn't meant as a dirge but under the circumstances it sounded that way.

Like many another Viking fan, Kassulke had just spent a long afternoon of disappointment. But for him the day held a special significance. He had been there himself: same time of year, same stadium, same game, same loser. He knew how it felt.

"It's a hollow and empty feeling. Now is the time if you're a Viking player, you want to go in some corner and be by yourself." He was the strong safety for Minnesota's first Super Bowl game—January 11, 1970. Kansas City won 23–7.

About 1:30 P.M. this Super Sunday, Kassulke was playing gin rummy with his accountant, Lowell Gordon, at the Kassulke home in Eagan. It was suggested he wasn't thus fiddling with the pasteboards five years ago.

"You mean you don't think Bud [Grant] let us play gin before the kickoff?" Kassulke said. And then he cackled out with the laugh that became his trademark as a Viking and has endured through his consignment to the sidelines and a wheelchair, the victim of a motorcycle accident in July 1973—just before he was to begin his eleventh Vikings season.

Soon Kassulke called off the gin, wheeled his chair down an incline and settled down in front of the TV set, notebook in hand, to more serious things—like covering the game for *Viking Report*, of which he is publisher.

His pregame prediction was a little hedgy. "The Steelers have a great defense," he said in what soon proved to be a summation of Pittsburgh's 16–6 victory. "But we've got to be positive. I think the Vikings are going to win."

With his sister, Mrs. Carmen Bolender, and a roomful of relatives and friends, Kassulke let the others supply the commentary much of the time. He laughed when someone remarked, after Pittsburgh's Roy Gerela missed an early field goal, "That's the best field position we've had so far."

"Son of a gun," he shouted when a long first-quarter pass to John Gilliam was ruled out of bounds. And "Get him, get him," when Bobby Walden picked up a bad snap on another Steelers field goal attempt and futilely tried to run the ball.

"Is that the same Bobby Walden?" he asked in disbelief about his Viking teammate of the mid-1960s.

"It's touch and go," he theorized when the first quarter ended 0–0, the best Super Bowl start the Vikings have had. It was 3–0 for Kansas City after one quarter in 1970, and Miami led 14–0 last January.

"Who's got the ball?" Kassulke demanded with tongue in cheek, when Randy Poitl, wearing the number 29 Kassulke made a Viking byword, recovered a fumble to give the Vikings their first scoring opportunity in the second quarter.

And then, minutes later, "Oh, Fred, you're horse (bleep)," when Fred Cox missed a field goal that would have drawn first blood for the Vikings.

Remarking on the 2–0 Pittsburgh lead at halftime, Kassulke said, "It's unreal. But the Vikings are impotent . . . so far."

Soon, of course, it was 9–0 instead of 2–0 and Kassulke agonized on the second-half kickoff. "Oh, Brownie." He was reminded that this costly fumble, which led to the first Steelers touchdown, was reminiscent of Charlie West's kickoff bobble that helped put Kansas City ahead 16–0 the other time the Vikings were besieged in New Orleans. A bad omen?

"We've got to get back in the ball game," Kassulke said, almost pleading. "We've got to get on the scoreboard."

"I'd go for the son of a bitch," Kassulke said on a fourth down and inches situation in the third quarter. Grant and quarterback Francis Tarkenton concurred but, after the Vikings' long-count play was ruled a no-play, a punt was ordered.

"I hate to say it," Kassulke said as he said it, "but the Vikings are going down to defeat." And then a characteristic, "Oh (bleep)," when a penalty nullified an interception by Jeff Siemon.

The Kassulke pessimism continued as the fourth quarter got underway. With 13 minutes to go and still 9–0, he said, "They're dead. You got to be (bleeping) me. There's no way it can happen."

Then suddenly it did. Matt Blair blocked a punt in the manner of Kassulke in the old days and Terry Brown recovered for a touchdown. Karl was shouting and cheering with the rest of the room.

He was still grinning when Pittsburgh, now pressured with only a 9–6 lead, got to a third down and three setup. "I'll bet they try a look-in pass," Kassulke said.

He was only half right. The pass was a long one to Larry Brown, who caught it—and fumbled it. The room was alive again and ex-Viking Kassulke was part of the short-lived delight. A quick whistle had voided the Minnesota recovery.

"Why not the Vikings' ball? Oh Christ," Kassulke moaned.

Quickly then, "Oh (bleep)." And after Terry Bradshaw's pass to Brown wrapped it up 16–6, Kassulke concluded correctly, "There's no way they can come back now."

It was supposed to have been a lively funfest afterward. It wasn't. The Kassulke cackle was stilled. "They worked so hard to get there," he said.

Was defeat easier to take now than then? "The other time [1970] I felt personally responsible. Now it's a little easier to accept."

But not much. Especially when it's three times and out.

●

The Vikings won 10 straight to start the 1975 season, and finished at 12–2. This looked like the best of Bud Grant's teams. The defense ranked first in the NFL in yards allowed and third in points. Paul Krause had 10 interceptions, just one below league leader Mel Blount of Pittsburgh, and Bobby Bryant tied for seventh with six. The offense ranked third in points scored. Fran Tarkenton had his best year and was voted the NFL's Most Valuable Player. He was first in most passing categories—a 64.2 completion percentage, 273 completions, 425 attempts, 25 touchdown passes (tied with Buffalo's Joe Furguson)—and second in passing yardage. To top that, during the season he surpassed Johnny Unitas to become the NFL's all-time leader in touchdown passes, completions and pass attempts. Chuck Foreman also had an amazing season. His 1,070 yards rushing was fifth in the NFL, and he led the league with 73 pass receptions. Demonstrating how potent the Vikings' passing attack was, fullback Ed Marinaro ranked sixth in the league with 54 receptions, while wide receiver John Gilliam was tenth with 50.

But the Vikings were stunned by the Dallas Cowboys in the divisional playoff game at Metropolitan Stadium, losing 17–14 on a 50-yard touchdown pass from Roger Staubach to Drew Pearson that came to be known as the "Hail Mary Pass." Dallas had fourth down and 16 yards to go with only 44 seconds left in the game when Staubach launched his pass downfield. To compound the pain, Tarkenton learned after the game that his father had died while watching the game on television. It was arguably the toughest loss in Vikings history.

St. Paul Pioneer Press, December 29, 1975
VIKES LOSE IN FINAL 24 SECONDS
COWBOYS PULL OUT 17-14 UPSET ON 50-YARD BOMB
Ralph Reeve
On a day that will live in infamy in Minnesota pro football annals, the Vikings had their season abruptly ended for them, 17–14, by the Dallas Cowboys in the 1975 divisional playoffs.

The Cowboys won on an unbelievable series of plays with barely more than a minute to go.

Then, after they had snatched victory from the jaws of defeat on a 50-yard bomb from Roger Staubach to Drew Pearson with 24 seconds left to play, the dark side of pro football became visible. The Vikings will argue long and loudly in the winter months ahead that they were euchred on that play and on a pass play previous to it, but they would rather forget the ugliness that surfaced in the waning moments of action.

One of the NFL officials, Armen Terzian, was struck flush on the forehead by a flying one-pint gin bottle from the right field bleachers, knocked down, bleeding and shaken.

"I wasn't unconscious at all," Terzian said later. "They tell me a couple people yelled 'Look out!' but I didn't hear them."

Terzian was visited in the officials' dressing room after the game by a number of writers wanting his version of the incident, plus Senator Hubert Humphrey, who told the stubby, grey-haired little field judge:

"I felt embarrassed, I just want to express my sympathy."

Bud Grant, who had one of his own players hit in the eye by a snowball eight days earlier in Buffalo, said:

"It was a terrible, terrible thing to happen. I apologize to him [Armen Terzian] and the whole country for this happening in our park."

The two critical plays in the Dallas 85-yard drive were both bitterly disputed by those players still in the dressing room by the time the door was opened to the press.

The first play was a desperation fourth-and-16 pass play with 44 seconds left to play on which Staubach hit Pearson at the 50-yard line.

The Vikings argued that Pearson caught the ball out of bounds and there's no question that Pearson landed out of bounds.

But Jack Reader, NFL assistant supervisor of officials, said after the game, "If he's knocked out of bounds and he could have landed in bounds, it's a completed pass."

The Vikings thought he would have landed out regardless.

Grant, the Viking coach, said afterwards:

"I'm sure if Nate hadn't pushed him he'd have landed out of bounds."

So much for that play.

Now the Cowboys had first down at midfield with 37 seconds left on the clock and the Vikings leading 14–10.

The first pass is incomplete and Drew Pearson came back to the huddle and told Staubach:

"Let's go."

Rifle-armed Roger let fly . . . Pearson caught the ball on the five-yard line, turned around and spun into the end zone for a touchdown which, with Toni Fritsch's conversion kick, made it 17–14 Dallas with 24 seconds left to go.

The Vikings protested vehemently that Pearson knocked down Nate Wright on the touchdown play and claimed that offensive pass interference should have been called on Pearson.

Terry Brown, the Viking strong safety, who was in the vicinity with Wright and Pearson said:

"Nate was right on him all the way. Suddenly, he was on the ground.

"Tell you what, I'd bet my playoff check Nate got knocked down. It was so obvious. They were running side by side and the next thing you know, Nate's on the ground."

"I kept telling the official [Jerry Bergman] he missed the call, but he said no, I was wrong."

Reader said later, "No official ruled there was any pushing. He [Pearson] made a play on the ball."

"I don't think I pushed off," said Pearson. "I was trying to get the ball and so was he. We both were fighting for it."

When they trotted off the field after the play, Nate Wright told Terry Brown he felt the play was an interception all the way for him . . . until he hit the deck in the battle with Pearson for the ball.

Two Vikings, Alan Page and Carl Eller, went off the field and into the dressing room while the last seconds were winding down, with the Vikings in possession.

Page had been hit with a 15-yard personal foul penalty shortly before, and apparently he left the field of combat of his own violation.

"He was not ejected," said Grant in reply to a question.

For only a brief period of time Sunday did it look like success was going to crown the Vikings' efforts.

The Vikings led 7–0 at halftime; it was 7–7 at the end of the third period and 10–7 for Dallas in the fourth period until the Vikings mounted their only sustained drive of the day, a 70-yard march that put Minnesota atop 14–10 until that ill-fated ending.

Minnesota's first touchdown was the product of a three-play, four-yard drive after Fred McNeil alertly recovered the ball after Neil Clabo's punt brushed Dallas receiver Cliff Harris on the back of the leg at the five-yard line.

"Autry [Beamon] got blocked into Harris," said McNeill, "and I saw the whole thing. The ball bounced right in front of me."

Harris had signaled for a fair catch, but when the onrushing Beamon was blocked toward him, he tried to shy away and the ball made contact with his leg.

The Vikings scored on a one-yard run by Foreman three plays later. Fred Cox kicked the extra point and Minnesota was ahead 7–0 with 3:11 gone in the second period.

The Cowboys tied the knot on a 72-yard, nine-play march in the third period, with the big play a 13-yard pass to Preston Pearson, to which was tacked 15 yards for a personal foul penalty on Viking linebacker Wally Hilgenberg.

Staubach also hit Billy Joe Dupree for 18 yards and Doug Dennison gained 10 on a blast up the middle, scoring three plays later on a four-yard smash, Fritsch converting at 6:41.

By the end of the third period the Cowboys had built up a 260–135 edge in net yardage and had dominated play to the tune of 62 offensive plays to 37 for the Vikings.

The Cowboys then drove from their 47 to the Vikings' seven by the final play of the third period and, on the first play of the fourth, Fritsch kicked a 24-yard field goal to make it 10–7 for Dallas. It was the only successful field goal attempt of the game as Fritsch earlier missed a 49-yard try and the Vikings' Cox was wide on a 45-yard shot.

Two series later, with 11:17 left, the Vikings started the 70-yard, 11-play march that put them ahead 14–10 and almost into the NFC title game next week.

The Viking march featured 29 yards on four carries by Chuck Foreman, who had been throttled most of the afternoon by the standout Dallas defense. Foreman also caught passes for 16 and 12 yards on the march.

The touchdown play was a one-yard smash by Brent McClanahan who hit at the left side of the line, bounced back and then slid outside into the end zone behind some blocking by Foreman, Steve Craig and Steve Riley.

It looked, as the seconds ticked away after the two-minute warning at the end of the period, like the Vikings were going to win comfortably by the same score they beat the Rams in the 1974 NFC title game.

But it didn't happen that way.

It came down, inevitably, to the final desperation pass by Staubach from midfield.

The two officials on the play were Terzian, this before he got hit with the bottle, and Jerry Bergman, who had been involved in a controversial play in the Miami–Buffalo game three weeks ago.

As Wright and Pearson were running upfield, Wright had the inside and Pearson said, "There's a 50–50 chance it would be underthrown, so I swung my arm to get inside him."

"It's the old basketball play," said Grant. "When you're coming down, you push off. He's only got one chance in 100 to get the ball, so he does what he has to do to get it. It was a well-calculated play on Pearson's part."

The Vikings objected violently and strenuously to no avail.

"From our point of view," said Grant, "he [Nate Wright] was pushed. That's the ball game."

Grant added, "Very coincidentally, it happened to be Mr. Bergman [the official on the play], quite a coincidence."

After getting hit just last week with a $500 fine, Grant's criticism of the officials was indirect, by innuendo and up to the listener's imagination.

●

The Vikings rolled through their schedule again in 1976, finishing at 11–2–1. The defense was number two in points allowed and Tarkenton and Foreman had strong Pro Bowl years again. Foreman was sixth in the league in rushing and fifth in pass receptions. Ahmad Rashad, obtained in an off-season trade from Seattle, caught 53 passes to tie for eighth. Rookie of the Year receiver Sammy White, the team's number two draft choice from Grambling, gave the team a new deep threat. White gained 906 yards—fifth highest in the league—on 51 receptions.

One of the casualties of the Rashad trade was popular backup defensive lineman Bob Lurtsema, who was waived after the first game of the season and picked up by Seattle. Lurtsema had not started a game in his nine years with the New York Giants and the Vikings, but became famous for his tongue-in-cheek television ads for Twin Cities Federal. Christened "Benchwarmer Bob," he was chosen to represent a bumbling but savings-conscious average Joe. He appeared in over 150 commercials. One of the most memorable showed him standing ankle deep in snow on the field at Metropolitan Stadium, delivering a speech at a fictitious "Bob Lurtsema" day. As the camera panned around to show an empty stadium, Lurtsema mumbled, "You'd think my wife and kids would have shown up."

Officials rush to the aid of field judge Armen Terzian, who was struck on the head and momentarily knocked unconscious by a liquor bottle thrown from the stands after Drew Pearson's game-winning catch in the Vikings' 1975 playoff loss to Dallas. Fans, angered when offensive interference was not called on Pearson, threw cans, bottles, and other objects onto the field. Terzian later said he was struck just after he had tossed a whiskey bottle off the field and as the two teams were lining up for the extra-point attempt. PHOTOGRAPH FROM *STAR TRIBUNE*. COURTESY OF THE MINNESOTA HISTORICAL SOCIETY.

FROM CHAPTER 1 OF *BENCHWARMER BOB: THE STORY OF BOB LURTSEMA* (1974)

Thomas Gifford

It was hot and windy in Anoka, a pleasantly green suburb about 15 miles west of the Twin Cities, and along the main drag there was a line of T-shirted boys and girls meandering toward the Twin City Federal Building, one of those brand-new colonial affairs which always make me think about Paul Revere and premiums for saving money. In the lobby, a wide-open space unbroken by anything but desks, a knot of 15 or 20 kids waited, self-consciously, shuffling, wondering what to do with their hands, feet, voices.

It was 3:15, and one of the firm's officials pulled on his pipe, smoothed his mustache and said, "If he doesn't get here soon, I'm going to put on my shoulder pads and helmet and pretend . . ."

At 3:25 the front door swung open and a man about the size of a tree came through, sandy hair slightly ruffled, a big smile at the ready, a cardboard sign in one hand and a purple football helmet with white horns on the side in the other. He was nattily turned out as is customary with big-time jocks: a denim sport coat, plaid slacks, open-necked shirt, white shoes, the perquisites of being better at games than the rest of us. There is a certain look of celebrity, robust health, the physical life, money. Yet the guy also looks like a foreman in a steel foundry. Or an engineer. Or a suburban father of two. Or a hustling young entrepreneur. And well he might. He's all those things and a professional footballer, too.

But that's not why he's here today. With the kids trailing eagerly in his immense wake, he moves to a centrally located desk while parents and office workers gawk. The kids close in on him, mysteriously sensing that in some way he's one of them; they're not frightened or shy. They watch him place two stacks of glossy photographs on the desk and set the poster up.

"Reserved for Benchwarmer Bob," it says.

Bob Lurtsema invites you to a TCF Benchwarming!

Come warm the bench with the most heralded second stringer of them all . . . Bob Lurtsema. He'll be here to chat with you, distribute autographed pictures and maybe even give you some valuable tips on the fine art of benchwarming. So join the fun! Join Bob at the TCF benchwarming.

See you at the Downtown Minneapolis Office
8TH & MARQUETTE AVENUE
Thursday, April 25
11:30 A.M. - 1:30 P.M.

TCF
THE THINK HAPPY PEOPLE
Minneapolis, St. Paul and Suburbs

Backup defensive tackle Bob Lurtsema's engaging personality and self-deprecating humor made him a media star. His advertisements for Twin City Federal were omnipresent, and he was in constant demand for personal appearances. PHOTOGRAPH COURTESY OF TWIN CITY FEDERAL.

The kids are lining up for autographs and repartee.

Bob Lurtsema, the Minnesota Vikings' fifth defensive lineman and Twin City Federal's private pied piper, has come to Anoka.

During the previous football season, Lurtsema became the best-known Viking of them all—not bad for a sub on a team larded with NFL superstars like Fran Tarkenton, Carl Eller, and Alan Page, to name three prominent All Pro veterans. But due to a series of joyously unpretentious television commercials extolling the manifold virtues of the savings and loan institution, Lurtsema became someone new, a self-effacing giant who began by realizing that nobody "reckanized" him with his helmet off or on and finished the season receiving bouquets of flowers in his dressing room as he applied burnt cork beneath his eyes, slipped on his helmet, and prepared to take the field when he was told by the stage manager, "Five minutes, Mr. Lurtsema." He became Benchwarmer Bob, football's answer to Dudley Dooright of the Mounties on Saturday morning television.

The impact of the commercials was enormous, both for Twin City Federal and for Lurtsema, who became an instant media celebrity and all-purpose Folk Hero. The demands on him grew exponentially: no pattern, but an explosion of interest. Everyone wanted him to be a guest at their banquet, give an after-dinner speech, reassure them that football was a fun place where a regular guy like Bob Lurtsema could get along just fine, thanks.

From February 3 until June 1, 1974, Lurtsema had three days off, three days with no appearances and no speeches, plus an additional 13 days of vacation. Sixteen days out of four months when "Benchwarmer Bob" didn't require attention, when Bob Lurtsema could just relax, if you call working out for four hours every day and having your arm taken apart and put back together again relaxing.

The day he wound up in Anoka had been typical. The obligatory four-hour morning workout: running, lifting weights, therapy on the arm. Off to the Sister Kenny Institute for a couple of hours with the kids being rehabilitated there, into the car and all the way out to Anoka. Arriving half an hour late from the Kenny Institute, he noted that it was the first autographing session he'd ever been late for and not to worry, he'd stay an extra half hour and you had plenty of time to go get your buddies and bring 'em down for a chance to chat.

A tiny kid, about 30 pounds and built along the lines of your basic soda straw, leans against the desk staring intently at the huge man signing autographs. Lurtsema looks up, notices the yellow T-shirt stretching well below the desk top and ending somewhere around the knees.

"Holy mackerel," Lurts exclaims, eyes wide. "The Washington Wildcats! Who are they?"

"Well," the kid says, laughing, "it's only a shirt, y'know."

"Hey, Bob, I'll take your position on the suicide squad . . ."

"Believe me, you can have it."

One husky kid confides that he's a paperboy and late already for his route: "But I don't care, I got your autograph . . ."

"Way to go, big fella," Lurtsema says, looking next up into the face of a 10- or 11-year-old girl who has one of those faces (with long legs to match) destined to break the hearts of a hundred halfbacks over the next 10 years. He takes another picture from the stack: "And what's your name?"

"Kathy."

"With a K is it?"

She nods and watches him sign the photo: "Best Wishes, Kathy—Bob Lurtsema." She takes it from him but pointedly holds her ground, peering at him as he signs again and again.

A woman arrives with a baby in her arms: "Oh, my God, he's gonna cry!" Her husband looks worried: "No, he's not, don't worry." The baby begins to cry.

"Hey, will you sign one for my sister?"

"Sure, for a buck and a half . . ."

"That's okay, I'll charge it."

And Benchwarmer Bob lets out a ring of laughter.

"How old are you, Billy? Fourteen?"

"Six, you dingbat!"

"Hey, Tom, I like your sweatshirt," to a boy in a Vikings souvenir. "I just bought a new sweatshirt myself—'Miami Dolphins' on the front of it. Always like to stick with a winner." And the kids crack up.

"Would you sign this one for Adam, please?" a mother inquires.

"Adam," he repeats. "A-D-A-M," he spells it out, "and they say football players are dumb."

He spies the boy in the long yellow shirt again: "Hey, Washington! Go, Wildcats!" And the boy grins, astonished.

A hoarse kid with thick glasses looks at his photograph: "Hunh," he says, "'Best Wishes, Billy'—is that what you write on all of them?"

"Only if your name is Billy," Lurtsema says, never breaking stride in the signing process.

"He does, too," the pretty girl with long legs says. She's moved behind him now, staring over his shoulder. "He always writes the same thing, 'Best Wishes, So-and-so.'" She's teasing him, reproof in her voice.

"Oh, I do, do I?" Lurtsema regards her coolly, then reaches out and grabs the picture out of her hand and carefully tears it into four pieces, then drops it in the wastebasket. A stunned expression flits across her face, but she hangs in gamely. "That's for being so mean to me," he adds and goes on sign-ing more pictures. She doesn't quite know what to make of it, and looks at her friend who shrugs. After signing several more he takes longer with one, shielding it as he writes, then turns and hands it over his shoulder to her.

"What does it say—?" Then she squeals: "Kathy," she reads, "I love you—Bob Lurtsema," and she collapses in outraged, mock hysterics. Chalk up one fan for life.

Later, one boy proudly informs him that his dad went to the Super Bowl.

"I wonder if he had as lousy a time as I did," Lurtsema says good-humoredly. But he's not kidding.

By the end of two hours, 700 photographs of Bob Lurtsema had been signed and delivered. Not bad for a Friday afternoon at the end of May.

●

When Lurtsema was traded, Jim Lovdahl, creative director for the TCF ads at Colle-McVoy ad agency, did some quick thinking and came up with a new ad showing Lurtsema leaving for Seattle in Lovdahl's rusty old Ford Falcon station wagon, complete with "Seattle-or-bust" painted on a win-dow. Lurtsema started in the 13 remaining games at Seattle in 1976, and in nine games in 1977 before retiring and coming back to Minnesota full time. He later established two "Benchwarmer Bob's" sports bars and is cur-rently the publisher of the print tabloid, *Bob Lurtsema's Viking Update*.

The Vikings opened the 1976 playoffs against the red-hot Washing-ton Redskins, who won their last four games to finish 10–4 and qualify for a wild card playoff berth. They had beaten the 11–2 Dallas Cowboys at Dal-las, 27–14, in the clincher, but the Vikings shut them down at Metropolitan Stadium. Brent McLanahan ran for 41 yards on the first play from scrim-mage to set up an 18-yard touchdown pass from Tarkenton to tight end Stu Voight. The Vikings led 21–3 at the half and 35–6 after three quarters. The Vikings' running attack controlled the game. McLanahan ran for 101 yards on 20 carries, and Chuck Foreman gained 105 yards on 20 carries. Tarken-ton sat out the fourth quarter as the Vikings cruised to a 35–20 victory.

The Vikings would face the Los Angeles Rams in the NFC champion-ship game. The Rams were hungry, having lost the last two NFC champi-onship games—to the Vikings in 1974 and to the Dallas Cowboys in 1975. However, the Rams had never beaten Tarkenton in Minnesota.

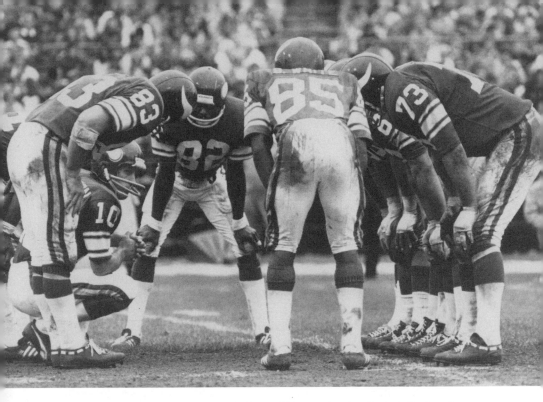

Fran Tarkenton, one of the last NFL quarterbacks to call his own plays, has the rapt attention of his teammates in this huddle. He was voted to the Pro Bowl nine times and was NFL MVP in 1975. He was inducted into the NFL Hall of Fame in 1986. PHOTOGRAPH COURTESY OF THE MINNESOTA VIKINGS.

Los Angeles Times, December 23, 1976

NOBODY SENDS IN HIS PLAYS

Bob Oates

Tarkenton, a quarterback's quarterback, is clever, commands respect and thinks exceptionally quick.

When the Minnesota Vikings beat Washington last week, 35–20, they fooled the Redskins on the first scrimmage play of the game—a running play that gained 41 yards.

"Was it sent in?" someone asked Fran Tarkenton afterward.

The Viking quarterback stared at the reporter for a moment, then asked coldly: "What did you say?"

"I said," the reporter persisted, "was that play sent in from the bench?"

Still staring, still hostile. Tarkenton replied: "Baby, no one sends in plays for Francis."

And that is probably the naked truth. After 16 years in pro football, Francis knows it all. What's more, he knows he knows, and his opponents all know he knows.

Says Hall of Fame quarterback Otto Graham: "The thing about Tarkenton is that he commands respect. He is a very clever fellow."

The National Football League consensus is that Tarkenton isn't the best of the game's active quarterbacks—and he certainly isn't the best passer—but that his aptitude for football outreaches everybody's.

Hall of Fame quarterback Sammy Baugh sums him up: "There may be stronger arms around but there aren't many that think as quickly."

All this is reflected today in an extraordinary and relevant statistic: In nine games since Tarkenton's rookie season, the Rams have never beaten him in Minnesota.

The Tarkenton jinx has lasted 16 years. And it is expected to run on for at least another game, in which Minnesota is a four-point favorite over Los Angeles Sunday with the National Conference title on the line.

HIS RECORD

- After eight regular-season games and one playoff, Tarkenton is 7–0–2 over the Rams in Minnesota.
- When the Vikings were an expansion team in 1961, he routed the Rams with four touchdown passes, 42–21.
- Tarkenton has a winning record over every Los Angeles coach since Bob Waterfield. He was 2–1 over Waterfield (1–0 in Minnesota); 4–2–1 over Harland Svare (3–0–1 in Minnesota); 1–0 over George Allen in a Ram–Viking game played in Minnesota; 1–0 over Tommy Protho in a game played in Los Angeles, and 2–1–1 over Chuck Knox (2–0–1 in Minnesota).
- As a Viking quarterback, Tarkenton is 10–4–2 overall against Los Angeles. Including two games with the Giants when he lost to Allen teams, Tarkenton's 16-year record against the Rams is 10–6–2.

The principal difference in the Chuck Knox era is that the Rams are now playing him closer. Tarkenton leads Knox teams by only a composite 51–49. In three games under Knox in Minnesota, the Rams lost two close ones (10–9 and 14–10) and tied Tarkenton last September, 10–10.

* * *

As a stylist, the thing Tarkenton has brought to football is a new way to play quarterback. He plays it on the run. His predecessors in pro football (and many of his contemporaries) work in a pocket formed by their blockers.

If John Unitas and Joe Namath are to be remembered as football's classic dropback quarterbacks—in a tradition best exemplified today by Oakland's Kenny Stabler—Tarkenton has invented a possibly more modern style in which he spends more time out of the pocket than in.

Says Willie Davis, the All Pro defensive end who played against him for years: "Francis operates that way not out of desperation like the other guys, but as a strategy."

It is a strategy that evolved out of the way he was forced to play quarterback on an expansion team early in his Minnesota years, where he began as a scrambler running for his life.

He was indeed the first of the scramblers, and he still holds the NFL record for most yards rushed by a quarterback, though he seldom ventures past the scrimmage line any more.

It was because of his small size (he is under 6 feet and less than 190) that Tarkenton became a strategic scrambler trying to stay in one piece.

He discovered that he could neither see over the giants in the defensive lines nor lick them physically. But he had the brains to run outside, where they had to lumber after him: he had the peripheral vision (including, some say, eyes in the back of his head) to duck and twist and run away from Willie Davis and Deacon Jones, and he had the quickness to throw the ball before they could catch him.

So he started doing all that routinely, and in the process became what he is today, a sprintout passer whose tactics are essentially those of a touch football quarterback.

On American sandlots, young passers have always run around madly, pointed down the field and either thrown the ball with all their strength or dumped it off to one of their backs. And this is fundamentally Tarkenton's style.

●

The Vikings blocked 13 kicks during the season and used two more in the NFC championship game to help defeat the Los Angeles Rams 24–13. In the first quarter defensive back Nate Allen blocked a 17-yard field goal attempt and Bobby Bryant scooped up the ball and ran 90 yards for a touchdown and a 7–0 lead. In the second quarter linebacker Matt Blair blocked a punt that was recovered by the Vikings on the Rams' eight-yard line. The Vikings couldn't push the ball into the end zone, but settled for a field goal and a 10–0 halftime lead. The Rams pulled to within 17–13 in the third quarter, but a third-down 57-yard pass from Tarkenton to Foreman moved the ball to the Rams' 12, where little-used running back Sammy Johnson—obtained from San Francisco in midseason—ran in for the clinching touchdown.

So, the Vikings were heading to the Super Bowl again—their third in four years, and fourth overall. Loyal Vikings fans were certainly not confident . . . hopeful was about as brave as anyone could be. The national press had no doubts, though. The Vikings were almost universally mocked for their big game ineptness.

Los Angeles Times, January 4, 1977
VIKINGS: SUPER LOSERS
Jim Murray

The Minnesota Vikings, the Harold Stassen of professional football, are in town to do their specialty this week—lose the Super Bowl. If they lose again this time, we put them on the road with the Harlem Globetrotters. They lose more often than guys going up against Perry Mason in court or John Wayne in a war.

The AFC loves the Minnesota Vikings. They've been in three Super Bowls and the score is AFC 63, Minnesota 20. Their best hope in the Super Bowl is a whole bunch of safeties. The last Super Bowl they were in, they scored on a blocked punt. For Minnesota, that's a scoring drive. In Super Bowl VIII, Miami didn't even know they showed up.

*

They play the Oakland Raiders on Super Sunday. Oakland is a pretty whacked-out outfit itself. It's like a kid with a machine gun. No telling who'll get hurt once they pull that trigger.

Still, Minnesota goes into such a coma in these things, you have to figure something must be done to keep a competitive balance, at least long enough for television to sell all that beer and razor blades. So I would respectfully suggest that Pete Rozelle invoke certain rule modifications for this game only so the Super Bowl XI won't end up LXX–II.

1—Oakland touchdowns will count only four points—up until it has scored 20 points. Then, they count only three. Oakland field goals count only one, and it is not permitted any extra points.

2—Oakland must kick off to Minnesota after every score, even in the unlikely event Minnesota makes that score.

3—No more than three Oakland men may be downfield under a kick-off or punt.

4—If Oakland is leading by more than 20 points at the half, it must play only 10 men at a time in the second half.

5—Oakland must furnish Minnesota with a notarized copy of its game plan. Any deviation and Oakland is penalized half the distance to the goal line.

6—Ken Stabler has to pass *right*-handed.

7—Cliff Branch must play in a potato sack.

8—Interceptions don't count if Oakland makes them. Ball returns to original line of scrimmage with no loss of down.

9—If Minnesota is behind at the end of regulation time, there must be two or more extra quarters, with Minnesota getting the ball on the Oakland 40. If Minnesota is behind by 30 or more points, give it the ball on the three-yard line.

10—No pass completion of more than 10 yards is legal for Oakland. Since Fran Tarkenton's average completion is only about 5½ yards, this is only fair. Oakland passing touchdowns of more than 10 yards shall be called back with loss of down and five-yard penalty. Any receiver 20 yards from line of scrimmage shall be considered an illegal receiver downfield for Oakland.

11—If Oakland is ahead at the half, it should be permitted no more than three passes per quarter in the second half. It will have to signify in writing when it wants to throw.

12—Start Minnesota with two touchdowns. In other words, start the game with "Minnesota 14, Oakland 0" showing on the scoreboard.

13—No Oakland player may run a pass route which has not been diagrammed and handed to each of the Minnesota safetymen one hour before the game.

14—Oakland must have martinis in the water bucket at all times. If the game gets really one-sided, the Oakland defensive line must play blindfolded.

15—Oakland may not punt—ever. This may boomerang, however, as having the ball four times on every series may result in Minnesota *never* getting the ball. So just give Oakland three downs.

16—If all else fails, take Oakland off the field for the second half and put Tampa Bay on it. If even this doesn't work, turn the game into a lo-ball. The team scoring least wins. I mean, *something* has to be done to keep all those poor Minnesota devils from having to go back and explain through another winter to all the lingonberry-lutefisk set why they keep going into the big city and losing their shirts because they can never find the walnut with the pea under it. There's another rule: On no account can it be legal to deceive the Minnesotans, because their eyes aren't too good. On every play, the Oakland guy with the ball must hold it up where they can see it. And point to where he's going with it. And, Minnesota gets the option of having 12 players for five downs inside the 10-yard line. And you still get 10 points if you want to bet on them.

●

Unfortunately, Jim Murray's sarcasm was not misplaced in Super Bowl XI. There had been a glimmer of hope for Vikings fans in the first quarter when Fred McNeil blocked a Ray Guy punt and recovered the ball on the Oakland Raiders' three-yard line. It looked like Minnesota's kick-blocking game might end their Super Bowl jinx, but the Vikings fumbled the ball back two plays later, and the rout was on. The Raiders scored on their next three possessions to take a 16–0 lead into halftime. Oakland set a Super Bowl record with 429 yards gained and won easily, 32–14. They piled up 266 yards rushing to control the game. The Vikings gained 282 yards passing, but most of these were after the game was lost. They didn't score until late in the third quarter.

It was another crushing blow for Vikings fans, but even more so for the players, 11 of whom had been on the roster in all four Super Bowl defeats—Bobby Bryant, Fred Cox, Carl Eller, Wally Hilgenberg, Paul Krause, Jim Marshall, Alan Page, Mick Tinglehoff, Ed White, Roy Winston, and Ron Yary. Middle linebacker Jeff Siemon kept a journal during the season, and writer Jim Klobuchar used it to capture the emotions of the team's ill-fated

The Vikings chose Southern California tackle Ron Yary as the number one pick in the 1968 NFL draft. He was a rock in the offensive line and was selected as an All Pro for six consecutive years (1971–76). He was voted into the NFL Hall of Fame in 2001. PHOTOGRAPH COURTESY OF THE MINNESOTA VIKINGS.

Super Bowl pursuit and to try to come to terms with the team's continued futility in the big game.

FROM CHAPTER 14 OF *WILL THE VIKINGS EVER WIN THE SUPER BOWL?* (1977)

Jim Klobuchar and Jeff Siemon

Mathematicians discount the theory that the Vikings cannot win the Super Bowl under any conditions, on any field and against any opponent.

The theory gained wide currency in the days immediately following Super Bowl XI and to this day it retains many stubborn adherents. Estimates of their strength vary widely, but a conservative guess might be 75 million—roughly the number who watched Super Bowl XI.

The mathematicians say no. They maintain that facts not now in evidence—whole new generations of data somewhere in the indistinct future—might be compatible with a Minnesota Viking victory in the Super Bowl.

They offer nothing specific. One theorized that the best hope for a Minnesota Viking Super Bowl championship lies in the potential return of the Ice Age.

"There's substantial evidence," he said, "that we are really living in an interlude between phases of the Ice Age and that the great glaciers will inevitably return, concealing most of the North American continent beneath layers of ice hundreds of feet thick.

"With time to prepare," he said, "civilization should be able to survive this vast entombment with some form of nuclear additive to keep society functioning underground. It follows that if life goes on in the next Ice Age, there will be football. If there is football, there will be a Super Bowl. If there is a Super Bowl in the Ice Age, the Minnesota Vikings have to be favored and one day might actually win."

He refused to cast that in the form of a flat prediction, pleading scientific restraint.

The history of the Super Bowl tends to support the scientists' conclusion that the Vikings thus far have not found the compatibility they need to win the big game. They are not compatible with the cities of New Orleans, Houston or Pasadena in January. To remove any doubt about New Orleans, they proved their incompatibility there twice. In New Orleans the first time they didn't like their hotel. In Houston there were sparrows in their shower room. In New Orleans the second time Howard Cosell showed up in their hotel the day before the game. In Pasadena they liked everything except Sunday. They have also shown themselves to feel awkward in the presence of the Kansas City Chiefs, Miami Dolphins, Pittsburgh Steelers and Oakland Raiders in January.

It is clear from this resume that the Vikings so far have functioned as disoriented waifs in the Super Bowl. The right environment obviously has eluded them. The Great Klondike Basin when the salmon are running has been suggested as a place more congenial to the Viking temperament.

The National Football League, for one, proceeded this fall on the premise that the Vikings actually are capable of winning the Super Bowl. The league office refused to honor the previously cited demands from the L.A. press to ban the Vikings from the playoffs, where they always eliminate the Rams, and from the Super Bowl, where the Viking presence has offended the artistic sensibilities of the California critics.

The league instead decided to continue the playoff system, which means the Vikings are almost certain to reach the postseason tournaments sometime in the next couple of years and probably eliminate the Rams again.

A lively mythology has already grown up around Viking futility in the Super Bowl. It demands some rebuttal from the truth. The Vikings have not been trampled in every Super Bowl. They lost one by only 10 points. They have not been held to two first downs rushing in every Super Bowl, only in three of them. They have not lost to the Kansas City Chiefs in 85 Super Bowls (an impression widespread among television watchers from the number of times Cosell exhumes the game on Monday night).

They have, however, played terrible football in the Super Bowl—or at least it has been made to look terrible. The Minnesota Vikings, in the four Super Bowl games they have played in eight years, lost to Kansas City, 23–7; to Miami, 24–7; to Pittsburgh, 16–6; and to Oakland, 32–14. There is no analogous record of failure at the highest level of major league competition in recent history. The Brooklyn Dodgers spread their misery over a longer period. In contrast, the Vikings have compacted their defeats. It is theoretically possible for some slow-moving sweethearts to have spent a substantial part of their courtship in front of a television set watching the Vikings lose the Super Bowl.

Before you attack the question of whether this team can ever win the Super Bowl, you should try to discover why they have lost them all. The juiciest bone for the analysts is not that they have lost four out of four—which is not all that improbable for a good football team—but that they have lost so dreadfully. In three of their defeats they trailed by at least 16 points at halftime. In the other, the Pittsburgh game, they lagged by only two points at halftime but were mauled physically from the start.

Were they outgeneraled technically?

In Super Bowl IV in January 1970, the slim one week of preparation time between the conference title games and the Super Bowl probably left the Vikings less ready than Kansas City. The Chiefs presented novel defenses and an attack Coach Hank Stram exuberantly described as the offense of the 1970s. Nothing so ambitious was required. So it actually became the offense of January 11, 1970, and it was adequate. Without a large file on the Chiefs, the Viking staff grubbed around and felt little comfort about its state of preparedness. The Viking defense, on the other hand, consisted chiefly of Alan Page, Carl Eller, Jim Marshall, and Gary Larsen, the best front four in football at the time. The Vikings lined up in a standard four-three defense on every play. They won their football games with better manpower, not complicated formations. Tactically, the Chiefs could have prepared for them between the national anthem and the kickoff. But the Chiefs won easily because Jan Stenerud kicked three long field goals in the first half, the offense of the 1970s produced two touchdowns and the Vikings, Joe Kapp and all, were duds.

Against Miami four years later the Vikings might have erred tactically by overhauling their offense to accommodate the Miami three-man line. But it wasn't the offense that lost the game. Larry Csonka and his herd scored two touchdowns in the opening minutes by caving in the Viking front and linebackers, and the crowd spent the rest of the game watching the blimp.

Against Pittsburgh the next year the defense didn't lose the game, the offense did—if you want to be parochial about it. If you want to be a Steeler about it, Pittsburgh devoured the Viking attack with L. C. Greenwood, Joe Greene, Dwight White and Ernie Holmes, Jack Lambert, Jack Ham, Mel Blount and anybody else you want to name. The game was close at the finish only theoretically. Franco Harris made over 140 yards, and the Vikings had to block a punt to score.

Against Oakland two years later the offense didn't lose the game and the defense didn't lose the game; the NFL did by scheduling the game on a Sunday.

It is almost impossible to imagine any wild combination of events that would have permitted the Vikings to beat Miami. The Dolphins may have been the best football team in pro history in the two years they won the Super Bowl in the 1970s.

The Vikings' loss to Pittsburgh was physical, deflating enough to convince some of the defeated players that sometimes survival is a legitimate end in itself.

Their only protest with Oakland was in trying to knot their ties after the game with Fred Biletnikoff's tar and jelly all over their hands.

They may have had a better team than Kansas City—but probably not.

The unremarkable truth their public has never been ready to consider is that the Vikings lost four Super Bowl games to superior teams. The world at large has no trouble with that conclusion. Certainly the Kansas City Chiefs,

Miami Dolphins, Pittsburgh Steelers and Oakland Raiders don't. The Viking fans, however, like fans from Lapland to McMurdo Sound, surround their football team with a montage of victorious symbols and visions, like a child's scrapbook: mobs on the field, goalposts falling, triumphant faces glistening in sweat through the birdcages, white hats, indomitability, immortality—the Super Bowl.

Don't tell the Viking fan his football team shouldn't or can't win there.

And don't make him watch while his football team makes a jackass out of his white steed of hope.

What kind of justice, what kind of gratitude is that, he demands, for all his valiant support in front of the television screen?

The best Viking team, in the context of the times in which it played, never reached the Super Bowl. This was the Viking team of 1971, which lost in the first-round playoff to Dallas, the eventual Super Bowl champion. It was the only time in the last nine years that a National Football Conference team won the Super Bowl, and the only year when the NFC was clearly the dominant conference. The Viking defensive stars were in their competitive and physical prime, and the offense was sound and balanced.

Throwing out the Super Bowl's first two years, when the AFC was a sacrificial offering to Lombardi's Packers, the old American Football League—now the AFC—plays better football than the NFC. It is a statement that is really beyond reasonable dispute. The best football teams in the NFL last year, for example, probably were, in order, Oakland, Pittsburgh, New England and Baltimore. The NFC offered the Minnesota Vikings and Los Angeles Rams, who played against each other twice last year without establishing much of anything except that the Rams don't seem to be able to win the NFC championship under two conditions: minus windchill (in Minnesota) and 75-degree weather (in Los Angeles, against Dallas, two years ago). They have not been tested in the Java rain forests or the Mongolian steppes.

The AFC's present superiority dodges easy explanation. It is really not a matter of style. If you want to argue that Oakland's roistering hearts and buccaneer camaraderie represent the AFC at its best, what about the Miami Dolphins under Shula a few years ago? The Pittsburgh Steelers are not the most suppressed spirits in football, but the whole orientation of the team, from the owner to the veteran players, has the old-league personality.

Critics have a tendency to lay down eternal truths on the evidence of last year's scoreboard. The Oakland Raiders, in the makeup of their team or the wily conduct of their management, aren't necessarily symbols or trailblazers. What they did was win Super Bowl XI. If Oakland was pure AFC, from management to coach to players, the Pittsburgh Steelers the previous two years weren't. Nor were the Miami Dolphins before that, in the coaching department. Shula wins in any league.

Neither conference has any special dominance in the category of chaotic management, although the NFC, with Atlanta, New Orleans, Detroit and New York has a slight lead over the AFC, with its New York and Houston. It's probably true that the AFC has stronger and bolder management from top to bottom, leadership more likely to turn a loser into a winner faster. Oakland's Al Davis maintains the AFC arrived at its current superiority in the last big draft before the leagues merged, when the AFC had fewer teams, chose wisely and did not have to spread its talent as thinly as the NFC.

The coaching certainly isn't any different. Owners being the impetuous perfection seekers and glory chasers they are, the coaches move with the wind in both leagues and, like wandering pollen, settle on the most convenient sprout in either league. The result, or course, is crossbred coaching. Thus Shula goes from the NFL citadel of Baltimore to the AFC sandbox of Miami and produces a Super Bowl champion. Joe Thomas, once strictly an NFL talent broker, leaves Minnesota to recruit a champion for Miami of the AFC. He wars with Shula and executive Joe Robbie in Miami and settles in Baltimore, where he turns an established and successful football team into a first-year franchise by tearing it up from top to bottom. Baltimore, now reconstituted as a typical AFC team, suddenly becomes a winner. And Thomas quits to join San Francisco of the NFC.

The AFC does have better quarterbacks in the aggregate (headed by Stabler, Bert Jones, Ken Anderson, Joe Ferguson and Terry Bradshaw). But the great running backs are evenly distributed (O. J. Simpson, Franco Harris and Otis Armstrong for the AFC, Chuck Foreman, Walter Payton and Lawrence McCutcheon for the NFC).

The difference, to the extent that it exists, may be largely in the management at that—the blunders that some make and others do not. The most dramatic illustration may be the Central Division of the National Football Conference, once the strongest in football. The Halas family, so distinguished in the formative years of football, allowed the Chicago Bears to deteriorate into squabbling nonentities on the field. They are being restored under the orchestration of Jim Finks. The Detroit Lions are still erratic administratively. The Green Bay Packers, with a couple thousand stockholders, sank to ineptness when Lombardi left. His departure threw the organization back into chancy thrashings of democracy-at-work.

Only the Vikings in the Central Division have stayed in their orbit through all this. They absorbed a major management upheaval when Finks quit in the spinoff of a power shift on the board of directors from Bernie Ridder, a St. Paul newspaper publisher, to Max Winter, a Minneapolis sports promoter and entertainment figure. But the fixed axis for the Vikings for 10 years has not been its management, or even some of its great stars, but the head coach, Grant.

Their stability is due to Grant's understated skills in achieving harmony and a team-oriented atmosphere around such individualists as Tarkenton, Page, Yary, Siemon, Foreman and Eller. With it the Vikings outdistanced all rivals in the Central Division and all but Dallas and Los Angeles in the conference generally. If much of the time they played like automatons, Grant did not object. It meant consistency. And consistency meant winning. And winning meant you reached the playoffs. Where other teams might have superior personnel in a given year or might play better much of the time, Grant's teams played acceptably well almost all of the time. This meant that now and then they might win a playoff game they shouldn't have won—especially if they played the game in Metropolitan Stadium in December against the Rams.

One reason the Minnesota Vikings lost four Super Bowl games is that at least once or twice they shouldn't have been there. That is, they beat a better team to get there. The Rams of 1976 probably were a better football team than the Vikings. They blew their chances to make the Super Bowl not on officials' lousy calls, as the Rams organization howled, but on the timidity of their coaching staff in going for a field goal from the three-inch line in the first quarter—which, in turn, had something to do with the Rams' prior failures on the Minnesota goal line.

But none of this explains why the Vikings look so irredeemably awful in the Super Bowl.

The temptation is to look for fall guys; and the most visible fall guy on a team that loses championship games is the quarterback. Against a truly great team, the argument goes, Francis Tarkenton's cunning and runabout quarterbacking can't win. This argument runs into trouble right away with its characterization of Tarkenton's style. He just doesn't run around much any more. And while he might not have thrown very far against Oakland, the Raiders' defense rarely can be attacked that way. He had to throw deep against Detroit and others, and he did. The accusation that Tarkenton can't win the big one belongs with the flying saucers and the abominable snowmen. It is an argument made of air. The same kind of charge used to be made against Tom Landry as coach of the Cowboys, and it wasn't much different for Al McGuire of the Marquette basketball teams.

And it's not the age of some of the Vikings' important players or the lack of heft in their defensive line (it went into the Super Bowl with an average weight not much greater than that of some of the bigger metropolitan high school teams) that offers clues to their unsightly pratfalls in the Super Bowl. They weren't too old or too light to win 11 games in the 1976 regular season—including an emphatic victory over the Pittsburgh Steelers.

What is it about the Super Bowl, then, that seems to unhinge this team?

Ed White might not be so far from the truth. The post-Pasadena ridicule infuriated him, but it also stirred him to an examination.

White is the 270-pound All Pro guard who has played in all four Super Bowls. He is one of the most powerful men in American athletics and a highly motivated competitor. Away from the caveman-in-ermine environment of the game, he is a thoughtful, even tender person, a youth counselor and a landscape painter.

He says he dies a little in playing in the Super Bowl. It has nothing to do with resolve or the quality of the competition or the bigger-than-us-humans scope of the game.

"I never like to talk about how I as a ball player react to the week of the Super Bowl," he said, "because it sounds like the lamest kind of alibi if you lose, and somebody always tells you, 'well, it's the same for both teams.'

"That's the point that bothers me. I don't think it's necessarily the same for both teams.

"We're pretty much a programmed football team. I don't think that's bad. The coach has eliminated just about all the extraneous stuff so that when we go to training camp we start a week after the other teams. When we practice during the season we get to the stadium a little before noon and we get out of there by 4:30. When we play a game on the road we fly out of Minnesota at the last possible hour that will satisfy the league rules. When we get in we have a team dinner, have a couple of hours off, have a meeting and a snack, go to bed, get up, have breakfast, get taped, go to the park an hour before the game, play, get out of there and go home.

"In other words, you get your football in concentrated form under Grant. The ball players aren't falling over each other all day, hanging around hotel lobbies or hanging around the dressing room for a half hour waiting for somebody to poke his head in the door and say 'come on, let's go.'

"When it's football under Grant, it's football and nothing else. When it isn't football, get out of there and go home or wherever you go.

"The schedule and the routine almost never vary. Same times, same things. You don't get bored with it because you don't have a feeling of struggling with time and monotony. Also, they pay pretty well—so where do you get off being bored? It's Grant's way of protecting against staleness, making everything move on schedule and preventing football from becoming a sort of hovering thing that occupies you even when it can't command your attention.

"And it works.

"The team is usually pretty sharp the last month of the year when a lot of other teams are hanging on or drifting already thinking about Hawaii.

"Then we go to the Super Bowl.

"It means a week in a hotel. It means two or three press conferences during the week, running around from hotel to practice field. It means you're going to a couple of parties during the week because there's nothing else to do with your time. They can't give you any more football than you usually play during the week, so you do a lot of card playing in your room or sitting around and calling home. And then you get a night with the wife on Friday and more contrived team meetings and a lot more card playing. You look around for diversions.

"Some of the more social creatures on the team come in contact with really beautiful diversions.

"So the fan might say, 'What the hell, I don't see that it's such a great hardship for guys hauling down 50 grand to 300 grand for one football game a week.'

"It isn't any hardship at all. But it is a helluva change. Without trying to make any self-serving excuse for how we've played in the Super Bowl, I'm just saying the change might affect us more than it does a team with a looser weekly routine during the season, where the programming hasn't been as close.

"I don't know if Grant would buy that kind of analysis. I think he's tried to adjust the team each time in a little different way to what it has to contend with, and I wouldn't second-guess it. Theories are easy—and meaningless. I wish I didn't have to try to explain, but when a thousand people ask you, and it's the first question they ask, you can't just stand there and stare like it's a stupid question."

Bud Grant does not consider it a stupid question. Why have his four National Football Conference flagships capsized so abjectly in the Super Bowl?

First, he doesn't believe there are any convincing explanations; second, he doesn't believe the team has played that badly.

Grant never mounts oratorical counterattacks against authors, commentators or fans who take offense at his football team's performance in the Super Bowl.

"Wiseguys and critics," he said, "or just plain teed-off fans aren't going to listen very seriously to the kind of explanation I've got. And I'm not going to cry about that. It's part of losing the Super Bowl—or losing it four times, if you want to go into history.

"I don't look at the games that way—I mean historically, or as part of some overall pattern or scheme. Why we lost to Kansas City may be entirely different from why we lost to Miami, and I'm sure it was. So each game has to be looked at for what it has to tell you.

"If I said now that in at least one or two of those games there were officials' decisions or a series of decisions that were just as important as any plays made, that sounds like the thinnest alibi in the world, and nobody will listen. That it happens to be true is just not relevant. If I said in one of the games, the one with Pittsburgh, it was a standoff most of the time, not many people are going to remember that or will be willing to consider it.

"So we hear a dozen explanations and theories because the record seems to demand them. But it's just a lot of talk, isn't it? If millions of people think the Vikings are a bunch of wilting flowers in the Super Bowl, talk isn't going to change their minds.

"You know, nobody thinks of Oakland that way now. Oakland went year in and year out losing in the AFC playoffs. They also lost the only other Super Bowl game they played in, to the Packers back in the mid-1960s. So I'm sure the Oakland press and the grandstands were full of theories every year about why Oakland lost the big game.

"The rest of the country didn't think much about it because Oakland didn't show up in the Super Bowl all those years. But they did last year, and won, and now nobody is ever going to hear those stories again. But nobody ever did get an answer to why Oakland lost that streak of playoff games. The same way, I'm sure Chuck Knox can't tell you why the Rams have lost three NFC championship games in four years. When we've lost, it's been in the Super Bowl, with 75 million looking at the game. So our losses go into the public domain.

"Nothing that happened in Pasadena can change the things we accomplished during the seasons. Almost everything we did, the trade for Rashad, the draft choices of Sammy White and a few others, the trades for Nate Allen, Windlan Hall and Sammy Johnson, avoiding serious injuries, winning the big games—all of those were sevens on the dice. And then it ran out. We threw craps. The Super Bowl turns the season into heaven or hell. It's glory or junk for two teams in football. Not for the others. They were judged by how many games they won, how they were at the finish, the crowds, all those normal things that decide whether you're successful or unsuccessful. In the Super Bowl you put the farm on the table and throw the dice and, as far as the country or even the shrewd guys are concerned, you're either the golden boys or the dogs.

"And I wouldn't change it. I really wouldn't be very surprised if the Vikings win the Super Bowl pretty soon. Even if they don't, I still wouldn't change the system.

"People ask me if I felt any personal chagrin late in the Oakland game, seeing we were losing another Super Bowl game. I did feel something. I looked down the bench one time and saw all the veterans who made this a great football team and I felt for them. It would be something to take away with you, winning the Super Bowl game. I never questioned that. But they weren't going to do it. Our fans have one coming, and I don't question that, either. It would be a tremendous trophy for them, and for the people who own the team.

"The coach doesn't really stew about embarrassing losses while he's coaching a game, especially if he knows the team he's coaching is a good one and has given him much all those years."

He still, after all, must coach. In the final moments of Super Bowl XI, when the crowd behind the Viking bench was venting its raspy judgment—and some in it wore purple eyeshades—Grant clasped Roy Winston by the arm and asked him if he wanted to finish out the game at linebacker. This was Moony, in his fifteenth season and probably headed for retirement, who took one of Grant's spirals in the snoot during a practice session but clowned about it later.

"Sure," he said. "Playing is what this is all about, isn't it?" So he ran into the ball game. And, like a rookie on opening day, Winston barged in to make a tackle. The game over, he thanked the coach.

Some day it would be nice to beam at the sight of a championship ring on his finger when the old clan gathers in some foggy bar on alumni day in the years to come.

But 15 years of football have filled his head with enough memories, his jeans with enough coin and his body with enough scar tissue to compensate for the empty pedestal in his trophy cabinet.

Pedestals don't mean much alongside Hilgenberg's cackle, Tarkenton's rolling a football on his hands and knees in the locker room or Yary's shaving in full uniform.

Moony had a suggestion as the last of the Vikings' corps left the Rose Bowl.

"Bud," he said, "maybe they really ought to schedule this damned thing on Wednesday."

●

Vikings fans by now were understandably gun-shy about hoping for another run at the Super Bowl, but things were looking good at midseason in 1977, when the Vikings were sitting at 5–2 and one game ahead of the second-place Chicago Bears in the NFC Central Division. Tarkenton's passing numbers were down from the marks he had set in his award-winning 1975 season, but he was still near the top in all categories. Chuck Foreman was on the way to his third consecutive 1,000-yard rushing season. In the four seasons from 1975 to 1978 he ran for a total of 4,086 yards and caught 227 passes—establishing himself as perhaps the greatest multipurpose back in NFL history.

The Vikings' fortunes looked bleak when Tarkenton was sacked and had a leg broken in a 42–10 victory over Cincinnati at Metropolitan Stadium on November 13. He was lost for the season. Under Bob Lee (four games) and Tommy Kramer (one game) at quarterback, the Vikings went 3–2 the rest of the way to finish 9–5 and tie the Bears for first place in the division. Rookie Kramer won one game when he came off the bench to throw three fourth-quarter touchdown passes to beat the San Francisco 49ers 28–27. The Vikings beat Los Angeles 14–7 in the NFC divisional play-offs, but lost to Dallas in the championship game, 23–6. The Vikings were held to only 66 rushing yards and managed only two second-quarter field goals.

In 1978 the NFL went to a 16-game schedule. The team defense continued its decline, especially in the defensive line. Although 41-year-old Jim Marshall started every game at his customary right end position, Carl Eller lost his starting position during the season to Mark Mullaney, and in a shocking development Alan Page was put on waivers and signed by Chicago.

St. Paul Pioneer Press, October 11, 1978
PAGE PUT ON IRREVOCABLE WAIVERS
Ralph Reeve

The Minnesota Vikings put veteran defensive tackle Alan Page on non-recallable waivers Tuesday night, culminating several weeks of speculation that the former All Pro standout of nine Viking championship teams was on his way out.

Reached at home shortly after the Page announcement, Page said:

"I don't have any comment. Really, I don't want to talk about it. I hate to cut you off this way, but that's the way it is."

Page's wife, Diane, who had been hospitalized Monday with acute sinusitis, answered the telephone. When the caller inquired about Mrs. Page, Alan said:

"She just got out of the hospital this afternoon. I can tell you she is not taking it too well. It's a real treat."

The Viking announcement was made about 7 P.M. Tuesday by public relations director Merrill Swanson. Swanson said:

"We placed Alan Page on non-recallable waivers. As a vested veteran, he can opt for free agency. Mike Lynn talked to a lot of teams about a lot of people, but was unable to make a trade. This puts our roster at 44 players, one below the limit, and Mike said the Vikings plan to sign another player before the Rams game this Sunday."

Speculation is that the player to be signed will be running back Sammy

Johnson, who has been on the "unable to perform" list stemming from an off-season injury to his ankle while playing basketball last March. The Vikings also plan to bring in a couple of offensive linemen for tryouts this week since that's an area that has been particularly hard hit by injuries.

"As you know, we have been carrying eight defensive linemen," said Viking coach Bud Grant Tuesday night. "We just didn't want to give up any of our young players.

"I think anything written about Alan should be qualified by the fact that he and I arrived here at the same time. He was drafted by the Vikings about one week after I got here. So we've been here together going on 12 years.

"On a football team nobody is the catalyst, but Alan's contribution was as great as anybody's to the success of this club the last 11 years. He played his position as well as anybody the last 11 years. I don't think anything being written or said now should take that away from him."

While Grant didn't say so, the impression was that Page's performance this year was not up to his standard of previous years. The waiver period on Page expires today at 3 P.M.

The Vikings put Page on waivers last summer during training camp and at least three clubs—Seattle, Houston and Chicago—claimed him at that time. But the Vikings were unable to work out a trade and withdrew waivers on Page then.

Last summer, after the Miami preseason game, Page was late reporting back to camp and was fined $50 by Grant. He subsequently filed a grievance with the NFL Players–Club Relations Committee. Ed Garvey, NFL Players Association executive secretary, also filed a grievance against the Vikings on the subject of days off during camp.

The Vikings tried to trade Page within the last three weeks and at one time a deal was tentatively set with Oakland. In fact, the Oakland players were talking about it in the locker room the day before Jimmy the Greek predicted on CBS television that Page would be traded. But that deal was apparently called off when Doug Sutherland suffered a sprained ankle in a Monday night game at Chicago. The Vikings figured the absence of both Sutherland and Page would deplete them too much at defensive tackle.

But Sutherland recovered quickly and Lynn started shopping around the NFL. Within two days of the Chicago game, he offered Page to at least three clubs—Seattle, the New York Jets and Houston—but got no takers.

An incident involving Page happened in that Monday night game in Chicago, a face-to-face confrontation with Grant.

During the game, the Vikings substituted Duck White for Page. Later, according to witnesses, when Sutherland sprained his ankle, Page was told to go back in and he replied, "What for?"

So Page stayed on the sidelines and rookie Lyman Smith was sent in at right tackle, with White playing left tackle. But when Noah Jackson of the Bears gave Smith a working over, the rookie was pulled out and Jim Marshall was inserted at defensive end and Mark Mullaney moved over to right tackle.

As a result, Minnesota finished the Chicago game with a front four that included three defensive ends—Marshall, Mullaney and Carl Eller.

But Page started the next two games, blocking a field goal against Tampa Bay and an extra point against Seattle, and the feeling around the club was that the storm had passed.

He has a six-figure contract, and he has said he would like to play a couple more years, but the last two years he has been playing at weights ranging from 218 to 222 pounds, which is well below the NFL standard for defensive tackles.

Page has finished his law studies, and when he passes his bar exam he has said he would like to practice law in the Twin Cities.

During his heyday, Page, who is now 33, was the top defensive player in the NFL, a performer of such awesome talent that he could, by himself, dominate an entire game. An all-out performer on the field and a player who never took a day off from practice, he was the NFL's Most Valuable Player in 1971, the first defensive player to win that award, and he was named to the Pro Bowl eight times.

●

The team had ranked second (out of 28 teams) in the league in fewest points allowed in 1976, but slipped to 13th in 1977 and finished in 20th in 1978. Despite Foreman's 1,112 yards in 1977 the team had ranked 21st in total rushing, and when Foreman was held to 749 in 1978—the team was dead last in total rushing—the Vikings almost abandoned the rush and put on an aerial circus. Tarkenton came back from his broken leg with no apparent ill effects. He led the league in total yards, pass attempts, and pass completions. Running back Rickey Young led the league with 88 receptions, while Ahmad Rashad finished fourth with 66 and Foreman caught 61 to tie for seventh place. Despite this offensive power, the team had trouble getting over the .500 mark. In a key matchup on October 22 at Metropolitan Stadium, the 3–4 Vikings beat the 6–1 division-leading Green Bay Packers 21–7 and then won their next three games to tie the Packers with a 7–4 record. Both teams stumbled down the stretch to finish with identical 8–7–1 records.

By virtue of the win on October 22—the teams tied 10–10 in their second matchup in Green Bay—the Vikings won first place on the tiebreaker, but lost to Los Angeles 34–10 in the NFC divisional playoff. Prior to this game, the Vikings had defeated the Rams four consecutive times in playoff games.

Fran Tarkenton and center Mick Tingelhoff retired after the season, and most of the other stars of the 1973, 1974 and 1976 Super Bowl teams had also retired or were beyond their prime years.

It had been a great run. From 1968—when the Vikings won their first divisional championship—through 1978, they had won 112 regular-season games. In addition they were divisional champions in 10 of 11 seasons and played in five NFL/NFC championship games. Only Dallas, with 117 wins, and Oakland, with 115, won more games in that time frame.

And only the Dallas Cowboys, who had won two and lost three, played in more Super Bowls during those great 11 years, but the Vikings were obviously going to be in a rebuilding mode in 1979.

The Magic Bounces Away

THE DIFFICULT 1980S

Bud Grant had succeeded in the 1970s by making annual minor adjustments to the Vikings roster—a college draftee here, a judicious trade there, complemented with an occasional free-agent signing. Optimistic Vikings fans hoped the 1980s would also be a time of successful evolutionary changes, but the odds were stacked against the team.

In 1979 there were only five starters on offense who had also started in 1976, the team's final Super Bowl appearance, and five on defense. Tackle Ron Yary was the only starter on offense left from the 1973 Super Bowl team, while Jim Marshall, Jeff Siemon, Bobby Bryant, and Paul Krause were the only holdovers on defense. The Vikings hovered around .500 all season in 1979, finishing with a 7–9 record and missing the playoffs for the first time since 1972. It was Bud Grant's first losing season since his first, back in 1967.

Marshall was the only holdover from the Vikings' first two seasons, back in 1961 and 1962. He retired just shy of his forty-second birthday after the 1979 season, having started every regular season and playoff game the franchise had played; a total of 302 games, including playoffs. He also started in 12 consecutive games with the Cleveland Browns in 1960, the year before he joined the Vikings. He set the NFL Ironman record in 1975 when he hit 224 consecutive regular-season games, and finished his career with 282, still a record. Safety Paul Krause also retired after the season.

His three interceptions in 1979 gave him an NFL-record 81 for his career, two more than prior record-holder Emlen Tunnell, who had played for the Giants and Packers from 1948 to 1960.

Tommy Kramer did a creditable job taking over the quarterback spot. He ranked in the top 10 in the league in most passing categories, but only four teams in the NFL scored fewer points than the Vikings and the defense gave up 100 more points than division-leading Tampa Bay. Receiver Ahmad Rashad and linebacker Matt Blair were the only Vikings to be invited to the Pro Bowl, quite a contrast to the heady days of 1975, when the team had 10 players selected.

Two longtime defensive stars retired after the 1979 season, but not before they racked up some all-time NFL records. LEFT: Free safety Paul Krause heads to the sideline after his NFL-record seventy-ninth pass interception in a game against the Rams on December 2, 1979. He was voted into the NFL Hall of Fame in 1998. BELOW: Jim Marshall is given a fans' salute prior to his last home game on December 9, 1979. He had started every game the Vikings had ever played, and his 282 consecutive starts by a position player is still an NFL record. PHOTOGRAPH OF KRAUSE COURTESY OF THE MINNESOTA VIKINGS. PHOTOGRAPH OF MARSHALL FROM *DISPATCH–PIONEER PRESS*. COURTESY OF THE MINNESOTA HISTORICAL SOCIETY.

Minneapolis Tribune, November 5, 1979

ROBERT T. SMITH'S COLUMN

The Minnesota Vikings lost Sunday, 37–7, to the St. Louis Cardinals, a team last in its division with a record of seven defeats and three wins. It was the fourth time the Vikes have been conquered in their last five games.

My friend George isn't eating much these days. He's pale and lethargic and has a critical case of down-in-the-dumps.

His problem? Minnesota sports.

You see, George is one of those Minnesotans whose lifeline is connected to his jock strap. You can recognize the Georges these days by the way they shuffle down the street, heads bowed.

Gone, at least temporarily, are the days when they quick-marched, eyes to the heavens, slapping folks on the back whether they liked it or not.

George's depression began when the Minnesota Twins finished fourth in their division.

"That's like being kissed by your sister," said George. For those who might not know, that's a sports cliché having something to do with tie ball games and finishing fourth.

(The Minnesota Kicks won their division, but then were eliminated from the playoffs after losing two straight. This did not affect George deeply, as he is a Minnesota sports traditionalist. He thinks soccer is a game for young people to watch, not a real sport. "You knock a guy down in soccer and they call a penalty," said George. "What kind of sport is that?")

Then the University of Minnesota Gophers. George never graduated from the university, or any university, but the Gophers still are his team.

"Look at them," said George. "They're in fifth place, and there's only 10 teams. They tie those sissies in Illinois, and Indiana handles them 42 to 24. We need Bernie Bierman back."

George doesn't read much at all. And his friends decided to never tell him Bernie is dead. (They also have managed to keep George ignorant of the fact Macalester College has lost 48 straight football games, a national record. Said one friend: "George is not particularly the suicide type, but . . .")

For George, it's too soon to place his life in the hands of the Minnesota North Stars. Hockey really has just begun.

Now to the Minnesota Vikings. "They're the straws that did it to the camel," said George. The Vikes, he said, are his major reason for life.

"But they're still in contention in the Central Division," I said.

"Everyone knows it's a lousy division," said George. "The Vikes are in second with a losing record. Even if by some miracle they should win the Central, they haven't a chance in the playoffs."

"Brighten up," I told George. "There are other things in life besides sports."

"Yeah, what?" said George.

I mentioned that the Minnesota Orchestra had Neville Marriner, a new quarterback. (You have to put everything to George in sports terms or his mind begins to drift.) "And Marriner has won every concert so far."

And there is good live theater around: the Guthrie, and a bunch of smaller operations. Or maybe, I suggested, George could take up a hobby, such as collecting coins or crocheting.

"O.K., wise guy," said George. "When do they have crocheting on Sunday afternoon TV?" It turned out George thought crocheting was a game you played with mallets and wooden balls.

I was tempted to suggest that George might read a book. But I felt that, in his present mood, he might hit me.

In fairness, I think there's a little of George in many of us. In some parts of the country, all the people know about Minnesota is its sports. And it's a bit nicer to be known for excellence in any activity.

(Television announcers of Vikes games, as you know, open up with "And now from Metropolitan Stadium in Bloomington . . ." As a result, there are those non-Minnesotans who believe Minneapolis is a suburb of Bloomington.)

I feel helpless in trying to get George out of the pits. About all I could come up with is another sports cliché:

Wait until next year.

And, in the meantime, George, remember there's more to life than sports.

Isn't there?

●

The Vikings returned to the playoffs again in 1980 with a 9–7 record, good enough to win the Central Division via a tiebreaker with the Detroit Lions. The team struggled to stay above .500 all season, and only clinched the championship with its ninth win in a 28–23 come-from-behind victory over Cleveland at Metropolitan Stadium on December 14 in the team's fifteenth game—thanks to the Vikings' own "Hail Mary" pass.

Minneapolis Tribune, December 15, 1980

VIKINGS WIN TITLE AGAIN, BUT . . . IT WAS NO LESS THAN ASTONISHING

Joe Soucheray

Maybe we have become too cinematic with this game of football and all its pretensions, but Sunday afternoon at Metropolitan Stadium the ball seemed to travel its arc through onrushing dusk as though in slow motion. There aren't many moments like it, when the season is on the twilight end of the

Vikings Sammy White (85) and Terry LeCount (80) scramble for a last-ditch "Hail Mary" pass from Tommy Kramer as time ran out in a game against the Cleveland Browns at Metropolitan Stadium on December 14, 1980. INSET: Ahmad Rashad (28), waiting just behind White and LeCount, caught the tipped ball and backed into the end zone, giving the Vikings a 28–23 victory that clinched the NFC Central Division championship. PHOTOGRAPHS FROM *DISPATCH–PIONEER PRESS*. COURTESY OF THE MINNE-SOTA HISTORICAL SOCIETY.

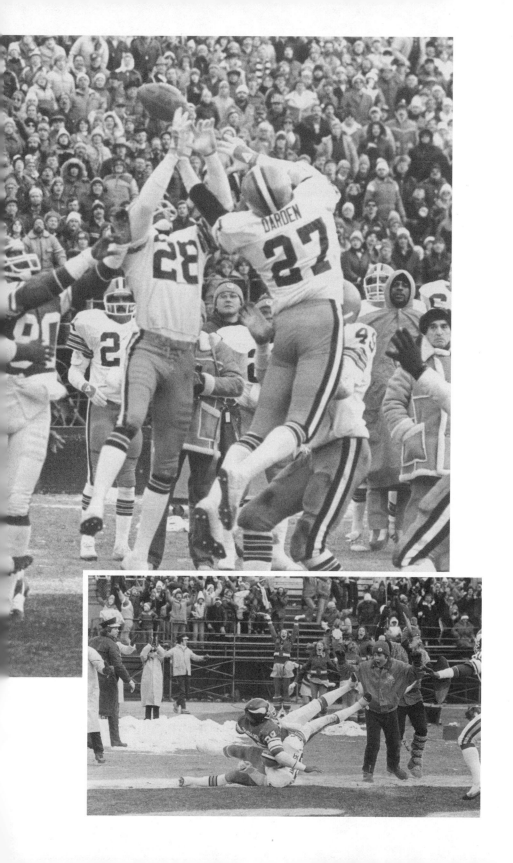

scale and the football is sailing through the air to upraised hands in the end zone and thousands of cold and unbelieving fans have stopped in their tracks at the exits.

The Vikings trailed Cleveland by a point, 23–22, and Tommy Kramer had just launched a pass from the Browns' 46-yard line into the right corner of the end zone, with four seconds showing on the scoreboard clock. Terry LeCount, Ahmad Rashad and Sammy White had been deployed to the right corner, LeCount in the middle as if it had been a wing formation. The clock ticked down to zero with the ball in flight. The Browns had responded by sending out a fleet of six deep backs, most principally Thom Darden, the eight-year safety out of Michigan.

"I chose to stick with White," Darden said later in his locker room. "I am sure the ball was intended for White to tip to Rashad. In my mind White was the tip man and I wasn't going to permit it."

"Where was Rashad?" somebody said.

"At that point I was between White and Rashad," Darden said. "Suddenly, White stopped. When he stopped, I stopped. And when he went into the air I went with him. I did get a hand on the ball."

"Where was Rashad now?" somebody said.

"By now he was in the vicinity," Darden said.

Rashad caught the ball, on what the Vikings insist was a tip off White's fingers. Rashad was near the two-yard line and he backed in, victorious in this astonishing and totally unlikely game of volleyball that had given the Vikings a victory and yet another Central Division championship. It was almost a replay of the ball Drew Pearson of the Cowboys caught in the shadow of Nate Wright at the Met in a 1975 first round playoff game.

"I wasn't going to allow Sammy to tip the ball, much less catch it," Darden was saying. "And I ended up tipping it to Rashad. It did not occur to any of us—me or Rashad or White—what had happened until we heard the crowd reaction."

In the Cleveland locker room later there was an occasional curse. Dirty laundry was flung this way and that. A television newsman discovered Cleveland coach Sam Rutigliano in the corner of the bathroom.

"Can we get a live interview?" the TV man said.

"How can you?" Rutigliano said. "I'm a dead man."

Rutigliano was more than gracious, almost bemused by what had just happened. He couldn't for the life of him remember Darden as his primary defender on the miracle catch.

"It was great concentration by a great player," Rutigliano said of the catch. "It was a 30-foot putt and he'll never make it again, but it was memorable. Neither team got much pressure to the quarterback today and the quarterbacks proved resourceful, didn't they?"

"Are you as cool on the inside as you appear on the outside?" Rutigliano was asked.

"I don't know," he said. "You'd have to perform an autopsy."

As interesting as the miracle catch—or more accurately, as astonishing—was a Brian Sipe pass intercepted by Bobby Bryant minutes earlier in the fourth quarter. Cleveland held a 23–15 lead with nearly five minutes left in the game and the Browns were cruising upfield when Sipe chose to pass on a second-and-nine from his own 41-yard line. The pass was intended for Reggie Rucker.

"That was an option screen play," Rutigliano said. "It worked well for us earlier in the game. We were thinking first down, we were thinking ball possession. I had warned the team at halftime that the Vikings were an extremely patient team."

"Were you surprised that Sipe passed at that point?" Bud Grant was asked.

"Not at all," Grant said. "They've always used the short pass as a form of ball control. Bobby Bryant just cheated a little. He knew that Sipe wouldn't throw deep and he moved in front of Rucker."

"Rucker was the intended receiver," Sipe said over in his quarters. "But in retrospect I wish I would have dumped it off to Cleo Miller, which was my option on the play. But hey, even after that I didn't think we were in trouble."

But the Vikings struck quickly with a touchdown to Rashad. Cleveland got the ball back and they eventually punted, giving Minnesota its final possession at Minnesota's 20-yard line with 14 seconds left in the game. The play that moved the team downfield was a pass to Joe Senser and the subsequent lateral to Teddy Brown, a play that moved the ball from the Vikings' 20 to the Cleveland 46, from where Kramer struck with the miracle throw.

"A flea flicker is what beat us as much as anything," Calvin Hill said afterwards. "A damn good flea flicker, that Senser-to-Brown play."

But it was the catch that people will remember, one of those great moments in sports that can be called up in the mind and played over and over again. It did take the chill off a winter day, all that heat and passion boiled down to the final play of a football game.

In the divisional playoffs the Vikings faced the East Division champion Philadelphia Eagles, who had pummeled them 42–7 in the second week of the season. The Vikings led at the half, 14–7, but doomed themselves with five interceptions and three lost fumbles in the second half to lose 31–16. The second half ended with a comedy of errors for both teams—seven turnovers in 19 plays.

The Vikings started slowly in 1981, losing their first two games, but then they went on a five-game winning streak and after 11 games had a Central Division–leading 7–4 record, two games ahead of Tampa Bay and Detroit, who were tied at 5–6. Unfortunately, the team went into a tailspin, losing its final five games to finish out of the playoffs.

The offense piled up a lot of yards, and "Two-minute" Tommy Kramer was always a threat—in his first three years as a starter he had guided the Vikings to nine late-game victories. Six of those came with less than 30 seconds on the clock. The team trailed only the San Diego Chargers in total passing yards, but ranked thirteenth in scoring and twenty-first on defense. Third-year man Ted Brown ran for 1,063 yards and finished third in the league with 83 pass receptions. Second-year tight end Joe Senser, from tiny West Chester State, was fifth in the league with 79 receptions. Wide receivers Sammy White and Ahmad Rashad collected 66 and 58 passes, respectively.

With the retirement of Fran Tarkenton and most of the rest of the Vikings' Super Bowl generation, Ahmad Rashad became the new image of the Vikings. His grace on the football field and his good looks attracted media attention, advertisers and fans—young and old, male and female.

Minneapolis Star, July 27, 1981
AHMAD RASHAD
VIKING'S 'GOOD LIFE' MATCHES HIS ELEGANCE, SAVVY ON THE FIELD
Joe Logan
To this day, Ahmad Rashad instantly recalls that day seven years ago. He was a gifted young receiver for the Buffalo Bills, still developing but clearly headed for bigger things. He and roommate O. J. Simpson were driving to the stadium for a preseason game.

"I remember driving, telling O. J., 'Hey, they can't hurt The Kid. I can never be hurt.'

"Athletics breeds that. You know, when you're in shape, hey, you're invincible. I went out that night and got my leg knocked out. I realized then that football could end anytime. I must have been 24. I went the rehabilitation route, but as I got my knee back together, I began to de-emphasize football."

Thus began the off-the-field exploits of one of pro football's premier receivers. And now, with the retirement of Fran Tarkenton and the trade of Rod Carew, probably Minnesota's most recognized, marketable athletic commodity.

Entering its 10th year, Ahmad Rashad's football professional career is soaring. Defensive backs marvel at his unassuming but effective moves, his timing, his shrewdness, his uncanny ability to be in a spot where they aren't. Quarterbacks marvel at his ability to anticipate, to catch and hold onto the ball, to make the big play.

Little surprise, then, working first with Fran Tarkenton, his friend and the man responsible for Rashad being in Minnesota, and now with Tommy Kramer, a rifle-armed youngster, that Rashad has caught more passes in the last five years than any wide receiver in pro football.

At 31, he appears to be at the zenith of his football career. He has carved out a career and lifestyle here to be coveted by most professional athletes in this country.

His home, a spacious two-story brick and cedar affair on three acres in wooded, suburban Lakeville, is a monument to what accomplishment can buy.

There is a tennis court, a pool and a small lake. There is a weight room and a Jacuzzi. In the driveway is usually a Subaru, which he drives when he's incognito. In the garage is a black Rolls-Royce, a motorcycle and some kind of Porsche under one of those canvas covers.

It's pretty much what you'd expect from a rich young bachelor. Amid the plants, the thick carpet and the stereo and video equipment, there is evidence of his other passion—tennis. Tennis shoes and clothes on the floor, tennis racquets leaning against this wall, against that stool.

Against one wall near the entrance are shelves with pictures of his parents, both of whom died last year, relatives and friends.

It is here, about 30 minutes from downtown Minneapolis, that he and some of his good buddies go to get away. O. J. Simpson comes every summer. Kareem Abdul-Jabbar was here for a week not long ago. When they ask him when he's shucking all this for his other home in Los Angeles, Rashad tells them he doesn't know, that he kind of likes it here in Minnesota. It reminds him of home—in Oregon—and it's his land of opportunity.

So this man, Ahmad Rashad, readily acknowledges that he has nailed down his corner of the good life here. He is worshipped by kids, envied by the ordinary men, chased by women and respected by oddsmakers. When he takes to the field, he changes the face of a game.

And, as his fortunes on the field have grown, so have his fortunes off the field. He is a goodwill ambassador for Jeno's pizza, a job that carries with it the title of vice president. He does local TV commercials. He endorses Nike products. He has a personal appearance contract with Dayton-Hudson, and he owns a football camp with Tommy Kramer.

But perhaps most important, he is an off-season and occasionally in-season sports reporter for WCCO-TV. When not catching footballs, he devotes great effort to polishing his television persona. Not surprisingly, it is as a sports "color man" that he believes his future lies.

His outside income now approaches his annual football salary, said to be in the $200,000 range. And once he hangs up his spikes, Rashad is confident his earnings will increase.

He is a smart man who knows the value of a smile and the importance of signing autographs. He'll show up practically anywhere he's asked. He's heavily into good deeds.

He is handsome, he has presence and style before the television cameras and he has people skills combined with a cheerful personality that will be with him long after he can no longer snare a high touchdown pass. He knows it. Hell, he readily admits it.

Indeed, he acknowledges he has an image to protect—an image he has carefully shaped and one he hopes to see maintained. He is aware of the influence he has on youngsters. Tales of doping and womanizing do not a wholesome star make. He knows that. He shrinks from controversy. In fact, dope, women and politics are the topics that make Ahmad Rashid ill at ease.

But he was willing to sit down in a patio chair by his pool last week, just days before the opening of another Minnesota Vikings summer training camp, to discuss his life off the field.

Dressed in a green golf shirt bearing the insignia of some distant, exclusive, tropical-sounding resort, a pair of designer jeans and sandals, Rashad was a vision of a man content. At his side was a portable radio telephone that enabled him to answer a constant stream of calls.

"I think everybody in Minnesota has my number," he lamented after about the fifth call.

Rashad seemed confident and relaxed about football and almost excited about his prospects of life after sport. It is those prospects that allow him not to worry constantly about football, about getting traded, about getting cut.

"Those are the things that worry players. Am I going to get drafted, who did they draft? Those things don't ever cross my mind anymore. I just go out and do the best I can. I think I've done an excellent job and now I have a lot of options."

Seven years ago, those options didn't exist.

"It was preseason and I was playing fantastic, everything was going great, we were flying high," he said of 1975, his fourth year as a pro, his second at Buffalo.

"I went out one night and got my knee banged up. I couldn't play the rest of the year, went into cast. My work went right down the tubes. I realized then that it was time to get something going, it was time to cultivate off-the-field stuff.

"Because, I don't care how big of a star you are, once you get hurt and can't help the team anymore, they've got to get another guy. The ship is sailing, so to speak. They don't hold up the ship for anybody."

Rashad winced. He has known far too many players who simply refused to acknowledge the future.

SIMPSON'S EXAMPLE

"It's a shame that guys play football for 10 years and then have nothing to do. I think the athlete has himself to blame for that. That's been drilled into my head since Little League. I remember early on, I found there was life after football practice and life after football—and *you* determine that quality of life."

Rashad learned how to make his move toward success beyond the field by watching Simpson, his roommate at the time and still his best friend. Only last week, they returned from a trip to Hawaii with their girlfriends.

"During that time [1975] was his hottest marketing time, and I watched him negotiate contracts. I watched him set himself up. I learned a lot. And I said that if I ever reach superstar status as a player, and a lot of those doors open up to me, then I'm going to take advantage of it."

But Rashad didn't get that chance in Buffalo. After being injured, he was dealt to Seattle. He never played a game. They traded him to Minnesota for Bob Lurtsema and a fourth-round draft choice.

"They [Seattle] got nothing for me. It was practically, 'Here, take this guy.' I had the knee injury and they thought I'd never get any better than I was right then. So they had to make a decision. They just made the wrong one."

After that statement, the smug grin on Rashad's face is so broad it would take two mean cornerbacks to wipe it off. But at the time, there was no grin.

"If it wasn't for Tarkenton, I wouldn't be here. I hadn't passed the physical and they were going to send me back to Seattle. My career was over. I was done. I was just going to take my stuff home and start working, probably try to get into television.

"I was on my way out the door and Francis said, 'Don't move. Let me see if I can work something out.'" Rashad grinned again. "It worked out. He is still one of my best friends."

The trade turned out to be what Rashad calls "the most important step" in his football career.

"Here you had a quarterback who was a household name all over the country, probably the best in the league, and all of a sudden I get to play on the same team with him and be his receiver—and be his *favorite* receiver." Rashad shook his head at the irony.

As Rashad spoke, Viking quarterback Bob Farra, a Claremont (California) College graduate who sat out last season with a shoulder injury, arrived. He and Rashad were to play tennis later in the afternoon, but for now Farra heads inside to watch old game films. A little later, Viking running back Ted Brown arrives and joins Farra.

Meanwhile, at poolside, the conversation turned to privacy and to being a celebrity. Is he besieged?

"Well, if we had done this interview in a restaurant, you'd see how different it is."

Autographs? He nodded.

"All the time. All the time. I don't love it. I don't hate it. It's just part of the job. It's nice because it must mean I'm playing football well.

"Besides, I remember something O. J. told me. When he was a kid he always wanted to be rich and famous. He thinks he'd be a total jerk now that he's achieved it to shun somebody. It's not a problem for me to write my name, and if it makes somebody happy . . ."

VIKING COMMUNITY

Nevertheless, it's common and understandable for those under public scrutiny for their work to seek privacy at home.

"It's so nice out here in the country. You don't hear cars. I've got great neighbors. Grady Alderman used to live right here," he said, pointing next door. "Dave Osborn lives in that house straight across. Bob Lurtsema lives two houses down that way. Paul Krause lives right over the hill. Mick Tingelhoff lives down the street. I just don't think I could live in a tight neighborhood with houses lining the street. Out here I get away. I've got a lot of room."

With a neighborhood like that, does he ever find thrill-seekers hiding in the bushes?

"No, but sometimes on Sunday people drive right up the driveway. It's not bad, though. It's private, but I've had intruders. I had a girl walk right in the house one night. *Right in the house.* I had some people from Channel 5 here shooting a segment for NFL films. They thought I knew her and I thought they knew her. I noticed everybody kept walking by her and nobody said anything to her. So she just sat on the couch until somebody finally said, 'Well, who is this?'"

Like any healthy, rich, professional athlete, Rashad has encountered his share of women throwing themselves at him.

"I'm a bachelor and I'm not ugly, and I'm young," he said, grinning again. "Therefore, there are all kinds of opportunities. When I was young I did take advantage of all the opportunities. But I'm older now. I don't want to know 1,000 girls. I just don't get myself in those situations anymore." So Rashad insists he is not on the make. Indeed, when asked who his closest friend is in the Twin Cities, without hesitation he names his steady girlfriend of three years: Diane Drummond, 24, of Minneapolis, a stewardess for Northwest Airlines.

So what does he do about rumors of women, of night stalking on the I-494 strip?

"I'm very careful about that. I don't show up at bars a whole lot. Being known, I don't want to embarrass my girlfriend. Not only would it embarrass her, but it would make me look like a jerk."

Whether Rashad actually carouses is irrelevant. What matters is that in this age of sexuality and in his profession of swollen egos, Rashad has the good sense and good taste not to acknowledge anything publicly.

His responses about drugs were pretty much the same.

"My statement on drugs would be, No, don't use any at all . . . Well, everybody's tried that stuff . . . Most people who get caught up in that go right down the tubes. I don't plan on going down the tubes."

So instead, for a good time, Rashad says he has a few friends over.

"Because of my schedule, I love being at home. My idea of a great night is to have a few people over, have some drinks, a little dinner, swim. It's not going to Maximillian's."

Unlike some of his acquaintances in football, Rashad is not a product of a ghetto or of racial tension. He was born in Portland, Oregon, was graduated from Mount Tacoma, Washington, high school and went to college at the University of Oregon. It is part of the country similar in many ways to Minnesota.

His mother was a housewife and his dad, a beautician, owned a 16-chair shop, which Rashad, then a kid named Bobby Moore, cleaned on weekends.

"I didn't come from a ghetto or have to walk 95 miles to anything," shrugged Rashad. Indeed, Rashad, who voted for Reagan, although he claims there is no party alliance, seems to have firmly placed middle-class values. "Maybe that's the reason I relate so well."

He was married for three years and has three children, who now live in Los Angeles. He won't be pinned down on future marriage plans.

His conversion from the Pentecostal Church to Islam, which came in his second year of college, was no big political statement, Rashad maintains, but rather the conclusion of his search for a religion that suited him.

As a Pentecostal, "nothing got in front of the church. And there were a lot of tenets that went unanswered. I don't know and you don't know, but God knows so we'll just do it blindly. That worked until I was 13 or 14."

So Rashad settled on Islam, which he says is "founded on how you live your life, not whether you are black or white, rich or poor. You're not judged on how you're born, but how you live."

Although he converted in college, Rashad didn't change his name until his second year as a pro. "I remember a guy telling me my marketability would go down. But it worked. Now I even think I look more like an Ahmad than a Bobby."

Rashad has never had a problem with racism in Minneapolis, perhaps, he theorizes, because he is a celebrity. Some local blacks suggest that Rashad's name doesn't come to mind when listing local black leaders.

Rashad's response is that he appears where he is asked, and that he's never been sought out by anyone on behalf of the local black community.

All things considered, Rashad seems to be a talented, personable man who has engineered his own success. Consistent play on the field has fueled the rise; good sense has assured him a future.

"At this point in my life, I don't see what could come apart. If my knee went out and I couldn't play football anymore, I could work at 'CCO full time. I could work at Jeno's full time. I can still talk. I still have my personality. That's the luxury of setting yourself up outside football—I can play football with all the gusto I've got and not worry."

And that's just the way he played last year in the Cleveland game, which he had planned to sit out with a bum knee. Remember Kramer's last-second desperation bomb to the corner? Remember Rashad's catch?

"It wasn't such a big thrill because I expected it all the way. As I ran down the field, I said to myself that if I don't catch it it's no big deal because they don't expect you to catch those anyway.

"But you know if they tip that ball . . . oh, my God . . . here it comes . . . I've got it . . . now all I've got to do is take two steps backward . . . now my knee is killing me and I've got to get out of here."

Rashad grins for the last time.

"It was just like that."

●

Metropolitan Stadium was built in 1956 to attract a major league baseball team, and had only 30,637 seats for the Twins' opening day in 1961. The addition of bleacher-type seating brought the capacity up to about 44,000 for football. The Vikings invested $600,000 in 1965 to build permanent seating in the left field area, bringing the seating capacity to an official 47,426. Later additions moved this up to 49,784.

By 1965 discussions about replacing Met Stadium had already begun, particularly by Vikings officials and supporters. The lease Senators' owner Calvin Griffith signed with the Metropolitan Sports Area Commission gave him 90 percent of revenue from concessions at Twins games, plus control of concessions at all other Met Stadium events, including Vikings games. The 1960s and 1970s saw a wave of stadium construction all over the country. Most of the stadiums were multipurpose, built for both football and baseball. The model seemed to be an 80,000 capacity stadium with artificial turf and sight lines laid out for football. Baseball fields looked cold and artificial in these designs, but the Vikings wanted one of them, and also wanted to control concessions revenues.

Talk about a new stadium was never far in the background throughout the 1970s, with arguments pro and con about public financing, and debates about where to build a new stadium. In the end, the Hubert H. Humphrey Metrodome was built in downtown Minneapolis to house the Vikings and Twins, and the University of Minnesota was seduced into moving Golden Gophers football games there as well. General Mills threw in a pot-sweetener for Vikings fans—to ensure that home games would be shown on local TV, the company agreed to buy all unsold home-game tickets when at least 90 percent had been sold 72 hours before kickoff.

The debates foreshadowed the stadium wars of the 1990s, when the public was beseeched once again to fund new facilities for professional teams—to replace the Metrodome with new football and baseball stadiums, as well as providing new hockey and basketball arenas.

"WHERE THE SUN DON'T SHINE," FROM *STADIUM GAMES: FIFTY YEARS OF BIG LEAGUE GREED AND BUSH LEAGUE BOONDOGGLES* (2000)

Jay Weiner

Met Stadium, the first Twin Cities major-league stadium, was conceived and built during the prosperous and calm days of the Eisenhower administration. The region had dreams of growing up. The late 1950s evoke images of *Father Knows Best*, of *American Bandstand*, and a time when America was hitting its post–World War II stride. This second cycle of stadium discussion, as the sixties turned into the seventies, came with a new set of circumstances. The Vietnam War was under way. Authority was being challenged from every direction. Citizens learned how to speak out against the war, against racial injustice, and, soon, against a male-dominated culture. The notion of "the public's interest" was always in mind, even if private interests continued to prevail.

Plus, Minnesota was becoming filled with, and jaded by, professional sports. The accessible warmth and stability of the early Twins and Vikings seasons, when players lived among the populace, was being shattered by expanding leagues, the creeping increase in players' salaries, and a facilities glut. Even as discussion commenced on a new stadium for baseball and football, Bloomington saw the construction in 1966 of a new arena to house the new National Hockey League franchise known as the Minnesota North

Stars. In St. Paul, where the fear was deep, a Civic Center was under construction to compete with Bloomington; a new, upstart professional hockey league faced off for fans against the NHL North Stars by 1973. Meanwhile, the University of Minnesota was in a continuous quandary about whether its on-campus Memorial Stadium was adequate.

In her 1982 book *Uncovering the Dome*, Amy Klobuchar, then a Yale University senior who went on to become Hennepin County attorney 15 years later [and who is now a United States Senator from Minnesota—ED.], detailed the key issues in the 10-year process to get the new major-league stadium in the Twin Cities. She wrote how the battle was, as always, about the location of such a unique facility, but also about Minnesotans' once strongly held trust in the political process, and how that was shattered by leaders who didn't listen. The fight, too, was over bringing baseball indoors in a culture where the outdoors in the summer is the only place to be. Finally, the public and some political leaders wondered why taxpayers' dollars should be put at risk or in use to aid professional sports in the face of other social needs. "If the jocks want a stadium, then the jocks can pay for it," was said as often between 1971 and 1977 as it has been since 1994, when talk of yet another Twins stadium began anew in the Twin Cities.

The stadium war of the 1970s centered on Minnesotans' sensibilities and their values, on and off the playing field. Should the sun be shining when our games are played? Should the cold weather be factored out of our lives? Should the core city be strengthened by our sports facilities? Should the safe, convenient suburb, with its parking lots and ease, be abandoned? Should the taxpayer's opinion be taken seriously when major community infrastructural decisions are made?

There was, then, not much discussion about what made a metropolitan area great. The Twin Cities knew how to do great things and seemed committed to it. Minneapolis–St. Paul wanted what other big cities had. There was no malaise in the Twin Cities in the 1970s. Unlike the late 1990s, when people always seem to find ways not to do great things, the atmosphere of the seventies wasn't a matter of *whether* we were going to build things to keep us special. It was a matter of *how* and *where*. The nationally known Guthrie Theater settled in Minneapolis in 1963. John Cowles Jr. (chairman of the Minneapolis Star and Tribune Company) was a driving force for it, too. Nicollet Mall made downtown special in 1967. The Walker Art Center signaled the region's fine arts strength in 1971. Orchestra Hall showed we wanted to be part of the symphonic major leagues in 1974. These were times when the Twin Cities were a model for the rest of the country. We spoiled ourselves then and came to believe we would always be special.

Thus there were conflicting interests shooting in from everywhere. City versus suburb. A culture of protest and authority-challenging versus a spirit of can-doism. An elite group seeking to build a covered sports stadium versus an ecological aesthetic that argued for sunshine and nature, not artificiality. It took six years to get a stadium bill passed in the legislature, to get politicians to approve the sale of $55 million in bonds to fund the construction. That dollar amount was barely enough to build what would become the Spartan Metrodome. Private dollars were necessary to complete the project, which today remains colorless and antiseptic. It took another year for the inevitable political decision that the stadium should be in downtown Minneapolis, after years of lobbying and years of the *Star* and the *Tribune*, Cowles's personal soapbox[es], arguing for such an eventuality in [their] editorial pages.

Klobuchar's book and an unpublished chronology of the Dome debate discovered in the files of former Chamber of Commerce vice president Krusell provide a picture that is shockingly familiar to anyone who has followed the Minnesota stadium war of the nineties. The opponents—anti-tax Republicans and socially conscious neighborhood-based progressives— fit a similar profile 25 years removed from each other. Some of the opponents, most notably Julian Empson, who led the Save the Met protest group, the most prominent anti-Dome group, lived long enough to oppose a new nineties Twins ballpark, too, for some of the same reasons. The legislature acted in similar ways back then and into the present tense, seemingly killing a stadium bill a thousand times before finally saying yes. The citizenry seemed eager to seek a solution to keep the teams, but news of the day or backlashes pushed and pulled public opinion to and fro.

A major player in the seventies that was missing in the 1990s was the business community. In the run-up to the Dome's political passage and financial creation, a cabal of Minneapolis's major business leaders determined that they would bring the Dome downtown, by hook or by crook. They didn't jump in at the very beginning. They jumped in when the political process turned a tad bit haywire. But when the business leaders decided to get involved, their involvement was deep and unswerving. They seriously put their money where their mouths were. Their throwing hundreds of thousands of dollars down the civic toilet with a snowball's chance in hell of getting any rates of return is legendary.

The effort to back a specific stadium site with a ton of private dollars didn't happen overnight. Three years after the first feasibility study to examine if Met Stadium could be refurbished, the downtown stadium idea suffered its first defeat. A citizen-led referendum to limit city funding for a stadium passed by a wide margin on June 12, 1973. It restricted the city's Board of Estimate and Taxation from allowing $15 million or more to be spent on a stadium. Opponents believed that would stop stadium advocates in their tracks. But city officials soon learned that bonds and taxes could be imposed by other city agencies, such as the Minneapolis Community Development Agency, thus circumventing the letter and spirit of the voters' decision. (In 1997 a similar referendum passed in Minneapolis, again to halt the next Twins stadium effort. This time, sports facilities opponents made sure their language was far more all-encompassing.)

Like all issues that powerful people want to see come to fruition, this stadium matter was revived soon after the referendum passed. Chamber vice president Krusell was the worker bee for the power elite who forged what would become the Dome plan. Krusell was an expert on affordable housing and urban renewal. It was he who (besides members of the Sports Area commission) first realized that the Met Stadium leases for both the Twins and the Vikings would expire after their respective 1975 seasons. In 1974, a go-getter named Harvey Mackay was named chairman of the Chamber's task force. He would eventually take a one-year leave from his company to wander the state and the boardrooms of the Twin Cities' corporations, personally selling the significance of a new stadium and its importance to downtown Minneapolis. Mackay also conceived an enduring slogan that Hubert Humphrey made famous: Minnesota without pro sports would be "a cold Omaha."

The same year [Mike] Lynn became the general manager of the Vikings and Max Winter's stadium liaison. Lynn was wily. He issued veiled threats that the Vikings would move without a new stadium. He had great power over Winter, or tried to. He was at the heart of designing what would become the Vikings' and Twins' new stadium, with the Vikings' priorities always satisfied. Lynn came out smelling sweet. In between, the odor he left behind was not always so pleasant. Meanwhile Twins owner Calvin Griffith was trying to make certain he wasn't left in the dust as Winter was wooed. With the Twin Cities' most powerful and egotistical men all engaged, the edifice complex was everywhere, and the testosterone was pushed into high gear.

Through four years of fighting in the legislature, a bill finally passed in 1977 to construct a facility that required no more than $55 million of public financing. The bill, conceived mostly by Governor Rudy Perpich, was "site neutral" and required that a new agency, to be called the Metropolitan Sports Facilities Commission, would determine within a year the location for the dual-purpose facility. A requirement was that the local unit of gov-

Fans swarm the field after the last game at Metropolitan Stadium, overwhelming security personnel. Souvenir hunters snatched up anything they could get their hands on, including signs, seats, and turf, even climbing on the scoreboard to remove speakers and other detachable objects. PHOTOGRAPH FROM *DISPATCH–PIONEER PRESS*. COURTESY OF THE MINNESOTA HISTORICAL SOCIETY.

ernment or local stadium backers had to supply the land on which any sta-dium would be built. Among the legislators who voted yes were two young Republicans, one from Albert Lea, the other from Minneapolis. The rural fellow was named Henry Savelkoul, an ardent Republican and a true con-servative; the city guy—a native New Yorker—was Arne Carlson, a former Democrat. Savelkoul was the minority leader of the House, and Carlson was his assistant minority leader. Little did they know that their 1977 stadium vote was small potatoes compared to a stadium game they would play—and lose—20 years later.

●

The Vikings lost their last game at the Met to the Kansas City Chiefs, 10–6, on December 20, 1981. After the game, rowdy fans tore up seats, speakers, parts of the scoreboard, sod, urinals, and anything else they could get their hands on for souvenirs. The 90 security guards from the Bloomington and Minneapolis police departments and Hennepin County sheriff's office were overwhelmed and could do little more than stand back and watch.

St. Paul Pioneer Press, December 21, 1981
PARTY'S OVER
VIKE GOURMANDS HOLD TAIL-END TAILGATE PARTY; MET TAIL-GATERS WONDER WHETHER PARTIES WILL BE SAME AT BUS STOP
Ozzie St. George
The Last Great Tailgate Party at Met Stadium, sandwiched around a mean-ingless football game in which the Kansas City Chiefs defeated the Minne-sota Vikings began very early and ran very late Sunday.

In fact, the first celebrants attending the more than 7,500 tailgate parties were waiting when the Met parking lot opened at 9 A.M. And a few vying for the title of Very Last Tailgater were hanging in there long after dusk.

In the interim, they burned thousands of pounds of charcoal—one party was provisioned with 325 pounds—and consumed steak, hamburger, hot-dogs, sausage, bratwurst, shrimp, fish, chicken, pig, raccoon, rabbit (plain and barbecued), potatoes, salads simple and exotic, beans, onions, sauer-kraut, breads, buns, rolls, doughnuts and soups.

Not to mention various libations: your basic beer, basic pregame Bloody Mary and other concoctions developed during the 1961–81 Tailgating Era—Viking Vroooooms, Met Mothers and Bohemian Bumps, among others.

It was, after all, as numerous veteran tailgaters noted in the course of pre-kickoff interviews, "the end of an era." Besides, a number said, it was "a perfect day for tailgating."

In case you haven't been tailgating lately, that's a mostly cloudy day with four inches of hard-packed snow in the parking lot, a high of 21, a stiff breeze and a four-below windchill factor.

Most of these tailgaters also lamented how "it'll never be the same—it won't be half as much fun—at the Dome."

And a few said they were "mad" rather than sad. They were the ones with the signs "Dome? Hell No, I Won't Go!"

But there were others, including a wild crew in a beat-up pickup truck with North Dakota license plates, who said tailgating is so much fun they'll never give it up.

"We have it all figured out," said Doug Koch, an Arthur, North Dakota, high school principal and one of several spokesmen for the group: "We're going to buy a $20 junker pickup, tow it down and park it near the Dome on Saturday night, then pack lunches, catch buses, meet at the junker and tailgate. And if the cops tow it away—well, no big deal."

"Right on!" said the rest of the crew, which by then had been tailgating for a couple of hours, sustaining life with an occasional beer, potatoes and "real Dakota steaks" cooked (or at any rate warmed) on a gas-fired grill.

Actually, Koch explained, this crew—Casey Hellenberg, Don Swearingen and others—is pretty much a "St. Paul bunch" that dates back to Highland Park High School.

Marlin Schutte is an "outsider" from Delano, but met Koch at Jamestown College in Jamestown, North Dakota. The crew has been tailgating together for about four years and all were wearing—as they peeled through several layers of clothing to prove—"Met Stadium Survivor" T-shirts.

Arthur, North Dakota, incidentally, is 30 miles northwest of Fargo, or a little more than 250 miles from the Met. Koch is, he agreed, a loyal Viking fan.

So is Dick Posthumus, an Albert Lea electrician who has been tailgating for about six years with a dozen friends "at just about all" the Vikings' home games.

"We've really enjoyed it," Posthumus said, "and we're really going to miss it at the Dome. I don't think we'll even try tailgating there. I suppose it might be possible, but half the fun of tailgating is you see the same people at every game.

"You take this area now [outside the Met's Section K]. It's mostly people from Albert Lea, Northfield, Faribault and Owatonna. We all come up I-35. I don't know what we'll do next year. Drive this far and take a bus to the Dome, maybe. But that won't be much fun."

But Posthumus said he does "come mainly to see the football game—the tailgating just makes it more fun—so I suppose I'll be there at the Dome."

Other members of the I-35 delegation weren't so sure, like Al Sevick, a Northfield barber, his wife Susie, and Nick and Kam Perry, all in Al's van.

The Sevicks have been tailgating at "almost all the home games" for about four years, but Al said he thinks he'll "wait and see about next year." He was one of those who thought it a "perfect day" for tailgating, but then he'd already had a Bohemian Bump.

(His recipe for same: 1 qt. Canadian Club, 3 qts. water; 6 oz. Rose lime juice, 1½ cups honey, mix well, heat to near boiling and drink as soon as possible. Guaranteed to prevent chills and trigger fond memories.)

And one of them did trigger—in Wayne Eddy, part-owner of radio station KWMN in Northfield—some fond memories of "really great tailgate parties." The one a "bunch from Northfield" put on in the mid-70s, for instance.

"We barbecued 12 20-pound turkeys on a single spit, all stuffed with a special dressing," he said. "We worked it out with the Minnesota Turkey Growers Association, set up the night before and fed 250 couples. Another time we did two whole pigs, stuffed . . ."

Eddy's memories, it should be noted, cover years and years of near-perfect attendance—he did miss one exhibition game—at the Met. And he gave high marks Sunday to another "great tailgate party" held by Anchor Block Co., North St. Paul.

Anchor fleet manager Vic Burski was running that one. He said Anchor has been running such parties for about 15 years. "This being the last one we decided to go all out," he said. "So we brought our display truck—that's a 44-foot semi-trailer with a gas furnace—and invited 300 contractors and their families. And built those grills—they're 55-gallon drums cut in half."

The trailer was equipped with color TVs, one with a six-foot screen, folding chairs for 30 persons and a videotape machine. Anchor will have a "permanent record" of this last game. The menu was hamburgers, bratwurst, onions, toasted buns, potato chips and beverages.

A short distance away, the Dirty Dozen, a St. Paul club headed by Harry Davis, was barbecuing ribs and chicken.

And next to the DD—at the far end of the tailgating spectrum—a lone can of beans sat unattended amid a few glowing charcoal briquets piled in the snow.

●

The 1982 season was chaotic. On September 12 the Vikings got off to a good start with a 17–10 victory over the Tampa Bay Buccaneers before a crowd of 58,440 in the inaugural home game at the new Hubert H. Humphrey Metrodome. Then the National Football League Players' Association (NFLPA) went on strike after the second game of the season. When the

The Vikings moved into the Hubert H. Humphrey Metrodome in 1982. The Dome never spurred the development its proponents had envisioned in the eastern downtown area of Minneapolis.
PHOTOGRAPH COURTESY OF THE MINNESOTA HISTORICAL SOCIETY.

strike was finally settled on November 16, the NFL decided not to try to make up any games, and reduced the season's schedule to nine games.

Eight teams from each conference were selected for the playoffs, seeded one to eight based on their records. No divisional records were considered. The 5–4 Vikings, seeded fourth in the NFC, beat Atlanta in the first round of the playoffs, 30–24, but lost to the eventual Super Bowl XVII champion Washington Redskins, in the second round, 21–7.

The 57-day strike was perhaps the most significant accomplishment in the history of the NFLPA. In the final settlement the Association won the right to obtain copies of all individual contracts. These formerly had been considered secret, and bringing them into the light laid the foundation for a rapid escalation in players' salaries. For example, after the "1982 NFLPA Base Salary Directory" was published, Tommy Kramer, who had thrown for 3,912 yards in 1981 and had a $100,000 contract, found out that San Francisco 49ers backup quarterback Guy Benjamin—who threw for only 171 yards—earned $130,000.

Kramer suffered a season-ending knee injury in the Vikings' third game in 1983. He was replaced by Steve Dils, a 1979 draftee from Stanford, who had started only three games in his four years with the team. The team was 6–2 at midseason, but went into a tailspin in the second half, twice losing three consecutive games, and finished 8–8 and out of the playoffs. Depletion of the receiving corps handicapped the offense. Ahmad Rashad had retired, tight end Joe Senser missed the whole season with a knee injury and three wide receivers, Sammy White, Sam McCullum, and Terry LeCount, each missed five games due to injury. In addition, Ted Brown, the Vikings' rushing and pass reception leader in 1981 and 1982, missed six games due to an injury.

In 1984 the Vikings made a big change in the sideline atmosphere at the Dome when they replaced the St. Louis Park Parkettes with a professional—read that "sexier"—dance line. The Parkettes were a high school dance line first formed in 1956. Several members of the group, called the Lakerettes, cheered at some Minneapolis Lakers games in 1959 and 1960, and the Parkettes became the official Vikings cheerleaders in 1964. The new Vikings cheerleaders would be modeled after the Dallas Cowboys Cheerleaders, who had been organized in 1972. Wearing skimpy outfits and performing well-choreographed routines, the Dallas Cowboys Cheerleaders became popular guests on television shows and made eagerly anticipated appearances on United Service Organizations (USO) tours. A made-for-TV movie, *The Dallas Cowboys Cheerleaders*, and its sequel were wildly popular in 1979 and 1980.

St. Paul Pioneer Press, May 11, 1984
VIKINGS BEGIN SEARCH FOR DANCE LINE
Theresa Monsour

Are you wholesome? Do you have personality, character and energy? Can you dance? Do you like purple?

If you're a female high school graduate who answered "Yes" to all of the above, the Minnesota Vikings want you.

The Minnesota Vikings are replacing the Parkettes, an extracurricular organization at St. Louis Park High School, with a professional dance line on the order of the Dallas Cowboys Cheerleaders.

Well, maybe not quite on that order.

"We want energetic girls who have that Minnesota-type wholesomeness," said Sue Matson, a dance instructor and choreographer who has been hired by the Vikings to coordinate the selection and preparation of the new Viking dance line.

Preliminary tryouts for the Viking cheerleaders will be held at 8 A.M. June 2 at the Metrodome. The semifinal auditions will be held at 5 P.M. June 11, also at the Metrodome. The final cheerleading squad of 32 plus four alternates will be selected after interviews.

Tryouts will be restricted to women who are high school graduates and who have had some dance training.

In 1984 the Vikings replaced the St. Louis Park High School Parkettes (shown above at a playoff game in 1974) with an adult dance line modeled after the famous Dallas Cowboys Cheerleaders.
PHOTOGRAPH OF THE PARKETTES FROM *STAR TRIBUNE*. COURTESY OF THE MINNESOTA HISTORICAL SOCIETY. PHOTOGRAPH OF THE DANCE LINE COURTESY OF THE MINNESOTA VIKINGS.

Those interested in auditioning are asked to send a non-returnable photograph and a resume or letter outlining their background to: Minnesota Viking Cheerleaders, 9520 Viking Drive, Eden Prairie, Minnesota, 55344.

Applications are due by May 24. Those who apply will be sent a confirming letter that will admit them to the preliminary auditions.

According to the Vikings organization, candidates will be judged on dancing ability, wholesomeness, personality, character, appearance and the ability to represent the Vikings in public. The 32 cheerleaders who perform at games will be paid $15 a game plus one ticket for each game, or two tickets for each game.

"Our aim is to create a unit that combines kick line with jazz dancing," said Matson, 26, owner and instructor at the Stage Door of Performing Arts in Blaine. "We want to have a group and music that is upbeat, innovative and crowd-pleasing."

Providing that music will be Bob and Chuck Elledge, a father-son team that has assembled a new Viking band made up of young musicians with pep band experience. They will feature the brass and percussion sounds popular with football fans.

Coordinating all this pompon pomp and circumstance will be Beth Obermeyer, the new entertainment coordinator for Viking games.

Just to give you an idea of how BIG Obermeyer thinks, she coordinated the World's Largest Marching Band (2,512 musicians plus 476 baton twirlers) and the World's Largest Tap-Dance Line (1,801 members).

After all that, coordinating a pep band and 32 wholesome cheerleaders should be a snap.

●

Bud Grant had surprised Minnesotans on January 28, 1984, when he announced his retirement. He said he felt no pressure to leave, but, in good health at age 56, he wanted to have more time to fish and hunt and be with his family. Les Steckel, the Vikings' receivers coach since 1979, was quickly appointed the new head coach.

Steckel, at 38 years, was the youngest coach in the NFL. Whereas Grant was fairly permissive in training, believing in saving players' strength for games, Steckel emphasized physical training. He held a grueling, compulsory Ironman competition on the opening day of the regular training camp.

Minneapolis Star and Tribune, July 22, 1984

IRONMAN TEST LEAVES VIKINGS ACHING

Bob Sansevere

Charlie Johnson was gasping, searching for air and the right words to describe what he had been through.

"I'm glad it's over. That was a nightmare," Johnson said.

The nightmare was the Vikings' eight-event Ironman competition that kicked off training camp and kicked in a few spirits Saturday.

"I tossed and turned all night thinking about it," Johnson said. "Never in my entire life have I been so nervous. Everyone was sort of shaking. I got up at two or three in the morning and Rickey Young was walking the halls shaking. I've never been through an event like this in my entire career."

That's quite a statement, considering the source. Two years ago, Johnson asked Philadelphia Eagles to trade him because Coach Dick Vermeil's training camps were too torturous. So, Johnson came to Minnesota and enjoyed every minute of the two years he spent under Bud Grant. Now he is bracing for what's still to come under new coach Les Steckel.

"Bud was from the old school," said Johnson, an eight-year veteran at nose tackle. "Playing for him gave my body time to recuperate, get my head together. I think I'm ready to go through with this."

He meant training camp in general. Not the Ironman events.

"I'll tell you what, I'd much rather go through two-a-days," Johnson said moments after completing the final event, maximum leg presses of twice his weight.

For the record, Johnson pressed 560 pounds 32 times. For the record, he never wants to go through another day like this one.

"It makes me tired even thinking about it," Johnson said. "It was like only 15 minutes, but it seemed like it lasted a year. When I got to the hip sled [the final event], it was like someone put my legs on fire."

So it went. The Vikings first day of training camp had a uniqueness to it. For one, there was not a football in sight. Just football players leaping and running and lifting and panting their way through the eight events with nearly $30,000 in prizes at stake.

"If I had to do it over again, I'd never do it," said offensive lineman Jerry Baker, the first player to go through the course. Baker was first because he was the heaviest player in camp, tipping the scales at 336 pounds.

Next to go was 325-pound lineman Curtis Rouse, who winced upon hearing what Johnson said about choosing two-a-day practices over the Ironman events. "I'll tell you what," Rouse said, "I don't want to take sides on either one. Both of them will get to you."

The 40-yard dash, the second event, got to defensive end Mark Mullaney and placekicker Benny Ricardo. They pulled hamstring muscles.

Punter Greg Coleman dressed in U.S. Marine Corps fatigues as a joke and reported to duty for new head coach Les Steckel at training camp in 1984. Steckel, a Vietnam veteran and Marine Corps reserve officer, promised a tough, physical camp and held an Ironman-type competition on the first day. PHOTOGRAPH FROM *DISPATCH–PIONEER PRESS*. COURTESY OF THE MINNESOTA HISTORICAL SOCIETY.

Running backs Darrin Nelson and Phil Frye collapsed during the 300-yard shuttle runs but recovered and were expected to practice today, when players put on pads for the first time.

Punter Greg Coleman, placekicker Vince Wagner and rookie wide receiver Lawrence Thompson of the University of Miami were too fatigued to finish the competition.

Before dropping out, Thompson had the best performances in the first two events—jumping 39 inches in the vertical leap and clocking 4.22 seconds in the 40-yard dash.

Tight end Steve Jordan was the overall winner, doing 127 sit-ups in a two-minute span and scoring 5,809 out of a possible 8,000 points. Jordan will receive a Buick as top prize if he makes the team. As the top finisher at one of seven position categories—tight ends and linebackers—Jordan automatically gets a video cassette recorder.

Other position winners were Dana Noel (defensive backs), Bob Sebro (offensive line), Paul Sverchek (defensive line), Jim Gustafson (wide receivers), Jan Stenerud (kickers-quarterbacks), and Rick Bell (running backs).

Gustafson, a first-year player out of St. Thomas, was second overall while tight end Bob Bruer was third. Bell, fifth overall behind Noel, had the top performance in the leg press with 86 repetitions of 440 pounds in two minutes.

While some of his teammates walked off with prizes, Mullaney limped away with the most serious injury. Steckel says he doesn't expect the 10-year veteran, who missed all but four games last season with a broken collarbone, to practice for at least two weeks. Mullaney was understandably upset, especially because he was negotiating with the USFL's Denver Gold on a contract that may be jeopardized by the injury. Ricardo said he was unsure how long he would be sidelined.

"Mullaney was determined to win," Steckel said. "And Nelson was one of the favorites. They did what so many athletes do—push themselves to the brink."

Stenerud did some pushing. The 41-year-old placekicker, the oldest player in the camp, turned in one of the best times in the shuttle run and turned out to be one of the best conditioned players of the 89 in camp.

"The last few years, when I realized each year could be my last, I've been running more," said Stenerud, the NFL's all-time field goal scorer who was acquired last week in a trade with Green Bay.

Said Steckel: "First time I met Jan was 1979 or 1980. I was at my brother-in-law's house. Jan and I grabbed two tennis rackets and ran five miles to the courts. We played an hour and a half and ran back five miles. What he did [today] is no surprise."

Coleman provided some levity to the otherwise humorless competition. He showed up wearing Marine fatigues, complete with helmet and boots. He snapped to attention to salute Steckel, a Vietnam veteran and a lieutenant colonel in the Marine Reserves who often likens football to war situations.

"It was a classic," Steckel said of Coleman's getup. "I welcome that kind of thing. You need some humor when the guys are so serious."

"I got it from the Marine Reserves. They were real cooperative," Coleman said. "They even were going to supply me with an M16 rifle."

A member of the Viking staff, seeing Coleman in fatigues, yelled that the club soon would be bringing in additional punters. Coleman replied: "You bring them in and I'll get out the M16.

"You've got to break the monotony," he said. "I was thinking one day wouldn't it be great if everyone dressed up as a Marine for camp."

"Only one idiot was dumb enough to do it," said linebacker Scott Studwell.

Steckel then ran six weeks of two-a-day practices, topped off by extra calisthenics and wind sprints. Steckel took part in the extra workouts with the team, but the boot camp atmosphere took a toll on morale as the season wore on. The team lost 11 of its last 12 games to finish at 3–13, its worst record since 1962.

Steckel was fired at the end of the season and Bud Grant was talked into coming out of retirement. Although the team finished at 7–9 in 1985, Grant coached the team back to respectability. They were competitive in all but two games. Four of the nine losses were by three points or less, and another was by seven. The wins were no laughers, either—five of the seven were by seven points or less. Many were perplexed when Grant resigned at the end of the season, citing the same reasons he had given at his first resignation in January 1984. General manager Mike Lynn was one of those, and he tried to woo Grant with a larger paycheck.

"A MOST ENJOYABLE YEAR," FROM *BUD: THE OTHER SIDE OF THE GLACIER* (1986)

Bill McGrane

The Vikings season ended on December 22.

Grant outlined his postseason routine during the week leading up to that final game.

"Monday, I'll come in and do the paperwork to tie off the season. Tuesday, I'll go Christmas shopping. Wednesday, we'll have all our family over for Christmas."

And Thursday, he would drive to the Simms Lake [Wisconsin] retreat. He didn't say so at the time, but he would go there to ponder his future.

Bud drove back to the Viking offices in Eden Prairie on Saturday. When he had signed his new contract before the 1985 season, it had included a clause giving him the right to notify the club within seven days of the conclusion of a season on whether or not he wished to continue as coach.

"I told Mike [Lynn] I thought it was time for him to find another coach," said Grant.

Why?

Grant laughed.

"The reasons I gave are real reasons," he said. "But a lot of people had trouble accepting them. Nothing had changed . . . the same things that were important to me when I left after the 1983 season were still there. I'm 58 years old, and I've been in professional sports for 36 of those years. I decided it was time to enjoy the fruits of those years."

Lynn, once again, suggested that Grant rethink his position.

"We talked throughout that next week," Bud noted. "And it would be incorrect to say I closed the door. We discussed possibilities that would have kept me in the job, we also talked about the direction the club might take without me."

The more they talked, Grant said, the more he came to believe that Lynn's direction, should Bud step down, would be to replace him with Jerry Burns, offensive coordinator and assistant head coach.

But first, Lynn made his effort to keep Grant in the job.

"Sometimes, it's hard for people who deal with money to understand that everything can't be bought," Grant said. "I don't mean money is a god to Mike, or anything like that, but he deals with it all the time, and a lot of that dealing is negotiation. In his job, you work under the assumption that, somewhere, there's a price for everyone. I think it was difficult for Mike to realize there wasn't a sum of money that would matter. I suppose if I had gone to most people and told them what he proposed, they'd say you're crazy if you don't take it. And if I needed this"—and Grant emphasized the word—"then I suppose I would be crazy. But how much money do you need? I have what I believe to be important for myself and my family. I don't need a yacht tied up in Miami . . . if I did, I'd have been beating on his door. But, I don't, so I didn't . . .

"The real reason I resigned again was because I wanted to get on with the other things that are important in my life," said Grant. "Unfortunately, real reasons don't make good copy, so people are going to question them.

"I left the Vikings once and returned to them because they asked me to. Maybe, it was because I felt I owed something to the club. If I did, I feel like I've repaid it."

Bud Grant had met Jerry Burns—who was then an assistant coach at Iowa—when he was recruiting college players to play for the Winnipeg Blue Bombers, and they developed a lasting friendship. When Grant went to the Vikings in 1967 he held a spot open for Burns, who still had a year left on his contract with Green Bay. Burns had been with the Vikings ever since, acquiring the reputation as an offensive genius on the same level as legendary 49ers coach Bill Walsh.

The 1986 Vikings finished 9–7 under Burns, but missed the playoffs again. They were 5–2 after a 23-7 victory over the defending Super Bowl champion Chicago Bears on October 19, but then lost four of the next five games—blowing leads with under two minutes to go in three of those losses. Tommy Kramer had a great year. In a 44–38 overtime loss to the Washington Redskins on November 2, he threw for 471 yards to become the first in NFL history to better the 400-yard mark two times. Injuries limited Kramer to 13 games, but his passer rating of 92.6 led the league, and he earned the only Pro Bowl selection of his career. Teammates Steve Jordan (tight end) and Joey Browner (strong safety) also made the team.

The NFLPA struck again in 1987, setting up picket lines after the games of week two—Sunday and Monday, September 20–21. NFL owners, who painfully recalled the 57-day strike of 1982, decided to hire replacement players to complete the season. Teams scrambled to contact players cut during the preseason and to conduct tryouts to evaluate new recruits. Skeptics were sure the scabs would be playing in empty stadiums. Where would the teams find the 1,120 players required to fill the rosters of the 28 NFL teams?

The schedule resumed on October 4. The fact that television networks decided to broadcast the replacement-players games helped convince NFLPA members to vote to go back to work after three games without them. The NFL, per its original plan, counted the replacement games, but cut the season to 15 games—eliminating the games missed at the start of the strike on week three.

Minneapolis Star Tribune, October 5, 1987

UNION WORKERS JOIN FOOTBALL PLAYERS ON PICKET LINES

THE BOREDOM/13,000 WATCH REPLACEMENT VIKINGS LOSE TO PACKERS 23–16

M. L. Smith

More than 500 union workers—some carrying placards, banners and an American flag—crowded outside the Metrodome Sunday, booing and castigating football fans who crossed the picket line to attend the Vikings–Green Bay Packers game.

"C'mon, show your wife you're a decent person," Jack Mogelson, a 6-foot-3, 250-pound business agent for Local 320 of the Teamsters Union, shouted at fans who waited to cross Chicago Avenue to the Metrodome.

"Hey, don't bring your kids over here. Don't make them into scabs," Mogelson shouted across the street. "Don't come over, son. You have a right to dignity."

But when the light changed, the group of fans crossed the avenue. Some walked with their heads down, trying to evade the catcalls and the glares from the pickets. Others walked with their heads up, pushing past the ranks of union members.

Mogelson, cigar in hand, stepped into the street to "talk" to the fans heading into Gate F at Sixth Street and Chicago Avenue.

"If you ever had a job, you wouldn't go inside," Mogelson said. But the group of football fans kept on walking and the crowd chanted, "Scab. Scab. Scab. Scab."

Almost 14,000 fans crossed the picket line to attend yesterday's game, which the Packers won 23–16. Some pushed their way through the pickets. Others were less conspicuous, entering gates away from the single gate the union members picketed. Fifty police—twice as many as usual—were on hand, but there was only one minor pushing incident, a couple of smoke bombs and no arrests.

Around the country yesterday, as National Football League teams played their first games since the regular players went on strike two weeks ago, attendance was way below the near-capacity crowds usually seen.

In Philadelphia, only 4,074 fans made their way into the game through a corridor of mounted police after pickets closed the gates. And in Detroit, where more than 40,000 advance tickets had been sold, only 4,919 people went into the Silverdome. Outside, seven people were arrested for disobeying a court order not to interfere with people entering the stadium . . .

Pickets from several unions joined strikers outside the Louisiana Superdome, where 29,745 fans showed up, the smallest crowd in the team's 21-year history.

Supporters demonstrated without arrest in Denver, Atlanta, Cincinnati, Washington, Buffalo, New Orleans and Pittsburgh.

Fans in Minneapolis had to endure their share of verbal abuse.

"This thing started way after I made plans to come here," said Steve Paulus, a union member from Oshkosh, Wisconsin. "I was going to come no matter what. Some guys are lipping off to me. I don't need that abuse. I don't feel any allegiance to these guys. These guys make $300,000; I make $20,000. I can't sympathize with this crap. I'm here on a bus tour. I'm here for a good time."

Jeff Nelson, formerly of Anoka and now stationed at Cannon Air Force Base in New Mexico, is a self-described diehard Vikings fan who also refused to stay home. Nelson marched past the pickets, wearing his purple Vikings T-shirt and jacket and carrying a small portable TV and radio.

"Football is football. These guys are idiots for striking. The players don't know when they've got a good thing," Nelson said. "The Vikings should've let everyone else go on strike and kept playing as long as they're playing so well."

As Nelson walked to his gate, the protesters began to chant again. "Scab. Scab. Scab."

"The real Vikings are out here."

"Take off your union clothes before you go in there."

"Don't miss the best part of the game: the huddle. That's when the players will introduce themselves."

The waves of shouts and taunts continued for three hours.

Chuck Mohr of Brooklyn Park wasn't really interested in the game or the picketing yesterday. He clutched his seven-month-old son and a new football as he ran across Chicago Avenue.

He was looking for autographs for his son and maybe a snapshot or two of Vikings players cradling the baby.

"He'll appreciate this when he's older," Mohr said.

Mohr got the autographs, but the four Gross brothers weren't so lucky.

They're Vikings fans from Wausau, Wisconsin, who came to town to attend the game. They wanted Vikings punter Greg Coleman to sign an autograph. But Coleman turned them away when they told him they were going to the game.

"At this point, I can't sign this for you. Maybe next week," he said.

Inside the Dome, fans had their choice of seats.

"Usually, this is the first game to sell out," said Mike Chandler, head of special events for Sims Security. "Today is a game when nearly everyone can sit on the 50-yard line if they wanted."

Typically, the halls would be jammed with people and filled with smoke. People would stand 15 deep at the concession stands. Fans would generally endure long waits outside the bathrooms.

Not so yesterday.

Outside the Dome, the crowd of pickets thinned as the minutes to the end of the first quarter ticked off.

Inside, spectators began to leave before halftime.

Tom and Mona Monroe of St. Cloud were among them. "We have season tickets, and we decided to go to see what was going on," Tom Monroe said. "Now I'm mad I didn't stay home to play golf. I've seen better high school games."

Mogelson wasn't discouraged by the number of fans who crossed the picket line.

"We can't force people to do what's right," he said. "But we're not going to sit back and watch the rich resources of a company destroy a union."

●

The Vikings, who had won their first two games, were 0–3 with replacement players, but went on a 5–1 streak after the strike ended. There was a big local and national publicity buildup for the cable TV broadcast of the December 6 Sunday night game at the Metrodome against the 9–2 Chicago Bears, who were striving for their fourth consecutive Central Division championship. Bears coach Mike Ditka helped stir things up when he called the Vikings stadium the "Rollerdome," better suited for a roller rink than a real sport. Vikings general manager Mike Lynn responded by sending Ditka a pair of roller skates. Ditka wore them at his next press conference, and the Vikings decided to put their cheerleaders on roller skates during pregame activities. They were actually on Rollerblades, but the product was new in the marketplace and not commonly known by its proper name.

(In 1996, when Robert Naegele Jr. sold his 50 percent share of Rollerblade to the Italian sporting goods giant Nordica and donated $1.5 million tax-free to the company's local employees, he gave credit to Ditka. Rollerblades at the time were just considered an off-season training tool for hockey players, but sales took off after the national publicity garnered by Ditka's stunts. Naegele refered to it as "the miracle of 1987.")

Vikings fans also waved "touchdown towels"—modeled after the "homer hankies" that Twins fans waved during the World Series that

Vikings cheerleaders enter the Metrodome on inline skates and roller derby helmets to taunt Bears head coach Mike Ditka before a Sunday night game on December 6, 1987. A week earlier Ditka had ridiculed the Dome in a press conference, calling it better suited for a roller rink than for a "real" sport like football. PHOTOGRAPH FROM *STAR TRIBUNE*. COURTESY OF THE MINNESOTA HISTORICAL SOCIETY.

year—and taunted Ditka when he walked onto the field during pregame warm-ups. Ditka reveled in the attention, however, and the Bears scored a touchdown in the last minute of the game for a come-from-behind 30–24 victory.

The Vikings struggled after this game, finishing with an 8–7 record, but they qualified for a wild card berth in the playoffs. They blasted the New Orleans Saints 44–10 in the wild card game and then upset San Francisco 36–24 in the divisional playoffs, thanks to a magnificent day by wide receiver Anthony Carter, who caught 10 passes for 227 yards, a new playoff record. The old record had been set by the Los Angeles Rams' Tom Fears way back in 1950.

The victory kindled Super Bowl dreams for many—maybe the Twins' World Series victory had broken Minnesota's apparent big-game jinx—but the improbable run ended with a bitter 17–10 defeat to the Washington Redskins in the NFC championship game.

Minneapolis Star Tribune, January 18, 1988
MAGIC BOUNCES AWAY
VIKINGS' HOPES DISAPPEAR
Doug Grow

The kind sporting fates don't live in Minnesota anymore.

Those fates of timely hits and good hops that suddenly had turned Minnesota sporting teams into remarkable winners slipped off Darrin Nelson's hands and fell to the turf of Washington's Robert F. Kennedy Stadium Sunday.

No, the Minnesota Vikings won't be following the Twins to the top. The Vikings were defeated 17–10 by the Washington Redskins in the National Football Conference championship game. In the end, their bid to at least tie the game—perhaps end up in the Super Bowl—fell six yards short. Less than that actually.

"I probably should have caught the ball," said Nelson.

There were 50 seconds left in the game. The Vikings were down to their final fourth-down chance. Four yards ahead was the promise of a first down. Six yards ahead was the promise of overtime—and maybe the Super Bowl.

Nelson slipped out of the backfield. Quarterback Wade Wilson spotted him and . . .

For a moment it appeared that it wasn't going to end. All the improbable winning that had begun with the Twins in October was just going to keep happening.

Over the Tigers. Over the Cardinals. Over the Saints. Over the 49ers. Over and over and over again.

The ball was in the air to Nelson. The coach of the favored Washington Redskins, Joe Gibbs, was on his knees. The 55,000 spectators in RFK suddenly were silent.

Surely the Vikings, who hadn't really played well enough to win on this day, somehow were going to tie the game and then there would be the trip to San Diego and more dancing in the streets in Minnesota.

And perhaps if the Vikings could have come to RFK with the attitude they had taken into games against New Orleans and San Francisco they would be plotting their trip to San Diego now. They had been underdogs in those games, too. But they had been raucous "we-got-nothing-to-lose" underdogs. They had played without a care and they had played superbly.

"We tried," said Vikings coach Jerry Burns, "to maintain that same attitude coming into this game."

But a game away from the Super Bowl, the Vikings took themselves seriously.

"The event," said rookie defensive lineman Henry Thomas, "was so big, we sort of got caught up in it. We got really serious. We were really intense. We'd walk around saying, 'We can do it.' Before, we were saying. 'To hell with it, we can do it.'"

Even more than most of the Vikings, Thomas was trying to deal with all sorts of emotions after the game.

A few months earlier, he had been an unheralded rookie. Now, he was a respected starting defensive lineman for a professional football team that had fallen just a few yards short of the Super Bowl.

Beyond that yesterday, Thomas had been sick. He'd awakened—painfully—with the flu yesterday morning. Hey, it wasn't supposed to be like this on the morning of the biggest day of his pro football life.

And now the pain of playing was over. Thomas had survived the game and could think about sitting back with his flu and think about how good it would feel in a few days when he could think back to all the wondrous things that had happened to him and his team this year and what might lie ahead.

So there weren't many tears in defeat for Thomas or other younger Vikings. Surely, they believed, other opportunities lie ahead.

Older players know, however, that's not necessarily so. Older players know that whole careers can come and go without ever climbing so close to the top as these Vikings had.

And so for the older Vikings, yesterday's might-have-beens overwhelmed the memories of the joy that had come with the playoffs.

"What's to feel good about?" said linebacker Scott Studwell, who in coming weeks will be contemplating retirement. "It's an accomplishment to get this far, but what good is the accomplishment when you don't do something with the opportunity?"

There had been so many opportunities for the Vikings. And even more for the Redskins. But neither team had been able to take advantage of the chances and very quickly the game became an ugly grunt and shove match, a game of failures, not of accomplishments.

But in time, even all the failures—the Washington sacks of the Vikings' Wilson, the inability of Washington quarterback Doug Williams to hit open receivers, the pathetic punts of the Vikings' Bucky Scribner and the awful field goal kicking of Washington's Ali Haji-Sheikh—took on an intriguing character all of their own.

And that the Vikings were able to hang close made it seem possible, maybe even likely, that a Hrbek or Gaetti or Baylor wearing purple suddenly would step forward to keep everyone dancing in Minneosta.

But in the final seconds of the game yesterday, the ball fell away from Nelson and onto the turf. And the people of Washington began dancing with joy and with the kind fates Minnesotans had enjoyed so much.

●

Success on the field had not been the only story in 1987. A power struggle in the club's front office was also in the news, dating back to a lawsuit filed in 1986 by local financiers Carl Pohlad and Irwin Jacobs, who had formed the PJ Acquisition Corporation partnership to purchase Max Winter's stock in the team. Winter owned one-third of the team's voting shares. Pohlad and Jacobs also purchased Winter's non-voting stock. They wound up with 50.6 percent of the team's stock, but were frustrated with their one-third voting share, and sued to force the team to adopt a more conventional one-share, one-vote ownership structure.

Players' DWI arrests also made headlines in 1987, and the team's off-field problems continued late in the season when three players were arrested in a nightclub incident—bringing the number of Vikings arrested to 11 in three years. Keith Millard had a series of publicized run-ins with police. One incident in 1986 might have been amusing if it hadn't been part of a continuing problem. The night before training camp began police were called to a motel to break up a disturbance created by a very agitated Millard, who apparently wasn't impressed by the men in uniform. "My arms are more powerful than your gun," he told one officer.

Coming into 1988, however, Vikings fans tried to ignore the front-office comedy and players' off-field troubles. After the two 1987 playoff wins, and despite the pain lingering from the heartbreaking loss to the Redskins and the knowledge of the team's 0–4 record in Super Bowls in the 1970s, they dared to begin to think about the big game again. Many national observers agreed with them. The team seemed to have the stars to do the job—while only one Viking had been named to the Pro Bowl in 1982, 1984 and 1985 and none in 1983, six made it in 1987 and nine were destined to make the squad in 1988. Offensive tackle Gary Zimmerman, defensive tackle Keith Millard, and defensive backs Carl Lee and Joey Browner were first-team All Pro selections, while defensive end Chris Doleman, linebacker Scott Studwell, tight end Steve Jordan, wide receiver Anthony Carter, and quarterback Wade Wilson joined them on the Pro Bowl team. Zimmerman, Millard, Carter, and linebacker David Howard came to the Vikings from the short-lived United States Football League.

A quarterback controversy dogged the team for the second consecutive year in 1988. Injury-plagued Tommy Kramer had started only 45 of 79 regular-season games during the previous five seasons, and backup Wade Wilson led the Vikings in their 1987 playoff successes, but Coach Burns had refused to name an "official" starter, frustrating Wilson. "I've given up trying to figure out what you've got to do to be a starting quarterback around here," he said at one point.

Kramer was slightly more flippant. "I just want to be in the right chair when the music stops," he said.

Wilson started on opening day in 1988, and in 10 of the 16 games. Led by a resurgent defense—which led the NFL in yards allowed and was second in points allowed—the Vikings improved to 11–5, but were second in the Central Division once again to the Chicago Bears, who finished 12–4. The Vikings won six of the last seven games and appeared to be peaking just in time for the playoffs. In a four-game stretch they had one shutout and gave up only a single field goal in the other three games. The Vikings beat the Los Angeles Rams 28–17 in the NFC wild card game, but were dumped by San Francisco, 34–9, in the NFC divisional round. It wasn't close, as the 49ers cruised to a 21–3 halftime lead.

The dashed dreams in 1987 and 1988 probably took a toll on the perpetually pessimistic coach Jerry Burns, as reported by award-winning national correspondent Jim Murray.

Los Angeles Times, September 7, 1989
IT'S NEVER WORSE THAN HE EXPECTED
Jim Murray

I always thought that when Don Coryell got out of coaching, the last of the great doom-sayers got out of the game.

You remember Don Coryell. He was the guy who used to stand on the sidelines with his hands on his knees and stare out at the line of scrimmage like a guy who just got a peek at his own coffin. Guys have gone to the electric chair happier than Coryell went to Charger games. He looked like a guy who knows the warden isn't going to call.

When he left, I thought the breed had died out.

Ladies and gentlemen, meet Jerry Burns.

Jerry is the coach of the Minnesota Vikings, which is enough to give anybody a worried look, but Jerry would have to cheer up merely to be considered lugubrious. His expression is not so much disdain or disgust as that of a man who wants to have nothing to do with the terrible things going on around him. He's like a guy who pulls the shades when he hears screams in the alley. He doesn't want to get involved.

You know how other coaches are? They stand on the sidelines and cup their hands and shout till the cords come out in their necks. They clap, cuss, pace, groan. Sometimes they grab a player coming off the field and yell in his ear or pat him on the back. They shriek at the officials, plead with the linesmen. Vince Lombardi used to look like a guy having a nervous breakdown.

Jerry Burns just distances himself from the whole mess. Look at him now on the sideline. He avoids all personal contact. He shuns the players. The ushers look more interested. His staff runs the game. Jerry acts as if he has better things to do. Or he can't wait for the game to be over so he can set about doing them. If he talks to a player, you get the impression he's asking him how the wife is.

He doesn't wear a headset. He never appears to be drawing a play on a slate. You'd figure the game was only mildly interesting to him. Plus, he expects the worst. Actually, he makes Coryell look like an optimist.

Burns just knows those guys are going to screw up. You draw all these lovely can't-miss schemes on the blackboard and then somebody forgets the ball. When that happens, Burns never changes expression. It's as if he expected it all along. He knows the next card will be a trey, the next dice craps.

You'd think a guy named Jerome Monahan Burns would have a sunnier outlook on life, but Jerry Burns is not your music hall Irish, wisecracking and butter-tongued. Pat O'Brien would never get the part.

It's not that Jerry Burns doesn't care. It's just that he knows what he's up against. People fumble. They drop passes, miss signals. Looking on the dark side of things is an occupational hazard with football coaches. They go down in lore as Gloomy Gil and Sad Sam. There has never been a football coach known as Lucky, or Horseshoes.

Burns is widely conceded to be the nearest thing to an offensive genius the game has, now that Bill Walsh has left. He draws these beautiful diagrams on the board. He doesn't really expect them to work. It's like giving Rolls-Royces to a tribe of savages. His blueprints are like the Austrian cavalry. They look pretty but they're no good in a war.

Not that Coach Burns is resigned. No matter how used to his team's blunders he gets, it just plunges him into more gloom. He expects them but he's not tolerant of them. He lost an exhibition game to the Rams here a couple of Saturdays ago and, in the locker room later, he drew a portrait of his team that was revealing, if unflattering.

"We stunk the joint out tonight," he growled. "I would say the defense played lousy 50 percent of the time, the special teams 75 percent and the offense 100 percent of the time. We didn't do anything but block a punt. That epitomizes our game.

"We get two touchdowns called back on the same series and then miss a field goal from the two-yard line. It was a sick operation all the way. You'd think we got our game plan out of a Cracker Jack box."

Onlookers were surprised he noticed. Coach Burns does not seem to be that much in a game once it has kicked off. He mopes along the side, hands in pockets, occasionally glancing out onto the field, as if to confirm his worst fears. The rest of the time, he looks like a guy trying to remember what he did with his keys or whether he locked the front door and put the cat out. He smiles twice a year but not during football season.

"Once the game starts, your preparation is over with," he says, shrugging. "It's too late to make over. The decision-making is up to others."

So, Coach Burns doesn't keep a low profile so much as he keeps no profile. But his brow darkens when they turn his melodramatic plans into comedy.

"We better take stock of our team," he warns. "We may not be the team we're cracked up to be. We're recognized as a heralded team. They're even talking of us as a Super Bowl team. We've got some good players. That doesn't always mean you have a good team."

If the Vikings do get in and win the Super Bowl, you'll have no trouble recognizing the coach. He'll be the one who looks as if he just lost his wallet—or heard the IRS called. If the team loses? Well, he'll be the one who doesn't look all surprised.

●

Early in the 1989 season, with the Vikings idling along with a lackluster 3–2 record, general manager Lynn engineered a deal that stunned the football world. He traded five players and seven future draft picks to the Dallas Cowboys for running back Herschel Walker, who had a spectacular debut in purple.

Coach Jerry Burns receives a Gatorade shower from his players as tight end Steve Jordan congratulates him after his last game in the Metrodome in 1991. Burns compiled a 52–43 record in his six years as head coach from 1986 to 1991. The Vikings made the playoffs from 1987 to 1989, losing the NFC championship game in 1987. PHOTOGRAPH BY RICK A. KOLODZIEJ. COURTESY OF THE MINNESOTA VIKINGS.

Sports Illustrated, October 23, 1989

SUDDEN IMPACT

A MEGADEAL SENT HERSCHEL WALKER TO MINNESOTA, WHERE HE RAN WILD

Peter King

So here was Herschel Walker riding along Route 169 outside Minneapolis. He was on his way to pick up a car in which to tool around this latest state to be in the palm of his hand. Walker was thinking. It was Saturday, 23 hours before he would touch the ball for the first time for his third professional team, and he was a little nervous.

"My father used to tell me I was only worth a quarter," he said with a nervous laugh. "That's still about what I'm worth, I think. I'm ashamed to be here, almost. Ashamed in a sense that the players here have earned their stripes and I haven't. I'm cheating. I'm sneaking in. But the situation's going to inspire me to work harder."

The largest Metrodome crowd ever to see the Minnesota Vikings play— 62,075—saw that inspired work firsthand on Sunday. The first time Walker touched the ball—it also happened to be the first time he returned a kickoff in the NFL—he advanced it 51 yards (it was brought back 24 yards because of a penalty). The second time he touched the ball, he took a handoff from Viking quarterback Tommy Kramer, skated right, burst into a hole punched out by tackle Tim Irwin, sprinted straight up-field, broke tackles by Green Bay Packers defensive backs Dave Brown and Mark Murphy, had his right shoe stripped off by Murphy and sprint-hopped a few more lengths before getting caught by linebacker Tim Harris. The gain: 47 yards. "Not bad," said Minnesota general manager Mike Lynn, the man who made the deal possible. "Two plays, a hundred yards."

Grateful Minnesotans found out what Georgians, New Jerseyans and Texans already knew: With Walker, all is possible. After two hours and 20 minutes of practice with the Vikings, he produced the best rushing game by a Minnesota back since 1983, gaining 148 yards on 18 carries in a 26–14 win over Green Bay. He did it while playing only 33 of the Vikes' 68 offensive plays.

The NFL is often maligned for its bland corporateness, but here was some real excitement. It was one of those you-had-to-be-there things. The crowd in the south end zone gave Walker a standing ovation when he lined up for the kickoff after Green Bay had scored to go ahead 7–0. The whole place went nuts on the lost-shoe run. And for no apparent reason—or maybe just because Walker was there—the joint broke into spontaneous applause for him during a TV timeout in the third quarter. "Herschelmania!" screamed some guy in Section 108 right about then.

"I had to take time away from my defense today because I had to see Herschel run," said Minnesota defensive coordinator Floyd Peters afterward. "He popped through the middle a couple of times, and—whoooooosh!—I thought he'd be gone."

And whoooooosh! was the way he had arrived from the Dallas Cowboys three days before the game. Ah, the trade—the weird, weird trade. It was one that had to happen, but it nearly unraveled at the last minute. Actually, to call the Walker deal a trade doesn't do it justice. Consider:

—Dallas received Minnesota's first-round draft choice in 1992, linebackers David Howard and Jesse Solomon, running back Darrin Nelson, cornerback Issiac Holt and rookie defensive end Alex Stewart. All five Viking players are tied to conditional draft choices—Solomon and Howard to first-round picks in '90 and '91, the others to second-and third-round selections in the early '90s in a complicated formula that neither team has fully disclosed.

By February 1, Dallas will have to make five decisions. If the Cowboys cut all five players, Dallas will get all five picks; if the Cowboys cut fewer they'll keep fewer picks.

—Dallas may try to keep the players and the picks by dealing with Lynn after the season. Here's where the trade gets weird. Cowboys coach Jimmy Johnson said, "We get players now, and we get ones and twos [in the draft] for the next three years to help us win. We're going to make those picks."

Dallas could approach Lynn in January with this idea: Look, we could cut these guys and take our five picks, and you would end up with neither players nor picks. Instead, let us give you some thing—say, five middle-round choices—and you erase the condition of the trade that says we have to choose either the players or the draft choices. When told this scenario was suggested on Sunday, Lynn arched his eyebrows and said, "No comment."

But Lynn is, ahem, a hardline fellow. When this deal was close to completion on the night of October 3, the guaranteed first-round draft pick in 1992 wasn't included. Johnson and Cowboys owner Jerry Jones told Lynn over the phone they liked the deal but needed something more. "I'll give you our number one in '92," said Lynn, "but if I do, that's it. There's nothing else. That has to be the deal, and we have to do it now." Jones and Johnson said they would do it. Now if they come back asking for still more, Lynn may well play hardball, even at the expense of all those draft picks.

—According to Lynn, he has already stared down Jones once, over a final, almost fatal snag early last Thursday morning. Jones had negotiated an agreement with one of Walker's agents, Peter Johnson, under which Walker would receive $1.25 million from the Cowboys to accept the trade. That is another remarkable part of this story: Walker didn't have a no-trade clause

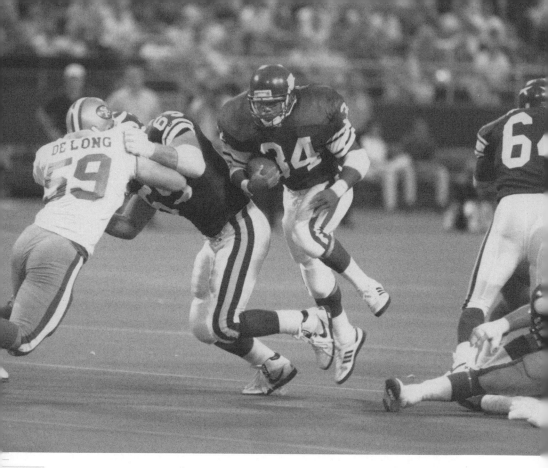

Herschel Walker tiptoes to the line. The Vikings traded five players and seven future draft picks to the Dallas Cowboys in 1989 in return for Walker, hoping that his running would complement their potent passing game and bring the Vikings back to the Super Bowl. Most observers consider the trade the worst in NFL history. PHOTOGRAPH BY RICK A. KOLODZIEJ. COURTESY OF THE MINNESOTA VIKINGS.

in his contract, yet Dallas had to pay to get him to report to the Vikings. After finishing negotiations with Peter Johnson, Jones got Lynn on the telephone at 8 A.M. Lynn says he was dumbfounded when Jones asked him to help cover the $1.25 million. Then, says Lynn, Jones wanted to talk about the terms again. Lynn feared Jones might start calling other teams, so he told Jones he wouldn't let him off the phone until they had made an absolute agreement. Walker had already come to clean out his locker at 6:15 that morning. Jones agreed to pay the entire $1.25 million. He wired the money to Walker's agents in Cleveland the next day.

—Walker, according to his Viking contract, gets two big perks: a house that must be comparable to his home in Dallas and "a new Mercedes-Benz automobile of the player's choice." Lynn said he planned to talk with former

Viking Ahmad Rashad, who lives in Mount Vernon, New York, about allow-ing Walker and his wife, Cindy, to live in Rashad's part-time home in Min-nesota this fall.

—Despite reports to the contrary, rookie Steve Walsh, Dallas's backup quarterback, who is expected to be traded after the season, isn't part of the Walker deal. "I can 100 percent give you my word that Walsh was never mentioned in the deal and is no part of it," says Jimmy Johnson. But who knows what will happen after the season? Five years ago, Walsh—then a quarterback at a St. Paul high school who was headed to the University of Miami—was told by Lynn at a sports banquet that someday he would come home to play for the Vikings. Although no groundwork has been laid for such a transaction, it's possible that Walsh could be sent to Minnesota in January in return for the Cowboys' being allowed to keep the five players as well as the five draft picks.

Trading Walker was the smartest move Dallas could make. They had gone 1–16 with him over the last 13 months, and he hadn't had a 100-yard rushing game since week 14 last year. "You always hate to lose a tremen-dous talent like Herschel," says Johnson, whose Cowboys fell to 0–6 on Sun-day with a 31–14 loss to the San Francisco 49ers in their first game of the Post-Herschel Era. "What saddens me more is to lose football games. The applecart was already upset, and it was going to be difficult to rebuild with-out trading Herschel."

Minnesota had been getting killed by its inept running game. Since the start of 1988, the Vikings have ranked 25th in the NFL in yards per rush (3.65). Until Sunday they hadn't had so much as one 80-yard rushing game by a back since '87. "We had to do something," said Lynn on Saturday. "We had the number one defense in the league, and we were keeping it on the field too long. Our guys were gasping. Look at the great teams of the '80s. They all had great backs. We needed one. As I told Herschel, 'We've got one missing spoke in the wheel, and you're it.'"

Walker got to Minneapolis at 5:30 P.M. last Thursday. Over the next day and a half, he would spend five hours talking to reporters, more than twice his practice time. Still, he learned 12 plays, most of them rushes taught to him by running-backs coach John Brunner. Walker was pleasantly surprised to discover that the Minnesota offensive system is numbered similarly to the one he had mastered under Tom Landry at Dallas, so the learning wasn't hard. Understanding Kramer's San Antonio drawl was another mat-ter. Kramer worked with Walker on the snap counts during Friday's practice. "Herschel had a hard time understanding me," says Kramer, who concen-trated on enunciating the counts more clearly. "He told me, 'The quarter-backs in Dallas talk slower.'"

The plan was to play Walker on 12 to 15 downs, giving him six or eight carries so he could get familiar with his blockers. He would have a big role beginning with the next game, against the Detroit Lions. By Saturday, Walker was pretty comfortable. "I can adjust to almost anything," he said. "My life has always been wild, always exciting. All I can do is make the best of this. That's the way I live. I lived that way at Georgia for three years, with New Jersey [of the USFL] for three years and with Dallas for three years."

And with Minnesota for how long? Walker says he doesn't want to extend his contract now. He'll be 28 next season, and he won't need the money. Next year will be his eighth pro season, and he will have earned, including incentive bonuses, something like $17 million directly from playing football.

He showed why on Sunday. Walker got hot, and he got the ball a lot more often than planned. "I'm not a complete idiot," said Coach Jerry Burns. "When I saw what he was doing, I said, 'Keep him in there and keep feeding him the ball.'" With five minutes left in the first half, Walker already had the Vikings' best individual rushing total of the season, 68 yards.

Beyond that, he simply made Minnesota better. Early in the second quarter Walker lined up in the backfield with Alfred Anderson, a six-year veteran. With Green Bay looking toward Walker, Anderson ran up the middle for seven yards. On the next play, Kramer faked a handoff to Walker and then threw for 19 yards to wideout Hassan Jones. The Vikings scored a field goal on that series to cut the Packers' lead to 7–3. Minnesota got a touchdown on its next possession—Walker played three of the four downs in that series—and the Vikings never trailed again.

Minnesota's defense shut down Green Bay's number-one-ranked offense in part because the Viking offense held the ball for a season-high 36 minutes and six seconds. "He's that main ingredient we've needed to take the heat off [wide receiver] Anthony Carter and [tight end] Steve Jordan, and to keep the defense off the field," says defensive tackle Keith Millard.

Lynn says the trade will only be a success if Walker leads the Vikings to a Super Bowl victory. Is that possible? With Walker, all is possible. Kramer found that out in the third quarter on Sunday. Walker was lined up as an I-formation tailback when the Packers suddenly shifted their defense, using two inside linebackers to fill the holes between guard and center. Kramer called an audible, changing from an inside run to a toss to Walker. Kramer looked back at Walker and almost froze. How will he know our audibles? thought Kramer. But because the terminology was familiar, Walker knew what to do. "I couldn't believe it," says Kramer. "He turned it into about eight yards."

●

The team won four out of the first five games with Walker in the lineup, but faded to finish 10–6, good enough for a first-place tie with Green Bay, and breaking Chicago's five-year run as Central Division champions. The defense was dominating again, finishing first in yards allowed, although it fell to sixth in points allowed. They racked up 71 sacks, a big improvement over the 37 achieved in 1988. Chris Doleman led the league with 21, while Keith Millard was third with 18.

Eight Vikings were selected for the Pro Bowl. Defensive players Millard, Doleman, Browner, and Lee were repeaters from 1988, as were Zimmerman, Anthony Carter, and tight end Steve Jordan on offense. Second-year guard Randall McDaniel began a remarkable 12-year run in the Pro Bowl. (He also made first-team All Pro in 1990, 1992–1996 and in 1998.) Millard was named the Associated Press NFL Defensive Player of the Year.

This star power was not enough, however, as the Vikings were clobbered by San Francisco once again in the NFC divisional playoffs, 41–13. If fans were looking for consolation, their last three playoff losses had been to Super Bowl champions—the Washington Redskins in 1987 and the 49ers in 1988 and 1989.

General manager Mike Lynn formed a players' council in January 1990 to deal with the Vikings' off-field problems, including the DWIs, player arrests, and unhappiness with Lynn himself. He was resented by many Vikings players for his tough salary negotiations and called racist by others. In May Lynn sent the team's players, coaches, and front-office personnel to a three-day training session at the Pecos River Learning Center outside Santa Fe, New Mexico. Participants attended classroom sessions and did physical exercises in small groups—climbing poles, scaling walls, and walking a high wire—designed to promote working together. It was the sort of team-building program in vogue with Fortune 500 companies.

Sporting News, June 18, 1990
ATTEMPT TO FOSTER UNITY PUTS VIKINGS ON HIGH WIRE
G.M. TAKES NOVEL APPROACH TO SOLVING TEAM'S PROBLEMS
Gregg Wong

Besides just sticking his neck out again, as he did last fall in trading for Herschel Walker, Minnesota Vikings general manager Mike Lynn also put his physical well-being on the line with his latest venture.

Lynn and most of those in the Vikings' organization—with a few notable exceptions—went to a self-help clinic near Santa Fe, New Mexico, in mid-May for three days of workouts and classroom exercises. The stated purpose of the trip was to improve the lines of communication at all levels (mostly between players and management), to foster team unity and to raise the quality of the entire organization.

"You know very well what happens in this business when management and ownership look for a change," Lynn said. "They fire the coaching staff. Well, maybe we've found a better way."

About 65 members of the organization, including 40 veteran players, went to the Pecos River Learning Center, trying to find that better way. They went to learn more about themselves and what they can do for each other to create a positive environment throughout the organization, something that was missing during a less-than-harmonious 1989 season.

Players and management alike climbed poles, scaled walls, walked a high wire—all in groups of two or three to promote working together. The participants were linked together and for the group to succeed, everyone had to contribute.

That was the physical side. Then came two days of classroom discussions and verbal problem solving.

Putting an entire organization through such a program was unprecedented in professional sports. But it was a gamble that Lynn believes paid off.

"It was a wonderful experience," said Lynn, who participated in all the exercises with the players. "We really came together as a team. Now, we have to stay together, and I think we will."

Togetherness was missing for the Vikings last season. Despite winning their first NFC Central Division championship since 1980, the team was divided by contract squabbles, a charge of racism and the disruptive mid-season trade for Walker.

After entertaining Super Bowl aspirations in the preseason, the Vikings sputtered from start to finish, never reaching their potential despite having the most Pro Bowl players of any team for a second straight year. Lynn felt something had to be done.

He started by forming a team council, made up of eight players, Coach Jerry Burns and himself. That group went to Pecos River in February for a one-day look to determine if the program there would be worthwhile for the entire team. The players voted unanimously to give it a try.

The early results of the program show that the risk was worth it, at least for those who were in attendance.

Unfortunately for the Vikings, the two most disgruntled players in 1989—safety Joey Browner and wide receiver Anthony Carter—chose not to go. Both were unhappy about contract negotiations last year and their play and locker room demeanor was affected all season.

Carter is now a conditional free agent, while Browner has an option year remaining that will pay him $385,000. A week before the trip to Pecos River, Lynn offered Browner $2.5 million for three years, but Browner wanted more.

Although Browner's agent suggested he go to Pecos River, he did not. In fact, at the very same time the team was returning from the three-day retreat, Browner was at Twin Cities International Airport leaving for a trip to San Diego.

"I don't have to be here [in Minnesota] now. We don't play until September," Browner said.

Two other veterans, both conditional free agents, also chose not to make the trip to Pecos River—center Kirk Lowdermilk and halfback D. J. Dozier. Lowdermilk was unhappy about his current contract negotiations, and Dozier, who has said he does not want to return to the Vikings, was playing minor league baseball.

Before the Vikings left for Pecos River, there naturally was some skepticism. One player said the trip was something "for Boy Scouts, not football players." Another player said, "The 49ers get to go to Hawaii, we go to Pecos River."

Upon their return, though, every player, coach and staff member called the three days an enlightening and worthwhile experience.

"It was one of the most powerful, explosive experiences I've ever been involved with," Burns said. "When we left, there was a unity that surrounded the team. Hopefully, this will carry on into the season. I won't say we'll be a better team because of it, but I think we'll be better people because of it and good teams are made up of good people."

Quarterback Wade Wilson called the retreat "beneficial."

"I really do think this was a positive step for the team. I think we dealt with some perceptions and got some things out in the open," he said. "I do think we made some progress."

Each person who goes through the Pecos River program is given a mountain climber's safety link as a reminder of what took place.

"You look at our safety links and they're a symbol of many things—support, creativity and courage. Put them together and there's strength in numbers," veteran fullback Jessie Clark said. "I've been with several organizations, and every organization has problems. The thing I admire about this one is that we're actively trying to do something about it."

And the Vikings aren't through trying. During training camp, they will be visited by Pecos River staffers to keep the idea of teamwork fresh in their minds.

"It's not like we're suddenly cured," said wide receiver Hassan Jones. "But that's not exactly why we went down there. We went down there to get to know each other better, to make us understand each other."

Such understanding was evident at the team's mini-camp, which immediately followed the trip to Pecos River. During one of the workouts, Lynn lined up in a three-point stance across from defensive end Chris Doleman.

Just a couple of months before, Doleman and Lynn had been in court trying to settle a dispute on whether an option year remained in the player's contract. Doleman lost the court battle, but a few weeks after the Pecos River trip, Lynn gave him a one-year deal worth $1.6 million.

In addition, before one mini-camp drill linebacker Mark Dusbabek and tight end Darryl Ingram hugged. Burns himself gave a hug to a TV reporter.

"I'll tell you what," said Burns. "After you get done with some of those high-wire drills, you're ready to hug anybody."

Players voted defensive coordinator Floyd Peters the "most fearless" on some of the exercises.

"He never even hesitated on any of that stuff," kicker Rich Karlis said.

Karlis added that the toughest assignment was a face-first free fall off a 160-foot overhang. Each participant wore a harness tied to a rope and had to rely on others to pull him back.

"I kept saying, 'Man, I'm not going to be able to do that.' But we all learned to overcome our fears," said Karlis. "I'd like to take my wife to that. You learn to further experience trust and to support each other. It's invaluable."

But will it mean a championship?

"We have to remember that it's not like this is going to get us to the Super Bowl," cautioned Wilson. "We have to do that on the field. Our key players have to do the job or all that other stuff isn't going to matter."

◆

Unfortunately, any newfound team unity didn't translate to success on the field, as the Vikings dropped to 6–10, and missed the playoffs for the first time since 1986. The quarterback controversy seemed to have been solved when Tommy Kramer was released after the 1989 season, but Wilson suffered a torn ligament in his right thumb, and played in only four games. Keith Millard suffered what was essentially a career-ending knee injury, and played in only four games. (Additional reconstructive surgery caused him to miss the entire 1991 season. The Vikings traded him to Seattle for a second-round draft choice in 1992 and he retired after spending the 1993 season with Philadelphia.)

Thanks to returning 44 kickoffs, Herschel Walker led the NFL in all-purpose yards—he had 770 rushing and 315 on pass receptions in addition to 966 return yards—but he didn't live up to the team's expectations. Early in the year he took some practice time off to try out for the Olympic bobsled team and that weekend gained only three yards on three carries, with two fumbles, against the Eagles.

If things weren't strange enough, in early October, with the team at 1–4, Mike Lynn resigned to become president of the new World League of American Football. (The WLAF was envisioned by the NFL as a development league, and operated in 1991 and 1992, with three teams in Europe. In 1995 the league was reincarnated as the World League, with all teams in Europe.)

Players and team staffers were stunned by the news. Dave Huffman probably summed up the reaction from the players. "What an early Christmas present," he said.

Lynn's departure didn't immediately solve the ownership struggles, either, which dragged on for several more years.

The Vikings finished 8–8 in 1991, and were never much more than a .500 team. Coach Burns went to a one-back offense in an attempt to make Herschel Walker more effective, but this was abandoned by midseason. Wade Wilson was benched during the fifth game and Rich Gannon, who had filled in when Wilson was injured in 1990, started the last 11 games, although many veterans thought number three quarterback Sean Salisbury should have been given a chance. Guard Randall McDaniel, tight end Steve Jordan, and defensive tackle Henry Thomas were the team's only Pro Bowl selections, compared to eight who had made the team just two seasons earlier.

Jerry Burns resigned after the season, and it was obvious that some changes would have to be made for the team to get back into the playoffs.

A New Sheriff in Town

DENNIS GREEN RESTORES WINNING WAYS

THE WHOLE VIKINGS ORGANIZATION WAS IN DISARRAY AFTER THE 1991 season. The team had no coach, the owners had engaged in a very public feud for over five years, and many of the players were angry and dissatisfied with their salaries or playing roles. The man with the responsibility for orchestrating the changes needed to restore the franchise was Roger Headrick, a career corporate executive—with no experience running a sports organization of any kind—who had once been the Chief Financial Officer at Pillsbury.

Headrick was originally brought into the Vikings ownership group in 1989 by his neighbor, Mike Lynn, to help engineer financing to purchase the shares of the H. P. Skoglund family. This consolidated two-thirds of Vikings voting stock into a single entity—out of the clutches of Pohlad and Jacobs—that was a virtual who's who of Minneapolis society: Wheelock Whitney, Jaye Dyer, Jim Binger, Betty McMillan, Bud Grossman, Skip Maas, Carol Sperry, and John Skoglund, in addition to Headrick and Lynn. (Six of the 10 belonged to the exclusive Woodhill Country Club in Wayzata.)

Headrick became the acting general manager when Lynn—who retained a role as executive vice president with the team—stepped down to lead the WLAF, and on October 29, 1991, over the objections of Jacobs and Pohlad, the board of directors selected him, by a 6–3 vote, to become the new team president, effective January 1, 1991.

The local media was not comfortable with the little-known Headrick, a self-confessed "corporate-suit guy" with no football experience, and wondered how he could help the Vikings. They gave him mixed reviews when the 1991 Vikings improved from 6–10 to 8–8.

The team ownership soap opera seemed to come to an end in December 1991 when Irwin Jacobs and Carl Pohlad sold their stock back to the Vikings. The sales agreement ended the court battles that had been going nonstop since 1985. In February 1992 Mike Lynn sold his stock back to the team. The team's ownership group now had 10 members with equal shares.

St. Paul Pioneer Press, December 17, 1991

VIKINGS TO BUY OUT POHLAD, JACOBS

Ray Richardson, Bob Sansevere, and Charley Walters

Irwin Jacobs and Carl Pohlad have agreed to sell their interest in the Minnesota Vikings to a group of investors led by executive vice president Mike Lynn, the team announced late Monday.

The agreement would end a longstanding ownership fight between the two Minneapolis businessmen and a group of controlling shareholders aligned with Lynn.

"The agreement provides that upon closing of the purchase there will be a complete dismissal of all litigation and a complete release of all claims by all parties," Vikings spokesman Merrill Swanson said.

KSTP-TV reported that Lynn's group paid $52 million for Jacobs's and Pohlad's share of the team.

Jaye Dyer, a part-owner, director and secretary-treasurer of the Vikings, and a member of Lynn's faction, said the deal was consummated at a board of directors meeting Monday night.

"There's not much I can say because there is a confidentiality agreement and stuff," Dyer said. "I wouldn't want to speculate on their [Jacobs's and Pohlad's] reasoning why it happened. Everybody agrees that it's a good thing and everything was done fair and amiably.

"It had to go one way or the other."

The sale will accomplish what courts and NFL commissioners could not. It will put an end to an often bitter ownership dispute that had Lynn and his allies on one side and Jacobs and Pohlad on the other. Former NFL commissioner Pete Rozelle and current league boss Paul Tagliabue attempted to help resolve the dispute, but with no success.

For the last several years, Jacobs and Pohlad have used the courts to try to take control of the Vikings from Lynn. Their dispute with Lynn goes back half a decade, when Jacobs and Pohlad purchased one-third of the team's voting stock from Max Winter, one of the franchise's founders.

Lynn and the holders of the other two-thirds of the voting stock, John Skoglund and the Bill Boyer estate, tried to prevent the sale to Jacobs and Pohlad by claiming in a highly publicized court case that they had the right of first refusal of Winter's stock. A Hennepin County District Court judge, however, sided with Jacobs and Pohlad and allowed the sale to go through.

After getting a foot in the boardroom door, Jacobs and Pohlad purchased significant amounts of non-voting stock, enough to give them more than half of the franchise's total stock. Their goal was to have the courts recognize them as the team's majority owners because they held so much of the overall stock.

Ever since Jacobs and Pohlad became involved as owners, there seems to have been a lawsuit pending. Jacobs has made no secret of his dislike for Lynn and has attempted several times to have him ousted. Lynn, however, strengthened his power base by setting up a trust that gave him control over two-thirds of the voting stock. He brought in other investors such as Wheelock Whitney, Dyer and team president Roger Headrick to buy up parcels of the voting stock he controlled. Most of the Boyer stock was divided up among the new owners.

"It was just one of those situations that couldn't go on," Pohlad said. "I'm not happy to be out, but it can't go on like this. It was either them or us."

Jacobs was in Boston on Monday night on business and was unavailable for comment. He is expected to return to the Twin Cities today.

A trial to decide the ownership dispute probably would have been scheduled for some time in 1992, but no date had been set.

Lynn's group includes Dyer, Whitney, Headrick, Jim Binger, Bud Grossman, Betty McMillian, Skip Maas, Carol Sperry, and Skoglund.

Will this make the Vikings' product on the field better?

"I sure hope so, but there's a long distance between the two," Dyer said.

Headrick said he expected final details of the settlement to be completed within 90 days.

Headrick's first big test on the field came when coach Jerry Burns resigned, as expected, after the 1991 season. Burns pushed for Tom Moore, his offensive coordinator, as his successor, while some board members favored Notre Dame coach Lou Holtz, who made many friends when he coached at the University of Minnesota in 1984 and 1985. Pete Carroll, the New York Jets defensive coordinator and a former Vikings assistant, was another popular choice.

Headrick irritated the local media by conducting the search for the new coach in secrecy, but he got the job done quickly. Headrick introduced his new coach, Dennis Green, at a news conference at Vikings headquarters

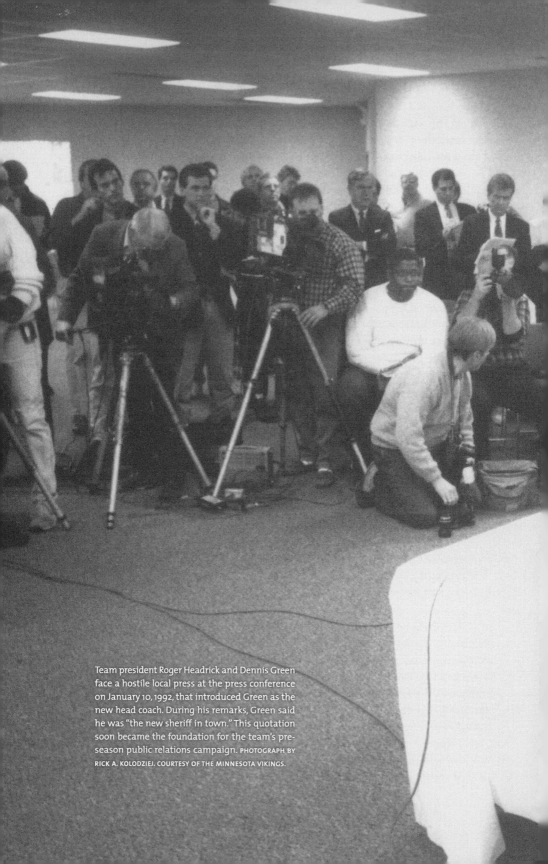

Team president Roger Headrick and Dennis Green face a hostile local press at the press conference on January 10, 1992, that introduced Green as the new head coach. During his remarks, Green said he was "the new sheriff in town." This quotation soon became the foundation for the team's pre-season public relations campaign. PHOTOGRAPH BY RICK A. KOLODZIEJ. COURTESY OF THE MINNESOTA VIKINGS.

on Friday, January 10, 1992. Headrick said Green, who became only the second African American head coach in the NFL, had been chosen because of his head coaching experience at Northwestern and Stanford, his experience as an assistant coach under legendary 49ers coach Bill Walsh, and because, as an outsider, he would not be bound by the past. Headrick and Green were given a severe grilling by the media assembled for the press conference. Green wrote about his initial reactions in his biography, published in 1997.

"GOING TO WAR," FROM *DENNIS GREEN: NO ROOM FOR CRYBABIES* (1997)

Dennis Green with Gene McGivern

For the first time in 25 years, when Bud Grant was lured down from Canada, the Minnesota Vikings hired somebody outside the organization as head football coach. This time it was a guy with a San Francisco 49ers flavor who wasn't afraid to make changes. A lot of people weren't taking it very well.

I was introduced at a Friday afternoon press conference at the cafeteria of our Winter Park facility. The room was packed. Roger [Headrick, president of the Vikings] and I took our seats in front of the team banner. I found it odd that very few if any owners were in attendance. They underestimated Roger.

I made brief comments about how excited I was to be the head coach. I had an appreciation for the National Football Conference having been in the system with the San Francisco 49ers. I mentioned the fact that the 49ers had won many Super Bowl championships. My hope was to bring a Super Bowl championship to the state of Minnesota. I spoke of what I feel is my aggressive and take-charge style and goal to build a great offensive tradition to match the past Minnesota defensive tradition.

The questioning turned nasty. The dean of Twin Cities columnists asked me, "Just when DID you accept the job?"

"Well, I am here now, and it shouldn't matter when it was finalized."

"Oh, it does," the columnist responded, "because Roger Headrick lied to me." The columnist went into a tirade on live radio, and the footage was played for TV, all because he wanted his close, personal friend Pete Carroll to get the job.

It was a short honeymoon for Dennis Green and the Minnesota media. I think I set some sort of professional sports record—I was getting ripped during the first few minutes of my initial press conference. Even though my background and proven record of success said otherwise, it looked like I would have to prove myself to certain people all over. It didn't set a very good tone for my relations with the media in Minnesota.

I sometimes wonder if my cool reception had to do with being a black man. I had a newspaper write that the only reason I got the job was because I was African American. There were nine NFL head coaching jobs open in 1992—apparently no African American should have gotten any of those jobs. Others suggested I got the job because the commissioner pressured Roger Headrick to hire me. Nothing could be further from the truth. Such stories were a total insult, and only a true bigot would come up with ideas like that. Since 1992, there had been 31 NFL head coaching jobs open, and only three went to African Americans. So much for NFL pressure.

An African American was not the head coach when the Vikings failed in the past. Favorites in three of the four Super Bowl games, they were outscored a combined 95–20 [it was actually 95–34—ED.] and never won the championship. Some believed that if Bud Grant couldn't go to the Super Bowl and win, then no African American could.

Minnesota has been rated one of the best places in the nation to live—if you are white. The Institute on Race and Poverty, a McKnight Foundation [the IRP is actually part of the University of Minnesota Law School—ED.], funded a national study that painted a different picture for African Americans. Subtle or blatant criticism implies that a black person needs permission to be ambitious or to seek top-level jobs. I didn't understand that. I was a citizen of the United States of America; I had the same rights and opportunities as anyone else. I should be appreciated for having the same ambitions as anyone else.

I wasn't afraid to prove myself, but I was surprised that in those first few months, some didn't even want to give me a chance to succeed. There were comments that I was a poor choice, and I was compared to Les Steckel, who was fired in 1984 after his first and only season resulted in just three victories. One reporter said I would not even match Steckel's three victories. I ignored such criticism and went to work.

One day during spring mini-camp, I watched as the players finished their stretching exercises, broke down for group drills, and jogged leisurely to their respective fields. I blew my whistle and I called them back. "From now on, all players will run from drill to drill," I said. I made the players start practice over. The next day a Viking player was quoted in the newspaper that I was "a college coach with a lot of stupid, rah-rah ideas." It didn't surprise me. Some tried to put me in the same mold as Steckel, who was labeled as more of a Marine drill instructor than a football coach in his short career in Minnesota, and said my coaching career here would be just as disastrous. It doesn't take very long to figure out what happened to those players—they weren't on the new team. I wouldn't tolerate crybabies on the team.

As for being a "rah-rah college guy," numerous NFL players come from my Northwestern and Stanford teams. My background with the San Francisco 49ers as an assistant coach was with a team that had won four Super Bowl championships, four more than the Minnesota Vikings' all-time total. The San Francisco 49ers also beat the Vikings five times in a row.

I didn't come to Minnesota to be intimidated by some people with their own agendas. I was a 42-year-old coach in his first NFL head coaching job. I was not going to follow old patterns or stereotypes. I wasn't trying to sound arrogant. I didn't underestimate my challenge.

My emphasis was two-fold. One, football was a business and we ought to be good at it. Two, we should be willing to work and enjoy what we do. Ideally, the two should go hand in hand. To turn a losing situation around, you have to start with a thorough and honest assessment of what it is you are inheriting. I spent a lot of time studying the roster and looking for the keepers.

The Vikings were labeled underachievers. There were some terrific players on the team, such as guard Randall McDaniel and wide receiver Cris Carter. I was up-front when I took over the Vikings. I felt we were a team on the rise. But we could only reach our potential with a team concept. My objective was fewer stars, better chemistry and more victories.

The person in charge has to possess two things—a clear plan on how to rebuild, and the courage to make the plan work. The head coach established the daily routine, and sets the tempo. I planned to inaugurate the new rules on the first day of spring mini-camp.

New criteria like making players run from drill to drill and making them repeat their calisthenics were small things, but it would send a clear message. What was good enough before wasn't good enough anymore. It helped players understand that a thorough and honest assessment of team attitude was underway to separate the winners from the whiners.

●

During the press conference Green told the audience that "There's a new sheriff in town," emphasizing that things would be different in the locker room and on the practice field. But he also said that the Vikings had a lot of talent. "The thing I want to do," he said, "is to bring some strong leadership to this team . . . This is not a team that has a 2–14 record."

The Vikings got pushed out of the headlines for the next couple of months by Super Bowl XXVI and the 1992 NCAA Final Four, both played in the Metrodome. It had been a remarkable year—sports-wise, anyway—for the Twin Cities. The St. Paul Civic Center had hosted the 1991 NCAA Hockey Frozen Four, the North Stars made it to the 1991 Stanley Cup Finals (losing to the Pittsburgh Penguins), Hazeltine hosted the 1991 USGA Open, and then in October the Minnesota Twins won their second World Series title, beating the Atlanta Braves in a seventh-game thriller in the Metrodome.

One of the least-surprising changes was Herschel Walker's release in May 1992. The 30-year-old running back was paid $1.7 million in 1991 in a one-year deal, but the team never got the production from him they had envisioned when they traded for him. The Vikings were a 21–23 team with Walker in the lineup. Coach Burns had been frustrated, Vikings fans were unhappy, and the local sports writers were unmerciful. Walker responded with a boycott of the local media in 1991. When attempts to trade him came up empty, Walker was given his unconditional release—leaving the team with absolutely nothing to show for the 1989 trade. (Walker soon signed a two-year contract with the Philadelphia Eagles. He rushed for 1,070 yards in 1992, but then fell to 746 and 528 in the next two seasons.)

Later that summer the Vikings' public relations department seized on Green's "sheriff" quotation and built an advertising campaign around a new "get-tough" policy adopted by the team.

Minneapolis Star Tribune, July 10, 1992
MOST FANS ENJOY VIKINGS' GET-TOUGH ADS
ONLY 30 PERCENT SAY THEY'RE TOO HARSH
Dennis Bracken

Apparently most Vikings fans don't think that last year's team had its head screwed on very straight. And fans don't mind a few laughs at the team's expense, especially if the humor involves former Vikings stars such as Keith Millard and Herschel Walker.

That's the logical conclusion to be drawn from responses to the *Star Tribune* Sports Line, which asked fans their opinion of the Vikings' new "get tough" television commercials. Of 319 respondents in the purely unscientific poll, 69.6 percent (222) said they liked the commercials, 30.4 percent (97) disliked them.

The two television ads, produced by Minneapolis' Bozell Advertising, combine criticism of last year's effort with humor. In the first ad, a receptionist informs callers that "Mr. Walker" and "Mr. Millard" are no longer Vikings. The ad closes with the receptionist telling a third caller, "No, we booted his butt, too."

In the other ad, an actor portraying new coach Dennis Green grabs a player's helmet and twists it in a circular fashion. The theme of this ad is that last year's Vikings didn't have their heads screwed on straight, but this year's team will.

Vikings vice president Jeff Diamond expressed satisfaction with the poll results, saying the intent of the ads was to convey the message that

1992 represents a new era "in an honest and humorous way . . . [70 percent] sounds like a ringing endorsement, since most politicians win with almost 52 percent of the vote."

What has to worry Vikings officials is the level of fan frustration that is evident in the responses. An article earlier this week suggested several Vikings players were embarrassed by the ads, but most fans were unsympathetic.

"I don't know why some current Vikings are embarrassed about a 30-second ad after having 3½-hour embarrassments every week on Sunday," said Ken Payet.

Said Sue Nichols of Buffalo: "I don't think the Vikings should complain about the ad because it's the only entertainment they've provided us for the last few years."

Diamond said the real purpose of the ads was to inform fans that tickets are available. Some fans said that fact alone should cause consternation for an organization that once routinely sold out every game.

"I think it shows exactly how far this team has fallen from its potential," said David Osberg of New Hope. "That's what I think is really embarrassing."

As for poking fun at departed former players Walker and Millard, some fans expressed hope the list of former Vikings might grow larger. "If there are any regrets in regards to the television commercials, it was the fact that they weren't also able to use the names of Chris Doleman and Joey Browner as having left the team," said Joe Schuth of Eden Prairie.

Fans who disliked the commercials generally felt the ads to be too harsh. "I agree with the players," said Darlene Pfahning of Farmington. "I think the ads are embarrassing and they're degrading. I think the Vikings could find something to make an appeal, not something to criticize players that are gone. If I were some of the players mentioned, I'd be on the phone to my lawyer."

Then there were the fans who didn't like the ads, but don't much care for the Vikings' recent efforts, either.

"I think the Vikings' promotional ads are terrible," said John Michael Anderson of Thief River Falls. "It's going to take more than cute promos to get me back as a fan. I once picked a fight with a good friend for criticizing Fran Tarkenton, and I wouldn't take phone calls during Vikings games. I mean, I was a fanatic fan. Now I'd rather watch the Home Shopping Network. It's going to take strong actions on the field and in the front office to get me to buy another Vikings ticket."

Said James Floan of Maple Grove: "I dislike the ads, the reason being that it gives me a scary resemblance to the Les Steckel era. I hope we're not headed back to that."

The Vikings had a sensational undefeated preseason under Green, outscoring four opponents 140–6 and looking nothing like the dispirited team that had limped to the finish in 1991. The "official" start of the era was also impressive—a season-opening 23–20 overtime win over arch-rival Green Bay at Lambeau Field.

The Vikings lost their next game to the Detroit Lions, but then ran off four consecutive victories. At the end of November they were 9–3, and a comfortable three games ahead of the 6–6 Packers.

Newsweek, November 23, 1992

IS IT EASY BEING GREEN?
A ROOKIE COACH PUTS THE VIKINGS BACK ON TOP

Frank Deford

The football coach is a hallowed American figure, by turns martinet and kindly godfather, the original exemplar of tough love. Uncle Sam in cleats. There used to be a bandleader on the radio named Horace Heidt, who would conclude every show with this sappy all-American aphorism: "It is better to build boys than to mend men"—and any of us who ever knew a football coach understood they were the prime ones in the crucial American boy-building business. Naturally, it was a football coach who first told a little baby-faced orphan in Harrisburg, Pennsylvania, named Dennis Green that he might actually go to college.

That precious image of The Coach remains with every built boy who grows up to watch *Monday Night Football*. But coaching football in the big time is a different thing altogether. To succeed, a Coach Chips must transmogrify himself into some sort of Perotian, Iacoccan-type: organizing, administering, media-ing. Football coaches are not like baseball managers, who keep wearing uniforms, just like their kid players, spit often and reside in the clubhouse; nor are they like basketball coaches, scrubbed, sartorial idols, the anchormen of sport. "What I miss the most is not being able to coach anymore," Dennis Green, 43, the new head coach of the Minnesota Vikings, says wistfully.

Coaching the actual game of football isn't even done any longer by people known as coaches. Coaching falls to men called coordinators. "A head coach has so many other things to take care of that if I tried to do the coaching, the offense and defense would have to slow down just to let me catch up," Coach Green says. So, as he lumbers up and down the sidelines, ursine, wired into the coordinators, he can retain only veto power . . . if he's quick. "Like this Sunday, there's a third-and-one on the 35. Jack [Burns, the offensive coordinator] tells me, 'Denny, we want to go for it. We'll try a play-action pass here, but if that doesn't work, we'll run on fourth.' So I say, 'OK,' and then I switch to my other line and tell Tony [Dungy, the defensive coordinator] to look out, we might be leaving his guys with bad field position, and then I tell special teams that we won't be needing them to kick. Then I watch."

If a head coach isn't secure in ceding such authority, then he cannot succeed. Yet it is his singular burden that he alone must set the team tone. "The first thing I told everyone here is hey, we're all on this ship together, and there better not be any son of a bitch getting on board with a pickax and a life preserver looking to break out by himself if things get tough. The only way a football team can work is everybody has to count on everybody else. Easy. But what I emphasize is that you have to come to accept this unconsciously. You can't worry about the man next to you. That's not your responsibility. You have to trust my evaluation for that. That's my responsibility."

"LOOK SQUAD"

Notwithstanding, Green does manage to indulge himself and coach a little, still. "I run the Look Squad when we practice during the week against the starters."

Coach Dennis Green holds up a sheet of plays for the scrubs during practice. He liked to coach the "Look Team," as he called them, against the starting team in practice. PHOTOGRAPH BY RICK A. KOLODZIEJ. COURTESY OF THE MINNESOTA VIKINGS.

"You coach the scrubs?"

A scowl. "Not the scrubs. I said: the Look Squad."

"Denny, a lot of people don't know what a Look Squad is. Can we live with 'reserves'?"

The scowl softens. "Well, all right. But it's important for me to coach the re . . . the Look Squad, because"—here he shakes a meaty finger for considerable emphasis—"it tells everybody that if the head man is coaching those guys, then there's no job in this organization that isn't important."

That's a most uncoachy thing to hear from a big-time coach, but it may be explained by the fact that Dennis Green recognizes better than other NFL coaches what it's like to be restricted to the fringes, limited in the reasonable dreams. All the time he was toiling as an assistant, developing a full, coherent coaching philosophy, he could never be certain that he could ever apply what he was constructing except, perhaps, to some Look Squad on somebody else's team somewhere. For Green is a black man, and until he was hired by the Vikings this year, no professional franchise had ever, in the history of the sport, gone out and sought the best head coach, and then declared that that man just happened to be an African American.

In days of yore, the Minnesota Vikings owned a reputation that would have pleased their stout Norsemen namesakes, for the Vikes were no-excuse brutes pounding the other NFL softies into their tundra. In the last decade, that noble reputation was turned upside down. Minnesota moved into a dome, and the Vikings became a bunch of climate-controlled prima donnas. There was racial bickering and general disgruntlement. "I guess they hired me because they were desperate," Green says. He shrugs. "But why not? Northwestern hired me because they were desperate, and so did Stanford." At Northwestern, in fact, in 1981, when Green accepted his first head position, succeeding a man who had gone 1–31–1, he actually had to declare: "I am not a wacko."

EXECUTIVE POSITION

Rather, he was simply black. Today, with Green gone to the pros, not a single major college football program is run by an African American. At least Green is preceded by Art Shell of the Los Angeles Raiders. But Shell was such an insider, with the Raider organization for two decades, that even blacks in the football community refer to him as an asterisk hire. As with general managers, college athletic directors might accept blacks to coach divertissements, such as basketball or track, but football is an executive position. A pro-football staff is larger than an entire basketball squad, and, as we know, backbones are formed in football. Football is serious, and therefore coaching football is best trusted to someone like, well—someone white, like the man doing the hiring.

"Whatever happened," Green says, "I always thought of myself as a leader. I believed that I could be a head coach, for anybody. You know, the philosophy is still the same, wherever you are. Sure, the atmosphere changes relative to the group you're in. But the principles of leadership remain constant."

And so, too, do the factors determining the choice of football leadership. It takes a confluence of rare, fortuitous circumstances. In Minnesota, Green got the call not only because the team was falling apart, but because the internal turmoil had thrown up a club president who was, in the eyes of the dubious football establishment, as lacking in the necessities as, say, any black coach. Although Roger Headrick had been an eminently successful financial executive, he was a patrician, with no experience inside the sideline stripes, and it was widely assumed that he was keeping the president's seat warm until a quote real football man unquote could be located. However, instead of looking through the usual pigskin ant tunnels, Headrick "applied the same sort of process as I did when I was seeking to find a manager at Pillsbury." This careful, deductive search produced one candidate who had just finished building Stanford back to an 8–4 season. And then Headrick met Green, and was terribly surprised at what he saw. "I expected him to be much taller," he says.

Green is not, in fact, a particularly prepossessing figure. He features a classic windbreaker ensemble, with turquoise jewelry and a stocky lineman's build (actually, he was a halfback at Iowa). Instead, Green is merely self-evident, at once unambiguous and full of fun, a rare combination that will take you a long way in football. A 7–2 record will take you the rest of the way. As the Vikings have moved into first place in the Central Division of the NFC, the Twin Cities have fallen utterly in the new coach's thrall. The *Minneapolis Star Tribune* gushed last week: "The Vikings believe everything that Green says and do everything he tells them to."

Green's speedy construction of this good Viking ship lollipop was based as much on subtraction as on addition. Very quickly, he eighty-sixed four of the brightest established heroes on the team—most particularly Hershel Walker, the unsociable running back who had been [obtained in a trade] that had gutted the team two years before. Jettisoning the four veterans not only moved four keen young players up, but it also called out an audible clearly to every other slacker on the desultory '91 Vikes. Green then brought in a new offense from the Redskins, and picked up a bunch of yeomen castaways. And left this way, with the second oldest roster in the league, the Dennis Green Vikings throw off resonances of the George Allen Redskins—those irreverent '70s outfits that captivated the corporate NFL with a bunch of grizzled old players producing for an original of a coach.

As has been the case in basketball for years, one line of coldly pragmatic reasoning says that hiring a black coach makes good sense simply because a vast majority of the athletes are black. In fact, as has also been proved in basketball, if things sour, black players will quit on a black coach every bit as quickly as they will on a white one. Dungy even reveals the ironic little secret that "it was some of the black guys around here who were the last ones to come around to Denny's way of doing things."

As for Green, he is himself already bored with all this first-black stuff. He's had to wear that jacket again and again, as he's found new and higher purchase in his profession. He holds out his turquoise-garnished hands. "Yes, yes, I know I'm a trailblazer," the coach of the Look Squad says. "I know all that. But I also know I've never had to apply for a job yet." The question remains, then, whether Green's success will finally force athletic directors and general managers to solicit applications from other black coaches.

The Vikings stumbled in December, losing two in a row, but clinched the Central Division championship with a tough 6–3 victory over the Steelers in Pittsburgh in game 15. The final game was at home against the resurgent Green Bay Packers, who had won six games in a row and needed a win to clinch a wild card playoff spot. The Packers had not been in a non-strike playoff—they made the 16-team playoffs set up after the 57-day players' strike of 1982—since 1972, and their play under new coach Mike Holmgren and new starting quarterback Bret Favre had excited and re-energized Wisconsin football fans. Strangely, the game didn't sell out until the last minute, and not until the NFL waived the 72-hour rule to sell tickets to prevent a local TV blackout. Consequently, there were many tickets available for green-and-gold-clad Packer backers.

With nothing to gain, the Vikings dashed Packer hopes with a convincing 27–7 win, to finish with an 11–5 record. Sean Salisbury, who had taken over at quarterback from Rich Gannon, had his best day in four starts. He had won a Grey Cup championship with the Winnipeg Blue Bombers in 1988, but sat on the bench without getting a snap during the 1990 and 1991 seasons as the Vikings' number three quarterback.

Minneapolis Star Tribune, December 28, 1992
VIKINGS SEND MESSAGE: PACK IT IN
A 27–7 ROMP ENDS PACKERS' PLAYOFF RUN
Jim Souhan
It was nothing more than an exhibition for the Vikings, a Pro(volone) Bowl to entertain Green Bay's cheese-adorned fans, unless you believed all that talk of momentum and mental edges, of purple pride and Packer prejudice.

The Vikings evidently did, because what they exhibited Sunday was power football, offensive diversity and raw ambition.

With their playoff spot secure, on a day they could have treated as an extended holiday, the Vikings bludgeoned a Packers team desperate for a victory and its first non-strike playoff berth since 1972, 27–7, before 61,461 at the Metrodome.

They set season bests by holding the Packers to 29 yards rushing and gaining 477 total yards, breaking the Packers' six-game winning streak and foiling Green Bay's playoff hopes.

The Vikings (11–5) will play a first-round playoff at the Metrodome 11:30 A.M. on Saturday against the Washington Redskins (9–7), who in their last two visits to the Dome beat the Bills 37–24 in the Super Bowl, and the Vikings 15–13 in November. The Packers (9–7), who needed a victory to make the playoffs and return to the Metrodome next week, finished a remarkable, if unfulfilled, season.

"I think our guys were a little ticked off because everybody, from Mike Ditka on down, seemed to believe that Green Bay had the best team in the division and we had something to prove," said Vikings defensive coordinator Tony Dungy, who was referring to Bears coach Ditka's declaration that the Packers were the division's best team. "We didn't want to wind up tied at 10–6 and have them saying we just won with the tiebreaker, and that they had won seven in a row and what they would have done in the playoffs. We wanted to make it clear that we were the champs."

Now, they get to face the real champs. Strangely, the Vikings will be the team entering Saturday's game with the more recently celebrated former Pac-10 quarterback. Yesterday, former USC product Sean Salisbury gave his old friend Mark Rypien, last year's Super Bowl MVP and a University of Washington alum, a reminder of what big-time quarterbacking looks like.

In his fourth NFL start, Salisbury completed 20 of 33 passes for a career-high 292 yards. More important, he ran the offense the way offensive coordinator Jack Burns wants it run. He threw to his backs and tight ends, found secondary receivers, tossed two touchdown passes, was sacked just once and didn't throw an interception.

But the Vikings might have won yesterday without a quarterback, their line play was so dominant.

"They sure kicked our ass," Packers linebacker Brian Noble said. When someone noted the Vikings were without injured receivers Cris Carter and Hassan Jones, he said: "You don't need weapons when you're jammin' the ball down somebody's throat."

That was the most apt description of the game. After the Packers took a 7–0 lead on their first drive when fullback Harry Sydney pounded in from the two, the Vikings responded immediately and often, scoring on their next three drives.

They tied the score with an eight-play, 79-yard drive that Salisbury ended with a perfectly feathered touch pass to the far corner of the end zone that tight end Steve Jordan took in over his shoulder.

On their next possession, the Vikings moved 51 yards in 12 plays, and after the Packers jumped offsides when Fuad Reveiz was lining up for a 51-yard field goal, Reveiz easily converted a 46-yarder to make it 10–7.

But it was a most unlikely hero—former Redskins tight end Mike Tice—who ensured the Redskins will revisit the Metrodome. On second-and-10 from the Packers' 34, Salisbury dropped back, was forced to roll left, away from his primary receivers, and found Tice standing along the sideline, waiting for a pigeon to land.

Tice, 6'7", easily caught Salisbury's high pass. Then Packers cornerback Vinnie Clark missed Tice completely—understandably misjudging Tice's, uh, speed.

"I was waiting for the safety to come over and knock my teeth out," Tice said. "When I saw he wasn't there, I knew it was going to be a cakewalk to get in, even with my exceptional 5.3 speed. Then I sat down and had some oxygen."

The Vikings added a field goal with a drive late in the first half, and Terry Allen dove over from the one in the third quarter to turn the game into a rout.

Allen rushed 20 times for 100 yards. That gave him 1,201 for the season, breaking Chuck Foreman's team record of 1,155 yards rushing in a season, which he set during a 14-game schedule in 1976.

But Allen's record was the stuff of asterisks compared to the one set by Packers receiver Sterling Sharpe. Sharpe caught six passes to give him 108 for the season, breaking Redskins receiver Art Monk's record of 106.

Sharpe set the record, but lost the war, managing just 45 yards against a defense intent on preventing big plays.

"We wanted to take him away," Dungy said. "He got his catches, but we didn't let him beat us."

Last week, when the Vikings clinched the division title, they celebrated quietly at Pittsburgh's Three Rivers Stadium. Yesterday, they anointed themselves champions by dumping ice water on coach Dennis Green.

"I thought it was significant that our guys didn't dump the Gatorade on me last week," Green said. "That shows that they had a fine focus on what we wanted to accomplish, that they realized the season wasn't over. They realized the Packers are our number one rival."

With his first regular season as Vikings coach behind him, Green still seems to think his job is far from finished.

"Anybody who thinks that there is a favorite in this race, they're mak-

Left tackle Gary Zimmerman was one of several players the Vikings signed out of the defunct United States Football League. He anchored the offensive line for seven years before becoming a free agent and signing with Denver. He was voted into the NFL Hall of Fame in 2008. PHOTOGRAPH COURTESY OF THE MINNESOTA VIKINGS.

ing a mistake," Green said. "It's wide open. Any of the six teams has a legitimate shot."

The last time the Vikings had swept Green Bay was 1986. The last time they had won their last two regular-season games was 1976. It was a regular season for milestones, even if the Vikings think they're weeks away from reflecting upon them.

"It's been a special season so far," Salisbury said. "But it's not over yet. If we can keep talking about this for another four weeks or so, that would be sweet."

●

The Vikings' hopes were dashed with a 24–7 loss to the Washington Redskins in the NFC wild card game at the Metrodome, however. The Vikings scored first, but were never in the game after that. Many fans who had dared to hope for a longer playoff run were unhappy, despite the team's big improvement from the disastrous 1990 and 1991 seasons. *Star Tribune* columnist Sid Hartman was critical of these "football geniuses," pointing out that the team had made dramatic improvements, going from thirteenth to fourth in scoring and from sixteenth to seventh in team defense. Six players were selected for the Pro Bowl—offensive linemen Randall McDaniel and Gary Zimmerman, defensive linemen Chris Doleman and Henry Thomas, and defensive backs Audray McMillan and Todd Scott. McDaniel, Doleman, and McMillan were first-team All Pro picks.

The 1993 season got off to a bad start when Terry Allen went down with a knee injury and did not play all year. Injuries to others also hampered the team. After a loss to the Dallas Cowboys on December 12, the team stood at 6–7. They had been within one game of .500 all year and the season's obituaries were already being written, but the Vikings went on a three-game winning streak to earn a wild card berth in the playoffs. However, the Vikings were eliminated by the New York Giants in a rough game on a cold and windy day at Giants Stadium, 17–10.

A blockbuster trade in April 1994 with Houston for 37-year-old quarterback Warren Moon—who was coming off six consecutive Pro Bowl appearances—tempered some of the criticism that had been aimed at Coach Green and team president Roger Headrick for the two first-round playoff losses. Moon was looked upon as a savior by Vikings fans, who once again started to dream about the Super Bowl. Many national writers agreed with them. Jeff Ryan set the stage for his interview of Moon in the December 1994 *Sport* magazine by recalling Mary Tyler Moore's arrival in Minneapolis:

"Warren Moon going from Houston to Minnesota? As soon as the trade was announced last April, the imagination began to run wild. Suddenly, it was possible to picture Moon driving to Minneapolis, à la Mary Tyler Moore, while a voice in the background sang, "Who can turn a world on with his spiral? Who can take a nothing game and suddenly make it seem worthwhile?'"

The 1994 season marked the end of the General Mills fund, created when the Metrodome was built in 1981 to help ensure that Vikings home games would be shown to local TV viewers. In the future, the Vikings, network television and local stations were forced to spend more effort to ensure that home games were sold out. Local blackouts were not only embarrassing, but also were costly in terms of lost advertising revenue.

Minneapolis Star Tribune, December 17, 1993
AHEAD FOR VIKINGS: BLACKOUTS
GENERAL MILLS FUND WILL SOON RUN DRY
Jerry Zgoda

That corporate umbrella protecting Vikings fans was, by design, supposed to ensure happy television viewing on Sunday afternoons for 20 years. But what do they say about the best-laid plans? They last, oh, maybe 12 years.

In a 1979 provision to the construction of the Metrodome, General Mills agreed to buy the unsold tickets for Vikings home games when at least 90 percent of them had been sold 72 hours before kickoff. The theory: People who couldn't afford tickets to the big, new publicly financed stadium could still watch games at home on TV. The original agreement with the Metropolitan Sports Facilities Commission said the "amount sufficient to assure the purchase of all such unsold tickets for a period of 20 years is $1,500,000."

Well, it's 1993 and that $1.5 million umbrella has dwindled to less than $100,000. The Vikings' final regular-season game against Kansas City on December 26 already is sold out, so fans need not worry this season. But with a playoff spot most unlikely, next season is a different story. Calculate one purchase of 6,000 tickets (about 10 percent of Metrodome capacity) at, say, $22 a ticket and the fund is bankrupt, with General Mills or any other local corporation showing little willingness to continue the program.

The outlook: Vikings fans should prepare to be like NFL fans elsewhere, some of whom rarely see their teams on home TV because they do not sell out.

The Vikings went 10–6 last season [1993] and won the NFC Central Division, yet four of their eight home games—Tampa Bay, Detroit, San Diego, New Orleans—required ticket buyouts. Next season, the Vikings almost certainly won't be riding the success of a division title. The likely result: Unhappy Vikings fans who want to see their team but don't want to pay $25 or $18 for the privilege. Since the General Mills agreement in 1979, only two regular-season games—one in 1989 and one in 1992—have been blacked out locally.

"The reality is that in a lot of markets fans almost never see their teams play home games," WCCO-TV sports director Kevin Smith said. "The day and age of local stations snatching up tickets is long gone."

●

The team started strong in 1994. Coming into their game on November 13 at New England they were 7–2 and riding a four-game winning streak. The Vikings dominated the first half, running up a 286–41 advantage in yards gained, to lead 20–3. Fox TV analyst Jerry Glanville practically guaranteed a berth for the Vikings in the Super Bowl.

The Patriots completely shut down the Vikings in the second half, however, and rallied to tie the game 20–20. New England won 26–20 in overtime. Quarterback Drew Bledsoe's 70 pass attempts and 45 completions were new NFL single-game records.

The shell-shocked Vikings lost their next two games to the New York Jets and Tampa Bay—two teams who ultimately finished with 6–10 records—but then rallied to win three of their final four games to finish 10–6, good enough for first place in the division.

The Vikings drew the Chicago Bears in the NFC wild card round. They had beaten the Bears twice during the season, by scores of 44–14 and 33–27. On this day, though, St. Paul native Steve Walsh quarterbacked the Bears to a 35–18 victory. Walsh, a Cretin High School graduate, led the University of Miami to the NCAA national title in 1987, but had been a journeyman in the NFL for four seasons with Dallas and New Orleans. National TV cameras were often trained on Walsh's family in the stands during the game.

St. Paul Pioneer Press, January 2, 1995

WALSH SAVORS PLAYOFF SUCCESS

Mike Augustin

Steve Walsh's visit with his family and friends from St. Paul was shorter Sunday than it was one month ago, when he was last in town with the Chicago Bears.

It was also much sweeter.

Walsh had only a few minutes in a Metrodome concourse for hugs, handshakes and family bonding after his outstanding performance led the Chicago Bears to a 35–18 playoff victory over the Vikings. Then the Bears' quarterback had to board the team bus for a trip to the airport and a flight back to Chicago. Something about another playoff game Saturday in San Francisco.

The kid from Cretin High School had left his hometown team behind, first-round playoff losers for the third consecutive year.

"This was very special, not just for me but for the whole team," Walsh said. "The Bears had not had much success recently against the Vikings, but we were still confident."

Minnesota had won six consecutive games in the rivalry, including an overtime victory on December 1, the only previous game Walsh started against the Vikings. That was on a Thursday, and Walsh was able to stay in the Twin Cities for a few days before rejoining his teammates. His hurry-up exit this time, however, was more pleasurable.

"We started slowly [turnovers on the first two possessions], something we do too often," Walsh said. "But we followed up with three solid quarters. I feel good about my role. I made all the right reads and all the right throws."

Walsh completed 15 of 23 passes for 221 yards and two touchdowns, with one interception. He settled into a rhythm as the Bears' offense kept the Vikings off-balance much of the day. Chicago had no turnovers after the two early ones, and Minnesota had four.

"Someone told me the last 31 playoff games were won by the team with the fewest turnovers," Bears coach Dave Wannstedt said. "I don't know if that's true, but I threw that out at the team before the game. Then the first two went against us, but we limited them to one field goal. After that, Steve did a great job."

Wannstedt said all last week he would not hesitate to pull Walsh, who had been struggling since the earlier loss to the Vikings. But it would take more than two early turnovers—only one of which could be attributed to the quarterback—and Wannstedt's patience was rewarded.

"Steve Walsh was under a lot of pressure this week, I mean a lot," Wannstedt said. "He knew he hadn't been playing like he can. This is his hometown. There were many factors.

"But he responded in a positive way. Steve is a winner. He knew he had to do some things to help his team win, and he went out and did them."

Walsh said talk of added pressure was "a lot of baloney." But he admitted to being on the spot.

"I knew I hadn't played well the last few weeks," he said. "But we opened up our package this week. You have to against these guys because they are so good against the rush. You can't pound it 40 times against them."

With the reins loosened on Wannstedt's close-to-the-vest offense, Walsh had a chance to make some big plays.

"Big plays are something you don't see very often from the Bears' offense," Walsh said. "But we know we always have the ability to make them. We hang in there by not having many penalties and by doing well on third down. Today we added the big play to that formula, and it worked out well."

The Bears converted four of five third downs in the first half as they established their attack. In the fourth quarter, Walsh accounted for a crucial fourth-down conversion, using a quick snap count to sneak three yards on fourth-and-inches. He hit Jeff Graham for a 21-yard touchdown on the next play.

The quarterback sneak was set up when Walsh, in the midst of loud crowd noise, turned to running back Raymont Harris before the snap as if to assure Harris of the count. The Vikings were lulled into thinking Harris was getting the ball, and didn't pinch on Walsh as he sneaked successfully to set up the TD that broke the game open.

"That was planned," Walsh said, breaking into a huge grin. "Guys from St. Paul are smarter than those from Minneapolis."

Statistically it had been a good year. Moon finished in the top three in most passing categories, Cris Carter led the league with 122 receptions (an NFL record that would be broken by Detroit's Herman Moore in 1995), Jake Reed was ninth with 85, and Terry Allen returned from his knee injury to gain 1,031 yards.

Coach Green was the first NFL coach to have his team make the playoffs in his first three years, but the local media and Vikings fans were unhappy about the three consecutive one-game playoff performances. In late January the *Minneapolis Star Tribune* published "Off the field, a grim game: Vikings' get-tough tactics cost team personnel, morale, results," a damning 4,200-word expose of Vikings' morale problems, based on interviews and research by reporters Selena Roberts, Curt Brown, and Paul McEnroe.

Neither Green nor general manager Roger Headrick would agree to an interview for the article. Green had often claimed that the media had it in for him, but columnist Pat Reusse defended his coworkers.

Minneapolis Star Tribune, January 31, 1995
BLAME FOR TEAM'S PROBLEMS LIES WITH GREEN, HEADRICK
DISCONTENT AMONG THE PLAYERS IS RAMPANT
Patrick Reusse
The Minnesota Vikings were the subject of 1,639 articles in the *Star Tribune* in 1994. There were only 19 days out of 365 in which they were not a subject in a *Star Tribune* article.

These articles concerned the organization's trade for quarterback Warren Moon, its successful use of extra draft choices, the annual bulletins from Mankato filled with optimism, and tributes to players Moon, Cris Carter, Jake Reed, Terry Allen, Randall McDaniel, John Randle, Jack Del Rio and rookies Todd Steussie and DeWayne Washington, to name a few.

Somewhere in those 1,639 articles, there were mentions of the impersonal manner in which the team ran off noble veterans such as Carl Lee, Tim Irwin and Steve Jordan. There also were articles on what was going wrong when the Vikings started to gasp, turning a 7–2 start and Super Bowl talk into a 10–7 finish that concluded with the playoff fiasco against Chicago.

The collapse caused Dennis Green to receive a modest amount of derision. Late in the season, Green said on his radio show that the media hated his guts and he shared that opinion of the media. Then, at season's end, Green said on his last TV show: "Just call me the battlin' coach. I'm not going to take any flak from players, fans and the media [in 1995]."

Green's expression of hostility toward the Minnesota media seemed to come from nowhere, since he had received volumes of praise—bound together, the pro-Green prose would have rivaled the Churchill memoirs in length—compared with several paragraphs of criticism during his tenure.

Down the season's stretch, reporters detected a strong undercurrent of discontent in the Vikings' locker room. Numerous players talked of incompetence on the coaching staff. And, the team president, Roger (Mr. Football) Headrick, and Green had operated the Vikings in a manner that made it seem as though they relished getting rid of people.

One of the fired assistant coaches said last summer: "The first conversation I ever had with Headrick, he told me, 'One of the things I do best is get rid of people.'"

Bob Hollway found that out when he was fired as a member of the football department. He has filed an age-discrimination suit. And, the settlement of another suit had been talked about in Vikings circles for more than a year. Headrick and the board of directors authorized a large settlement to a former front-office intern in order to stop a sexual-harassment claim against assistant coach Richard Solomon.

The *Star Tribune* decided to take an in-depth look at what was going on at Winter Park. Three reporters worked on the story.

Last Sunday, these reporters revealed that $150,000 had been paid to fend off the sexual-harassment claim, that Headrick had taken away Hollway's dignity and then his job, and that a low regard for Green's operation was widespread among both current and former players.

The current players chose anonymity, and for good reason. Green has sent players down the road for far less than public criticism of the team. Frank Cornish, who could have been helpful when the offensive line started to go in the tank down the stretch, was dumped at midseason because Green and company found him annoying.

The Vikings would like to have people believe that the current brouhaha is based strictly on the disenchantment of Dan Endy, a fired employee. The Vikings offered several non-denial denials to the news reports, and in those denials Endy has become the Disgruntled Former Employee.

Endy gave the affidavit in support of the intern's claim of sexual harassment by Solomon. The affidavit—never filed in court because the Vikings chose to settle the case—included some allegations Endy had heard concerning Green. Those allegations did not involve the woman who received the settlement.

The Vikings had paid a lot of money to get a confidentiality agreement from the intern and her lawyer. Members of the organization started to hyperventilate last week, when they learned that the *Star Tribune*'s investigation was going to cause the cover-up to come unglued.

Headrick went into a sulk and refused to respond to the questions from *Star Tribune* reporters. This newspaper's Vikings writer tracked down Headrick and confronted him on Saturday night in Miami. He refused to comment and said, several times: "I have no respect for you."

Headrick has seemed to take pride in firing front-office people. Green has dismissed veteran players with such disdain that a sequel to "North Dallas Forty" could be filmed here and titled "Eden Prairie Fifty-Three."

There has been such a revolving door on Green's staff that, at the end of this season, players at some positions were left feeling they had been coached by amateurs.

There was all of this, and there were age-discrimination complaints, and there was the $150,000 paid in an attempt to cover up a sexual-harassment claim. When that story finally surfaced in the wake of the *Star Tribune* investigation, the Vikings responded with a statement that read, in part:

"As an organization, we have a firm policy of protecting the privacy of the individual by maintaining strict confidentiality about internal personnel matters."

Yes, in the arrogant world that has been created at Winter Park in recent years, a $150,000 sexual-harassment settlement can be explained away as an internal matter.

Respect was Headrick's word to a reporter, and it leaves a question: How would he recognize it?

●

The controversies didn't stop during the 1995 season, when the team struggled to an 8–8 record and missed the playoffs for the first time in Green's tenure. The team was fourth in the league in scoring, but twenty-seventh (out of 30) in points allowed. Warren Moon started all 16 games, the first time a quarterback had done this for the team since 1979, and Cris Carter had another great year. His 122 catches matched his 1994 total, but fell one short of league leader Herman Moore of Detroit.

As the start of the 1996 season approached, off-field controversies were still dogging coach Dennis Green. For the third time he was being linked to sexual harassment. In September, KSTP-TV said it had obtained court documents containing allegations that Green had impregnated a woman in an extramarital affair, and then paid her to have an abortion. A Vikings employee was apparently the go-between man.

Green responded that he was prohibited from publicly discussing the claims by a Hennepin County Court confidentiality order. In a prepared written statement he said that he was seeking court approval to discuss the incidents with Minnesota Vikings owners.

Fortunately for Green, the Vikings won their first four games, and the controversy faded. The four wins were not easy, however. Quarterback Warren Moon sprained his ankle in the second quarter of the home opener against the Detroit Lions. Brad Johnson came in and threw a touchdown pass to Cris Carter with 1:06 left on the clock to win 17–13. Johnson started the next game against Atlanta—his first start after four years in which he had only thrown 73 passes as a backup—and was NFC Offensive Player of the Week after a 23–17 win. Moon came back the next week, but re-injured his ankle in a 15–13 loss to the Bears.

Green made Johnson his starter for the last six games of the season, and the team responded with four wins to finish 9–7 and earn a wild card playoff berth. Green and the front office rewarded Johnson with a new four-year, $15.5 million contract just prior to the last regular-season game with Green Bay, keeping him out of the postseason free-agent market, where he would have been a hot property. Although team president Headrick said no decisions had been made, it was obvious that the Vikings could not afford to keep Moon, who had signed a three-year, $15 million contract the previous year.

St. Paul Pioneer Press, December 22, 1996
VIKINGS FANS WILL PONY UP FOR JOHNSON
Bob Sansevere
The Two Great Myths about Vikings quarterback Brad Johnson are that he's a) just a kid and b) lucky.

Quarterback Brad Johnson twice took over for injured starters: for Warren Moon in 1996 and Daunte Culpepper in 2005. Between those two stints with the Vikings, he won a Super Bowl with Tampa Bay in 2002. PHOTOGRAPH BY RICK A. KOLODZIEJ. COURTESY OF THE MINNESOTA VIKINGS.

At 28, he is a year older than Green Bay quarterback Brett Favre. He's eight months older than Dallas Cowboys running back Emmitt Smith. And he's almost four years older than New England quarterback Drew Bledsoe.

Johnson just seems younger because he has been obscure for so long. Until this season, he was the backup quarterback nobody had heard much about. He became a Viking before Bill Clinton became President.

Johnson has been with the Vikings as long as coach Dennis Green, and longer than every other starter except Cris Carter, Jake Reed, Randall McDaniel and John Randle. Johnson has been understudy to Rich Gannon, Sean Salisbury, Jim McMahon and Warren Moon. And now he's richer than any of them.

Johnson signed a four-year contract worth $15.5 million Friday. With the scrawl of a pen, he increased his salary 10 times over.

Some would say he's lucky.

Johnson agrees. Sort of.

"The harder you work, the luckier you get," said Johnson, who leads the Vikings into Green Bay today for their regular-season finale against the Packers. "I just hope to get lucky."

The Vikings are lucky to have Johnson. He is a fresh squirt of air in a franchise that, over the past few years, has reeked of scandals and bickering among the owners.

A couple of seasons ago, the Vikings tried selling season tickets with an ad campaign that featured comedian Jonathan Winters. That turned out to be a swing and a miss. Jonathan Winters doesn't appeal to anyone born after the Spanish-American War. If the Vikings want to sell season tickets for next season, they should build a marketing strategy around Brad Johnson.

Him they can sell.

All the years Carl Pohlad has owned the Twins he has been a skinflint, but there were players on the field who deflected attention away from his parsimonious ways. For most of the past decade, when people thought of the Twins, they thought of Kirby Puckett and Kent Hrbek. Not Pohlad.

These past few NFL seasons, when people thought of the Vikings, it was Green and scandals and President Roger Headrick and the team's lousy management that came to mind.

That could change if the Vikings are smart enough to shove Brad Johnson in front of the ticket-buying public.

He's everything Minnesotans admire in their heroes. He has worked hard to get where he is. He doesn't brag or boast. He doesn't have a rap sheet. He says things that are, really, quite endearing. The morning he signed his deal, Johnson was asked during an interview on radio station KQRS-FM what he would do with his newfound wealth. He said he might buy a nicer shirt. And he wasn't joking. He meant it. How can you not root for a guy like that?

How can you not run out and spend a few hundred bucks for the chance to root for him in person?

The Vikings desperately need someone for fans to rally around. Whether Green returns or not, there will be discontent among the fans. Many Vikings fans could not bring themselves to buy tickets to games because they object to Green and his reputation, real or concocted, for scandalous behavior.

And if Lou Holtz became coach, fans wouldn't be setting up any vigil outside the Vikings' ticket office waiting for the doors to open. A large number of folks, including Headrick and Vikings players such as linebacker Jeff Brady, believe Holtz is strictly a college coach who doesn't belong in the National Football League. They don't believe his presence will help sell tickets.

Nor will Headrick and his fellow owners. Last week, Headrick went before the Metropolitan Sports Facilities Commission and, basically, claimed his team was impoverished. Well, whose fault is that?

Headrick wants at least $100 million of improvements made to the Metrodome. Or, he wants a new stadium. In the latest issue of *Sports Illustrated*, Headrick made a veiled threat to move the Vikings to Cleveland or Los Angeles if he doesn't get what he wants. Blackmail and extortion don't exactly make fans feel warm and fuzzy or put them in a ticket-buying mood.

About the only thing that could get fans to pony up for tickets is somebody fresh and new and likable, somebody talented who offers hope for the future of the franchise.

Somebody such as Brad Johnson.

●

The season ended on two sour notes, unfortunately, as the Packers, who were on their way a victory in Super Bowl XXXI, dumped the Vikings 38–10. Then the Vikings were soundly beaten by Dallas, 40–15, in an NFC wild card game.

Green was pilloried in the off-season by fans and the local media, angry over his 0–4 playoff record and the continuing off-field woes of players and administrative personnel. One bright spot was Brad Johnson, who was the white knight heading into training camp.

As expected, the Vikings released Warren Moon in February. For backup quarterback they signed Randall Cunningham, who had retired in 1995 after an 11-year career with the Philadelphia Eagles, and did not play in 1996.

The Vikings started the 1997 season with two wins, followed by two losses, but then launched into a six-game winning streak. Their 8–2 record put them in a tie with Green Bay and one game ahead of Tampa Bay in the tight Central Division race.

In the middle of this run Dennis Green's autobiography, *No Time for Crybabies*, hit the street. Obviously still angered by rumors that some owners had courted Lou Holtz to replace him at the Vikings, Green ended the book with a bizarre threat to sue the team unless they sold him 30 percent ownership of the team. It included a letter he said he could distribute at the Vikings' November 11, 1997, board of directors meeting, plus a draft lawsuit, as well as a stock purchase agreement.

FROM CHAPTER 19, "IF IT LASTS UNTIL TOMORROW," FROM *DENNIS GREEN: NO ROOM FOR CRYBABIES* (1997)

Dennis Green with Gene McGivern

Dear Directors:

I am purchasing the nine percent shares of the two individuals sitting in this room who contacted Lou Holtz, the former Notre Dame head coach, without authority last year and deliberately interfered with my ability to coach the team.

I will not single you out even though most of the people in this room know who I am talking about. Your solicitation of Lou Holtz was a major distraction on a local and national level. It caused harm to me and my coaches and players, as well as our families. This disrespect for my position as head football coach of the Minnesota Vikings hurt my football reputation and undermined my leadership capabilities.

As a career coach of 26 years, who can be expected to coach for another 15 years, these two board members may have damaged my future career opportunities. In other words, I AM BUYING OR SUING. My claims in damages are compensable under Minnesota's Tortious Interference law, separate and above the damages ordinarily available for such tortuous conduct, as specifically held in *Swaney v. Crawley*, 157 N. W. 910, 911 (Minn.1916). Please do not misunderstand or underestimate what I am saying. In my opinion, everyone in this room—including the other eight board members—can be held accountable and responsible for the actions of these two.

I look forward to your immediate response.

Sincerely,

Dennis Green

●

The uproar was instantaneous, with many calls for Green's firing. NFL Commissioner Paul Tagliabue talked separately by phone to Green and Vikings President Roger Headrick and told them to settle the dispute quickly and quietly—he imposed a gag order on both sides. Green, for his part, said he "was just thinking out loud" in the book, and sent a letter of regret to Tagliabue.

Pro Football Weekly, November 30, 1997

WARNINGS

CAN GREEN, THE EMBATTLED UNDERDOG, WEATHER CONTROVERSY FROM HIS BOOK?

Paula Parrish

Viking coach Dennis Green likes fighting out of corners, against the odds, uphill both ways, barefoot, backward and on sharpened fence posts, if possible.

THE EMBATTLED UNDERDOG

"It's never been a picnic around here," said Green, in the midst of his sixth Viking season. "It's always been a battle. I'm an underdog fighter. I've been coaching a long time, and a lot of people don't appreciate my style. But, wherever I've been, players want to play for me, and that's the bottom line."

Another bottom line is that the Vikings are winning, and it's hard to find fault with a team one game out of first place in the NFC Central, possibly the toughest division in the NFL.

But controversy has dogged Green's steps since he arrived in Minnesota prior to the 1992 season, and this year is no exception.

Last month Green stung the Vikings' ten-member board of directors/owners with the final chapter of his book, entitled *No Room for Crybabies*.

In the chapter, described by the author himself as a "bombshell," Green details a plan to sue the Vikings' board unless it allows him to purchase a 30 percent controlling interest in the team. Green threatened to sue on the grounds that his reputation and future job opportunities were harmed last season by two unnamed directors who Green believes, during a midseason slump, floated the name of former Notre Dame head coach Lou Holtz as his possible successor.

The astounded owners were peeved by Green's detailed plan, and his job security was openly questioned. Green responded by saying he was only "thinking out loud" in the book. NFL commissioner Paul Tagliabue stepped into the controversy, placing a gag order on both Green and the owners. He requested that Green issue a statement to defuse the situation.

Green did, stating he regretted the furor and assuring that "I have no intention of trying to force my way into the Vikings' ownership."

Just days later, the controversy was pushed aside to make way for another: News broke that the owners had secretly been shopping the team for months.

Winning is always a good thing. But winning in the wake of this recent breach with ownership is even more important, as far as Green's tenure is concerned.

Green's contract extends through the '98 season, for which he is slated to be paid $900,000.

But his job security, which rests in large part on this season's success and the Vikings turning around their 0–4 playoff record during his regime, has crossed the minds of players.

"I don't think we need to win the Super Bowl for Denny Green to stay here," Viking MLB Jeff Brady said. "I think a lot of people think we need to win in the playoffs for Green to stay here. I really don't feel that way.

"There are a lot of organizations every year that don't make the playoffs who would love to have a contending team year in and year out, like this team has been. I think all you can ask for, year in and year out, is to be a contender, to make that shot at the playoffs and roll the dice to get in the Super Bowl.

"For people to put that on top of him, there are a lot of coaches who haven't even gone to the playoffs."

Fierce loyalty to Green is inspired by his upfront approach, meticulous organizational skills and a mutual respect factor.

"We all respect Denny, and I think everyone enjoys playing for him," RB Robert Smith said. "From the people that I know who have been on different teams, they always talk about how organized it is here, and how we always know what is next, and what's coming, and what's expected of us. That would seem to be common sense, but I guess it isn't. I guess there are other teams around the league who aren't like that."

Green has repeatedly reiterated that, contractually, he is working in an unusual situation.

"I'm not really thinking about what's going to happen next year," Green said. "I'd love to keep coaching. I've coached for 26 years. But let's face it: [Next year] I'm basically working on the last year of my contract, and that doesn't happen very often.

"Of the 30 coaches in the league, I'm the only one whose contract expires after the '98 season. And that affects your players, and new players coming in. There's a lot to putting a good football team together. I just haven't seen it done very well with guys that are in the last year of their contract."

Several players who are free agents after this season, including WR Jake Reed and DT John Randle, will be making their decisions with Green's presence—or absence—in mind.

"Coach Green has been very good to me and very loyal, and I have a tremendous amount of respect for him," said WR Cris Carter, whose contract ends after the '98 season. "It's something I'll look at, and I know other guys will, too, like the guys who are free agents next year [including Reed, Randle, Smith and OLT Todd Steussie]. We all love playing for Denny. So it's going to be a difficult situation for management. That is something they have to think about."

The postseason could hold many headlines for the Vikings, including Green's status, a playoff run and a new owner or ownership group.

"As I've said to the team, 'Do all of us expect to be here next year?' No, it's not realistic," Green said. "We've got 53 players and 14 coaches. It doesn't happen that way in the NFL, and we all have to keep that in mind."

●

Meanwhile, things were not going well on the field. Brad Johnson sprained his ankle in the last minutes of a 23–21 loss to the New York Jets on November 23. Then, in a marquee Monday Night Football match-up in the Dome against the Green Bay Packers, Johnson was ineffective in a 27–11 loss. It turned out he had a herniated disc in his neck, and was sidelined for the year. Cunningham, just two weeks from arthroscopic surgery on an injured knee, started and lost the next two games, running the team's losing streak to five. What had once looked like a cinch playoff run came down to a must-win against the hapless Indianapolis Colts (3–12) to finish with a 9–7 record to ensure a wild card berth.

The Vikings responded with a 39–28 win. Cunningham threw four touchdown passes, although he did have three interceptions. Cris Carter caught three of the touchdown passes. He led the league with 13 touchdown passes and had more than 100 receptions for the fifth consecutive year. Robert Smith, whose injuries had limited him to seven starts in each of the previous two seasons, had his sixth 100-yard rushing day of the year. He finished with 1,266 yards, good for seventh in the league and a new Vikings record.

Green finally got his first playoff win when the Vikings scored 10 points in the final 90 seconds to beat the New York Giants 23–22 in an NFC wild card game in Giants Stadium, but the victory did nothing to soothe Green's relationship with Minnesota media.

In a pregame interview with ABC-TV reporter Lesley Visser, Green said he had proof that three columnists from the *Star Tribune* and *Pioneer Press* were working with an unnamed Vikings official to try to run him out of town. Green did not disclose his proof, however.

Visser said that both papers denied the allegations. Green refused to discuss the interview after the game. But he did gloat a bit about the victory, especially his decision to punt on fourth-and-seven from the Vikings' 40 with only four minutes remaining and trailing 22–13. Several Vikings players on the sidelines threw down their helmets in disgust when the team didn't go for a first down.

Newsday, December 28, 1977
EMBATTLED GREEN LAUGHS LAST
Bob Glauber

Minnesota Vikings coach Dennis Green's week began with a tirade against the local media for its incessant criticism of his 0–4 playoff record.

It escalated into his contention that three Minneapolis columnists recently conspired with a Vikings official to run the coach out of town.

And it ended with a defiant fist thrust into the snow-filled air of Giants Stadium after a breathtaking 23–22 comeback victory over the Giants.

"I feel great, but not because it's my first playoff win," said Green, who has reached the playoffs in five of his six seasons in Minneapolis. "A lot of guys that are tremendous coaches in this business have never been in the playoffs, whether it's assistant coaches or head coaches. It's great because it's a win, and it gives our guys a chance to continue playing. People will be talking about this game for a long time, and I can't think of a better place to do it than the number one city in America, New York City."

Green, who has been rumored to be on the coaching hot seat several times in the last three seasons, may have saved his job in the process. He became the target of intense criticism in October when he openly wondered in his autobiography what it would be like to own the Vikings. It was a foregone conclusion that he would be fired at the end of the season, considering the mutinous tenor of his remarks.

But now that he has finally won a playoff game, it may be more difficult for the Vikings to let him go. Especially in light of the team's unsettled ownership. The Vikings have been up for sale for several months, and a new owner could force Green out. But the NFL is attempting to broker a deal that would allow team president Roger Headrick, one of Green's staunchest supporters, to gain a 30 percent controlling interest in the Vikings.

Even so, the coach may have turned up the heat even more yesterday, when he told ABC television reporter Lesley Visser that he was told three Twin Cities columnists met with a Vikings official to outline a smear campaign against Green that would force him out.

After the game, Green did not name the columnists, nor the team official. When asked if the official was Headrick, he vehemently denied it was the team's president.

As for the game itself, Green was at his best, especially down the stretch. The key decision: Faced with a fourth-and-seven from the Vikings' 40 with four minutes left and the Vikings trailing 22–13, Green punted rather than go for it. Several Vikings players, most notably wideout Cris Carter, went ballistic on the sideline because Green didn't attempt to pick up the first down.

Defensive tackle John Randall, from tiny Texas A&M–Kingsville, was an inside force in the 1990s, earning first-team All Pro honors six consecutive years (1993–98). PHOTOGRAPH COURTESY OF THE MINNESOTA VIKINGS.

But Green was vindicated by what happened next. The Vikings stopped the Giants on three plays and forced them to punt from their 23 with 2:06 left.

Four plays later, Randall Cunningham hit Jake Reed for a 30-yard touchdown to pull the Vikings within 22–20.

The Vikings recovered the onside kick and then drove for the winning field goal with 10 seconds left.

"The worst mistake I could have made was not punting on fourth down," said Green, whose team will face the 49ers on Saturday in San Francisco. "I thought about it, but that's not the way I've developed the game of football. You have to know how to play the game, you have to know how to manage the clock and you have to make plays, and we did that. A head coach shows himself when he has to use timeouts properly, when he has to make decisions on field position, when he has to make decisions on blitzing and all those other things.

"Today you saw my stuff."

●

The *Star Tribune*'s Dan Barreiro didn't see Green's stuff—he said he had been incredibly lucky and compared him to Richard Nixon. The paper was flooded with letters criticizing Barreiro's strong words, prompting Lou Gelfand, the paper's reader representative, to draft a reply.

Minneapolis Star Tribune, January 4, 1998

IF A PAPER'S GOING TO HAVE SPORTS COLUMNISTS, IT CAN'T TELL THEM WHAT TO THINK

Lou Gelfand

Several hundred readers, many with passion and venom, attacked Dan Barreiro's column on last Sunday's sports cover that vilified Minnesota Vikings football coach Dennis Green, comparing him to "the last great paranoid leader, Richard Nixon."

Displayed near Barreiro's searing words was the news report of the Vikings' like-fiction finish that upset the New York Giants.

After quoting Green that "luck is when preparation meets opportunity," Barreiro wrote, "The guess here is that the coach got that one from inside the fortune cookie he used to clean the plate after a big helping of moo goo gai pan."

The message Barreiro conveyed was that the Vikings won a playoff game for the first time in six years in spite of Green, because New York "quite possibly is the worst division champion" in the league's history.

A sampling of the responses:

"The newspaper is not the place to be carrying on with a private vendetta." —Jackie Dohn.

". . . truly a blatant assault on the character of Green and reeks of underlying racism." —Israel Morrow.

"If we wish to read that type of personal diatribe we can purchase the *National Enquirer.*" —Toni and Tonette Gehrking.

Many callers insisted that the newspaper has a responsibility to support the hometown team. One said, "No wonder pro sports are in trouble in Minnesota. It's because of columnists like Barreiro."

Stewart Widdess, Vikings marketing vice president, lamented the placement of Barreiro's column near the game story.

"It was a disappointment at a time when the team pulled off a major upset. Barreiro could have written the column from home." He, too, blamed Barreiro for "a personal vendetta."

Barreiro's column ended with a comment on Green's charge on national TV that three Twin Cities sports columnists and a Vikings official, all unnamed, conspired to formulate a plan to force him to resign.

Barreiro wrote to me that his column "has never been intended as the last word, or the only opinion. Offering opinion occasionally means stepping on toes, and taking the heat for doing so. If I have difficulty with the manner in which a coach conducts himself—either by what he says or does—then I am going to consistently offer my opinion on that conduct. Sometimes in a more reasoned way, other times in a more biting or satirical way.

"But when a columnist observes an individual over time, and then develops a point of view about him, the columnist runs the risk of being accused of having a vendetta against that person. When, in fact, all that the columnist is doing is remaining consistent to his point of view—especially when the individual continues to behave in a way that tends to confirm the conclusion. The conspiracy theory is merely the latest example."

Comment: Whether Barreiro has the license to savage Green is not an issue. It is his duty to render opinion. Were newspaper managers to constrain his judgments, they would reduce him to a lackey.

The soundness of his judgment will be determined over time by the court of public opinion.

Surely, as the Vikings' Widdess said, positioning his column last Sunday on the cover near to a report of Minnesota's victory was not good judgment. What readers preferred on the cover was more insight and background on the Vikings' ability to score 10 points in the last 90 seconds of the game to win by one point.

The column that begs to be written is one challenging Green to name the three Twin Cities daily newspaper sports columnists he says conspired with a Vikings official to get rid of him.

There are seven such columnists, and by not naming the three he's indicted all of them. If Green speaks from knowledge, four innocent people have been maliciously fingered. In fairness to the four and their families, he should name the three he says committed what should be, if proven, career-ending bungles.

If this is a case of Green behaving in the manner of Sen. Joseph McCarthy, spinelessly injuring the reputations of innocent people, he should be exposed.

That the media have an obligation to support the hometown team, as many callers insisted, is nonsense. When the day arrives that the *Star Tribune* is the public relations arm of a business it covers, the newspaper will be a licking puppy, not a watchdog.

The playoff one-game winning streak ended the following week with a 38–22 loss at San Francisco. Cunningham threw for 331 yards and three touchdown passes, but his one interception was returned for a touchdown by Ken Norton Jr., giving the 49ers a 21–7 halftime lead, and San Francisco coasted home from there.

The Vikings ownership struggle heated up after the playoffs, and pushed Dennis Green's threat to sue the team off the radar screen. Minnesota football fans had been shocked back on October 29 when *Star Tribune* writer Don Banks broke the news in a page-one story that the Vikings had been secretly for sale since August.

It was no idle rumor—part-owner and Vikings board vice chairman Philip Maas told Banks that four potential buyers had already met with the team and that the board had received and rejected one bid for $150 million. The interested parties were from Los Angeles; Toronto; Birmingham, Alabama; and one other unidentified area, raising the specter of the team leaving Minnesota.

The Vikings ownership situation had slipped under the radar back in 1992 when the Pohlad/Jacobs sale had been completed and Mike Lynn sold his shares back to the team. That left the team with 10 equal partners as owners. In July 1991 NFL commissioner Paul Tagliabue reportedly had advised Lynn that the Vikings' ownership structure would have to come in line with NFL requirements before any sale would be approved. That would have required that one of the partners own at least 30 percent of the club's outstanding stock, but no mention of Tagliabue's demand was made when the sales were finally approved. In fact, general manager Roger Headrick claimed that the Vikings were permitted to "grandfather" that demand, since the team had always had multiple owners and had never had a single owner with a 30 percent interest in the voting stock.

The NFL never did like this situation, though, and in January 1997 forced the Vikings owners to sign an agreement guaranteeing that one of them would own at least 30 percent of the team. Tom Benson, owner of the New Orleans Saints and chairman of the NFL finance committee, told *Star Tribune* columnist Sid Hartman that "We have a league rule that must be lived up to. We expect this problem to be worked out at our March meeting." Vikings owners assumed they had until the end of the year to make the changes, but in April commissioner Tagliabue expedited the mandate to the end of June. By June, however, he backpedaled a bit, and put the issue on hold until the team's stadium issue was resolved, prompting *Pioneer Press* writer Tom Powers to wonder what the real deadline was.

St. Paul Pioneer Press, August 1, 1997
VIKINGS WON'T PRODUCE LEAD OWNER UNTIL NFL CEMENTS DEADLINE
Tom Powers

It seemed like a logical enough question. But the fellow in the NFL information office seemed perplexed. All I wanted was a clarification of league policy.

Our gaggle of Vikings owners, I explained, is under an NFL mandate to come up with a head cheese. Instead of 10 people each owning 10 percent, the league wants someone from the group to step forward and take control of 30 percent.

I think that's because, when things go wrong out here—as they inevitably do—Commissioner Paul Tagliabue would like to be able to pick up the telephone in New York and holler at just one person. As it stands, he has to make 10 calls.

Frankly, this whole scenario of finding a "lead owner" is frightening. The last time our Gang of Ten tried to restructure its hierarchy, in 1993, it cost them $50 million to pay off Carl Pohlad and Irwin Jacobs. The organization still is buckling under the weight of that debt.

Anyway, what I wanted to know was: What happens if they can't work this out among themselves? Most Vikings owners shun the spotlight the way a vampire shuns the daylight. And for good reason. The Vikings' decade-long history of playoff failure coupled with their terrible image has resulted in the majority of the proprietors wearing fake nose-and-glasses in public.

As you can imagine, there isn't a long line to be the captain of the [HMS]

Bounty. Or the Pequod, depending on your literary bent. The current system of sending the dividend checks to unmarked post office boxes works quite well for most of them.

So, if and when they can't come up with a head cheese, will the league fine them? Suspend them? Shoot them?

"Policy, policy . . ." the NFL spokesperson said. "We'll certainly look into this. We'll get back to you."

This year?

"As soon as possible. We'll put this question in the right hands and go from there."

Actually, it probably doesn't matter. The NFL again has extended the deadline. This is about the fourteenth time. The league now has decreed—privately—that the Vikings don't have to come up with a 30 percent owner until after their stadium issue is resolved.

Considering CEO Roger Headrick is most likely to come up with enough outside-investor money to control 30 percent, some may consider the NFL's latest ruling to be a reprieve.

Under the current regime, the franchise has reached a Metrodome-era low in season-ticket sales. Interest is flagging, partly because the public is chilled by the head coach. And partly because of the playoff failures.

Furthermore, the Vikings have declared themselves to be the first "small-market" team in NFL history. That's despite receiving more than $40 million a year in national broadcast revenue.

In any event, we will know when the NFL is serious about the Vikings having a lead owner. We'll know because the huge squabble that will ensue within the Gang of Ten will spill over into public view.

The dispute probably will boil down to a war between the pro-Headrick and anti-Headrick factions. If you were to poll the Gang right now, you'd probably find three pro, three anti and four trying to find the Metrodome.

In the past, the league has levied huge fines on franchises that do not comply. And the NFL doesn't send a bill in the mail, either. It withholds TV money.

When the Seahawks threatened to bolt Seattle, for example, the league issued a $500,000 fine that stopped them in their tracks. Maybe that's what it will take to get something done about the ownership situation here.

But first, the NFL will have to set a deadline it plans to enforce.

●

Oh yes, the stadium issue. Minnesota sports fans have been dealing with football, baseball, hockey, and basketball stadium issues almost continuously since 1988. That's when Minnesota Twins owner Carl Pohlad activated an escape clause in his 30-year Metrodome lease. The Twins lease agreement actually permitted the team to terminate its lease if one of two conditions were not met: 1. If the team didn't sell 1.47 million tickets (the American League average in 1978 had been 1.47 million per team) or the league average for three consecutive seasons; or 2. If the team had a cumulative net operating loss for three consecutive seasons. The Vikings had also signed a 30-year lease for the Metrodome—extending through the 2011 season—but they had no escape clauses.

Pohlad was able to prove that the Twins had net cumulative operating losses during the three-year span from 1985 to 1987. Coming one year after winning the World Series and after drawing over 3 million fans in 1988—second only to the New York Mets in the major leagues—the complex, but legal, accounting rules for depreciating players' salaries and interest expenses were met with skepticism by the public. Nevertheless, the Twins negotiated a new 10-year lease that eliminated stadium rents and gave the team other revenue improvements, while retaining the two escape clauses.

Sports franchise problems in the next few years put new stadiums front-and-center in local media and in the legislature. In 1993 owner Norm Green moved the Minnesota North Stars to Dallas. A move to attract a new NHL franchise began almost immediately. Then, the financially-strapped owners of the NBA Minnesota Timberwolves, Harvey Ratner and Marv Wolfenson, appealed for a public buyout of their privately-financed Target Center. The state legislature approved the buyout on the last day of the 1994 session, but the deal was not completed until March 1995, when Mankato businessman Glen Taylor bought the team.

The Twins fired the next salvo.

"I GOTTA GET ME ONE OF THESE," FROM *STADIUM GAMES: FIFTY YEARS OF BIG LEAGUE GREED AND BUSH LEAGUE BOONDOGGLES* (2000)

Jay Weiner

Seeking a new Twins stadium in 1994 was simply not in the cards. The lack of ripeness of the baseball stadium issue dogged the Pohlads' efforts. In 1994, while Pohlad was shaking his head about the future of the Dome, the legislature was beating up on Wolfenson and Ratner. Those guys were about to lose $50 million of an empire that wasn't much larger while billionaire Pohlad was beginning to lay the groundwork for a plan that would guarantee that he would lose not one dime of his investment in the Twins. Bell [Twins general manager Jerry] knew that Pohlad couldn't just join the Marv-and-Harv train that was making stops and starts at the capitol.

Cris Carter grabs a pass despite interference by a Houston Oilers defender. In his 12 years with the Vikings (1990–2001), he averaged 84 pass receptions per year. He led the NFL with 122 receptions in 1994, and he made the Pro Bowl eight consecutive years (1993–2000). PHOTOGRAPH BY RICK A. KOLODZIEJ. COURTESY OF THE MINNESOTA VIKINGS.

"We could see all that was going on over there for a grand total of $750,000 a year," said Bell of the 1994 legislative session and the effort to get state money to buy out Target Center. "For $750,000, I wouldn't waste my time. We were looking at hundreds of millions. We decided then and there, we'd better not go to the legislature with a crisis. We'd better go with an explanation and a plan." They knew that their lease, with its ever-present escape clause, expired in 1998. They knew that in 1997 they could trigger that escape with a year's notice. They assumed, given the operating losses that were mounting with increased salaries and the lack of new revenue streams, that they would reach—or fall to—the thresholds needed to escape.

As the plan developed, a vision solidified. Camden Yards in Baltimore was the first successful new ballpark, merging the synergies of a downtown with the new fan services of elite suites and creature comforts, a carnival atmosphere in a background that felt like the good old days. On April 4,

1994, Cleveland's Jacobs Field was opened, named after Pohlad's pal Dick Jacobs, owner of the Indians, who paid $13.8 million of his own dough to place his name on the city-built stadium. Soon afterward, Pohlad visited what has become one of the jewels of the nation's ballparks, a facility that rejuvenated the sport in Cleveland. A former Twins employee remembers Pohlad coming back from that visit and telling some Twins staff members, "This is what we need." He was, said the high-ranking staff person, "Like a kid in a candy store after seeing Jacobs." Pohlad didn't know where it would go or who would pay for it, but he knew he wanted it soon. In July 1994 Pohlad officially began his effort, saying, "Me, too," in the chorus of sports facilities.

On the one hand, this was wise and fair. The legislature and Minneapolis City Council, while tired of addressing pro sports matters, certainly had to appreciate an attempt at a reasoned approach. Pohlad was making his needs and plans known earlier rather than later. In a sense, Pohlad was kicking off the conversation to allow many ideas to flow. That was good. On the other hand, it was as if the hits just kept on coming. As in a crowded delicatessen, the Twins' number was up, and there stood Pohlad waving his little deli ticket high so that the workers behind the counter—the elected officials—could serve up some public-finance lunch meat. The beginning of the Twins' campaign added oil to the North Stars and Target Center fire.

Just 10 weeks after the legislature passed the ill-fated Target Center buyout plan, Pohlad, [Jerry] Bell, and financial adviser Bob Starkey of the Arthur Andersen accounting firm appeared before the Sports Facilities Commission and said that the Twins were facing dire financial straits. "Unfortunately, the current controversy regarding the North Stars and Timberwolves understandably leaves little sympathy for major league sports in the state of Minnesota," Pohlad told the commission, which listened intently in its tiny, Spartan conference room on the first concourse level of the Dome. "Our purpose in appearing before you today is to explore opportunities for the stadium commission and the Minnesota Twins without deadlines or media hyperbole and without threat of relocation."

Whenever a banker suggests he wants to "explore opportunities," it's time to guard your wallet. Whenever a team owner desires a conversation "without threat of relocation," beware—the threat will arrive sometime soon.

●

In June 1995 the state legislature directed Sports Facilities Commission chairman Henry Savelkoul to set up the Minnesota Advisory Task Force on Professional Sports to study pro sports and the stadium issues as a whole. Shortly thereafter the Twins made a presentation to the task force, arguing that the Dome was no longer a viable facility for the team.

The Vikings quickly got into the act. In September, Roger Headrick, with support from NFL commissioner Paul Tagliabue, told the task force that the Vikings needed a restructured lease to remain competitive. Headrick didn't demand a new stadium or threaten to relocate, but he did insist a change was required.

Within a year, though, the Vikings grew more assertive. In October 1995 Minnesota governor Arne Carlson had proposed a metro-area public referendum to build a new baseball stadium and talked about a public subsidy to relocate an NHL team to Minnesota. Through most of 1996 much of the public focus was on the Twins since they could activate the escape clause in their lease and threaten to stop playing at the Metrodome after the 1998 season, but St. Paul mayor Norm Coleman's drive to attract an NHL team to downtown St. Paul was also gaining some traction. In early October Headrick told *Star Tribune* reporter Jay Weiner that the Vikings felt left out of stadium planning. He said it looked like the Twins would get a new stadium, a new NHL team would get money to refurbish the Civic Center and the Timberwolves are already playing in a refinanced Target Center. Then he dropped the bombshell—the Metrodome, even with the Twins gone, would not be acceptable to the Vikings! Headrick suggested a new football stadium could be built east of the Convention Center.

Headrick's suggestion angered Governor Carlson, who was trying to steer a Twins stadium proposal through the legislature. The *Star Tribune* editorial page also sounded a warning to Headrick, arguing that the team's demands could undercut overall stadium planning efforts.

Minneapolis Star Tribune, October 16, 1996
VIKINGS STADIUM?
OUR PERSPECTIVE: ONE SPORTS PALACE AT A TIME, PLEASE
Editorial

When officials in Cincinnati's Hamilton County concluded that the city's Riverfront Stadium no longer met the needs of the baseball Reds and football Bengals, they didn't settle for halfway measures. They proposed, and last spring voters approved, $540 million in public bonding to build two new stadiums—one for each team.

A word of advice, however, to Vikings president Roger Headrick: Don't look for the same result in Minnesota. In fact, don't even suggest it. Just by floating his "dream" that the Vikings might get a new stadium to go along with any new baseball park built for the Twins, Headrick may well have undercut both possibilities.

It's true that the Vikings are affected by the same revolution in sports economics that has rendered the Metrodome financially untenable for the

Twins. The Vikings too are at a disadvantage there in keeping up with the competition for dollars and talent. To solve the problem, adjustments will be necessary that sweeten the team's lease and provide additional revenues.

But first the Twins have to move out of the Metrodome. Once that happens, the Vikings' problem can be addressed—and probably solved—in that venue, and at considerably less cost than the price of a completely new stadium.

That's the best Headrick should hope for, given the controversy surrounding the proposed Twins project.

Most of the legislative candidates who are now falling all over each other to oppose public financing for a new baseball park will, if elected, probably find reason to break that promise rather than risk having the Twins leave Minnesota. But their current opposition reflects real and deeply held public reservations about spending tax dollars or even public credit on the construction of sports palaces. It would be a mistake for anyone—whether on behalf of the Twins or the Vikings—to push those reservations too far.

Rather than looking to Cincinnati for his model, Headrick might better take a lesson from Denver. By almost any measurement, that area's public investment in Coors Field as a home for the Colorado Rockies baseball team has been a huge success. But despite that success, a subsequent bid by the Broncos for similar financing of a new football stadium was widely viewed as an attempt by a greedy team owner to horn in on a good deal. The issue is to be decided by referendum next year, with passage by no means certain.

As Governor Arne Carlson has cautioned the Vikings, there's a risk in Minnesota as well that taxpayers can be pushed beyond the limits of tolerance. The Vikings need to be patient and understand that the first step in solving their stadium problem is to solve the Twins' stadium problem.

Then the needs of the Vikings can be objectively assessed and dealt with in a manner that best serves the public interest along with the team's. In the meantime, Headrick and other Viking officials might want to scale down their stadium "dream" to something more likely to come true.

●

Headrick was undeterred, and on December 19 told the Metropolitan Sports Facilities Commission that the Vikings would not wait its turn in the ongoing stadium-finance game. He proposed three alternatives: a major refurbishing of the Metrodome, a new dual-purpose retractable-roof stadium to house both the Twins and Vikings, or a new football-only stadium for the Vikings. Commission chairman Henry Savelkoul, who was working with the Twins to introduce a stadium-financing bill in the 1997 state legislative session, rejected the suggestions. But the legislative session ended in May with no new stadium bill. A bonding bill for $65 million for a new hockey arena in St. Paul was also defeated.

Governor Carlson said he would call a special legislative session in early fall to consider stadium issues. Twins owner Carl Pohlad called a press conference to challenge the legislature to come up with a solution by October 1, when the Twins could activate an escape clause in their lease. He said he would not wait until the 1998 legislative session, and followed up by meeting with the Major League Executive Council to request permission to relocate the team. Meanwhile, Roger Headrick continued to irritate the governor with his push for a new dual-purpose stadium for the Vikings.

Then, in early August, Kevin Garnett, the 21-year-old Timberwolves star, rejected a six-year contract extension worth $103.5 million. The public was stunned . . . and then angered. Many callers to sports and news talk radio shows claimed they were done with sports. The furor gave anti-stadium forces a shot in the arm and stadium boosters had to wonder if the economics of big league sports had finally reached the breaking point.

Team president Roger Headrick and coach Dennis Green were the favorite whipping boys of the local media, and loyal Vikings fans were outspoken in their criticisms of the team, its owners, coaches, and players, but the news report in October 1997 that the team might be sold to an outside owner was devastating. Despite all the hate mail, booing and cynicism, the Vikings were still family . . . they might be despicable, but they are OUR Vikings!

Thus, fans waited out the winter of 1997–1998 with nervous anticipation, hoping that a white knight would show up to keep the Vikings in Minnesota.

Purple Pride

AN OFFENSE FOR THE AGES

THE SALE OF THE VIKINGS WAS THE HOT TOPIC IN PRINT AND TELE-vision news for the first half of 1998. The 10 owners, once the intent to sell the team had became public—and raised such an outcry—established a formal bidding process, with bids to be opened on February 2, 1998.

The bidder previously unidentified by Philip Maas in October turned out to be Red McCombs, a San Antonio businessman—ranked 190 on the *Fortune* magazine list of the 400 richest people in the country—whose empire included Clear Channel Television, owner of Twin Cities television station WFTC Channel 29. Vikings fans were nervous when they learned that he had once tried to get an expansion NFL team for San Antonio, but McCombs claimed he had no interest in moving the team.

In a surprise development, bestselling novelist Tom Clancy's $205 million bid topped those submitted by team president Roger Headrick ($177.5 million) and McCombs ($175 million). It was the first time Clancy's name had surfaced in the Vikings' ownership saga.

Headrick immediately matched Clancy's offer, claiming that team bylaws gave any partner the right to match an offer from an outside party. He filed a grievance with NFL commissioner Paul Tagliabue to block the sale to Clancy.

Tagliabue took almost two months to make a decision, but in the end denied Headrick's appeal, clearing the way for the sale to be finalized.

But then, in another bizarre twist to the saga, in late May Clancy withdrew his offer, indicating that his financing arrangements had fallen apart. It turned out that he did not have the personal wealth it was assumed he had, and he had been trying to leverage only $5 million of his own money into a 30 percent share of the team.

McCombs revised his bid to an estimated $250 million and became the new owner when Headrick chose not to bid. McCombs made friends in his initial press conferences in early July, and tried to reassure Vikings fans who feared he might have a secret plan to move the team to San Antonio. "Let me be very straightforward with this," he said. "The Vikings belong in Minnesota. If . . . they have an equal opportunity to participate and compete in the NFL, they're going to stay in Minnesota. If I come to the conclusion that I can't meet the challenge, then maybe we'll find somebody else in Minnesota. I think it's always preferable to have hometown ownership."

Houston Chronicle, July 6, 1998
WITH RED IN SADDLE, VIKINGS SITTING PRETTY
Mickey Herskowitz
When Lou Holtz landed on the campus of the University of Minnesota for one of his several coaching stops, he explained how easy it was to recognize the natives: "They all have blond hair," he said, "and blue ears."

If you ask us who had the red, white and bluest Fourth of July in the land, we can assure you it was the fans of the Minnesota Vikings.

If white stands for purity, or at least clean sheets, the shakiest franchise in the NFL got a fresh start this week. In the new deal, the dominant color is red.

When the much applauded bid by author Tom Clancy fell apart, it led to The Hunt for Red McCombs, a tall Texan who is both humble and extroverted, impulsive and persevering.

Mercy, but the fans in Minnesota are going to have fun in this and future football seasons.

McCombs has a rich, mellow voice which, in full boom, can frighten the fowl off the San Antonio River. He is going to be a terrific NFL owner because he has been through the NBA three times and the Big State League once, and he delivered good teams and happy crowds.

The players loved him because he wasn't a tyrant, he truly cared about them, and his word was better than most contracts.

He is smart and self-made, but doesn't belabor either. He went to Southwestern University in Georgetown to play football and to the University of Texas to study law, was too skinny for one and too hungry for the other.

He found he could make more money selling cars than working as a first-year law clerk.

GREEN THUMB

Red built one of the largest Ford dealerships in the country, moved into oil, cattle, movies, sports and broadcasting. His friend Lowry Mays wanted him to buy one radio station in San Antonio. The company grew into the largest in the industry, with outlets here and in Mexico and eight or nine TV stations.

He wasn't the richest guy at the table when he owned the basketball teams in Denver or San Antonio (twice), and certainly not in the bush leagues of baseball. In the past five years, Clear Channel Communications has made him a billionaire. He gives the credit to his partners, Mays and Gary Woods.

"The only difference between the majors," he says, "and a Class B team are the number of zeroes on the checks you write."

This isn't a story of "Only in America." It is a story of "The Best of America."

McCombs was born in Spur, Texas, where the train stopped and turned around. When the family moved to Corpus Christi, Red didn't want to give up his job as a soda jerk or his status as the most popular kid in school. His mother changed his mind by swatting him over the head with a tennis racket.

His father worked nearly all of his life as a mechanic for Ford, one of its best and most loyal, who caught errors in the new-car manuals. He never fully supported his son's decision to cancel his Edsel franchise. This is a fellow who came from prime Texas stock.

Red is a hearty, good-looking character, who at the age of 70 still doesn't know what he wants to do when he grows up.

I met Red McCombs the year of the first Super Bowl. He was pushing hard even then to bring an NFL team to San Antonio. In those days, the NFL brass knew nothing about the city and had forgotten the Alamo.

If that history makes Minnesota fans nervous, they can relax. When he bought the Vikings for about $250 million, McCombs acknowledged the stadium lease, which binds the team to Minneapolis to 2012. His fans in South Texas pointed out that he could afford the buyout.

As clearly as one can recite the English language, Red said, "You don't break a lease just because you have the money."

DISHEVELED BUT NOT DISHONEST

In the same week, he was boosting San Antonio to the Republicans for their next convention. He was a force behind the Alamodome, debt-free when it opened its doors.

Back in 1968, he helped organize the HemisFair. When Ford balked at being a sponsor, Red called John Connally, the governor of Texas, who called Lyndon Johnson, who called Lee Iacocca. The Ford pavilion was one of the Fair's big attractions.

Everybody seems to know Red. Nor is he hard to reach. He sits behind a large desk in an office that has the intimate, closed-in feeling of a trailer at a construction site. It is paneled, and almost every inch of it is filled with western art, sculptures and artifacts, except the space devoted to his striking wife, Charline, their daughters and grandkids.

On one wall is a portrait of Red by artist LeRoy Neiman. It was commissioned by Sidney Shlenker, who had just bought from him the Denver Nuggets. Red is fond of repeating the story, literally, behind the painting.

"There is a letter on the back," he says, "from Neiman, saying, 'I went to the NBA offices looking for a good photo of you, but everything I could find had you looking disheveled.'"

He laughs. This is his usual look, at 6'4", maybe taller in his anteater boots. Big man. Big heart. Big Red.

●

McCombs seemed to be everywhere. He bunked down with the team for one week in the training camp dormitory in Mankato, and became the team's number one cheerleader with his exhortations to restore "purple pride." He brought his family to the first home exhibition game, glad-handed fans on the Metrodome plaza, gave the team a pep talk in the locker room before they took the field, stalked the sidelines during pregame introductions, hugged team mascot Ragnar, and invited former coaches Bud Grant and Jerry Burns, as well as former Vikings stars Carl Eller, Bill Brown, and Mick Tingelhoff, to join him in his luxury suite. Adoring fans treated him like a conquering hero wherever he walked in the stadium.

The unpopular Roger Headrick resigned on August 21 to preempt being fired by the new owner. When he turned up at team headquarters with a U-Haul the next day—a Saturday—to retrieve his personal belongings he found the lock on his office door had been changed. The irritated Headrick hired a locksmith to break into his old office.

Local media hopes that the team would also get rid of coach Dennis Green were dashed when McCombs offered a contract extension to Green, who was in the final year of his contract. McCombs, who had been dodging questions about Green's future, said he came up with the idea the week before the first regular-season game, while on his treadmill back home in San Antonio. (The hard-driving, hard-drinking McCombs had quit drinking and started exercising back in 1977 when he had nearly died of hepatitis.)

That particular morning he was trying to think of something he could do to boost team morale.

"I realized that the only thing that could ruin this season was the situation with Denny's contract," he told *Sports Illustrated* writer David Fleming. "At that point I had seen enough to make up my own mind. I got off that treadmill, grabbed the phone and offered him an extension." The three-year, $4.7 million deal was very popular with the players.

The Vikings, who had won all four exhibition games, got the regular season off to a good start with a 31–7 win over Tampa Bay in the Metrodome. In the next game in St. Louis, quarterback Brad Johnson suffered a broken right fibula when he was sacked early in the fourth quarter with the game tied. Backup quarterback Randall Cunningham threw a 19-yard touchdown pass to Cris Carter with 2:09 remaining to win the game 38–31.

The offense didn't miss a beat with Cunningham under center. The Vikings won the next five games to sit at 7–0, and were averaging 34.4 points a game. Running back Robert Smith was on his way to his second consecutive 1,000-yard season, and sensational rookie Randy Moss was teaming with veterans Cris Carter and Jake Reed to terrorize defensive backs.

Moss's troubles with the law, including a positive test for marijuana, had cost him major college scholarship offers from Notre Dame and Florida State. He wound up at Division I-AA Marshall University in his home state of West Virginia, where he caught 25 touchdown passes in 1997. Nineteen NFL teams, fearful of his troubled background, passed on Moss in the 1998 draft. Dennis Green felt that Cris Carter, who once had a cocaine problem himself but was now a born-again Christian, would be a good mentor and role model for Moss, and snapped him up with the twenty-first pick of the first round.

Moss could outrun any defensive back, and Cunningham wasn't afraid to throw to him in double coverage because he was confident that Moss could use his 6'4" height and 39-inch vertical jump to beat defenders to the ball. Moss came to national attention in a battle of 5–0 teams in a Monday Night Football game at Green Bay's Lambeau Field on October 5, when he destroyed the Packers' secondary with five receptions for 190 yards, including touchdown catches of 52 and 44 yards.

The Vikings dropped from the unbeaten ranks in a tough game in Tampa Bay, losing 27–24. Although Cunningham had a good game, completing 21 of 25 passes for 291 yards, two touchdowns and one interception, a possible quarterback controversy was brewing as Brad Johnson was restored to the active roster for the next game against New Orleans.

New team owner Red McCombs (shown with quarterback Randall Cunningham) helped pump up public enthusiasm with his appeals for "purple pride." PHOTOGRAPH COURTESY OF THE MINNESOTA VIKINGS.

The controversy didn't last long. Cunningham injured a knee in the first quarter and Johnson returned to action to lead the Vikings to a 31–24 victory with 28 completions in 38 attempts, for 316 yards, one touchdown and two interceptions. It wasn't easy—he broke his right thumb on the first play of the third quarter, but gutted it out the rest of the game. The postgame prognosis was that he would miss at least two weeks, and that third-string quarterback Jay Fiedler would start the next game. Cunningham, however, came back six days after surgery to remove bone chips from his right knee and directed a 24–3 win over the Cincinnati Bengals.

Sports Illustrated, December 7, 1998

SECOND COMING

REJUVENATED AFTER A YEAR IN RETIREMENT, RANDALL CUNNINGHAM
IS SETTING THE LEAGUE ON ITS EAR AND LEADING THE VIKINGS TO
NEW HEIGHTS

Austin Murphy

It didn't feel like a sabbatical. At the time, it felt like the rest of his life. Two years ago Randall Cunningham was out of football and on his knees in strangers' houses. He was cutting marble and granite for kitchen counters and bathrooms. "Have you ever tried to cut black granite?" asks Cunningham, the Minnesota Vikings' starting quarterback. He does not await your answer. "Now, that's hard work." Another tough job: convincing Cunningham's critics that he has radically improved since returning in '97 from his one-season hiatus. Try telling them that he is staying in the pocket longer, seeing more of the field and making better reads than he ever did in 11 seasons as a Philadelphia Eagle. Talk about hard work.

What's the difference between the Cunningham who retired after the '95 season because teams evinced hardly any interest in him and this year's model, the 35-year-old who is on the short list of candidates for the league's MVP award? What's the difference between that washed-up Eagle and this fired-up Viking, whose 23 touchdown passes and 109.2 quarterback rating lead the league, and who pureed the Dallas Cowboys' secondary like sweet potatoes on Thanksgiving Day, throwing for 359 yards and four scores in Minnesota's 46–36 win? What's the difference? When we posed the question to Rodney Peete, the Eagle who displaced Cunningham in Philadelphia, he was not in a generous mood.

"What's different about Randall? Randy Moss, Cris Carter, Jake Reed, Robert Smith. That's really it," said Peete, ticking off the names of Minnesota's trio of big-play wide receivers and its superb running back.

Cunningham digests, then rebuts, this analysis. "Rodney is a jealous person," he says. "He's stabbed me in the back before." A pause follows, then Cunningham, perhaps realizing that those are strong words to be emanating from the mouth of such a godly man as himself, adds this: "But I've forgiven him."

God knows Peete has suffered enough. While Cunningham has gone on to star for the best team in the NFC, his successor in Philadelphia has alternately struggled and borne a clipboard for the league's lowest-scoring offense. Rodney's sour-grapes explanation for Randall's success is as understandable as it is inaccurate. Cunningham admits that he wasn't the most astute reader of defenses during his days as an Eagle, but he also points out that he wasn't asked to be, particularly from 1986 to 1990, when he played for coach Buddy Ryan, a defensive specialist who had as much interest in offense as he did in Ashtanga yoga.

"Buddy basically asked me to make five or six big plays a game, and the defense would do the rest," says Cunningham, who nonetheless made three consecutive Pro Bowl appearances beginning in 1988. When he pulled the ball down, bolted from the pocket and commenced freelancing, he says, "I was doing what I was told."

In Minnesota, where the 11–1 Vikings have won nine of the 10 games he has started since replacing the injured Brad Johnson, Cunningham's orders are different. "Here," says Minnesota offensive coordinator Brian Billick, "we've asked him to drop back and go through a progression of receivers. We've asked him to be smart, to make reads and make plays within the system. It's what a lot of people around the league told me he wouldn't be able to do, and it's exactly what he's done. Anyone who thinks Randall has been successful just because he throws a nice deep ball doesn't get it."

Which is not to say the Vikings will be de-emphasizing their big-play offense anytime soon. His advancing years notwithstanding, Cunningham still throws the NFL's most beautiful bomb. And as he proved again last Thursday at Texas Stadium, where he caught three passes, all for touchdowns, Moss is, at 21, as good as or better than any other receiver in the league at beating defensive backs deep and then outleaping them for the ball.

When Moss was his primary receiver and the Cowboys (who were playing without Deion Sanders) rolled their coverage toward the rookie, Cunningham calmly went to his second and third reads. He has been much more comfortable with the offense in '98 than he was late last season, when he started five games—two in the postseason—in relief of the injured Johnson. Back then Minnesota coaches streamlined the game plan for Cunningham, reducing it to 60–70 percent of what Johnson was asked to master. This season, says Billick, "we go into the game with the same number of plays."

Whereas Cunningham only occasionally made it to his second read last season before fleeing the pocket, this year he has shown far more poise and patience. On October 5 at Lambeau Field, the Green Bay Packers focused on confining him to the pocket, figuring that was where he posed the least threat to their 25-game home winning streak. Four Cunningham touchdown tosses and 442 passing yards later, the streak was toast, as was the notion that Randall isn't a pocket passer.

When Johnson fractured his right fibula in the second game of the season, Cunningham came off the bench to throw the game-winning touchdown pass in a 38–31 win over the St. Louis Rams. If the Vikings were still concerned about Cunningham, he eased their minds the following Wednesday. In preparing for his first start of the season, against the Detroit Lions, he completed 18 of 19 passes against Minnesota's first-string defense. The sole incompletion was a drop.

More so than a year ago, when he was still learning Billick's system, Cunningham has projected a quiet, contagious confidence this season. Just before kickoff against Dallas, Billick, afflicted with butterflies, approached his quarterback on the sideline and said, "You're gonna have to keep me calm today." Cunningham smiled, then threw first-quarter scoring passes of 51, 54 and 56 yards as the Vikings bolted to a 21–6 lead.

Cunningham's newfound serenity transcends the football field. "There's been a lot of grace poured down on me," he said last Saturday while overseeing work on his new, 14,000-square-foot home outside Las Vegas. "I have peace in my heart." He went on to describe a kind of spiritual awakening that occurred in him during his year away from the game.

"I've been a Christian since 1987," he said, "but I was a hypocrite for a lot of the time. I was built up to be this superstar, and I spent all my time trying to live up to that." In hindsight, he sees that his motives were selfish. "I was doing it for man, rather than for God," he said. "I needed to humble myself."

General managers around the league helped him reach that goal by expressing little interest in him after the '96 season. Additional humility awaited as he started his new business, grinding and hoisting slabs of expensive stone. He had long since ceased to take football for granted when the Vikings informed him in April 1997 that they wanted to bring him in as Johnson's understudy. He took their interest as a sign from God.

Of course, Cunningham takes it as a sign from God when he can find a parking place without driving around the block. Born-again Christians often speak of their desire to let Christ's "light" shine through them. Cunningham's nickname, in that case, should be Klieg. Two days before a divisional playoff against the San Francisco 49ers last season, a reporter concluded an interview with Cunningham by wishing him luck. "Pray for me," came the reply.

Give the man credit—he isn't just bearing witness, he's leaving as little as possible to chance. During TV timeouts, after Billick gives him the play, Cunningham sometimes steps from the huddle and offers a short prayer for its success. If a bomb has been called, for instance, "I'll ask God to anoint the play, to complete it, to give him glory."

Admittedly a selfish player in Philadelphia, Cunningham appears to have traded in his ego for a purple jersey. He has been exemplary in Minnesota, never taking it the wrong way when younger Vikings recall seeing him on television while they were in elementary school. He always says the right thing, and appears to mean it. For instance, when he's asked who should be the starting quarterback once Johnson, who broke his right thumb while spelling the injured Cunningham during a 31–24 win over the New Orleans Saints on November 8, regains his health, Cunningham always insists that he'll happily resume his role as a backup. Eagles wide receivers coach Gerald Carr believes Cunningham's season away from football was the key. "He finally realized it wasn't all about Randall," says Carr. "Once he realized it wasn't all about him being a superstar, he became one."

This season Cunningham has thrown eight touchdown passes of 50 or more yards. At the same time, he has been careful with the ball. He did not throw an interception in his first five games, though he has since thrown seven. His 60.9 completion percentage is a career best for a season in which he has thrown at least 200 passes. He may have played his best game in Minnesota's lone defeat, completing 21 of 25 passes in a 27–24 loss to the Tampa Bay Buccaneers on November 1. He threw two touchdown passes, and another was dropped. He was intercepted once, when a blitzing linebacker hit him in the back as he released the ball. He threw one ball away to avoid a sack. For his fourth incomplete pass, the ball glanced off Carter's hands.

"I think the time off gave him peace of mind," says Bucs coach Tony Dungy, who insists that Cunningham "has to be the MVP of the league."

How to stop him? "Get pressure on him without blitzing, without giving up any coverage," says Dungy. "Get him in a rush, get him to make a bad decision. So far, that hasn't happened."

"Two-deep zones don't seem to bother him as much as they used to," adds New Orleans defensive coordinator Zaven Yaralian, a former New York Giants assistant who faced Cunningham twice a year when both were in the NFC East. "You can't just sit back in zone coverage and let him throw it. You have to come after him."

The Saints could have had Cunningham on their side following the '96 season, when they came close to signing him before he opted to go to Minnesota. No great loss, the Saints told themselves; they picked up Heath Shuler and Danny Wuerffel instead. "Come to think of it," Yaralian was saying last week, "we also had a chance at [drafting] Randy Moss. Jeez, we could have ruined their whole season."

Under the terms of the two-year, $2 million deal Cunningham signed last March, he will become a free agent after this season if he plays more than half of the team's snaps. That is all but assured. Will Cunningham, who has said money is not of paramount importance, accept less than he could get elsewhere to stay in Minnesota?

"The Bible says tomorrow is not promised to us," he says. "I'm just thankful for what I have now. I will pray that God puts it in the Vikings' heart to do what is right."

Believe this: The loss of Cunningham might spark a mini mutiny in Minnesota's locker room, where respect and affection for number 7 run high. The criticism in Philadelphia that he was too focused on himself doesn't wash with the Vikings. Not after his performance on November 15—six days after having two dime-sized bone chips removed from his right knee—when he led the team to a 24–3 win over the Cincinnati Bengals.

Never one to miss an opportunity to deflect a bit of glory to the man upstairs, Cunningham gave the bone fragments—in a small jar—to team chaplain Keith Johnson. At a Sunday morning service preceding the game, says Cunningham, Johnson brandished the bone chips while extolling the healing power of the Almighty.

Cunningham's season has been a reminder of the healing power of a sabbatical. It has also been a revelation. He is awash in grace, so he won't be offended by our admission that he is smarter than we thought he was. Not only is Cunningham not soft, he is as tough and durable as black granite.

Brad Johnson got back into action in the third quarter of the 50–10 rout of Jacksonville in game 15, six weeks after he broke his thumb, but it was now clear that the team was planning to stick with Cunningham going into the playoffs. On Christmas Eve the Vikings signed him to a five-year contract extension worth $28 million. On December 27 the Vikings beat the Tennessee Oilers 26–16 to finish with a 15–1 record, and their 556 points scored was a new NFL season record.

The Vikings beat the Arizona Cardinals in methodical fashion, 41–21, in an NFC divisional playoff game. Their first score set the tone. It came on a 13-play, 80-yard drive, consuming 7½ minutes. The Vikings led 24–7 at halftime and coasted from there.

The stage was set for the Vikings to return to the Super Bowl for the first time in over 20 years, and to avenge the team's four Super Bowl losses. All they had to do was defeat Atlanta at the Metrodome—fans discounted the Falcons' 14–2 record and their 20–18 win over the San Francisco 49ers in their divisional game.

Vikings mania had been building all season, gaining momentum with each victory, but place kicker Gary Anderson missed a 38-yard field goal attempt in the fourth quarter—his first miss all season—that could have clinched the victory. The Falcons drove for a touchdown to tie the game, and then won it 30–27 on a field goal in overtime. It was arguably the most crushing defeat in Vikings' history, rivaling those in Super Bowl IV and the "Hail Mary" playoff loss in 1975.

St. Paul Pioneer Press, January 18, 1999

PURPLE WIDE

THE LAST LEG OF THE VIKINGS' SEASON WILL BE REMEMBERED FOR MISSED OPPORTUNITIES AND AN OVERTIME LOSS TO ATLANTA

Jeff Seidel

The victory platform constructed in the middle of the Vikings' locker room was not needed. There was no celebration, merely stunned silence.

"We were a few minutes from the Super Bowl, and it's just taken away," running back Robert Smith said after the Atlanta Falcons upset the Vikings 30–27 in overtime Sunday in the NFC championship game at the Metrodome. "It's about as bad as it can get athletically."

In the far corner of the locker room, Gary Anderson quietly took off his uniform.

"I'm very, very disappointed," he said after his missed 38-yard field-goal try with 2:07 left in regulation allowed the Falcons to score a tying touchdown before winning on Morten Andersen's 38-yard field goal in their second possession of overtime.

In the hallway, owner Red McCombs, having witnessed a Vikings loss for the first time, couldn't describe his disappointment. "I couldn't measure it," he said.

For the Vikings, it was a game of squandered opportunities, dropped balls and a missed field goal try.

In the first half, it appeared the Vikings were headed to a rout until they got greedy. Instead of running out the last 1:17 of the half, Randall Cunningham passed three times—or at least tried to. On his third attempt, defensive end Chuck Smith hit Cunningham's arm, knocking the ball out of his hand, and teammate Travis Hall recovered at the Vikings' 14-yard line. The Falcons scored a touchdown on the next play.

In the second half, the highest-scoring team in NFL history managed only seven points.

The final blow was the most surprising: Mr. Perfect missed a field-goal attempt.

Leading 27–20 late in the fourth quarter, the Vikings had a chance to put the game away, but Anderson's kick went wide left.

"It just goes to show that no one is perfect," Cunningham said.

It was Anderson's first miss since December 15, 1997, when he played for the San Francisco 49ers. He had made 46 consecutive field-goal tries, including the playoffs.

"All I know is that I didn't get to see the kick because I was lying on my back with a couple of their guys on top of me," Anderson said. "I was lying down, which is sort of unusual."

Holder Mitch Berger said it was a perfect snap from Mike Morris.

"The snap was very good," he said. "It was a perfect snap. I didn't have to rotate it. Not everybody makes every kick. It was his turn to miss, I guess. It happened at a crummy time."

Eight plays after Anderson missed, Falcons quarterback Chris Chandler threw a 16-yard touchdown pass to Terance Mathis, their second hookup for a TD. Andersen kicked the extra point—twice, because of a penalty—and the Falcons tied the score 27–27.

"The drive down, with just the one timeout, ranks right up there with the drive that we had in Cleveland," Atlanta coach Dan Reeves said, comparing the Falcons' effort with the famous John Elway–led drive for the Denver Broncos in the January 1987 AFC championship game, which also went into overtime.

The Vikings had the ball one more time at the end of regulation but decided to run out the clock with 30 seconds to play.

"We didn't feel the odds were in our favor," offensive coordinator Brian Billick said. "We would rather go with the 50-50 chance of the coin flip."

They won the coin flip, but it didn't do them much good. The Vikings couldn't move the ball and had to punt.

So the Falcons took a turn and didn't do much better, punting it back to the Vikings.

Once again, the Vikings failed to move the ball. On five plays, Cunningham threw four incomplete passes, and the Vikings had to punt again.

This time the Falcons took advantage.

Atlanta crossed midfield when Chandler threw a 26-yard pass to tight end O. J. Santiago to the Vikings' 48 when linebacker Bobby Houston pulled a quadriceps muscle.

After crossing midfield, the Falcons simply pounded the ball, giving it to Jamal Anderson four times to set up Andersen's 38-yard, game-winning field goal.

"It just hit it pure," Andersen said. "I mean, right down the pipe."

Right down the pipe?

That's what happened to the Vikings' offense after halftime.

Through the second half and overtime, Randy Moss caught only one pass for four yards. "I think we got a little rattled in the end and we couldn't make anything happen," he said.

Cunningham was one for seven in his final three possessions.

"I don't think we tightened up. I think that we didn't make the plays that we needed to make at the end, offensively and defensively," he said.

Injuries played a part as well. At the end of the game, Smith was on the bench with contusions on his knee and thigh.

And the Vikings' defense was so banged up late in the game that linebacker Dixon Edwards was forced to play despite a hamstring injury.

"They made the plays when they had to, and we didn't," defensive coordinator Foge Fazio said. "It was as simple as that. You have to give them a lot of credit. We had our opportunities. You don't lose the game at the end. The game is played out from the beginning, and everything accumulates. They made a lot of nice plays. They caught the ball. I'm not making any excuses. They just made the plays, that's all."

The Falcons opened the game by picking on cornerback Jimmy Hitchcock, completing three passes to his side. And they converted a third down when Chandler hit Tony Martin for nine yards.

On third-and-goal from the five, Chandler threw a swing pass to Jamal Anderson, who beat Dwayne Rudd for the touchdown.

The Vikings answered with a scoring drive that lasted only 2:48. Ray Buchanan was called for a 30-yard pass-interference call while trying to defend Moss. On the next play, Moss faked a move to the corner, and Cunningham threw a 31-yard touchdown pass to him over the middle. Moss tiptoed through the back of the end zone, tying the score 7–7.

Late in the first quarter, Chandler threw a one-yard pass to Harold Green, who stumbled to the ground and fumbled. The ball was recovered by Ed McDaniel at the Vikings' 40.

That set up Anderson's 29-yard field goal, which gave the Vikings a 10–7 lead.

On the next play, Chandler threw a 13-yard pass to Santiago, who fumbled after a hit by Orlando Thomas. Robert Griffith recovered on the Falcons' 42. Six plays later, Cunningham plunged into the end zone on a one-yard run, giving the Vikings a 17–7 lead.

The Vikings extended their lead to 20–7 when Anderson kicked a 35-yard field goal.

And the rout was on . . . only it wasn't.

With 1:17 left in the first half, Chuck Smith caused the fumble by Cunningham, and on the next play, Chandler threw a 14-yard touchdown pass to Mathis.

"It was 20–7, and we were trying to put them away," coach Dennis Green said. "That's been our style all year. You just have to go out and play like you have played. We came out and tried to move the ball. We had plenty of room. We weren't backed up. We were on the 20-yard line. We had plenty of room. We are probably one of the most successful teams in the league in a two-minute offense, and we had three timeouts. Unfortunately, they got the ball back."

In the second half, the Vikings' offense disappeared.

Cunningham threw a five-yard touchdown pass to Matthew Hatchette, but nothing else worked.

Chandler completed 27 of 43 passes for 340 yards and three touchdowns. Cunningham was 29 of 48 for 266 yards with two touchdowns, but he fumbled three times, two of which were lost.

●

A sign above Vikings shirts and caps at a souvenir shop at the Minneapolis–St. Paul International Airport said it all: "25 percent off." Vikings jerseys were being boxed up at Sportmart and other sports merchandise stores. Demand went to almost zero. Caps already printed with "NFC Champions" had to be packed up and returned to the manufacturer to be destroyed—per NFL rules. At Heartland Apparel in north Minneapolis, 18 employees who had been waiting to begin printing NFC championship T-shirts turned out the lights and trudged home. Travel agencies scrambled to cancel charter planes they had already reserved, and local media companies also altered their plans. The *Star Tribune* had planned to send 28 folks to Miami for the Super Bowl, but cut the list to four and even cancelled a plan to print a souvenir book on the Vikings' season.

St. Paul Pioneer Press, January 19, 1999

FACING THE UNFORTUNATE TRUTH: WE'RE MINNESOTANS, SO WE LOSE

Nick Coleman

The sun—despite the fears of Vikings fans—rose Monday. But it failed to dispel the gloom. There is no joy in Slushville. The mighty Norsemen have struck out.

If a state can bleed, Minnesota bled purple. People moved slowly, eyes glazed, faces downcast. Four dozen football-playing mercenaries—most of whose names we didn't know last September—had failed to fulfill our vicarious hopes. The stink of defeat seeped out of the Metrodome and left a sour taste in the mouths of Minnesotans. We were left with reality, and January. There will be no Super Bowl for Minnesota. There will be no three-week bacchanalia of Purple Pride TV programs and purple-prose newspapers. Turn out the lights and get the ice augur out, Sven. The party's over.

No one does a mass mope better than Minnesota.

From International Falls to Albert Lea, from Afton to Ortonville, Minnesota was in mourning: The Vikings lost to Atlanta and a curtain of grief came down with a crash, ruining the best-laid plans of the fans and the million-dollar hopes of souvenir T-shirt makers. Minnesota will spend January 31 in a frozen funk, drilling holes through the ice while muttering what ifs:

What if we had tried to score at the end of regulation? What if we could've gotten the ball to Randy Moss in the second half? What if Mr. Perfect, the field-goal kicker, could've made the one that counted most? Or—oh-oh—what if all that talk about God being in our huddle backfired?

If God were watching Sunday, He saw 60,000 purple-painted maniacs waving towels that had one of the Big Guy's least favorite words on it: pride, the thing that goeth before an overtime upset. For the angst-ridden faithful in fly-over land, our purple shame might seem like divine comeuppance. But next time, let's go for a more exciting sin, shall we? How about purple lust?

Recriminations, second guessing, finger pointing. We are wandering once more in the desert, condemned by the failure of a football team—and by our hyped-up emotional entanglement with its fortunes—to a feeling of futility. In truth, most of our heroes are just journeymen athletes who would have meant nothing special if they hadn't gelled into a wonderfully entertaining team that captured our fancy. But they made us forget the oaths we swore years ago never again to let our hearts be stepped on by the bums with the horns on their heads.

Lucy has yanked the ball away again, and Minnesota has fallen on its duff, again. We knew it would happen. But we wanted to believe it would be different this time. We never learn.

Sunday's goat, fittingly for a state where half the population was wearing fake Heidi braids, was a hired gun named Gary Anderson. That's right, that funny little fella who talks like he comes from Fargo but who is from South Africa, and who could tee it up and kick it right down the middle all day long or even all season long unless the bleeping Super Bowl was on the line.

Perfect: The Vikings could've gone to the Big Show, but the closest thing to a real-danged Viking on the team stubs his toe and shanks one, dooming us to another long winter's night with no hope of a vice time in Miami. Instead of piña coladas on the beach, it's back to snow and sleet, slush and snirt. Our primary consumption of alcohol won't come with little umbrellas in the glass. It will come in blue jugs of windshield washer, chugged by the gallon.

We forgive Gary Anderson, of course. He tried his darnedest. It's probably for the best. We might've gotten to Miami and lost the big one, and I don't think Dad's heart could stand another one of those deals. God must have a plan. But how come He always lets the other guys win?

We're not good with pain.

Our gladiators were sobbing after Sunday's defeat, a teary display of manly emotion that made even hug-giving Lutherans blanch and probably made an old Viking like Norm Van Brocklin spin in his grave. Well, don't cry for Cris Carter, Minnesota. Save your sorrow for the children, by which I mean anyone born since the last time the Vikings fell on their faces.

The children, uninitiated in the ways of Minnesota near-misses, second-

place finishes and losing (interrupted only by two fluke baseball championships), were left unprepared for defeat. Bedazzled by Red McCombs's
car-dealer sales pitches and the God-is-with-us sky-pointing of God-fear-
ing Vikings players, we grown-ups forgot where we came from. Dang it.

Sit down, kids. Mom and Dad need to tell you something: You're Minnesotans. And Minnesotans lose. A lot. We're sorry we forgot to tell you. We
know this Vikings thing hurts, but we'll be OK. We survived Fritz Mondale's
defeat and Hubert Humphrey's defeat and we survived Bud Grant's multiple defeats and we'll survive this, too. No, we aren't going to the Super Bowl.
But look what we got out of this deal: Another chapter in our noble Nordic
saga of defeat. This is what we live for, kiddos. It's our myth, our subcon-
scious view of ourselves: star-crossed losers.

Victorious Vikings? We wouldn't know what to do with them. But van-
quished Vikings are our bread and butter, the ancient story we hand down
from generation to generation, an heirloom like Dala horses, deer rifles and
the lake cabin. Just think of losing like lutefisk: It's hard to swallow. But we
have to have it on our table every year, just to remind us where we came
from.

Someday—maybe not today or tomorrow, but someday—you'll be grateful for this. This is the kind of thing we can chew on for the rest of the winter, and for winters yet to come.

Go Vikes.

●

Fans could find some consolation in the postseason accolades rung
up by Vikings players. Cunningham led all quarterbacks with a 106.0
quarterback rating and was given the Bert Bell Award as the NFL Player
of the Year, and Randy Moss was voted the NFL Offensive Rookie of the
Year. Moss led the league with 17 touchdown receptions, tying Tom Fears's
47-year-old record of 10 touchdowns greater than 40 yards, while Cris
Carter was fourth with 12. Kicker Gary Anderson led the league in scoring
with 164 points, and was a perfect 59-for-59 for extra points and 35-for-35
in field goals during the regular season. Ten Vikings were selected for the
Pro Bowl, a record for the franchise—Cunningham, Moss, Carter, Anderson,
running back Robert Smith, center Jeff Christy, guard Randall McDaniel,
tackle Todd Steussie, as well as defensive end John Randle and middle linebacker Ed McDaniel. Five players made the Associated Press All Pro team:
Cunningham, Moss, Anderson, Randall McDaniel, and Randle.

In a move that surprised no one, the Vikings traded quarterback
Brad Johnson to Washington in mid-February in exchange for three draft
choices. Johnson and his agent had been working for a trade ever since
Cunningham signed his long-term deal in December, and the team saved

a $1.15 million roster bonus due Johnson on March 1, as well as $2.48 million towards the team's salary cap.

The NFL salary cap came out of negotiations with the National Football League Player's Association in 1994. It is a "hard cap," unlike Major League Baseball's "luxury tax," which permits teams like the New York Yankees to exceed the cap by paying a penalty back to the league. If an NFL team exceeds the cap, on the other hand, the last contracts the team signed are voided and the players involved become free agents. The NFL agreed to free agency in return for the NFLPA accepting salary caps.

The salary cap per team was set at $34.6 million in 1994. That figure was originally arrived at by determining the broadcasting revenue and gate receipts for all NFL teams, applying a percentage and then dividing by the number of teams. In later years merchandising revenues and money from web enterprises have been added to the mix. In 1999 the salary cap was $58.4 million, based on 63 percent of gross revenues. The 2008 cap is $116 million.

Under salary cap rules, if a player under a long-term contract is cut before June 1, the balance of his contract is not paid nor is it applied to the team's salary cap. To induce free agents and key players to sign long-term contracts, teams began to offer large signing bonuses, which were paid upon signing, but pro-rated against the life of the contract for salary cap purposes.

The team was largely intact coming into training camp for the 1999 season and their high-powered offense made them the preseason favorites to repeat as Central Division champions and challenge once again for a Super Bowl berth. Some labeled the Vikings the "Team of the New Millennium." Vikings vice president of player personnel Frank Gilliam might not have been that bold, but he was confident the team was set for a sustained run of excellence. "If we can keep our guys together," he said, "I feel confident we can put together that type of run." Indeed, all 10 Pro Bowlers were coming back and most of the key players were locked up with contracts extending through the next three seasons.

The Team of the New Millennium won its opener in a squeaker against the Atlanta Falcons—in a revenge game of sorts—but only by a 17–14 margin. The offense continued to sputter and after five games the team had a 2–3 record and was averaging only 19 points per game, compared to 35 in 1998. By the end of a desultory 24–22 loss to the Chicago Bears at the Metrodome on October 10 half the seats were empty and signs appeared calling for backup quarterback Jeff George. An 18-yard touchdown pass by Cunningham with two seconds remaining made the game seem closer than it actually was.

George, who had been the number one overall pick in the 1990 college draft, had been signed for a mere $400,000 to be Cunningham's backup. George had never fulfilled his promise on three teams in nine years in the NFL, at least partly due to his arrogance and antisocial behavior. Teams were still in awe of his quick release and golden arm, but none bid against the Vikings for him, figuring he was beyond reclamation.

Dennis Green finally pulled the plug on Cunningham at halftime on October 17 in Detroit, trailing 19–0. George completed 10 of 14 passes in the second half, for two touchdowns and rallied the team to a 23–22 lead, but the Lions scored on a field goal in the last minute to pull out a narrow 25–23 win. When Green named George his new starting quarterback, Cunningham was strangely acquiescent. "I support the decision 100 percent," he said. "It's not my time anymore. It's Jeff's time now."

A more humble Jeff George, surrounded as never before in his career by a star cast of receivers and runners, guided the team to an 8–2 record the rest of the way to finish 10–6 and earn a wild card playoff spot against the 8–8 Dallas Cowboys. Behind a solid game by George—12 for 25 passing for 212 yards, three touchdowns and no interceptions—the Vikings defeated the Cowboys, 27–10. A 58-yard touchdown pass to Randy Moss at the end of the first half gave the Vikings the lead for good at 17–10. Robert Smith gained 140 yards on 28 carries to help control the ball, and also scored a touchdown on a 26-yard pass from George.

The Vikings led the St. Louis Rams 17–14 at halftime in a divisional playoff the next week at St. Louis, but were outscored 35–20 in the second half to lose 49–37.

Minneapolis Star Tribune, January 17, 2000
RAMPAGE
ST. LOUIS BLITZES VIKINGS WITH 35-POINT SECOND HALF
Jim Souhan

So this is how quickly and pathetically Super Bowl hopes can die, with a former Arena Football League quarterback in a baseball town that had never before been host to an NFL playoff game flicking away the Vikings as if they were so much lint.

When it was mercifully over, after he had shredded the Vikings secondary for five touchdown passes in the Rams' 49–37 NFC divisional playoff victory at the Trans World Dome, Rams quarterback Kurt Warner was asked if he could believe it.

"Hey, I saw that sign," Warner said, referring to a fan's banner. "We still haven't played anybody."

That was the rap against the Rams entering this game—they hadn't played any good competition during their magical 13–3 regular season. Sunday, the Vikings changed that for, oh, about 15 minutes.

"We came to play 60 minutes of football, and I thought we did that," Vikings coach Dennis Green said.

He's arguably only 25 percent right, but after the Vikings took a 17–14 halftime lead with one of the most impressive quarters in franchise history, they collapsed in every possible way.

From the second-half kickoff until midway through the fourth quarter, the Rams scored 35 more points than the Vikings had first downs (35-0).

"We were doing well," receiver Cris Carter said of the Vikings outscoring the Rams 14–0 in the second quarter. "We played the first half a lot like we usually do. We feel the team out, the team scores, gets the lead, then we come back."

Unfortunately for the Vikings, they came back on the field for the second half.

The Rams had trailed for only 4:28 of their eight home games, and they had to spend halftime wondering about their legitimacy.

Then Tony Horne took the kickoff, cut left, stumbled and yet ran 95 yards untouched for the go-ahead score. Suddenly the crowd and the Rams' confidence were revived.

"The kickoff return for a touchdown, and a couple of turnovers, made all the difference in the world," Green said. "We went into halftime with the lead, and we did not come out with the lead."

Picking out key plays the rest of the way is difficult. How do you decide which snowflake causes an avalanche? During their 35–0 blitzkrieg, Warner completed passes to 10 receivers, and five Rams scored touchdowns: a kick returner (Horne), backup tight end (Jeff Robinson), running back (Marshall Faulk), a center lined up at tackle (Ryan Tucker) and another tight end (Roland Williams).

"We just didn't make enough plays," Carter said. "In the playoffs it's all about turnovers and big plays, and we just didn't play well in the second half as a team.

"I felt like we could beat St. Louis. You realize it's a difficult task, but we felt we matched up well with them. They put some pressure on us, but we knew their defensive backs couldn't cover us—and they had a hard time covering us, but they put pressure on us.

"A couple of series in the third quarter were big. If we could have gotten something going there—even if we had just gotten two or three first downs and punted them down deep, it's big."

After the Rams took a 14–3 first-quarter lead by scoring touchdowns on their first and fifth plays of the game—a 77-yard pass to Isaac Bruce and a 41-yard screen to Faulk—the Vikings put together what had to be one of the gutsiest quarters in franchise history.

With the Rams threatening to blow open the game early in the second quarter, Vikings cornerback Jimmy Hitchcock made a spectacular interception on a jump ball to Bruce, giving the Vikings the ball at the four.

Jeff George converted a third-and-14 with a 41-yard pass to Jake Reed and finished the 96-yard drive, as Rams fans created a maelstrom of noise, with a 22-yard touchdown pass to Carter. It was 14–10.

The Vikings defense held, then George threw an interception, but Faulk fumbled the ball away on the next play, and the Vikings drove 53 yards in seven plays, with Leroy Hoard scoring from the four. The Vikings led 17–14.

"We were in our comfort zone," defensive end Chris Doleman said.

Frighteningly, the Rams could have scored far more than 49 points if not for two turnovers and a missed field goal. In the decisive third quarter, the Vikings held the ball for only 2:35 and lost two fumbles.

"When you have a kick return to open the second half, and you fumble another kick and fumble a snap all in one quarter, are we good enough to overcome that?" Carter said. "No. It's breakdowns, mental breakdowns, mistakes, players just not making plays.

"What it boils down to, it's just man on man . . . They won more of the battles than we did. They're a good football team."

Carter thought he and Moss could beat the Rams' secondary, and he was right. George passed for 424 yards and four touchdowns. Moss and Carter combined for 299 yards and three scores.

Many of those yards, however, came on desperate fourth-quarter heaves, and the Rams' passing yardage was more meaningful.

Warner's five touchdown passes was one short of the NFL postseason record, and he completed 27 of 33 passes for 391 yards. Of his six incompletions, one came on a dropped pass and another when his arm was hit while he was throwing. His quarterback rating of 142.99 was the eighth-highest in postseason play.

"So much for playoff experience," Rams coach Dick Vermeil said.

So much for the Vikings.

●

Contract issues would dominate Vikings headlines for the next few months as salary cap problems made it nearly impossible for the team to keep all its veteran players. Wide receiver Jake Reed and tight end Andrew Glover were released, and free-agent center Jeff Christy—a Pro Bowl player in 1998 and 1999—signed with Tampa Bay. The most painful loss was 36-year-old Randall McDaniel, who had started in 11 consecutive Pro Bowls and had been first-team All Pro seven times.

Randall McDaniel (64), out of Arizona State University, was the Vikings' number one draft pick in 1988. He made the Pro Bowl 12 consecutive years (1989–2000) and was All Pro seven times. He was inducted into the NFL Hall of Fame in 2009. PHOTOGRAPH BY RICK A. KOLODZIEJ. COURTESY OF THE MINNESOTA VIKINGS.

Minneapolis Star Tribune, February 12, 2000
LEAVING WITH CLASS
RANDALL McDANIEL WAS A MAN OF FEW WORDS, BUT HE WILL
LEAVE AN IMPACT IN THE COMMUNITY, ESPECIALLY AT A PLYMOUTH
GRADE SCHOOL

Patrick Reusse

Randall McDaniel speaks in a soft and deliberate manner, yet his voice reso-
nates as though his dials are turned to bass. If he were to sing in the shower,
it might sound as though a young Barry White was in there.

On Friday, the media were invited to Pilgrim Lane Elementary School in
Plymouth, to listen to McDaniel say goodbye to the Vikings and their fans
after 12 seasons as a star left guard.

There was a full turnout of Twin Cities television stations and sportswriters. Several reporters made it obvious with their questions they had
attended to find out if McDaniel would have anything controversial to say
about his unhappy parting with the Vikings and coach Dennis Green.

Others among us had a more basic curiosity: We wanted to hear how
Randall's voice sounded.

Yes, on rare occasion during his 12 seasons in Minnesota, McDaniel had
uttered a couple of quiet sentences in response to reporters' questions. And,
if you ran across McDaniel away from football—say, at one of the charity
golf tournaments in which he has beat the ball around during recent off-
seasons—you would get a polite, "Hello . . . how's your summer going?"

Everyone who has been in the sports business here for the past decade
knew McDaniel was A, an outstanding football player, and B, an outstanding human being. We had the unanimous assurances of coaches and teammates on Point A, and the unanimous assurances of teammates and people
who had worked with him in various community causes on Point B.

What we didn't know, since when he had talked it was in snippets, was
how that voice really sounded. It's a rich voice, one that Randall has been
sharing with third graders at Pilgrim Lane for several years—and he shared
with Twin Cities reporters for 45 minutes while taking questions Friday.

The third graders of Pilgrim Lane also were in attendance, sitting on the
floor behind the minicams. The kids didn't have a good view and McDaniel's
responses were tough to hear. They did hear enough to cheer loudly when
"Mr. McDaniel" said the Twin Cities were going to continue to be his family's home, and he would continue as a volunteer teacher at Pilgrim Lane.

McDaniel was recruited for this duty by Nancy Benz, who teaches a
third-grade class at Pilgrim Lane. She also has been a Vikings' employee,
serving as the team's training camp coordinator for the stay in Mankato.

McDaniel has volunteered every other Tuesday (the players' day off) during the season and a couple of days per week for the remainder of the school year. He has a degree in physical education from Arizona State. He said Friday his post-football plan is to finish whatever requirements remain to become an elementary school teacher.

What he didn't say is that his career is over, despite Green's decision to cut him Thursday, four days after McDaniel had appeared in his 11th consecutive Pro Bowl (a record). He sounded like a man who wants to play a couple more years—perhaps maybe in Tampa Bay for Tony Dungy, his latest Pro Bowl coach, and a gentleman saluted by McDaniel several times in this media session.

Friday's audience included Mike Morris, McDaniel's road roommate with the Vikings. Morris' NFL future is also up in the air, but all he wanted to do on this morning was talk about his friend as a sensational football player and grand person.

"I've watched all the films," Morris said. "Randall McDaniel's the only football player to ever have a 190–0 record. There's never been a game when, after four quarters were over, an opposing player could say to himself, truthfully, 'I beat Randall McDaniel today.'"

Last year, a reporter talked to Bob Gray, one of McDaniel's coaches at Agua Fria High School in Avondale, Arizona. Gray told this story:

"After he played in the Rose Bowl for Arizona State, we were able to get him to speak to our students at an assembly. All the things Randall had accomplished—All American, outstanding lineman award in the Pac-10, helping Arizona State to the Rose Bowl for the first time and winning—were mentioned.

"Then, Randall got up and said the accomplishment of which he was most proud was from his first day of kindergarten until he graduated from high school, he never missed a day of school."

Several of Miss Benz's third graders were asked for their attendance records since their first day of kindergarten. Terri Grimlund came in with the low number: one day missed, "last year, when I had pink eye."

She was asked if she could imagine never missing another day before graduating from high school. "No," she said, as though the old bald guy talking to her had asked a very silly question.

"Well," said the old bald guy, "Mr. McDaniel never missed a day of school from kindergarten through high school graduation. Not one."

Young Miss Grimlund and several of her classmates looked at one another in disbelief. Then, Terri summarized the third-grade reaction by saying, "That's scary!"

McDaniel did sign with Tampa Bay, and he and Jeff Christy returned to the Pro Bowl once again after the 2000 season.

And, to no one's surprise, the quarterback position was up for grabs again. Dennis Green had used seven starting quarterbacks in his first eight years with the team, and Warren Moon had been the only repeat opening-day starter. Jeff George clearly was going to command more than a $400,000 salary in 2000, but Randall Cunningham—now a backup—was locked up in an expensive multiyear contract. Green, who was now the Vikings' personnel director, tried to get Cunningham to renegotiate his contract. He also advised George to shop around, and talked to Miami great Dan Marino about coming to the Vikings. Green eventually offered George a $440,000 contract with incentives up to triple that amount, but George turned him down and signed a four-year, $18.25 million deal with Washington to back up Brad Johnson.

Green became committed to Daunte Culpepper—his first-round draft choice out of Central Florida in 1999—as his starting quarterback. His long-term plan had originally been to have Culpepper study under Cunningham for two years, but Green now signed 13-year journeyman Bubby Brister, who had started for Pittsburgh in the late 1980s, as backup, and then released Cunningham.

Sports Illustrated, August 28, 2000
SCOUTING REPORT
COACH DENNIS GREEN IS PUTTING ALL HIS EGGS IN THE BASKET OF YOUNG, STRONG-ARMED QUARTERBACK DAUNTE CULPEPPER
Josh Elliott

Daunte Culpepper had scarcely completed his drop-back before the pocket collapsed, forcing him to hurry a throw that a Chiefs cornerback picked off. Because the 23-year-old Culpepper has never thrown a regular-season pass, such mistakes are to be expected. What was unexpected was the next decision he made in the informal scrimmage. Surveying the defense and recognizing a formation he didn't like, Culpepper changed the call from a safe run to a quick slant. He threw a strike but didn't celebrate the completion. He was too busy being—however unbelievably—the Vikings' starting quarterback, and NFL starting quarterbacks don't exult at well-executed audibles in August.

"When Daunte made that call I thought, We've got something here," says wideout Matthew Hatchette. "He showed a lot of poise and understanding. Every day he looks more like a veteran." Several teammates echo Hatchette's view and attest to Culpepper's maturity or his athleticism or his moxie, while coach and general manager Dennis Green expresses his utter comfort with Culpepper at the controls. "I absolutely think he's ready for what we're asking of him," says Green.

But then Culpepper has to be ready, because Green failed to sign an alternative in the off-season. First he cut loose Randall Cunningham, runner-up in the 1998 NFL MVP voting, then he balked at keeping Jeff George, who won nine of 12 starts last season. Only after his flirtation with Dan Marino went nowhere did Green go after George, who instead signed with the Redskins. Even for Green, who's prone to making enigmatic personnel decisions, banking on Culpepper smacks of desperation. A team that two years ago went 15–1 and that still possesses a talented core of skilled players is in the hands of an untested second-year man. "This is why we drafted him when we did [No. 11 in 1999]," says Green. "He will succeed. Randall came here and flourished. Didn't Jeff have his best year as a starter last year? I have faith in our system."

Indeed, in Green's eight years as coach the Vikings have never finished with a losing record. In seven of those seasons they have gone to the playoffs—with six starting quarterbacks. With wideouts Cris Carter and Randy Moss, a blossoming third receiver in Hatchette and former Pro Bowl running back Robert Smith, Culpepper will have a supporting cast few first-year starters have enjoyed. "It's nice knowing those guys are there if I get in trouble," says Culpepper. "But I was surprised I didn't play last year, to be honest. I feel like I belong with these guys, talentwise. I know I do."

Based upon his career at Central Florida, where he threw for 11,412 yards, broke 30 school records and set the NCAA single-season completion-percentage mark (73.6), Culpepper's quiet confidence seems reasonable. Moreover, Culpepper is a physical marvel: At 6'4" and 265 pounds he is perhaps the biggest NFL quarterback ever. With his size, strong arm and mobility, he is often compared to the Titans' Steve McNair, who held a clipboard for two years, then ran an ultraconservative offense for two seasons before leading Tennessee to the Super Bowl last January. Minnesota, however, can't afford such a leisurely timetable. "I know we'll be expected to win," says Culpepper. "That's fine. That's not pressure."

In a way he's right: Pressure on Culpepper will come on the field, where defenses—looking to neutralize the Vikings' superb intermediate and deep passing routes—are certain to blitz him relentlessly. Their job was made easier after center Jeff Christy and guard Randall McDaniel signed with the Bucs. Perhaps sensing impending chaos, Culpepper spent 10 weeks in Boca Raton, Florida, during the off-season sharpening his timing with Carter, Moss and Hatchette. Carter came away cautiously optimistic. "I believe Daunte can do it," he says. "How fast he learns and how much he wants to work, those things are up to him. But I believe he's going to be a great quarterback."

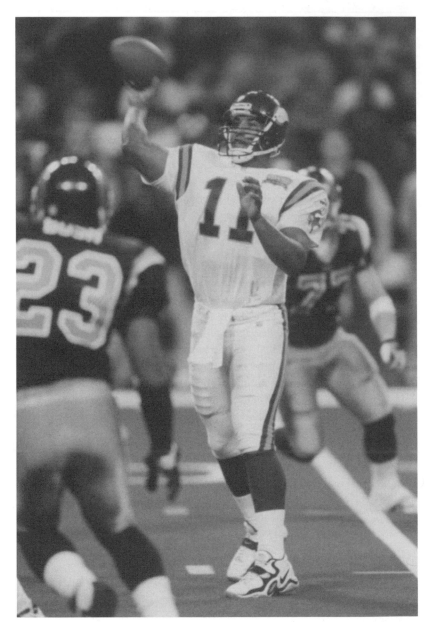

Coach Green was criticized in 2000 for not signing experienced quarterbacks Jeff George and Ran-dall Cunningham and for selecting Daunte Culpepper, from little-known Central Florida, as his starter. Culpepper, who had not thrown a pass in his rookie season in 1999, rewarded his coach with a Pro Bowl year. PHOTOGRAPH COURTESY OF THE MINNESOTA VIKINGS.

Following an afternoon practice at the team's Mankato, Minnesota, training camp, as the players trudged through the hordes of autograph hounds that lined the path to the locker room, only Moss was more sought after than Culpepper. Each time the quarterback stopped, a screaming frenzy ensued, until finally he had to go: Meetings, a quick dinner and more meetings awaited.

As he was stepping into the locker room, two kids pleaded with him to return. After a long moment, Culpepper—wearing an apologetic half grin—did just that and signed the wide-eyed boys' hats, shook their hands and posed for pictures with them.

In doing so Culpepper looked every bit a gracious, civic-minded NFL star. Maybe Carter and Green and the rest are right. Maybe he will be great someday. Then again, defenses won't be as easily impressed as a couple of eight-year-olds.

The Vikings were an unimpressive 1–3 in the preseason, but Daunte Culpepper gave the NFL a preview of what was to come in the season-opening 30–27 victory over the Chicago Bears. A raucous Metrodome crowd celebrated as he ran for 73 yards and three touchdowns, and completed 13 of 23 passes for 190 yards.

The team ran off six more victories before losing, and after a Thursday night 24–17 win over the Detroit Lions, stood at 11–2. The Vikings were the surprise of the NFL and Daunte Culpepper was the darling of the national press, who branded the 6'4", 260-plus pound hulk the "quarterback of the future." Vikings fans still suffering from the NFC championship game loss to Atlanta were jumping back on the bandwagon.

Minneapolis Star Tribune, December 4, 2000
VIKING FEVER ON THE RISE
MINNESOTA GETS THE HOME-FIELD ADVANTAGE FOR THE PLAYOFFS IF IT WINS SUNDAY
Randy Furst
John Zephirin delivers Sheetrock.

Thursday night, however, the 30-year-old Rosemount truck driver was in another world, the crowded Metrodome concourse before the Vikings–Lions game.

His face was painted purple, a horned helmet was atop his head and gold braids dangled past his ears. He was hand-in-hand with his 11-year-old daughter, Ashley, also decked out in Viking regalia.

"Super Bowl all the way this year!" shouted Zephirin, pausing to buy a

Enthusiastic Vikings fans make Metrodome Plaza an exciting place on game days. PHOTOGRAPH COUR-
TESY OF THE MINNESOTA VIKINGS.

beer from a vendor. "We got the two greatest wide receivers in NFL history, the MVP running back and the next Joe Montana at quarterback."

"You should see our house," Ashley added.

"My downstairs basement is dedicated to the Vikings," her father said.

Whether you are watching the game at eardrum-splitting volume from the perch of a Metrodome seat or taking it all in horizontally from a home sofa, a subtle viral infection is starting to take hold in the Minnesota populace. It's known in the local sports-medicine community as Viking Fever.

With or without a certain purple tinge to the skin, it is accompanied by great amounts of hope and a sudden desire to visit local merchants in the dead of winter and buy short-sleeved shirts with such names as "Culpepper" on the back.

As a holdover from previous outbreaks, there's also a touch of paranoia that it might end prematurely.

There is other evidence that the fever may be rising with anticipation of a possible Vikings entry in Super Bowl XXXV on January 28 in Tampa, Florida.

First off, the Vikings have a real shot at it. They have an 11–2 record, the best in professional football, and they clinched a playoff spot Thursday by defeating Detroit.

A victory Sunday over the St. Louis Rams would give the Vikings the Central Division championship, a day off for the first week of the playoffs and a guarantee that their playoff games, until the Super Bowl, would be in the Metrodome.

COULD BE SOME CRUISIN'

There's an excellent chance the Vikings would only have to win two playoff games to get into the Super Bowl and, if they maintain the best record in the National Conference, both of those games would be at the Metrodome next month.

That prospect has Paul Ridgeway of Minneapolis, who ought to have a charter membership in the Hypester Hall of Fame, even more hyped than usual.

Ridgeway, who is in charge of Super Bowl transportation and parking logistics for the National Football League, has a plan—if the Vikes are in the big game—to float a Viking ship into Tampa Bay the day before the game, with such folks aboard as Vikings owner Red McCombs and Governor Jesse Ventura, outfitted in Vikings garb.

"He [Ventura] would look great as a Viking," says Ridgeway. "I mean a Viking Viking."

The boat would then ride on wheels through Tampa's annual Gasparilla Pirate Fest parade, which typically draws 100,000 people.

Ridgeway is dickering with a group in Philadelphia that owns and staffs a 40-foot Viking boat about bringing it to Tampa. The only problem is that Minnesota might have to beat the Philadelphia Eagles to get into the Super Bowl, which could cause some ambivalence for the oarsmen aboard the ship.

"We might have a riot on the boat," laughed Dennis Johnson, a Philadelphia architect who is part of the group that operates the ship. Johnson is a graduate of the University of Minnesota, so the idea of promoting the Vikings doesn't annoy him.

The cost of renting the boat is $10,000, which Ridgeway figures he can swing with a corporate sponsor.

SIGNS OF THE OUTBREAK

Charlie Dahl, general manager of Nick's Sports World in downtown Minneapolis, recalled the intensity of fan interest in the 1998 season when the team had a 15–1 record and came within a missed field goal of beating Atlanta and going to the Super Bowl.

"This time the fans are little tempered because of the heartbreaking loss against Atlanta," Dahl said.

Nonetheless, he added, sales are "very good" and growing. He's sold about 700 Vikings jerseys this season, about 500 of them with quarterback Daunte Culpepper's name on the back.

"Every time they win, people get more excited about the postseason," Dahl said. "This could be the year."

Robert Smith and Randy Moss jerseys are hot items at Galyan's in Woodbury. "We can't keep them in stock," said Kim Gilbertson, a floor manager. "They are selling very well." Receiver Cris Carter's shirt has been another hot seller in stores along with Chris Walsh, a receiver who plays on special teams.

Jeff Wistrom, store manager of Champs Sports at the Mall of America, is gearing up for another onslaught. If they clinch the division title next Sunday, he plans to have several hundred division championship T-shirts in stock.

They have a short shelf life. If the team wins the conference championship January 14, fans will want shirts with that title on them.

As always, Super Bowl tickets will be an expensive commodity and particularly hard to get if the Vikings are in the game, according to longtime Super Bowl observers. Many Minnesotans winter in Florida and will want to get their hands on tickets.

Jim Steeg, the NFL's senior vice president for special events, said that the price of a Super Bowl ticket will be $325, or $400 for club seats. Those are seats where fans have access to a bar and other amenities. If the Vikings wind up in the Super Bowl, the team will receive 10,000 to 11,000 tickets.

According to Phil Huebner, director of Vikings ticket sales, season-ticket holders will be put in a lottery drawing, and if the Vikes are in the Super Bowl, those whose names are drawn will have an opportunity to buy two tickets.

Long-term loyalty to the Vikings will count: Huebner said the number of lottery slips will be based on the number of seats a ticket holder has, multiplied by the number of years he or she has been a ticket owner. Someone who has four seats and has been a season-ticket holder for 30 years would be entered 120 times, he explained.

For the most part, however, Super Bowl tickets for the general public will only be available through out-of-state ticket brokers, such as Ticket Exchange in Phoenix. Expect to pay $2,100 for an upper-level end-zone seat or $4,500 for a seat on the 50-yard line. Raymond James Stadium seats about 71,000 people.

Twin Cities–area companies already are looking into chartering trips to Tampa. Steve Erban, marketing director for Creative Charters in Lake Elmo, figures he'll send at least one planeload of fans to Florida, maybe more, if the Vikings make it.

"I think there will be a very big interest because we were so close a couple of years ago and the reality of going to a Super Bowl for Minnesotans is big," Erban said.

Bob Hagan, Vikings public relations director, pointed to the increasing crush of national media interest in the team, reflected in the cover story on Culpepper in the current issue of *Sports Illustrated* and a recent cover story in *ESPN The Magazine*. "Our press box has been virtually full for every home game and on the road, too, because a lot of national press want to follow us," Hagan said. "Sometimes the media room is kind of crowded from people coming in from elsewhere . . . Obviously the fans are getting pumped up."

Dennis Green basked in the glow of the team's success. He had taken a lot of heat for the tough 1999 season and the internal bickering on the team that spilled out onto the playing field at times, but the team's success had once again quieted his critics. Fox TV announcer John Madden declared Green the Coach of the Year.

Los Angeles Times, December 10, 2000

VIKINGS' GREEN REWARDS MCCOMBS, WHO STOOD BY COACH AGAINST ALL ADVICE

Bill Plaschke

The bear of a man could stare down thundering John Randle, straighten up raucous Cris Carter, shut up rowdy Jim McMahon.

But he couldn't do anything about the whispers.

The raucous atmosphere inside the Dome gives the Vikings a big home-field advantage. Team mascot Ragnar (aka Joe Juranitch) stirs up fans when he blasts out of the inflatable Viking ship on his motorcycle. PHOTOGRAPH COURTESY OF THE MINNESOTA VIKINGS.

Whispers about his intelligence. Whispers about his personal life. The constant, droning whispers about his color.

In 1998, six years after Dennis Green of the Minnesota Vikings became the second black head coach in the history of the NFL, the whispers reached the ear of his new boss.

"Some of the other NFL owners told me that the good news was, Dennis Green only had one year left on his contract," recalled Red McCombs, the plain-speaking Texan who bought the Vikings that summer. "They said I would not get along with Dennis. He was too strong-willed. He was too much for himself, and not enough for the organization."

Too often in society, this is where the racism meets the road. A whisper becomes a gospel. Another opportunity is lost.

"Except, I'm the kind of guy, I only believe what I see," McCombs said.

Thirty minutes after buying the team, he called Green. He later hung out with him at training camp. He listened to his meetings. He talked to his players.

What he eventually saw convinced him to, against all popular opinion, extend his coach's contract.

What he sees today is not only football's best team, but its best active coach.

What the diverse sports world should see is business the way business should be done.

"I'm only here because Red McCombs threw me a lifeline," Green said. "He is fair and upfront. We share the same beliefs."

Mainly, that people should not be surmised in a look, or judged by a whisper.

Today Green leads the Vikings, with a league-best 11–2 record, against the defending Super Bowl champion Rams.

There will be much talk about Daunte Culpepper and Randy Moss and Robert Smith.

There will, once again, be little said about the guy who leads them.

It is time that changed.

"Dennis has the best football mind in the game," his boss said.

McCombs phoned approximately four minutes after being faxed a request to talk about Green.

Green phoned less than 10 minutes after being given a request to talk about, among other things, McCombs.

Said McCombs: "Bottom line is, I just like the hell out of the guy."

Said Green: "It's all about being given an opportunity."

Since he became a head coach in 1992, he has made more of that opportunity than any other coach in the game. He has the league's longest current coaching tenure with one team, and the numbers show it.

He has won 92 games in that span, the most by any active coach.

By clinching a playoff berth last week, he has led his team to eight post-season appearances in that span, the most by any team.

Probably his most impressive statistic, though, is that he has gone to the playoffs with seven different quarterbacks.

Mike Shanahan is generally considered the game's best boss, but until this season, his entire success was based on John Elway.

Mike Holmgren is another Super Bowl champion coach, but has failed miserably without Brett Favre.

Green does not have their rings. His teams have won only three of 10 postseason games.

But nobody has been more consistent, and consistently right, than this guy who is rarely publicized, rarely complimented, and, frankly, lucky to still have his job.

"I coach the same way I've always coached," Green said. "This is about continuity."

A couple of seasons ago, when a freak missed field goal by Gary Anderson kept the Vikings out of the Super Bowl, everyone thought Green was being propped up by offensive coordinator Brian Billick.

Billick left to run the Baltimore Ravens, and Green continued to win.

Last season, when they lost in the divisional playoffs to the Rams, everyone thought Green was being propped up by quarterback Jeff George.

George left, and Green continued to win.

This season he has a new quarterback, new offensive coordinator, new defensive coordinator, and two new offensive linemen replacing longtime veterans Jeff Christy and Randall McDaniel.

The Vikings were picked to finish in the bottom of the NFC Central.

But they continue to win.

"This game is all about taking risks, moving forward, being decisive," Green said. "You can't be afraid."

He is surrounded by a league that disagrees.

Even though nearly 80 percent of the players are black, there are only two black head coaches (Terry Robiskie of the Washington Redskins is an interim).

The other full-timer, Tony Dungy of the Tampa Bay Buccaneers, remembers that when interviewing for jobs, he was told by one owner he couldn't hire many black assistants because the community wouldn't accept it.

Green's two new coordinators? Both are black.

"This is not about hiring a black coach," Green said. "It's about hiring the best coach. The problem is, too often, people don't take the time to find the best coach."

In the past, he has rarely spoken about the racial imbalance in the league's hierarchy, preferring to crusade with victories. But as that imbalance grows, so does his impatience.

"It is hard to believe that there are only two full-time [black] head coaches out of 31 jobs, especially in this day and age," he said. "I'm always trying to make sure we have equal access to the jobs. It's all about equal access."

For more than just coaches.

Many in the league still don't like playing blacks at quarterback.

Green's new quarterback? A linebacker-looking guy named Daunte Culpepper, who also happens to be black.

"You can't listen to what everybody is saying," Green said. "You have to do what you believe."

Green won't talk much about it, but there was a time when he heard every word. Early in his tenure with the Vikings, every loss was scrutinized, every action was questioned.

Off the field, there were reports—one that even appeared in a book—of off-field indiscretions. Although he made the playoffs in five of his first six years, there was talk of a firing.

Shortly before McCombs purchased the team, Green even wrote his own book, *No Room For Crybabies*, in which he threatened to sue two minority owners for undermining the team.

One of the first questions posed to McCombs was, what did he think about the book?

"I knew that question was coming, and I was ready with my answer," McCombs said. "I didn't read it, and I wasn't going to read it. I was going to judge Dennis starting right now."

Coincidentally, all of this happened about the same time that Green ignored past reports on a guy named Randy Moss, who he drafted twenty-first overall. You know what happened next.

McCombs was so impressed with Green's evaluation skills that he gave him complete football control of the operation.

For his part, Green says he has matured beyond his past personal troubles, and is remarried with two young children.

Yet some things haven't changed.

Many mornings before practice, Green relaxes by playing the drums in his office.

Every day during practice, Green relates to his players by running the scrub—or "scout"—team.

He is the only coach in the league who bothers.

"It's important to look at everyone, to know your players," Green said. "It is important to give everyone an opportunity."

There's that word again. Opportunity.

Dennis Green received one, so he's giving them out by the handful.

Red McCombs gave one, and is being rewarded by the week.

An unusually simple, incredibly smart proposition.

One would think.

●

The Vikings limped into the postseason, however, with three straight losses, to finish at 11–5. The Rams exposed the Vikings' defensive weaknesses in game 14 at St. Louis on December 10, racking up 508 yards and winning 40–29. Culpepper suffered a high-ankle sprain late in a 33–28 loss in the Metrodome against Green Bay, and played only a few series in the final regular-season game at Indianapolis. The Vikings lost 31–10, and gained only 236 total yards, their worst output since September 29, 1996—coming only one week after setting an NFL record with 30 consecutive games above 300 yards.

Culpepper had two more weeks to heal, and the team seemed to recapture its early-season form while defeating the New Orleans Saints in a divisional playoff game at the Metrodome, 34–16. Randy Moss had touchdown catches of 53 and 68 yards, and Cris Carter had one of 17 yards.

The NFC championship game in New York was a 41–0 disaster. The Giants received the opening kickoff and took only 1:57 to drive for a touchdown. Then, on the following kickoff, return men Moe Williams and Troy Walters couldn't handle a short kick, and the Giants recovered on the Vikings' 18-yard line. Giants quarterback Kerry Collins threw a touchdown pass on the next play, and the Vikings found themselves down 14–0 before their offense had taken the field. The Vikings trailed 34–0 at the half and were never in the game.

Minneapolis Star Tribune, January 15, 2001

NFC CHAMPIONSHIP: UGLY PLAYOFF LOSS, NOT SEASON, WILL STAY WITH FANS

Sid Hartman

True, the Vikings won the NFC Central Division title, and they posted an unexpected 12–6 overall record this season.

But unfortunately what could have turned out to be a great season went down the drain Sunday when the Giants buried the Vikings 41–0, the first time a Dennis Green team has been shut out in his nine seasons as the Vikings' head coach.

It's sad, but all the fans are going to remember is one thing—the one-sided loss to the Giants. The Vikings went to four Super Bowls and lost all four. Well, you never heard the Vikings had won the NFC title. All the fans talked about were the Super Bowl losses.

That is going to be the same story again.

The Giants had scored 30 points or more only three times during the regular season, including a season-high 33 in beating Philadelphia on September 10.

The Giants finished near the bottom of the NFL in passing and have been a team that has won low-scoring games, such as a 14–7 victory over Chicago, a 13–6 victory over Atlanta and a 9–7 victory over Washington.

So, when the Vikings coaches studied film of the Giants, they looked for New York to run the ball with Ron Dayne and Tiki Barber as it has all season.

Vikings receiver Randy Moss mentioned the fact the team didn't enter Sunday's game with much respect for the passing ability of Giants quarterback Kerry Collins and a receiving corps that didn't have close to the ability of Moss and Cris Carter.

The Vikings defensive game plan could not have included any real concerns about the Giants' passing game. And nobody in their right mind expected Collins to throw for five touchdowns in a record-setting performance.

But once the Giants had success on their first two drives—scoring on Collins' 46-yard touchdown pass to Ike Hilliard and then on an 18-yard TD pass from Collins to Greg Comella after New York recovered a fumble on the ensuing kickoff—they proceeded to do what the Rams, Packers and Colts did to the Vikings defense in the final three regular-season games.

A ROUGH STRETCH

Having spent a lot of time at Winter Park last week and watching how upbeat and confident the Vikings were they could handle the Giants, I expected Green's team to win this game by three touchdowns. But the Giants apparently wanted this game more than the Vikings.

Eliminating the Vikings' 34–16 playoff victory over the Saints, Minnesota gave up 145 points in a four-game span. And all the losses were the result of a hot quarterback—St. Louis' Kurt Warner, Green Bay's Brett Favre, Indianapolis' Peyton Manning and Collins—picking the Vikings' pass defense apart.

As in their losses to the Rams, Packers and Colts, the Vikings were able to get little pass rush and Collins was hardly touched all day.

The Vikings are anywhere from $12 million to $20 million over the salary cap. They need to improve the entire defense. But the big problem is going to be signing running back Robert Smith and Moss, leaving little money for defensive help.

The 49ers, Cowboys and Packers have found out how tough it is stay on top of the standings because of the salary cap. It could be the same story for the Vikings.

Green has done a great job keeping the Vikings competitive despite salary-cap problems, but it's going to be much tougher for him in the future.

TOUGH ON MCCOMBS

Charline McCombs, wife of Vikings owner Red McCombs, said there were a lot of tears in the family's executive box Sunday.

"It's really tough," she said. "It feels like I've been kicked in the chest. I was looking forward to a win, this championship and then the Super Bowl. I wanted it so badly for Red. We all did. It's pretty tough. It hurts. I think if we had been at home, we would have had a better chance. I really do. But you can't take anything away from the Giants. They played very well."

Following the game, Red McCombs told the players: "I support Dennis and everything that he does. My job is to pay the players, so we can put the best team on the field."

McCombs expanded on his comments after he left the locker room. "I can tell you we are committed to what we were the very first day we got here, and that's to win the championship," he said. "I have no idea [what went wrong]. I'm sure we won't be making any decisions in the emotional state we are right now. I don't even know what to say. Some days it rains, and some days it floods. Today, we got a flood.

"Nobody's job is in jeopardy. I love all of them, and they're great football players and great coaches. Dennis makes all of those decisions, and I'll be supporting him 100 percent. I'm not unhappy, I'm hurt."

SMITH CONFIDENT

Smith, who rushed for 44 yards on seven carries, said he didn't lack any confidence entering the game.

"I felt as confident going into this game as I have any game this year," he said. "I just felt everybody was ready to play. I thought we'd come out with a lot of fire. I think the guys were pumped up. But you get down quickly like that on the road . . . You can't take anything away from the Giants. They obviously played a great game offensively and defensively."

Smith said nobody panicked when the Giants took a 14–0 lead before the Vikings offense had even taken the field.

"It wasn't the first time for us, and I don't think anyone was panicking," he said. "You go down and score a touchdown right away, and that's 14–7. We turned the ball over there early as well, that hurt us, but we were still in the game."

Asked about his impending free agency, Smith said, "I don't know what I'm going to do."

DID A GOOD JOB

Linebacker Kailee Wong said the Vikings expected the Giants' offense to try to control the ball.

"We definitely knew they were going to try to start fast and keep our offense off the field," he said. "So we kind of suspected that. But the way they came out throwing the ball I think it did surprise us a little bit.

"Collins did a really good job. He knew what coverages we were in and was throwing to the parts where you're vulnerable in certain coverages. He did a good job out there."

Wong said that in the past the Giants have tried to establish the run first.

"Watching the film, they always tried to establish the run a little bit more," he said. "With us, they tried to establish the pass today."

●

Seven Vikings were chosen to play in the Pro Bowl: receivers Randy Moss—who also made first-team All Pro—and Cris Carter, running back Robert Smith, quarterback Daunte Culpepper, center Matt Birk, tackle Korey Stringer, and defensive back Robert Griffith. Culpepper tied Peyton Manning of the Colts with 33 touchdown passes, and ranked fourth in passing yards and in the quarterback passer ratings. Smith had his best year, finishing second to the Colts' Edgerrin James with 1,521 yards rushing, but the 28-year-old confounded the team by announcing his retirement. It wasn't the only unexpected decision Smith had made in his career.

Sporting News, February 19, 2001
GOODBYE, MR. SMITH
Dave Kindred

The first time sports writer Bob Fortuna saw Robert Smith, here's what Robert Smith was doing: running with a football. A high school sophomore, 16 years old. And not just running.

Running the way O. J. Simpson ran. High strides on long, skinny legs. Strong, smooth, fast. The first time Bob Fortuna saw Robert Smith run, here's what Bob Fortuna said: "Whoooaaa." The sudden sound of serendipitous discovery.

Twelve years later, the telephone rings in Bob Fortuna's home in Euclid, Ohio.

"Where's your dad?" It's Robert Smith talking to Jessica, the sports writer's daughter.

"I don't know."

"Could I talk to your mother, please?"

Donna Fortuna says her husband is covering a gymnastics meet, and she's not sure when he'll be home.

"Have him call me, please. I need to talk to him."

About nine o'clock that night, as Fortuna tells the story, "Donna says, 'You better call Rob, it sounds serious.'"

Running back Robert Smith surprised fans when he retired at age 28 after the 2000 season. Injuries hampered him early in his pro career, but he rushed for over 1,000 yards in each of his final four seasons. PHOTOGRAPH COURTESY OF THE MINNESOTA VIKINGS.

For a long time, Robert Smith was the NFL's best invisible running back. Only now have we noticed his transformation from sprinter to the full package. A free agent after eight seasons, he became the subject of high-dollar speculation: $40 million for five seasons, perhaps on a team less dysfunctional than the Vikings?

Fortuna calls him, and Robert Smith says: "I'm going to retire, and I want you to have the story."

Whoooaaa.

Even for his friend, Smith answered no questions. In fact, he retired by e-mail—sort of. When his e-mail showed up garbled, Smith called back to Fortuna, who dictated his farewell to football and thanks to friends.

No fancy news conference. No public displays of sentiment. No contract negotiations by threat of retirement. Just a phone call to the man who'd written him up for the suburban weekly *Euclid Sun Journal* and now covers scholastic sports for the *Cleveland Plain Dealer*.

Such commonsense behavior, alien to today's egomaniacal athlete, is in keeping with the character, personality and intelligence of Robert Smith. Leave the trash talk to Randy Moss. Leave the money talk to Deion Sanders. Leave God to Reggie White. Robert Smith became an NFL star the old-fashioned way: He earned it.

He ran for more yards than any Viking ever. He scored touchdowns on runs of 40 yards or longer in six seasons. The Giants' Jason Sehorn called him "Eddie George with another gear." The trauma of life as an NFL running back was such that doctors often explored his knees, and yet Smith running with a football was an act of athleticism so beautiful it moved at least one journalist to drop Smith's name into a sentence with Joe DiMaggio's.

The *New York Observer* columnist Michael M. Thomas remembered DiMaggio's running style, "effortless, powerful, above all, smooth." Then Thomas added, "The way Robert Smith of the Vikings runs reminds me of Joe D."

DiMaggio retired at 36. Beleaguered by heel and knee injuries, he no longer could make the hard work look easy. It would be no surprise to learn that Robert Smith has retired at 28 because he acknowledged two truths athletes often ignore: 1) the hard work was no longer easy, and 2) if you play now, you pay later.

"When Robert hurt his knee this last time," says Paul Serra, once a Euclid High baseball coach and Smith's legal guardian, "he told me, 'I want to be able to walk when I'm 40.'"

After playing hurt the last month of the Vikings season, Smith underwent surgery for the fourth time on that knee. He had left Ohio State eight years earlier with no long-range NFL plans, and Serra says, "Robert always said, 'I'm only one injury away from not doing anything.'"

So Smith has walked away while he still can walk.

Nor is it the first time he walked.

He enrolled at Ohio State with plans to go to medical school, perhaps to study orthopedics. His curiosity encompassed genetic research, molecular biology and astronomy (friends call him "Copernicus"). As admirable as all that is in a student-athlete, there's evidence one coach thought, "And how does that beat Michigan?"

Smith said offensive coordinator Elliot Uzelac demanded he miss two classes to attend practice. Rather than bend to what he considered an unreasonable order, Smith sat out his sophomore season. Coincidentally or not, the coach was fired the next winter. Smith then suited up and told *The Plain Dealer*:

"If I go out this fall and rush for 2,000 yards, if we win the Big Ten championship and I win the Heisman Trophy, if I go on to become a doctor and find a cure for cancer, then become president of the United States, there will still be people that will call me 'that prima donna that got Coach Uzelac fired.'"

There is that. Even now Smith often stands accused of arrogance. Dan Barreiro of the *Minneapolis Star Tribune* once quoted Smith on the religious zealotry in the NFL. First Smith said of the evangelizing Reggie White, "I find many of Reggie's comments incredibly ignorant. His statements on gays are embarrassing and speak to how little he knows . . ."

As for Cris Carter and Deion Sanders saying religion saved their lives, fine, "But wearing it on your sleeve to where it dominates the whole part of you, to where some guys seem to say they're better than you because of their religious faith, that bothers me."

Smith has created the Robert Smith Foundation supporting children's hospitals and funding cancer research. He might yet become a researcher himself. Bright and articulate, he also might do television football commentary.

The wonder is not that such a man quit football so young.

The wonder is that he played at all.

●

Smith wasn't the only starter lost for the 2001 season. Six-time All Pro defensive lineman John Randle and seven-year starting offensive tackle Todd Steussie were lost due to salary cap woes, and linebacker Duane Rudd was lost to free agency. Hopes were high that speedster Michael Bennett, their first round draft choice (twenty-seventh overall) out of Wisconsin, would fill Smith's shoes, and the passing attack seemed set with Culpepper throwing to Randy Moss and Cris Carter. The pair had combined for 173 receptions and 2,711 yards in 2000, and Moss's 15 touchdown receptions led the league. In May, Carter announced it would be his last season, but he was in great shape, thanks to his rigorous off-season training program, and the team was counting on him for his ninth consecutive 1,000-yard season.

USA Today, July 3, 2001

VIKINGS STAR CARTER SAVING BEST FOR LAST
RECEIVER WORKING HARDER THAN EVER FOR FINAL SEASON
Jarrett Bell

Soaked in sweat after a grueling two-hour workout on a nearby high school field, Cris Carter returns to his immaculate, Mediterranean-style house and promptly heads to the pool. He slips into a weighted flotation device, then slides into the cool water to unwind with . . . more exercise.

This water therapy represents a new twist to Carter's regimen. And it's evidence that despite the Hall of Fame credentials the Minnesota Vikings star receiver has achieved—heading into his fifteenth season he's the only player in NFL history other than Jerry Rice with more than 1,000 catches—he's still open to new tricks.

"Bye, Crissy," Carter's wife, Melanie, shouts from the patio. "I'm going shopping."

"Don't forget your resolution," Carter hollers back.

"Which one?" she asks.

"The new one," he says. "This is definitely my last year in the NFL. What do they say when you leave church? 'Govern yourself accordingly.'"

She heads for the mall with a laugh. And Carter spends the next hour twisting, stretching and jogging in the water—which helps his muscles recover faster. At 35, anything that will reduce soreness is a good thing.

"This is the first time I've tried it," Carter says. "I do feel a difference."

Carter just hired a new speed coach, too. And about a month before the Vikings open training camp, he insists he's in the best condition ever at this point of the year, because he started his off-season training—a boot camp so revered that it attracts about 30 NFL players to work out with him—a month earlier than normal.

And this guy is retiring? Carter has played in eight consecutive Pro Bowls. He ranked third in the NFC last season with 96 catches. A crafty possession type, he shows no sign of slippage. He says he can do more now, physically, than he could at 30.

But rather than daydream about a farewell tour, Carter has been proceeding with the zeal of a long-shot free agent. This approach tells you as much as anything about how a man who climbed from the depths of career turmoil—the Vikings got Carter off waivers in 1990 for $100 after drug and alcohol addiction got him kicked to the curb by the Philadelphia Eagles—to status as one of the league's most respected elders.

Never mind the attractive post-playing career options that loom, including the management services company Carter owns with a brother that recently signed a lucrative partnership deal with ADT Security Systems. Carter still is driven for one last, big splash on the playing field.

"There's a side of me that says when I do retire and look back, there won't be any regrets," he says. "There won't be anything else I can do from a physical standpoint to play at a higher level. So I'm putting myself in position to play at the level I'm used to."

WORKING ON WEAKNESSES

He hasn't caught a football all off-season—not even horsing around with his kids, 10-year-old son Duron and seven-year-old daughter Monterae.

"The human being normally likes to work on things that they do well," Carter explains. "People wonder why they don't get different results from doing the same thing. As far as my catching is concerned, all I want are the same results. As far as my running speed, agility and quickness, I want some different results. I only work on my weaknesses, not my strengths."

Carter has become quite the guru for extracting the most from one's talent. His FAST Program—a patented speed, strength and conditioning routine that is run by a full-time staff—has become popular with athletes from varied sports and levels.

Carter says the program has had more than 3,000 participants the last two years, and for every big name, such as NBA star Vince Carter, there have been dozens of college players prepping for the NFL combine and hundreds of high school soccer players. When Randy Moss was drafted by the Vikings in 1998, he enrolled in Carter's program, then later called it a key to his explosive rookie season.

"There are a lot of different ways to do it," says Carter, who credits former teammates Roger Craig and Herschel Walker for inspiring him to upgrade his emphasis on conditioning earlier in his career. "My program is just one of the ways. It's not the best way or the only way. But we've had tremendous results."

To Carter, an ordained minister, it's another way to share his knowledge and experience with his fellow man. He laughs when he remembers how former Vikings receiver Anthony Carter used to tell him he would wind up losing his job to one of the many young receivers he has shared tips with.

Carter never did lose his job to a younger receiver but has encountered one in Moss who is capable of someday surpassing Carter's Vikings records. Says Carter, "Randy's the only guy I've played with that I couldn't teach everything I know."

The lessons Carter shares, though, are on a variety of life issues, and the message usually hits home because he took such a hard, comeback path to greatness. Getting cut by the Eagles jolted Carter into putting his fast-lane lifestyle in the rearview mirror.

While running his total of career receiving touchdowns to 123 (second only to Rice) and becoming a community pillar (he was named the NFL's Man of the Year in 1999), Carter has maintained his sobriety for more than 10 years.

"But I live with that every day," he says. "People say, 'Look at the end result. It turned out so great.' But to me, I live with it every day. There's no day that I get up that I'm not a drug addict, an alcoholic. So I would change that. That's not my desire to wake up every day with that pressure on me.

"It gives me a tremendous ability to understand other people. But for me, personally, no, I wouldn't have drawn it up that way."

Carter's now more focused on mapping out his future rather than dwelling on his past. His agent, Mitch Frankel, marvels at how meticulous Carter has been for the last five years in preparing for life after football. Carter announced his intention to retire in early May during a banquet in his hometown of Middletown, Ohio.

"There's only one thing that would make me reconsider," Carter says. "Finishing in a way with an injury or something that I didn't like. Not based on performance."

Says Frankel: "The decision to retire was very difficult for Cris. He's still playing at a level most people dream of playing at. He's smart enough to walk into the arena of big business and be as successful as he is on the field. I can't say that about most athletes."

SUPER BOWL RUN?

But there's also unfinished business on the field that is calling Carter back for another run that includes a regular-season finale December 30 at a fitting venue: Lambeau Field, pitted against the NFC Central rival Green Bay Packers.

Carter has never played in a Super Bowl. The Vikings were one victory from the Super Bowl in January but were blasted away by the Giants in their second NFC title game loss in three years. In obvious disgust after the game, Moss even suggested that Carter not return if he wanted to win a Super Bowl. A shaky defense that wasn't significantly upgraded this off-season may add further doubt about the Vikings' ability to get over the hump.

Yet Carter rolls his eyes at the thought of making his final run a Super Bowl or bust mission.

"Randy was accurate," Carter says. "I'm not coming back just to win a Super Bowl. What he was saying was, 'Cris, I love you so much, I don't want you to put all of your hope into winning and be disappointed.'"

Still, in Carter the Vikings have at least one man primed to do his part one last time.

◉

Tragedy struck the team when offensive tackle Korey Stringer collapsed of heatstroke during practice on July 31. He died the next morning. "Big K" had been one of the most popular players in the locker room. Right tackle is not the most glamorous position in football, and stars like Stringer often labor in obscurity. Many Vikings fans were surprised to read about the 6'4", 350-pound giant's gentle nature and sense of humor.

Over 1,000 mourners gathered in 90-degree temperatures outside the Washburn-McCreavy Funeral Chapel in Edina for the visitation. At the private funeral service Cris Carter and Randy Moss struggled to find words to express their emotions. Coach Green said that the team was taking baby steps to deal with his loss, while line coach Mike Tice said that "I've got a hole inside of me that I don't know will ever heal. I've got a scar on my heart."

Sports Illustrated, August 13, 2001
REQUIEM FOR A VIKING
IT TOOK HIS UNTIMELY DEATH FOR THE WORLD TO LEARN ABOUT KOREY STRINGER
Steve Rushin

I always liked Korey Stringer, but only for his hair, which exploded from his head in mini-dreadlocks, like novelty spring snakes from an opened can, and for the way—in his purple Vikings uniform top—he put me in mind of a hip-hop Barney the Dinosaur. Beyond that I knew almost nothing about the Minnesota offensive tackle until he died on August 1 at age 27 and I learned that he had lived year-round in Bloomington. That's my hometown, and the place where all my friends and I had become, like it or not, permanently em-Purpled. As adults we can no more shake our lifelong allegiance to the Vikings than we can shed our ties to one another, or to Bloomington, or to our families. To this day my computer password is V-I-K-I-N-G, and the single item in my home that betrays my profession is a Vikings road jersey, number 88, that was signed and sent to me by my all-time hero, Alan Page. (When, as a 33-year-old, I opened the box that the jersey came in, the hair on my arms stood on end.)

So I was looking forward to last weekend with greater excitation than is perhaps strictly healthy in a grown man. Ron Yary, the right tackle on the four Vikings Super Bowl teams of my childhood, would be inducted into the Pro Football Hall of Fame last Saturday, 24 hours before Twins centerfielder Kirby Puckett—the most popular person, now or ever, in the state of Minnesota—would be enshrined in the Baseball Hall of Fame. St. Paul native and former Twin Dave Winfield would join Puckett in Cooperstown on Sunday, making the weekend one of the most anticipated in the sports history of my home state. It was especially resonant for me that each of the athletes involved was retired. The Vikings of today, while I rooted for them, were not real. They were cartoons, almost literally so in the case of Stringer, with the Barney build and Sideshow Bob hair. I admired the preposterous talent of wide receiver Randy Moss, but was put off by his arrogance, which appeared to be equally outsized.

Those shallow assumptions changed when Stringer, in essence, worked himself to death in practice last week and, hours later, Moss stepped to a

Coach Green comforts Randy Moss as Cris Carter speaks at a news conference following the death of Korey Stringer, who collapsed and died of heat stroke at the Vikings training camp in August 2001. AP PHOTOGRAPH BY JIM MONE. COURTESY OF AP IMAGES.

microphone to remember his friend. He got only as far as this halting reminiscence: "After the games I'd see his wife and son in the lounge . . ." Then grief bent him double like a jackknife, and Moss was led away from the podium, sobbing. In that instant, two comic-book figures stepped off the page and became—for the first time in my eyes—fully human.

In the days following his death, news reports revealed Stringer to be the best-liked player in the Vikings' locker room. The compliments were not the customary kindnesses that eulogists grant to anyone who hasn't been convicted of crimes against humanity. We read, rather, of countless instances that brought Stringer, in death, fully to life. A caller to a Twin Cities radio station told of Stringer's stopping, after a Vikings game, to help the fan change a tire. While visiting a youth football program in his hometown of Warren, Ohio, Stringer retrieved from his truck his $15,000 Pro Bowl appearance check and—on an impulse—endorsed it over to the organization. He was, of course, father to three-year-old Kodie, so the 335-pound Stringer sat on his Bloomington porch on Halloween and insisted that timid children take more candy from the bowl: Take a "Korey handful," he told trick-or-treaters.

He was, in other words, exceedingly difficult to dislike. Tom Powers of the *Saint Paul Pioneer Press* recalled a tense postgame locker room in which Moss lashed out at reporters who were waiting at his locker after a shower. "Why don't you go over there and watch Big K get dressed?" Moss told the throng. To which Big K replied, "Have to put a dollar in the G-string if you want to watch. I'm not going to perform for free." Everyone—reporters and Moss alike—roared.

"The hardest thing I had to do was ask him to be a tough guy," Vikings offensive line coach Mike Tice said of Stringer at Friday's memorial. "You know why? He wasn't a tough guy. He was a sweetheart. He was a teddy bear. He was a little kid."

Evidently Stringer tried at one time to be more menacing, getting a tattoo that read FTW (F—— the World). But he didn't have it in him, and Stringer began to tell people that the tat really stood for Find the Way. He seems to have done so before saying goodbye. Or not goodbye, really, for Stringer never said that. In parting, he always said, "Peace."

It's a tragedy that someone as young as Stringer had to speak his final Peace last week. At the same time, it was a privilege, finally, to have met him.

●

The noisy, capacity crowd that showed up at the Metrodome for the first game of the season were stunned when Carolina rookie Steve Smith took the opening kickoff and ran 93 yards for a touchdown. The Vikings struggled to a 13–10 lead early in the second half, but lost 24–13. It was to be Carolina's only win for the season.

The nation was stunned by the terrorist attacks on the World Trade Center and the Pentagon two days later, and the sports world grappled with the proper response. On Thursday, NFL Commissioner Paul Tagliabue, mindful of the criticism his predecessor Pete Rozelle received for not calling off games two days after President Kennedy was assassinated in 1963, called off all games on the weekend. Most other sports organizations, professional and amateur, followed suit. It was not that simple a decision. Many wanted to defy the terrorists by refusing to change our daily lives. Others called for us to keep sports in perspective.

Minneapolis Star Tribune, September 14, 2001
PLAY–DON'T PLAY DEBATE MEANS VERY, VERY LITTLE
Dan Barreiro

The NFL announced Thursday it has called off all games for this weekend.

"We in the National Football League have decided that our priorities for this weekend are to pause, grieve and reflect," Commissioner Paul Tagliabue said. "It is a time to tend to families and neighbors and all those wounded by these horrific acts of terrorism."

With this announcement, the league will be spared the wrath of the self-important sports moralists ready to bludgeon the NFL for even considering the possibility of playing football five days after New York and Washington were violated by a gang of bloodthirsty cowards.

Most colleges and universities, who also have postponed games this weekend, will also be spared. So will Major League Baseball. The University of Minnesota had planned to go forward with a home football game against Baylor on Saturday night. On Thursday afternoon, it changed course, also averting the moralists' wrath.

You see, the moralists want us to know that in the current backdrop, the games don't matter. As if this is some sort of profundity. As if the games ever truly matter. They want us to know that in comparison with what is happening in New York and Washington, games pale in importance.

Then again, so does going to a movie theater, though the moralists have not yet asked that all multiplexes be shut down through the weekend. So does going to a park for a pickup basketball game, though the moralists have not asked that our parks be closed.

To play or not play? The reality is that both positions are perfectly defensible. What is downright laughable is the endless teeth-gnashing and agonizing over the so-called "moral dimensions" of trying to decide whether to play the games.

By pretending the decision matters at all, the self-important sports moralists merely reinforce the condition they think they are decrying.

By pretending the decision matters, they are not diminishing sports, or even putting them in their proper place, they are further inflating their importance even more out of proportion. And that would be the real affront to those who are suffering over the loss of loved ones or friends, or to any of us lamenting a loss of innocence.

To say that to play the games too soon does not show proper respect for the injured and dead is to attach, again, too much significance to sports in the first place.

Does anybody think that those who have lost a relative or a friend to this unspeakable tragedy are going to notice or care whether football or baseball games are played later this weekend, after today's national day of mourning? Will doing so—or not doing so—lessen or alter their unthinkable pain?

How did the moralists arbitrarily decide that Sunday is too soon to play, but Monday is perfectly acceptable?

There is no right or wrong here. Once the two significant issues clearly worth weighing—security and logistics—are dealt with, each league should come back when it feels ready. Each fan should come back to sports when he or she feels ready.

For some fans, even the thought of working up any emotion about whether the Vikings can rediscover their winning formula may be distasteful.

For others, there may be a kind of therapy attached to plowing forward with the kind of mindless acts that we all engage in to force ourselves through difficult days. Though anybody who believes watching—or playing—a game makes any kind of "we're-carrying-on" statement to the cowards is also kidding himself.

It is worth noting, though, that five weeks after Japan sneak-attacked Pearl Harbor on December 7, 1941, President Roosevelt sent a memo to the baseball commissioner. "I honestly think it would be best for the country to keep baseball going," Roosevelt advised, and baseball kept going the following April through almost all of World War II. [Major League Baseball played a full schedule throughout the war.—ED.]

There are no rules written to guide sports leagues, franchises and fans through this sort of thing. There should be one: Play the games. Postpone the games. But stop the silly, overwrought agonizing and moralizing that it really matters all that much either way. Not with the slightly more crucial decisions that must be made in the coming weeks.

The NFL resumed play one week later. Each stadium displayed red, white, and blue banners above the NFL logo, with the slogan "United We Stand," and held special observances and presentations. It was an emotional restart to the season. In Kansas City the visiting New York Giants, who trained 10 miles from the World Trade Center, were given a standing ovation when they took the field.

The Vikings returned to action in Chicago, losing 17–10 in a game marked by angry sideline outbursts by Cris Carter and Randy Moss. This set the tone for the season, as the team never got their vaunted offense going. They went from fifth in scoring in 2000 to twenty-fourth in 2001, primarily because their yards rushing fell from sixth to twenty-fifth.

Daunte Culpepper hurt his left knee in the December 2, 13–6, loss to Chicago. He tried to play with a brace the next week but the knee stiffened at halftime, and backup quarterback Todd Bauman, from tiny Ruthton, Minnesota, and St. Cloud State, took over. Culpepper ultimately had arthroscopic surgery on the knee and was out for the season. Bauman was 21 for 31 passing the next week, for 348 yards and four touchdowns, in a 42–24 win over the Tennessee Titans. Unfortunately, Bauman hurt his thumb in the next game at Detroit, and little-known Spergon Wynn took over at quarterback.

Meanwhile, sideline and locker room bickering between players became common, and Randy Moss's boorish behavior, tolerated when the team was winning, was blasted by the local media, as well as by fans at the Metrodome and on local talk radio shows. Much of it was triggered by an interview with the *Tribune*'s Sid Hartman following the Vikings' 28–16 *Monday Night Football* win over the New York Giants on November 19. Moss caught 10 passes for 171 yards and three touchdowns in that game, but had been criticized for his lackluster play in other games. When asked if he got himself fired up for a nationally televised game, Moss replied, "I play when I want to play." Taken in context with the rest of the interview, the comment was not as inflammatory as headlines made it appear, but Moss refused to back down or clarify his remarks in subsequent interviews. Tom Powers spoke for most Vikings fans when he told Moss to grow up.

St. Paul Pioneer Press, December 10, 2001

THE MOUTH THAT ROARED

WE'VE HAD IT UP TO HERE WITH RANDY MOSS, WHO NEEDS TO GET HIS ACT TOGETHER IMMEDIATELY

Tom Powers

Maybe somebody stole Randy Moss's bicycle a long time ago. Or maybe his fourth-grade teacher was mean to him, three years in a row.

Whatever his deep-seated problems, he needs to get over them.

With all the dough he has, he could hire a psychologist to sit inside his locker at Winter Park and dispense soothing words. Or he could order the Time-Life self-improvement book series, and have someone read it to him.

But he needs to act quickly before he messes up the best gig he'll ever have.

Randy Moss could own the Twin Cities. He could own the state. People want to embrace him. All he has to do is be civil. All he has to do is refrain from saying the first dumb thing that pops into his head.

Instead, a rudimentary thought starts to form, rattles around in all the empty space and then comes shooting out:

"I play hard when I feel like it."

Oops.

Moss is immature, petulant, shy and apparently very unhappy. Add $75 million to that volatile mixture and you can see why we have a human Molotov cocktail.

The Cris Carter mentoring program isn't working. The Dennis Green approach—"Problem? I don't see any problem. Just the media stirring things up."—isn't working.

Someone needs to figure out why a guy with so much talent, and so much ownership-given money, can't make it through the day without ticking off half of the free world. The guy is blessed and yet acts as if he is cursed.

At the rate Moss is going, his estate is going to take a big hit someday when the executor of his will has to hire pallbearers. Not one or two, either. All of them. The executor might even have to go to Manpower to try for a group rate.

If I were Vikings owner Red McCombs, I'd protect my investment by hiring a professional to look under Moss's hood. The guy definitely is in need of a tune-up.

◆

Fan discontent reached its peak at the final home game on December 23 in a lackadaisical 33–3 loss to Jacksonville. It was billed as "Fan Appreciation Day," but fans booed the team when they took the field; they booed when Red McCombs and Dennis Green delivered video greetings on the Jumbotrons. The lone video message that drew cheers was from former Viking Robert Smith. Most of the crowd left the Metrodome by the fourth quarter.

McCombs, after having denied for several weeks that he was considering making any changes, bought out Green's contract January 4, just three days before the team's final game at Baltimore.

Minnesota Public Radio, January 4, 2002
GREEN IS OUT AS VIKINGS COACH
Brandt Williams

The Minnesota Vikings have fired head coach Denny Green. Green announced that he has accepted a contract buyout and will not be on the sidelines for the season's final game Monday night. The Vikings are 5–10 and will not make the playoffs for only the second time in Green's 10 years with the team. However, Vikings owner Red McCombs says the team's dismal record wasn't a factor in his decision.

"I will no longer be the head football coach and vice president of football operations for the Minnesota Vikings," said Dennis Green. With his trademark stoicism, Green announced his departure from the Minnesota Vikings at a hastily called news conference at the team's headquarters.

Green says he reached agreement with team owner Red McCombs over the final two years of his contract, which is worth about $5 million.

As members of the team stood solemnly in the back of the Vikings weight room, Green expressed his admiration for the players he's worked with over the past 10 years.

Green has been credited for developing the talents of players who were cast off by other teams. He says he's glad to have worked with them.

"Some guys who most people never thought would have played in the National Football League, but they were looking for an opportunity. Those are the type of players that made up the 10 years that we've been here with the Minnesota Vikings. What we try to do is treat them all the same. We try to give them all an opportunity to reach their goals to reach their dreams to be successful. And that's something I've enjoyed," he said.

Green's project players include standout receivers Randy Moss and Cris Carter, both of whom came to the Vikings with troubled pasts.

For a while, Carter and Moss controlled their attitudes and focused on catching passes and scoring spectacular touchdowns. However, as the Vikings began playing poorly and losing games this season, both became known more for their behavior on the sidelines than on the field.

Fans and commentators speculated that Green lost control of his star players.

Owner Red McCombs was not specific about what led to Green's departure, but acknowledged he and Green had some issues that they couldn't resolve. McCombs was more specific on how the next coach will be judged.

"The criteria for the next coach is real and is established and that is to go to the Super Bowl," McCombs said. McCombs named offensive line coach Mike Tice as the interim head coach. He will lead the Vikings in their final game of the season against the Baltimore Ravens Monday night.

Tice says he's glad to take the team's reins, but does so with mixed feelings. "You know, this is a very tough situation for me because of the admiration I have for Dennis Green and his program. I've been with Dennis a long time. It's a great opportunity to lead Dennis Green's football team into Baltimore with all the great players and coaches we have to try and beat an old friend, Brian Billick, and knock him out of the playoffs," Tice said.

Dennis Green was the most successful Vikings coach besides the legendary Bud Grant, who led the Vikings to four Super Bowl appearances. Green achieved a record of 97 wins, 62 losses, four NFC Central titles and eight playoff berths. But unlike Grant, Green was at the center of several controversial incidents during his tenure with the team.

In 1995, the coach was accused of sexually harassing women associated with the team. Green denied any wrongdoing and he and the team refused to confirm a settlement.

Two years later he published an autobiography with a chapter that appears to threaten a lawsuit for controlling interest.

Before this season, the most frequent on-field complaint has been Green's failure to take talented teams to the Super Bowl.

Green's first losing season gave fans something new to grumble about.

Former Viking Jim Marshall says he thinks fans today are a little more impatient than the Vikings fans of old. However, he can understand their frustration. "You got some very highly paid players here who are paid to go out and put on winning performances and certainly if I were a fan and I were looking at it from the standpoint of how much I had to pay to go see a game, I would be outraged," Marshall said.

Marshall says he thinks Green did a great job as coach. He also says Green stayed longer with the Vikings than most NFL coaches stay with teams today, regardless of how many championships they win.

"Look at Dallas and what happened down there. Here's a guy who comes in and wins a couple Super Bowls for them and they turn around and get rid of them. You never know," he said.

Owner McCombs said he hadn't had time to compile a list of potential replacements for Green.

◈

McCombs gave no specific reasons for the firing, except to say that it was time to move on, framing it as a type of Texas witticism that had endeared him to fans back in the honeymoon days of 1998. "There's never a horse can't be rode. Never a cowboy can't be throwed," he said.

The Vikings lost at Baltimore to finish 5–11—Green's only losing season in 10 years with the club, but the worst for the team since Les Steckel's 3–13 season back in 1984.

All Day Long

NEW OWNER AND NEW STARS

DENNIS GREEN WAS A CONTROVERSIAL FIGURE, BUT HIS TEAMS WON divisional championships four of his 10 years as Vikings' coach. His only losing year was his last. Green's 97 wins are second to Bud Grant's 158 in team history, and his overall .610 winning percentage is just below Grant's .622.

But owner Red McCombs didn't give the media much time to eulogize Green or speculate about a successor—within a week of the final game of the 2001 season he elevated 42-year-old interim head coach Mike Tice to become only the sixth head coach in franchise history. Some questioned Tice's experience—he was a 14-year NFL veteran who had never been an offensive or defensive coordinator—but he was a popular choice. The media were confident the gregarious 6-foot-8 former college quarterback and pro tight end would be much more accessible than the embattled and reclusive Dennis Green, and players expected him to be a "players' coach."

McCombs also made a significant front-office change by giving Frank Gilliam, who became the Vice President for Player Personnel, the authority over player decisions formerly held by Green.

In his first press conference, Tice said he would demand a better work ethic from his players. He challenged quarterback Daunte Culpepper to spend more time preparing for games, and said none of his players

In his first year as head coach in 2002, Mike Tice implemented the "Randy Ratio," intended to direct two of every five passes to wide receiver Randy Moss. He caught 24 more passes than in 2001 but averaged 5 yards fewer per catch. PHOTOGRAPH COURTESY OF THE MINNESOTA VIKINGS.

would loaf on the field. He also pledged to throw more passes to Randy Moss, a thought that would soon become a strategy known as the "Randy Ratio."

Minneapolis Star Tribune, April 26, 2002

GIVE THE BALL TO MOSS

HOW DOES A ROOKIE HEAD COACH REVIVE A ONCE-POTENT OFFENSE AND REINVIGORATE A SULKING SUPERSTAR? TO THE VIKINGS' MIKE TICE, THE ANSWER IS SIMPLE

Kevin Seifert

The goal is simple, if not bold. A year from now, Randy Moss would rest atop the NFL record book for receptions in a season. All he has to do, the Vikings figure, is get open for two of every five passes they throw.

They call it the Randy Ratio, and after three months of playbook construction, the Vikings will begin implementing it when mini-camp opens today at Winter Park. Moss's well-documented travails last season helped bring down his team and coach, but new coach Mike Tice has placed much of the Vikings' success, and perhaps his own career, in the hands of the enigmatic superstar.

Upon assuming his job in January, Tice commissioned a game-by-game study of the 2001 season. The results were indisputable. "When we throw the ball in Randy's direction," Tice said, "we win football games."

In fact, the Vikings went 4–1 when they threw toward Moss at least 40 percent of the time. In a January meeting with Tice, Moss argued the same point.

"Randy feels like he can control the ball and the flow of the game," Tice said. "And that study, to me, proved it . . . You can really mold stats any way you want. But it's four out of five."

Tice hired offensive coordinator Scott Linehan based largely on Linehan's ideas for keeping Moss involved throughout games, regardless of defensive formations. Linehan, a bookish ex-quarterback, has developed an offense that will feature Moss at all three receiver positions as well as a system that will keep track of his involvement during games.

If everything goes according to plan, the Randy Ratio should result in about two Moss receptions per quarter. Extrapolating over a full season, Moss would finish with 128 catches, five more than the record set by Detroit's Herman Moore in 1995.

Moss might never shake his "I play when I want to play" reputation, but the Vikings hope the Randy Ratio will do what neither a $75 million contract nor wide locker room latitude could do before: motivate him to play hard.

"He reminds me of every really good receiver I've been around, and he's obviously the best of any I've been around," Linehan said. "Their energy level just rises when they get the ball. He's a receiver. He's not here to block. We ask him to block and do those things, but his job is to get the ball and put it in the end zone. By doing that, I think that helps him determine his role, and now the other little things that are involved in being an all-around player are going to become a factor. He's going to buy into that."

Tice's relationship with Moss, forged over four years through a mutual respect of people who speak their minds, has given the Vikings a head start. During their January meeting, Moss acknowledged his erratic play last season but pointed out the need to be more consistently involved.

Tice concurred and explained his ideas for the Randy Ratio, apparently persuading Moss to the point where he spent the majority of the off-season in the Twin Cities, meeting with Tice and Linehan and following the Vikings' off-season conditioning program.

"The connection is honesty and a lack of patronization," Tice said. "I'm not going to patronize him, and he's not going to patronize me. I don't want him to, and he doesn't want me to. That's kind of the basis of our relationship. There's a certain trust there."

While trust and good intentions might have bred an early benefit of the doubt with Moss, ultimately the issue will evolve into one of X's and O's. The bright light of the Randy Ratio will not suddenly force opposing defenses to drop off the consistent double- and triple-teams they applied last season.

Tice, the old tight end and ex-offensive line coach, said implicit in Moss's success is a strong running game. Linehan's will emphasize balance almost as much as it focuses on Moss.

"There is no way that I've seen in this league, ever, that they can double receivers when you're able to run the ball successfully," Tice said. "You'd have to draw something up for me that I haven't seen. We have to have balance. We've also got to eliminate the predictability of our offense."

To that end, Linehan has reworked the Vikings' playbook to put Moss in the quarterback's "progression" more often. He is learning the flanker, split end and slot positions, and Linehan will keep track of Moss's touches minute-by-minute during games.

"We're not going to force the ball to Randy," Linehan said. "The thing we've got to avoid is the two-quarter, he-hasn't-touched-the ball, what's-going-on-here? thing. . . . We've got to say, 'Hey, we've got to get Randy involved and this is how we're going to do it.' And we have to have a way of doing it, as opposed to, let's just start throwing the ball."

Record run?

The Vikings project two receptions a quarter for Randy Moss in 2002. If that happens, and Moss equals his career yards-per-catch average of 17.5, he will set two NFL records: Most receptions, season: 128; and receiving yards, season: 2,240.

●

Unfortunately, the Vikings lost their first four games to begin the 2002 season, extending the team losing streak to eight. The defense was porous, giving up an average of 35 points per game over the four-game stretch, while the offense was averaging 25 points per game, an improvement of seven points a game from 2001 and back to the levels they had achieved in 1999 and 2000, when they ranked fifth in the league in scoring. However, Moss's production was down. He was catching more passes per game, but was averaging only 59 yards per game, compared to his four-year career average of 91. Many were wondering if the "Randy Ratio" was taking away the long pass threat.

After a close 26–22 loss at Green Bay on December 8—marked by a bench-clearing brawl on the last play of the game—the Vikings were 3–10 and Tice was in danger of matching Les Steckel's 1984 record for futility. However, the team rallied to win its last three games—by margins of one point, three points, and two points, respectively!

The 32–31 victory at New Orleans on December 15 broke a 17-game losing streak on the road, and was also the first time that a team won a game on a two-point conversion since its adoption by the NFL in 1994. (The American Football League had used it from 1960–1969, but dropped it when the two leagues merged for the 1970 season.) A 13-yard touchdown pass from Culpepper to Moss with five seconds remaining on the clock brought the Vikings within one point. During the final drive, Tice had instructed his assistants to go for two points if they scored, instead of playing for the tie and overtime. On the extra point attempt, Culpepper set up in a shotgun formation with an empty backfield in hopes that the Saints would be expecting a pass. In fact, it was a run play all the way. Culpepper was so surprised to see the wide lane open for the run that he dropped the snap from Matt Birk, bobbled it while attempting to pick it up, but finally grasped it and dove into the end zone for the victory. The team ran onto the field and celebrated like it had won a playoff game.

In the off-season, McCombs signed Culpepper to a 10-year contract extension worth up to $102 million, making him one of the five highest-paid quarterbacks in the NFL. Only $16 million was guaranteed, however, a feature that would become a sore spot for Culpepper in only two or three years.

The Vikings started 2003 with six consecutive victories, and everything seemed to be going their way. When Culpepper suffered a lower back injury late in the second quarter in game three against Detroit, backup quarterback Gus Frerotte came in to preserve the 23–13 win. Frerotte had a remarkable game the next week in a 35–7 win against San Francisco, going 16-for-21 for 267 yards and four touchdowns—three of them to Randy Moss. He threw two more touchdown passes to Moss in a 39–26 victory at Atlanta.

Culpepper came back after a bye week to lead the team to a 28–20 victory over the 5–1 Denver Broncos, but it took a miracle play to make it possible. With the game tied 7–7 and the clock winding down in the first half, Culpepper's desperation pass was caught by Randy Moss on the Broncos' 15-yard line. Moss was immediately hit by three defenders, but tossed a lateral over his shoulder—without looking—to running back Moe Williams, who had been trailing the play. Williams ran it into the end zone to complete the 59-yard scoring play.

The magic disappeared, though, and the Vikings promptly lost four in a row. After a 13–10 loss at Chicago on December 14, they had an 8–6 record and needed to win their last two games to make the playoffs. They accomplished the first with an impressive 45–20 win over the high-powered AFC West–leading Kansas City Chiefs, who had won their first nine games and were now at 12–2. All the Vikings needed now was a victory over the hapless 3–12 Arizona Cardinals.

St. Paul Pioneer Press, December 29, 2003
GONE IN A FLASH
THE FULL-OF-SURPRISES VIKINGS TAKE A LAST-SECOND FALL FROM PLAYOFF CONTENTION AND COULD LOSE THEIR COACH
Bill Williamson

In historical context, this sudden death in the Desert wasn't the most devastating last-second defeat in the history of this seemingly cursed franchise. But for the current program, it had the same meaning—the end of a season.

Typical in this most atypical season, the story line was unfathomable. One minute, 54 seconds earlier, the Vikings were imagining a home playoff game next week (team employees were getting the word out about ticket availability) and celebrating a major step in the brief Mike Tice era. In year two of a three-year plan, Tice appeared on track to what he had planned—and predicted.

However, in a blurry flash—and two fourth-down touchdowns that were reviewed and upheld—everything stopped for the Vikings. There won't be any playoff—after a 6–0 start—and the promise of the Tice era suddenly was thrown into flux.

Supplying one of the wildest finishes of the NFL season, inexperienced Arizona quarterback Josh McCown hit receiver Nathan Poole for a 28-yard touchdown pass as time expired to give the Cardinals an 18–17 victory and send the Vikings into a stupor, à la 1975, when Dallas shocked the Vikings in the divisional playoffs on a Roger Staubach–to–Drew Pearson touchdown pass to end the Vikings' season.

After the players picked themselves off the Sun Devil Stadium grass, thoughts immediately went to the future of Tice, who had guaranteed that his team would make the playoffs. The Vikings became the first team since the 1978 Washington Redskins to start the season 6–0 and not make the postseason. All the Vikings needed heading into Sunday was a victory over Arizona, or a Green Bay loss to Denver, to qualify for the playoffs. The Packers ended up routing the Broncos 31–3.

There was speculation going into the Vikings' game that mercurial team owner Red McCombs seriously would consider firing Tice if the Vikings didn't make the playoffs. After the game, McCombs did nothing to quell the speculation.

Scurrying to a van that would carry him and his family (some of whom were in tears) to the airport to fly home to San Antonio, McCombs declined to answer reporters' questions.

"I will talk to you tomorrow," he said four times, replying to various questions, including those about Tice's status. McCombs has given Tice several lukewarm endorsements since November.

McCombs spoke to the sullen team in the locker room after the game. Those who heard the short speech said he was positive. That was a departure from his speech October 26, when he told the team it had humiliated itself and the franchise after losing to the New York Giants, its first loss of the season.

Tice discussed his status after the game.

"One more play," he said, "and you guys wouldn't have to speculate."

Tice has never been one to sway from pressure. The day after last season ended, he predicted the Vikings would win 10 games this season and be a serious playoff contender. Then, in the November 11 *Pioneer Press*, Tice guaranteed that the Vikings would make the playoffs. This came after a startling four-game losing streak that immediately followed a six-game winning streak to open the season.

Sunday, Tice, who has one year remaining on his contract, said he hadn't thought of his future.

"I'm a good coach. I'm not worried," he said. "Right now, I'm more worried about my wife and daughter and about how they feel. They were at the game, and I haven't seen them yet. I'm sure they're upset. That's what I'm worried about right now."

Still, Tice said he will turn from preparing for his first playoff game as a head coach to preparing "a state of the team" report.

"I need a few days to regroup," he said.

Although Tice generally has earned praise for the job he has done in his first two years, McCombs is unpredictable, and those close to the situation have noticed tension between the two in recent weeks. It would cost McCombs—who is now done paying Dennis Green the $6 million he owed his former coach after firing him after the 2001 season—about $750,000 to relieve Tice of his final season.

"I would hope not," linebacker Henri Crockett said about the possibility of a coaching change. "We have a good thing going here. The coaches have us on the right track."

Added quarterback Daunte Culpepper: "Me, personally, I don't want that. I think he has what it takes. He motivates us, and he gives us 100 percent."

However, after what happened in the final 1:54, nothing is certain.

Center Matt Birk (78) and guard Steve Hutchinson (76) anchor the Vikings offensive line. They each have made six Pro Bowl appearances, while Hutchinson has been voted first-team All Pro four times. PHOTOGRAPH BY RICK A. KOLODZIEJ. COURTESY OF THE MINNESOTA VIKINGS.

The game's final play was set up by a recovered onside kick with 1:54 left after Arizona had scored on a two-yard pass from McCown to tight end Steve Bush on fourth and one to make the score 17–12. After recovering the kickoff, the Cardinals cruised downfield until the Vikings' defense rallied with back-to-back sacks to set up the fourth-and-25 final play.

As time expired, McCown rolled out and hit Poole, who was being covered by Denard Walker and Brian Russell. The officials ruled that Russell forced Poole out of bounds.

A review examined only whether Poole had possession of the ball. After about three minutes, it was determined that the play stood, and several Vikings lay on the field in disbelief.

"I was telling guys on the field that the game was over," Tice said.

Until the Cardinals' stunning final two touchdowns, it appeared the Vikings would win the NFC North, securing their first division title since 2000. They would be the number 4 seed in the NFC playoffs and host number 5 seed Seattle next weekend at the Metrodome.

Instead, rival Green Bay, which was 3½ games behind the Vikings in October, will host the Seahawks next weekend as the division champion.

"This really hurts," Vikings safety Corey Chavous said. "We gave it away. We gave the division championship away."

Several players cried in the locker room, and most players sat in their uniforms, staying at their lockers for several minutes. Just like that, the Vikings are now preparing for an uncertain future.

"Hopefully, we can all get over this," center Matt Birk said. "It won't be easy."

●

Four Vikings made the Pro Bowl—Culpepper, center Matt Birk, Randy Moss, and defensive back Corey Chavous. Moss, who had 111 catches and led the league with 17 touchdown passes, made first-team All Pro for the third time.

At a time when the next misbehavior by a professional athlete was only a headline away, St. Paul native Birk was a breath of fresh air. In 2001 he had signed a seven-year contract extension worth $30 million. It included a $6 million signing bonus and was the largest contract ever for an NFL center. In spite of these riches, he considered himself just a regular guy, and fans considered him one of the family. His self-deprecating humor reinforced these feelings. He once said "I'm just a big, fat guy with red hair who wears flip-flops and baseball caps. I wish I took more pride in my appearance."

St. Paul Pioneer Press, July 18, 2004

MORE TO BIRK THAN MEETS THE EYE

Bob Sansevere

Training camp cranks up for the Vikings at the end of the month, and you will be learning all sorts of things about all sorts of players. Of course, there are some players you already know plenty about.

Anyway, you think you know plenty. But there is a lot you don't know. Take Matt Birk.

Most Vikings fans know Birk grew up in St. Paul, graduated from Cretin-Derham Hall and went off to Harvard, where he played football and got a degree in economics.

Many also know he used to give stock tips on a local radio station and wears the same T-shirt every day of training camp.

But how many know he once cheated on a test at Harvard? Or that he and his brothers used to steal candy? Or that he claims to eat a spicy shredded burrito from Chipotle every day of the week?

There's a lot more to Matt Birk than you may know. Or may want to know.

Consider: He once was so drunk in college he relieved himself in his roommate's clothes drawer.

"On his shirts," Birk says. "When I'm drinking, I like to drink the hard stuff. Johnnie Walker. Jack Daniels. I just drink it with water or soda. The sugar in mixed drinks will mess you up. That's a great tip."

Here's another great tip: If you're going to steal candy, as Birk did from a candy store in his Highland neighborhood when he was about eight years old, throw out the wrappers after you're done wolfing down the candy.

"My two younger brothers were my partners in crime," Birk says. "My parents found all the wrappers. They busted us and grounded us."

Birk never did get busted when he cheated at Harvard. Until now.

"I don't want Harvard to revoke my degree, but here's what happened. We had a final coming up, and guys on the lacrosse team were going to the NCAA tournament, so they took the test early. It kind of got out what was on the test," Birk says. "I still got a C-minus."

He gets an A-plus, though, for persistence. Get a load of how he met his wife, Adrianna.

"She was in college working at Key's Cafe, and I was single and liked to eat. I would go in there quite often, and that's how we met," Birk says.

Adrianna was a waitress, and Birk made sure to sit at a table in her section.

"I'd keep sucking down iced teas so she'd have to keep refilling the glass," he says. "I'd go there four times a week. I'd talk to her and get some grub."

Picture this now. Birk is 6-foot-4 and 300 pounds, and one of the best centers in the NFL. There's nobody he fears on the football field. Yet he ate a lot of grub before mustering the nerve to ask Adrianna out.

"I probably ate there 50 times before I asked," he says. "We were married eight months after we started dating."

And now they have a two-year-old daughter, Madison. Birk changes diapers, by the way. But only when the sun is up.

"I don't know if I'm proud to say it, but I've never gotten up in the middle of the night with Madison," Birk says. "Once I fall asleep, a freight train could come through the bedroom and I wouldn't know it."

Birk does know this (and now you will, too): If he could swap places with any teammate, it would be quarterback Daunte Culpepper.

"Just to see what it's like to be the superstar quarterback and have all those women ogling you," he said.

He already knows what it is like to be mistaken for another teammate.

"Half the time people think I'm Chris Hovan. They say, 'Hey, Hovan,'" Birk says. "The other day, somebody came up and said, 'You're Todd Steussie, right?' Todd Steussie? He hasn't been with the Vikings for years."

Over the years, Birk has worked a variety of jobs, including caddy, forklift driver, movie theater ticket-taker and member of a bathroom cleaning crew. He did all that before he became a pro football player.

His dream job: Professional bass fisherman.

"If I wasn't married and not playing football, that's what I'd want," Birk says. "But I'm married and have a kid and have to pay the bills. I love to fish, I'm just not very good."

As we speak, Birk is in Canada fishing for walleye with former Twins star Kent Hrbek. They're filming a segment for Hrbek's upcoming TV show about fishing and hunting.

And speaking of TV, don't ever invite Birk over to watch *Survivor* or *The Apprentice* or any other reality TV show.

"Reality TV is going to be the downfall of the human race," he says. "I hate it. I hate reality TV."

He isn't too fond of President George W. Bush, either. Or John Kerry.

"I'm for [Ralph] Nader," Birk says. "I hate politics and all the b.s. associated with politics. I'm definitely not liberal, but I can't stand politics. I don't like the two-party system."

He doesn't like people who are rude or mean, either. Those people are his pet peeve.

"It's just as easy," he says, "to be nice as to be a jerk."

And now it's also easier to say you know plenty about Matt Birk.

Stadium issues were front and center throughout Red McCombs's ownership era. He was often frustrated with the lack of action by the state legislature. In 2002 he tried to escape his Metrodome lease, but NFL Commissioner Paul Tagliabue said the league would stand behind the letter agreement signed by Commissioner Pete Rozelle in 1979, stating that the NFL would not approve a franchise relocation until the lease expires after the 2011 season.

The site for the Vikings training camp became an issue, as well, when McCombs entertained bids from Duluth, Sioux Falls, South Dakota, and others to replace Mankato, where the team had held its training camp since 1966. In the end, although Sioux Falls presented the best bid, the Vikings decided to sign a new four-year contract with Mankato after being warned by governor Tim Pawlenty that choosing Sioux Falls would doom any chance the team had for securing a new stadium.

In August 2004, team vice president Gary Woods said the Vikings were suspending their five-year effort—costing about $400,00 per year—to lobby for a new stadium. In late October McCombs told *Sports Illustrated* writer Michael Silver that he would love to move the team to Los Angeles. He said he was tired of lack of support by Minnesotans.

The Vikings got off to a good start once again in 2004, winning four straight after splitting their first two games. But then they lost three straight. Randy Moss pulled a hamstring muscle in the game five win at New Orleans. He tried to come back too soon, and eventually missed three games. After 106 receptions in 2002 and 111 in 2003, he was destined to fall to 49 in 2004. Culpepper had his best season, on the other hand.

The game of the season was a match-up at the Metrodome on Friday, December 24, against the Green Bay Packers. The two teams were tied for first place in the NFC North Division with 8–6 records. Although some church officials in Green Bay and Minnesota objected to scheduling a 2 P.M. game on Christmas Eve, the game was a sellout. St. Paul Archbishop Harry Flynn had earlier declared that the game would not disrupt the Christmas celebration, and most other church officials took a philosophical view.

Minneapolis Star Tribune, December 24, 2004
THANKS TO FOOTBALL, A REALLY SILENT NIGHT
Reverend Peter Geisendorfer-Lindgren, Lord of Life Lutheran Church, Maple Grove

'Twas the night before Christmas and all through the church,
Not a creature was stirring; I know, 'cause I searched:
The Packers and Vikings at two in the aft —
A Friday? The Yuletide? Was Tagliabue daft?

The faithful were nestled in front of their tubes,
No worship, no carols, no church for these rubes.
They believed in their Vikings and because of their meds,
Visions of Super Bowls danced in their heads.

Mom with her Norse braids and Dad his Vikes cap,
They all settled down for Matt Birk's first snap.
When what to their glazed-over eyes should appear,
But a miniature sleigh, holding eight tiny beers.

On the field was their driver, more naughty than nice,
It was clear in a moment it must be Mike Tice.
With his pencil in place and a scheme for this game,
He whistled and shouted and called out their names;
"Now, Daunte! Now, Randy! Now, Mewelde and Mixon!
Good offense, bad defense, oh well, just go blitz 'em."

The chess match with Sherman began in the first,
But if Tice had two choices, he always chose worse.
By halftime the score was so on one side,
That the exits were filled, no more Purple Pride.

In a suit all in purple, from his toe to his head,
With a map of Los Angeles, it had to be Red.
The governor! The legislature! There was no one to blame,
So Red gathered his family and got back on his plane.

When the third quarter started with a touchdown by Favre,
Dad started looking for a turkey to carve.
Mom said, "Why rush it? No need to be nervous,
If we hurry we'll make it, the 4 o'clock service."
So Dad sprang from his armchair, gave the family a whistle,

He was ready to trade his remote for a missal.
When back at the church there arose such a clatter,
I sprang from the pulpit to see what was the matter.
Away to the window I flew like a flash,
And saw hundreds of people, some in a mad dash.

They wore face paint and jerseys, 84 and 11,
Their sole focus now was on worship and heaven.
They spoke not a word, but went straight to their seats.
Chagrined and repentant they were soon off their feet.
The crowds they kept coming, some glad, others lonely,
No scalpers, but still, it was standing room only.

I tightened my cincture and welcomed the throng,
Then "Joy to the World," an exuberant song.
The lessons and carols, the Lord's sacrament,
The game now forgotten in this blessed event.
No steroids, no trash talk, no outrageous salaries,
Just a stable and shepherds. Just Joseph and Mary.

For a few too short moments there was peace on the earth,
Experiencing the glory of our dear Savior's birth.
The benediction was sounded and I dwelled in the sight,
Merry Christmas to all, and to all a good night!

[Pastor Geisendorfer-Lindgren wrote this poem before the game was played—ED.]

The Vikings led at halftime, 21–17, but the Packers came back in the second half to win 34–31, which meant the Vikings had to win their final game against the 5–10 Washington Redskins to ensure a playoff berth. During the week, owner Red McCombs ended the speculation about Coach Tice's future by picking up his $1 million contract option for 2005. Many had expected Tice to be fired because of the team's late-season fade.

The signing didn't change things on the field, however, as the Vikings lost 21–18 to fall to 8–8 for the season—making it the second consecutive season they had lost seven of their last 10 games. Randy Moss created another media storm when he walked off the field with two seconds left on the clock . . . with television cameras following his every step. An angry Matt Birk ran Moss down after the game and chewed him out. Culpepper and other players voiced their disapproval, as well.

Thirty minutes later the Vikings backed into a wild card berth via a tiebreaker when New Orleans beat Carolina. Their reward was a rematch with Green Bay, this time at Lambeau Field.

Minneapolis Star Tribune, January 10, 2005
FREAK SHOW
CULPEPPER TORCHES PACKERS FOR FOUR TOUCHDOWNS WHILE FAVRE FLOPS. MOSS'S TWO SCORES ALSO HELP IN FIRST PLAYOFF VICTORY SINCE '00 SEASON.
Kevin Seifert
Mike Tice had but one request. As players began a raucous sideline celebration Sunday evening, Tice looked over at his superstar-slash-headache. Do one thing for me, Tice later recalled telling Randy Moss. The cameras are on us. Get over here and hug me.

Manufactured as it was, the moment—broadcast nationally—proved genuine and symbolic. It melted a week of disarray into a sense of accomplishment, an all's-well-that-ends-well philosophy the Vikings now believe can carry them deep into the NFC playoffs.

Moss, who embarrassed his coach and organization a week ago, redeemed himself with a pair of touchdown catches in the Vikings' wholly improbable but somehow believable 31–17 wild card playoff victory over Green Bay. An announced crowd of 71,075 at Lambeau Field sat stunned as the Vikings overlooked history and their own shortcomings to produce their most impressive top-to-bottom performance of the season.

Holding a lead they took one minute and 40 seconds into the game, the Vikings became only the second 8–8 team in NFL history to win a playoff game. Their recent record on grass fields now 3–20, the Vikings earned a trip to the grassy confines of Philadelphia and will take on the NFC's top-seeded team at noon Sunday.

One of those losses came September 20 against the Eagles, but the Vikings were eager to avenge that 27–16 defeat. "We knew we could beat anybody anywhere," tight end Jermaine Wiggins said. "On grass or wherever else. All of that garbage. And today we proved it."

At game time Sunday, however, history and the week-long Moss distraction suggested a quick and painless end to the Vikings' season. While Tice professed a "new" season had begun, it was difficult to imagine the Vikings could move past a 3–7 end to their regular season—especially against a Packers team that won nine of its final 11 games.

According to Moss, however, players accepted Tice's pleas and put themselves through an intense week of practice. While Moss absorbed the attention, his teammates quietly prepared for the Packers. Six players, Moss included, took out the braids in their hair to "let it all hang out," Moss said.

Real or imagined, Moss's new role as a sponge left quarterback Daunte Culpepper to riddle the Packers' secondary for 284 yards and four touchdowns. It left the defense to intercept Brett Favre four times and sack him twice, and it might even have helped Onterrio Smith to run out the game with 36 fourth-quarter rushing yards.

"In all honesty," he said, "I'm glad the pressure and all of the talk was about me. I can take the criticism. You didn't see one thing in the paper about the Washington loss. All you heard was Moss. That was a good thing. I feel very comfortable about being able to take the heat . . . I think that was a relief from the players' standpoint."

Said center Matt Birk: "It seems like there's always something going on around here. But we were able to look at this game and say, 'Hey, nobody is giving us any chance to win.'

"So all the pressure was off. We could play loose and fast, and not get tight, as we have had a tendency to do this season." Often, such tentativeness was the result of early trouble, and Tice pleaded this week for players to come out of the tunnel blazing. Heeding his request, the Vikings took a 7–0 lead on the third play of the game; Moe Williams took a dump-off pass, eluded Packers safety Darren Sharper and scampered 68 yards for a touchdown. The lead ballooned to 17–0 with 6:06 remaining in the first quarter after Moss's 20-yard touchdown reception and Morten Andersen's 35-yard field goal.

The Packers ultimately were stymied by a Vikings defense that had given up a combined 894 yards and 68 points in the teams' regular-season meetings. "I feel terrible, and that is an understatement," Favre said after his four interceptions led to 10 Vikings points.

"That's the way we should have been playing all season," said defensive coordinator Ted Cottrell, who was feted to a Gatorade shower courtesy of cornerback Antoine Winfield and linebacker Keith Newman. Tice received the game ball, presented by owner Red McCombs in the postgame locker room.

The result was still in doubt, however, after the Vikings offense stalled in the second half. They managed only six yards of offense in the third quarter, and Najeh Davenport's one-yard run cut the deficit to seven points with 13:37 remaining, but Moss—playing despite a sprained right ankle—put the game away by hauling in a 34-yard touchdown pass at the 10:18 mark.

On the play, Moss reacted to a Culpepper audible and used his healthy left ankle to cut past Harris on a fade route. Although he was limping noticeably, Moss created enough separation to catch Culpepper's moon ball.

His subsequent celebration—Moss pantomimed pulling down his pants toward the Lambeau crowd—will carry the Vikings' news waves for the remainder of this week. Not that Moss, or the Vikings, would have it any other way. Nothing that a hug can't cure.

●

Predictably, Moss's "moon shot" was controversial. Moss said he was just having a little fun. Though some called for charges or a penalty— he eventually was fined $10,000—most national observers dismissed it merely as another tasteless gesture by Moss. Matt Birk, who had a verbal altercation with Moss the previous week, said, "That's Randy. You take the good with the bad. He'll probably never be a model citizen."

The Philadelphia Eagles easily defeated the Vikings in the divisional playoff the next week. The Eagles scored touchdowns on three consecutive possessions and led 21–7 at the half and coasted to a 27–14 victory.

Only three Vikings won postseason awards—Culpepper, center Matt Birk, and defensive tackle Kevin Williams made the NFC Pro Bowl team.

Williams, whose specialty was stopping the run, also had 11.5 sacks, and was also voted to the All Pro team. Culpepper lead the league in pass completions and yards, and was second in pass attempts, touchdown passes and in the passer rating, just behind NFL Most Valuable Player Peyton Manning of the Indianapolis Colts.

Randy Moss was traded to the Oakland Raiders in February. All the Vikings could get for the troubled receiver was Oakland's number one pick—seventh overall—in the 2005 college draft, linebacker Napolean Harris—a part-time starter in 2004— and a future seventh-round draft choice. The biggest benefit of the trade was to the bottom line—saving $36.5 million in the four remaining years of his contract—as well as making more room in the team's salary cap, but fans were tired of his attitude and glad to see him go, despite his performance on the field. He had been to five Pro Bowls and named to the All Pro team three times in his seven years with the Vikings.

It was no surprise that 30 other teams passed on the chance to obtain Moss. Oakland—where the Raiders and their iconoclastic owner Al Davis had long been the bad guys of the NFL—seemed the perfect place for him. NFL business ventures spokesmen revealed that Randy Moss Raiders jerseys had been the bestseller on its web shop since April 1, the start of the league's fiscal year. And Moss was one reason the NFL chose to spotlight the Raiders (5–11 in 2004) in the Thursday night, September 8, prime-time television kickoff of the 2005 season at New England, the defending Super Bowl champs.

Moss took the attention in stride. He made it clear he wasn't planning to change.

Oakland Tribune, May 1, 2005
MOSS ARRIVES, BUT HE WON'T BE UNPACKING HIS BAGGAGE
Monty Poole
He has no desire to become the new face of the Raiders or the face of the New Raiders, even if many in the Raider Nation have glued his mug to the shield.

He has no plans to ingratiate himself with the organization, other than among teammates, and he shuns the idea of being a spokesman.

He won't demand a section of the locker room, or furnish his surroundings with a leather recliner and big-screen TV.

Randy Moss, new to Oakland, does not anticipate moving here—and he's only vaguely aware of the Bay Area's exorbitant housing market.

The NFL's most dangerous deep threat is reporting for duty, simple as that. If we can accept that, Moss contends, everything's cool.

"I'm coming here to work," he said Saturday between practices at the team facility. "As far as me living here . . . my family is in the South and on the East Coast. That's where I want to be, around my family.

"But I have a job to do, and that's here on the West Coast. I plan on coming here to work. When my work's finished, I'm going back to the family. That's the way I see it."

So the position of unofficial owner of the town, open since Dave Stewart retired from baseball, remains available. Maybe Baron Davis will take the job Chris Webber held ever so briefly and Jason Giambi never quite nailed down.

Moss? Nope. Wants no part of it. He's a country kid, still adjusting to life in the big city. From his college career at Marshall to seven years in Minnesota, he has toiled in relatively small markets.

Not that Moss ever could go unnoticed. He has been far too good a wideout to be ignored, establishing himself as the man most feared by NFL secondaries. He has at the same time performed too many silly acts to be overlooked, showing he is on the slow road to maturity.

In both cases, though, Moss himself was bigger than the room.

"I think it's a challenge for me to be in this big state with a lot going on," he said. "Hopefully I can make the best of it. In Minnesota, it was a small fishbowl, where you had athletes such as myself, Daunte [Culpepper], Kevin Garnett and a couple of baseball players like Torii Hunter making a lot of noise. It was hard, from endorsements to going out in public.

"Now, here, it's just more about getting used to how the Oakland Raiders do things and how the players do things and how the fans do things."

This ain't Minnesota, a place where stars can't escape. Midwestern sports heroes become local royalty, gaining the adoration of some, the envy of others—and the attention of all.

Which didn't help Moss, who too often found himself embroiled in controversy, sometimes warranted.

"Some of the things he did were blown completely out of proportion," said new teammate Jerry Porter, who crossed paths with Moss while at West Virginia. "A lot of things, he should not have done."

Porter quickly added that Moss's history is best left in West Virginia or in Minnesota.

For this is a different land, with different circumstances. The Bay Area is home to six professional sports teams, making it the nation's number two sports market, trailing only greater New York.

But we aren't nearly as obsessive as Noo Yawk. There are fewer screaming headlines, far fewer irrational fans and nothing like the *Post*'s "Page 6," on which the tabloid details late-night escapades and various other activities celebrities would prefer to keep under cover.

We tend to be more tolerant around here, maybe because we've seen so much. This is where the Raiders hatched their outlaw reputation, where the A's brawled their way to championships.

We joked about Jose Canseco's demonic driving habits, laughed off Jerry Rice's infamous massage, summarily dismissed Jon Gruden's brush with DUI.

Here is where people still debate the significance of Terrell Owens' increasingly pathetic ramblings and where Barry Bonds is allowed to create his image.

We gave and continue to give Bonds his . . . space.

Moss, it seems, is seeking exactly that.

"If you all give me my space, let me do what I want to do—and that's playing football—we're going to have a good time here," Moss said.

Not an unreasonable request, especially if it provides him with a chance to be the player who helps the Raiders rediscover winning.

If he is to be believed, Moss is ready to accept advice from receivers coach Fred Biletnikoff, enjoy running back LaMont Jordan's forays between the tackles and catch the occasional pass.

Nothing more. On the field or off.

●

And after several months of intrigue, Red McCombs sold the team to a New Jersey businessman, Zygmunt (Zygi) Wilf, in May. McCombs had earlier accepted an offer from Arizona businessman Reggie Fowler, who would have become the first African American owner in the NFL. Fowler began talks with Wilf in the fall of 2004, when he realized he would need some additional support to secure financing for the purchase. He also talked to Glen Taylor, the Timberwolves owner, but Taylor had no interest in becoming a minority owner of the team.

McCombs was asking $600 million for the team. Taylor made an offer on his own, reported to be substantially lower than McComb's target, and on February 9 Fowler signed a contract to purchase the team for $600 million. Wilf and two others were limited partners with Fowler.

McCombs had just sold the team for $350 million more than he had paid for it seven years earlier!

Within a month, though, Fowler's world started to fall apart. Several items in his resume were found to be untruthful. In addition, the cash flow from his private companies turned out to be vastly overstated, and his expected financing was not forthcoming. In a meeting at Wilf's offices in late April, Fowler confessed that the deal was falling apart, and Wilf made the decision to take the lead, with Fowler assuming a minority role.

Minneapolis Star Tribune, May 22, 2005

WILF IS READY TO BRING VIKINGS INTO THE FAMILY

Jay Weiner and Randy Furst

Zygi Wilf sips a can of Diet Coke, paces in his third-floor office and carefully answers questions about this new project.

It's called the Minnesota Vikings football team and it will force him to shed his cocoon of familiarity—his family-centered, New Jersey–based, real estate–driven bubble—and confront the cacophony of pro sports ownership.

If all goes as expected at National Football League owners' meetings Tuesday and Wednesday in Washington, D.C., Wilf—grandson and son of immigrants, father of four, owner of more than 100 shopping centers and strip malls—will become the general partner and primary owner of the Vikings. He, too, will become the planner and developer of a new Vikings stadium, exact solution unknown.

Once the $625 million deal with Vikings owner Red McCombs closes, Wilf and his family—actors and heirs in a saga of Holocaust survival and capital accumulation—will never be the same.

"He's not a limelight kind of guy," said his friend, Leonard Bielory.

"They go under the radar," said Daniel Forman, development vice president at New York City's Yeshiva University, to which the Wilf family has donated a reported $10 million.

But this deal is about more than a football team.

"I am interested in making sure the fans of Minnesota are able to enjoy their football experience in a stadium and environment they can be enthusiastic about," said Wilf, who renewed his promise to keep the team in Minnesota.

This Vikings purchase isn't just about square footage or cash flows. There's some passion for the game in there.

AN NFL FAN

Wilf, 55, has been a New York Giants fan all his life, a season-ticket holder for 30 years and a luxury-suite holder for almost as long. A football, emblazoned with 1960s Giants great Sam Huff's autograph, among others, sits on Wilf's cluttered desk.

His brother, Mark, 43, who will be involved in operating the team, was the football play-by-play announcer for Princeton University's radio broadcasts when he went to college there. The two have attended a handful of Super Bowls.

And in the 1990s, Zygi Wilf was part of a group that considered buying the New York Jets.

In an interview, he praised the Vikings' recent defensive acquisitions, and he pledged to bring a championship team to Minnesota. "I want a Super Bowl, and I will do whatever I can" to help the Vikings reach that goal, Wilf said.

In his business and philanthropy circles, he mingles with pro sports investors, such as Alan Landis, who owns a small piece of the New York Yankees and who last year introduced Wilf to an enthusiastic man named Reggie Fowler, who wanted to own the Vikings.

But Wilf, in a series of interviews with the *Star Tribune*, was reticent to discuss many details of the Vikings' sale, his life, his personal net worth, the specifics of his design or finance plan for a new stadium or his relationship with Fowler.

Wilf and his family haven't revealed much in the 50 years since Wilf's father, Joseph, and uncle, Harry, began to build a business that now stretches from New Jersey to California, from Florida to Israel to, perhaps, Minnesota.

WEALTH AND THE WILFS

Wilf's wealth is difficult to quantify, but visits to some of his shopping centers and housing developments, an examination of his family's philanthropic activities and published reports provide some insight.

The Wilf family companies are privately held and tightly controlled by Zygi, his brother Mark, father Joseph, cousin Leonard Wilf and Leonard's son, Orin.

Garden Commercial Properties, the Wilfs' retail arm, owns at least 109 shopping centers with about 25 million square feet of leasable space, making it the eighteenth largest shopping center developer in North America, according to the International Council of Shopping Centers.

While the old-fashioned strip mall has hit on hard times, the Wilfs seem to be adjusting, in recent years linking up with so-called "big box" retailers, such as Wal-Mart, Lowe's and Home Depot. That, said one retail analyst, shows a certain sort of corporate nimbleness needed in today's retail landscape.

Zygi Wilf said the shopping centers are 95 percent leased. A company website showed 28 of the shopping centers are 46 percent vacant, according to the *Star Tribune*'s calculations, but the website appears to be out of date. A visit last week to some of the malls that were listed on the website as unfinished or empty were actually full and thriving.

Others, such as Oakwood Plaza in Edison, New Jersey, appeared in poor shape, with the anchor store shut down.

Besides their retail operations, the Wilfs' housing arm, Garden Homes Development, has built thousands of homes and apartments in New Jersey, New York and California.

They are developing high-end housing properties on New York City's Upper East Side and in the financial district of Manhattan.

The company's townhomes and single-family homes, some built with partners, dot the central and north Jersey suburbs and range in price from $250,000 to $2 million, with generally positive reviews but some dissatisfaction from owners and tenants.

The family's philanthropic foundations offer a glimpse at its holdings. The Wilf Family Foundation, set up by Joseph and Elizabeth Wilf, has assets of nearly $88 million. Zygi Wilf's foundation has assets of about $6.5 million, according to federal documents. Combined, those two foundations have about the same amount of assets as the McCombs Foundation, established by the current Vikings' owner.

Families don't buy NFL teams, however; individuals do. The NFL requires one man to control 30 percent of the franchise's assets. Zygi Wilf said he will use his own money to cover 30 percent of the team's $625 million price tag. With league-approved lending, that means he will have to lay down at least $150 million.

When asked about that the other day, he didn't miss a beat responding: "Yes," he would handle that financial load.

FAMILY MATTERS

Zygi is not a lone Wilf. He is part of a tightly knit, consensus-oriented family that, until now, has operated generally behind closed doors.

In this family-based company, there are no grand labels.

"We don't use titles," he said, a certain non-corporateness woven into a hierarchy determined by genes, not by outside hires.

Family ties are so precious and family history so rooted that the office of Harry Wilf, Zygi's uncle, sits untouched at Garden Properties headquarters, just down the hallway from Zygi's.

Harry Wilf died 13 years ago.

Maintaining Harry's office, said Forman, the Yeshiva University official, "signifies Harry will always be in the minds of those who were closest to him. It's a little sign of how they operate. What really counts is family teamwork, shared responsibility, the whole-is-greater-than-the-parts and consensus."

It is a family whose collective consciousness and culture was sculpted by the experiences of the Holocaust.

"Understanding what my parents and grandparents went through to survive the Holocaust, I was instilled with a desire to excel," Zygi Wilf said.

The family's experiences have been reported most extensively by the American Society for Yad Vashem, which has helped to build the New Holocaust History Museum in Israel. The Wilfs, according to public documents, have contributed more than $4 million in the past five years to that cause.

The Vikings are a family affair for owner Zygi Wilf (center). His younger brother Mark (left) is team president, while cousin Leonard is vice chairman and nephew Jeffrey is an ownership partner.
PHOTOGRAPH COURTESY OF THE MINNESOTA VIKINGS.

According to the Yad Vashem organization's newsletter, Joseph Wilf and his family were deported from their Polish home during World War II by the Russians to a Siberian labor camp. After the war, Joseph met his wife, Elizabeth, in an American-occupied sector of Germany; she and her family had survived the Nazis.

Upon arriving in the United States, Joseph and his brother, Harry, began a used-car business and then began renting out apartments, according to Shopping Center World, an industry publication.

Apparently, the Wilf enterprises were relatively small potatoes until the 1980s. They controlled only four shopping centers as late as 1982, according to one published report that quoted Zygi's nephew, Orin Wilf. Orin Wilf didn't return the *Star Tribune*'s phone calls.

Zygi Wilf said he didn't grow up feeling like a rich kid. "I never thought of myself that way," he said.

But there were perks. "I used to take him to Giants games," said Ralph Loveys, 76, a family friend and business partner. "I used to take him into the locker rooms to meet the ballplayers. He was nine or 10. It was a thrill for him."

Wilf didn't go to particularly prestigious schools. His choices were Fairleigh Dickinson University in Madison, New Jersey, where he was an economics major, and New York Law School, which began as a haven for immigrants and working people seeking law degrees. He graduated from both institutions, registrars from both schools said.

Wilf said he chose Fairleigh Dickinson because it was close to home.

A decade later, Mark Wilf graduated from Princeton and attended New York University Law School, one of the nation's most prestigious.

Meanwhile, with the family wealth came a practice of philanthropy and political giving.

POLITICS AND THE LAW

An analysis of political contributions shows a family placing its bets on many sides, although it has tilted slightly toward Democratic candidates. According to a *Star Tribune* examination, since 1980, Wilf family members and key employees of their companies have given $848,000 to various national and local political campaigns and candidates; $491,000 of that went to Democrats.

However, Zygi Wilf has given $96,800 to Democratic candidates and committees and $32,600 to Republicans since 1980.

"We decide to support the leadership that is committed to our goals of better and stronger communities," Wilf said of his political funding, adding that the contributions weren't made for the purpose of influencing elected officials.

But Wilf was one of 28 influential developers who were revealed last year to have easy access to former New Jersey governor James E. McGreevey [who had resigned amidst charges of sexual harassment and admitted having a homosexual affair with a political appointee—ED.]. The *Newark Star-Ledger* reported that McGreevey was meeting with developers at the same time he was signing legislation giving them quick building permits and environmental waivers.

Asked about it, Wilf said, "I may have gone to one meeting for input." He had no further comment.

Otherwise, the most controversial legal entanglement for Wilf was a race discrimination lawsuit involving three of his company's apartment complexes in Parsippany, New Jersey. In 1999, the U.S. Justice Department filed a lawsuit against Garden Homes Management for refusing to rent to black tenants. The case was ultimately settled. In an interview earlier this month, Wilf called it "an unfortunate incident."

"We investigated it, addressed it, and in a timely fashion, corrected it," he said.

Mitch Kahn, vice president and director of organizing for the New Jersey

Tenants Organization, a statewide advocacy group, said he was unaware of any major conflicts between Garden Homes and its tenants.

A review of court files in Essex and Middlesex counties found no recent major lawsuits.

Visits to a handful of other housing developments built by Wilf and his partners found homeowners mostly satisfied with the craftsmanship and the way they were treated, although some dissented.

"Once they close on a house, they wash their hands of it," said George Mercado of West Orange, New Jersey, who is upset that Wilf did not return phone calls about a legal matter concerning his new $300,000 house. He said developers did not repair some construction defects.

Up the block, however, Ed Ayuso praises the "great construction" of the house Wilf's company built and calls the developer "very cooperative."

Wilf insists that most customers are satisfied and says he always returns phone calls.

Away from his real estate holdings and on the campus that bears the family's name, some students expressed enthusiasm for Wilf's endeavor. "I think it's pretty impressive," said Jacob Sassoon, 21, a senior at the Wilf Campus at Yeshiva University. His roommate, Jason Silverman, 20, a junior and a Vikings fan, said he e-mailed Wilf, asking if he could become an intern for the Vikings.

QUICK STUDY

When he's deep in conversation, Zygi Wilf paces. He is cautious, speaks slowly and chooses his words carefully. He smiles to himself as he thinks through an idea and occasionally asks his younger brother to answer a question. But he also does his homework and learns fast.

That's what public officials from Anoka County have been saying about his instant knowledge of the real estate market around Blaine. That's what they're saying at Albert Einstein College of Medicine these days, too.

Wilf was recently named to the board of directors at Einstein, which is affiliated with Yeshiva and is known for its research into infectious diseases. Wilf has poured himself into the job and has wanted to spend time with the medical school's dean and with scientists working on cures.

"He's starting to become an activist, an expert in this new area," said Forman, the Yeshiva fundraising vice president. "I do believe that people who are successful in one area of life have an interest in making a difference, a mark in another area, to round out a life, to have fun, to have an inspirational impact. We ask the question, 'Why are we here?'"

Who could have known that one of the reasons Zygi Wilf is "here" may be to run a pro football team, to build a stadium, to attempt to transform his family's business culture into a sports company that has had its share of woes, from suspended drug-test dodgers to ticket-scalping coaches to armed wide receivers.

"I hope to make a team feel more like a family," Wilf said, "so that we can meet all the challenges that face us."

Those may be the words of a novice, but come Tuesday or Wednesday, they will probably be the aspirations of the new Vikings owners. Wilf will step out of the shadows of shopping centers into the house-to-house battles of NFL ownership. The secure cocoon will drop away. Ready or not, Zygi Wilf will go prime time.

●

Freed of the divisive Randy Moss and with a chance for a fresh start with a new owner, circumstances appeared favorable for coach Mike Tice to come into his own as head coach. Tice was open—too open, according to his boosters—with the media, who had battled for years with the tight-lipped and belligerent Denny Green. Reporters loved their access to Tice, and appreciated the tough job he inherited—Red McCombs pinched pennies the last few years he owned the team, running $20–30 million below the salary cap and generally cutting administrative expenses.

Tice was by far the lowest-paid head coach in the league, and he was in the final year of his four-year contract. He was clearly under pressure to improve on the team's combined 23–25 regular-season record the past three years. Wilf said he would "see how the season unfolds" before making any decisions about Tice's future.

Sporting News, August 26, 2005
MR. BIG'S SHOT
Paul Attner

Mike Tice is oversized, colorful and fun, a lot like the loudmouth on the next barstool. But on the sideline, he's still fairly nondescript. It's about time his New York personality starts to rub off on the Vikings.

Hey, you. Yeah, you.

I want to talk to you for a minute. It's about Mike Tice, OK? You probably think you're some football genius so you know this Tice guy. Really tall and coaches the Vikings and got in trouble with the league for selling his Super Bowl tickets—what's the big stink anyway?—and trades away his best player, that numbskull Randy Moss.

So you know the easy stuff. Big friggin' deal. If you have any brains, you oughta be pulling for him. I mean, it's like taking the guy sitting at the bar, the one with all the loud opinions because he knows everything about everything, and giving him a whistle and a head coaching job. He's one of

Mike Tice was a likable coach, but his 32–33 won–loss record and the off-field behavioral problems with Vikings players spelled his doom. New owner Zygi Wilf fired Tice just after the final game of the 2005 season. PHOTOGRAPH COURTESY OF THE MINNESOTA VIKINGS.

us, you know what I mean—even if he's like a foot taller? Hand him a beer and a cigar and put a Knicks game on and he's the best company.

Did you see him walking around in the off-season with a cast on his foot? Know what happened? You're not so smart after all. Well, here's the scoop. He's playing in an end-of-camp touch football game with Vikings interns and ballboys last summer and tears up his ankle but doesn't have surgery until winter. Could just as well have happened to you or me on a Sunday afternoon on the playground. But here's my point: Could you see Parcells or Belichick playing a game with the interns at camp? No freakin' way. Tice's wife, who likes to bust him to keep him humble, which is like asking Larry King to be modest, tells him to grow up. As if that's going to happen.

He has been gone, what, 24 years from Central Islip, New York, right in the middle of Long Island, and you'd never know it. Talks like he still lives there, you know what I mean? He hasn't forgotten his roots; he's damn proud of them. Tell me what other NFL coach would describe himself like this: "I am a big, tall, deep-voiced, loud, arrogant New Yorker who thinks he is right all the time. That rubs some people the wrong way. I don't mean anything by it. But I am opinionated."

Toss in gutsy, too. This being a family publication, I can't be more ana-tomically specific, but you get my drift. I mean, he has no contract after this season, which gives him the security of a mosquito at a Raid demonstration. Even close friends concede the Vikings need to go deep into the playoffs for him to be retained. He knows that, too, yet he gets rid of Moss. What's more, he does it even though he is about to gain a new owner, which doesn't make for the swiftest first impression, even if the new big man, Zygi Wilf, is an East Coast guy.

But what the heck. You might as well give it your best shot surrounded by guys who buy into your rules and play hard all the time, not just when it suits them, and respect authority and understand loyalty. I mean, Moss never got it. Tice believes in this loyalty thing big-time—go ask anyone in Central Islip about loyalty—and he starts right off as coach by declaring the "Randy Ratio," which really is a love offering to Moss, only the jerk never understands. He rewards Tice by various displays of stupidity, whether it's a run-in with a meter maid or mock mooning Packers fans or leaving the final regular-season game last January before it's finished and, dumbest of all, responding to a question about Tice's future by saying, "I don't know if Coach Tice is the coach for this team, and I don't know if he isn't."

Talk about sticking a knife into someone who actually likes you and stands up for you and even to this very minute won't bad-mouth you because that's the honorable thing to do. If Moss had his way, Tice and Daunte Culpepper would be ex-Vikings and his own loud mouth and mer-curial personality would be in Minnesota, where his teammates still would be disgusted with both his churlish behavior and his special set of rules.

Instead, Moss is gone, and this now is Tice's team, you know what I mean? Only five starters, all on offense, remain from when he replaced Denny Green in January 2002, but it's more than that. When Tice was named coach, he said he wanted the squad to take on his personality. But with a wimpy defense and an offense too intent on keeping Moss happy, the Vikings never have played with a tough, physical, New York attitude. He says that's changing this year.

It's a team that finally has his back. Got a problem with that?

The little man walks across the field, greeting players and coaches. He stops next to the very tall guy with a pencil behind his ear. Mike Tice spots him, bends down and embraces Billy Klinke. They talk and laugh. All's well. Billy's here.

Klinke is a dwarf who grew up across the street from Tice in Central Islip. He was the best man at Tice's wedding. His sister is married to Tice's brother John, a former NFL tight end who now is the Vikings' tight ends coach. Billy was a jockey, which is why Tice once owned a bunch of second-level racehorses. Billy rode the horses; they didn't get rich but they had some laughs. Tice also once owned two delis in the Seattle area, called them "Fill Yer Belly Deli." Billy, who retired after too many injuries, spends every training camp with the Vikings.

They know people stare but, hey, if you don't like it, take a hike. Billy is family, and you don't mess with family. "Father, forgive me, I'm Catholic and go to church, but my order of priorities is family, church and football," Tice says. "That's maybe why I look at what is going on around here a little differently. Don't get me wrong. Football is very, very important, but there are other things in life I care very deeply about, too."

Tice has two kids, Adrienne, 18, who's named after the woman in *Rocky*, and Nathan, 16. For the longest time, Tice drove a 1998 Buick Roadmaster station wagon when he could have afforded better. But he coached Nathan's youth league teams in football, basketball and baseball; he needed the wagon to haul players and equipment. With the hours you work in the NFL, it's nearly impossible to coach your kid, too. But he figured out a way because it was family.

He likes being the man, but it's nice how he doesn't act snotty or any of that garbage. You just always know where you stand with him. He has this bellow, and his personality is pretty strong. He's also funny, profane, sincere, blunt, stubborn, trusting, volatile, emotional, likable, difficult, great company and truly caring. He holds parties at his house so just about everyone who works for the Vikings gets to mix with him in a different setting. He hands out generous Christmas gifts to who knows how many. And so what if he makes $1 million a year? He still sees himself as a regular guy. Hey, another of his closest friends is a bartender at a pub where he and his wife, Diane, like to eat breakfast so often that he now has his own parking space.

But he's right, not everyone loves him. It has something to do with all those opinions. No one is exempt. "I get up in the morning coaching," he says. "Sometimes, stuff comes out of this New York mouth that I would like to yank back right away." He introduced President Bush during a campaign appearance in Minnesota, a blue state. He got plenty of critical letters, but you know what, a man can't be afraid. "I like the guy," he says. "I would have introduced Clinton, too. I liked him. Besides, what guy from Central Islip, New York, has ever introduced the President of the United States? I'm proud of that."

Now that Super Bowl ticket mess—that wasn't smart. He unloads tickets and someone rats on him, and even though it's common practice among coaches and players, Tice shouldn't have done it. The league fines him $100,000, 10 percent of his salary. I mean, what was he thinking?

Something else, too. When then-owner Red McCombs promoted Tice from assistant head coach–offensive line coach, he wasn't ready. A player for 14 years but an assistant coach for just six, he wasn't prepared for the totality of his new position. He wanted to be everyone's friend, please everyone, not hurt anyone's feelings. Other times, he would make quick, emotional decisions that could have used more thought. And his game decisions, well, you gotta know some of them baffled even his players. In all these areas, he has improved.

Not that Tice always has gotten a fair deal. McCombs, who sold the team in May, was an erratic tightwad who constantly had the Vikings on the market while trying to persuade local politicians to build a stadium. In a media conference call to discuss the Moss trade, McCombs revealed he almost fired Tice instead of dealing Moss. Great vote of confidence, that. Tice also functions as an unofficial general manager in a very thin Vikings front office that supports the lowest-paid coaching staff—and head coach—in the league.

"It seems like sometimes Mike is all by his lonesome," says *Sporting News* and FOX TV Sports analyst Brian Baldinger, who does Vikings preseason games. "Where is the G.M.? I think it is too much. By the end of the season, he looks awful. There's no question he can coach, and the guys love him. But Moss wore everyone out. The whole team took its cue from him. When he pouted, they pouted. No one could yell at him or he would go in the tank, so they coddled him. He was a front-runner. I know those guys won't miss him."

He's right. "It seemed like he wanted to move on, and it was time," says center Matt Birk. "A lot of what was going on was getting old, for [Moss] to do or say something outrageous and not make himself available to the media and leaving us to try to explain it. It'll be different around here, but I think we will be OK."

That's what Tice thinks, too. And he needs to be right. "He continues to grow, but he is so much more comfortable in the job," says Scott Studwell, the Vikings' director of college scouting. "Now he's at a critical juncture in his career as a coach. This is a huge season. We have worked hard as an organization to build this team, but we know what is at stake. The new ownership is going to make a lot of good and hard decisions based on how we do this year."

After three-plus years, you'd think you could quickly define Mike Tice. I mean, I say Joe Gibbs and you immediately think Super Bowls and offense. Parcells? Taskmaster and winner. Belichick? Eccentric genius. Vermeil? Lots of tears. But Tice? Other than being 6'8", what defines him? That's what this season is all about, too. Because if he can fill in the blanks as a coach and give us a complete picture of his skills, the Vikings will do well enough to save his job.

Tice is so much of what should be good about coaching. "He's trying to do this with a human touch—with compassion for others—and it makes him different in a good way," says Studwell. This tag of being a players' coach is so overused it has become a joke, but this guy really does like his players. As an assistant, he spent so much time in the locker room that they had to remind him occasionally to stay away. Now they love his Friday meetings, which are nothing more than laughfests, usually featuring comical pictures from the past of players and staff. It's impossible for him not to talk, not be friendly. And what's not to like about a coach who has fresh flowers delivered weekly to his office and plays everything from Springsteen to Bocelli on his sound system?

Still, there are contradictions. He was smart enough to be recruited by the Ivies yet never finished his degree at Maryland. He understands the marathon that is a season, yet his practices have been among the longest in the league. He is incredibly organized, living by lists he compulsively compiles daily, but he constantly has gone off-schedule during workouts.

But he's trying to change. He considers himself a terrific offensive coach. But last fall, coordinator Scott Linehan called all the plays. The Vikings didn't run as much or as efficiently as Tice wanted, and now Linehan is with the Dolphins and Tice intends to be deeply involved in the play-calling. His coaches and players pleaded with him to shorten practices. He agonized for days about it before finally agreeing. Now, counting walkthroughs, they'll be on the field some 65 minutes less each day. Plus, he has altered how he practices special teams and, for the first time, has asked veteran starters to join those squads. And toss in the defensive remake with at least five new starters. He wants a top-ten defense so the Moss-less offense won't have to score as many points for the Vikings to win.

"He's like a proud papa," says Rob Brzezinski, the Vikings' vice president of football operations. "He's pretty excited about showcasing this team."

So many of the changes are geared toward sustaining excellence for a whole season.

"I know how to rock and roll coming out of training camp, but it's those 3–7 finishes that I have to figure out," Tice says. That has been the pattern under him—quick starts followed by collapses, both in 2003 and '04. The Vikings managed a playoff berth last season and then his first postseason victory by beating the Packers, but Minnesota still was only 8–8 and is 23–26 in his tenure.

But, hey, Tice once was the ninth-string tight end with the Seahawks in his rookie year after joining the team as a quarterback. Wound up as the starter week one. "I've always accomplished what I've set out to do," he says.

You want to bet against him on this one?

●

Unfortunately, the Vikings didn't rock and roll out of training camp in 2005, and were 1–3 when they reached their bye week after an ugly 30–10 loss to Atlanta on October 2. Daunte Culpepper was struggling. He didn't throw his first touchdown pass until the team's third game—and he had already thrown 12 interceptions, compared to 11 in all of 2004. The team had scored only 31 points in its three losses.

Then came the "Love Boat"—a cruise on October 6 for Vikings players on two boats rented from Al and Alma's Charters on Lake Minnetonka. The party was part of a long-standing Vikings bye-week tradition, with first-year players paying for an activity planned by some of the veteran players. This one got out of hand. Charter boat employees complained of harassment and described graphic lap dances, open sex acts, and other shocking lewd behavior. The two boat captains finally decided to cut the cruise short and return to the dock. About 20 team members had been on the cruise.

The event created a media firestorm. New owner Zygi Wilf was rightfully embarrassed. He promised appropriate actions against any player charged with misdemeanors or other illegal activities in the investigation by civil authorities. The public outcry over the Love Boat and other Vikings' misbehaviors may have derailed Wilf's proposal for a new stadium project in Blaine that he had unveiled in September, calling for $510 million in public funds. Governor Pawlenty had been supportive, and there was talk of a special legislative session to work on the Vikings' proposal, as well as plans for new Twins and Gophers football stadiums.

The Love Boat wasn't an isolated event. In their 1998 book, *Pros and Cons: The Criminals Who Play in the NFL*, authors Jeff Benedict and Don Yaeger said that "the Vikings may have been the most out-of-control team in the NFL." Using the Freedom of Information Act, they searched police records in the greater Twin Cities metropolitan area and found many incidents that never became public, thanks to aggressive work by Vikings security personnel—getting charges dropped for problems including drunken driving, sexual harassment, domestic violence, rape, larceny, illegal guns, and concealed weapons.

Minneapolis Star Tribune, October 14, 2005

VIKINGS SHOW DISRESPECT TO STATE
AFTER 20 YEARS ON THE POLICE BLOTTER, IT'S TIME FOR REFORM
Editorial

Respect is something that professional athletes say they crave, both on the field and on the street. You hear the word a lot. To have respect is perhaps an NFL player's greatest yearning.

Yet, if the latest allegations are true, the Vikings players who engaged in lewd behavior on two Lake Minnetonka cruise boats last week showed no respect for their teammates, coaches, organization, fans—or for the citizens of Minnesota who, like it or not, find themselves inextricably linked to the Vikings' national brand.

How do you explain lap dance to an eight-year-old who loves wearing her purple jersey to school? How do you account for nude women mingling in the crowd, then getting sexually occupied with players on the decks? How do you react when your waitress daughter is trapped on a boat, forced to fight off aggressive propositions from hulking, drunken football players? Real respect runs both ways. You don't get it by threatening vulnerable people or urinating on people's lawns.

We are not prudes about this. What consenting people do behind closed doors is their business. But this wasn't like that. The cruise line never expected this kind of party. After only 40 minutes the boats were ordered back to shore not because things happened to get out of hand, but because someone had planned it that way.

Perhaps the NFL should end the pretense that football players are role models, worthy of the adoration that goes with caps, shirts, TV commercials and the other trappings of fandom, and market them simply as violent entertainers, expensive gladiators whose careers could end at any point and, therefore, shouldn't be expected to behave as anything other than arrogant fatalists with no sense of decency or mutual respect.

But we are not that cynical. Instead, we hope that the team sets out to repair not only its image but its reality. Zygi Wilf, who may already regret paying $600 million for this zoo, shouldn't hesitate to clean house if the allegations are true. The new owner may have the opportunity to lead, something coach Mike Tice has failed at.

Wilf should fire any players found to be implicated in misconduct aboard the boats. What happens on the big lake cannot stay on the big lake if the safety and integrity of innocents were jeopardized. After 20 years on the police blotter, it's time to resurrect a team that, we hope, has finally hit rock bottom and whose only remaining path is upward. Football players don't have to be Boy Scouts, just reasonably good citizens.

Most tragic is this disgraceful episode's impact on Minnesota's governor and legislators who wake up every day looking for excuses not to do things.

It's understandable that the Vikings stadium project has now been set back months, perhaps years. It's unfair if the Twins ballpark and University of Minnesota football stadium are tarred by the same brush. What happened on Lake Minnetonka has nothing to do with them. Those teams have earned the respect of Minnesotans. Atonement has not yet arrived for the Vikings.

The Vikings came off the bye with a lackluster effort in a 28–3 loss at Chicago, and fearful team officials—worried about a hostile crowd reaction—decided to forgo pregame introductions at the first post–Love Boat game at the Metrodome on October 23. Despite this, the booing and catcalls started early—and got louder when the team went into the locker room at halftime trailing the Green Bay Packers, 17–0.

Daunte Culpepper rallied the team in the second half—looking like the Culpepper of 2004 for the first time in the season—and the Vikings won 23–20 on a 56-yard field goal by Paul Edinger as the clock ran out, a kick described in a *Minneapolis Tribune* headline as "The Love Boot." The Vikings celebrated like they had won the Super Bowl.

The euphoria was short-lived. Culpepper suffered three torn ligaments in his right knee when tackled on a scramble in the first quarter of the next game at Carolina. He would soon undergo surgery that ended his season. The seriousness of surgery caused some medical experts to wonder if he could be ready for the start of the 2006 season.

In an amazing stroke of déjà vu, the 37-year-old Brad Johnson—signed in the spring to back up Culpepper—took over as starting quarterback. Johnson first became a Vikings' starting quarterback in 1996, replacing the injured Warren Moon, and was replaced by Randall Cunningham due to his own injuries in 1997 and 1998. He was traded to Washington in 1999, and led them to the playoffs and was voted to the Pro Bowl team. In 2002 he quarterbacked Tampa Bay to a Super Bowl victory and earned his second Pro Bowl berth.

Johnson led the Vikings to six consecutive victories, salvaging what looked like a disastrous season. Some argued that those wins came in the softest part of the team's schedule. Nevertheless, he was 7–2 as a starter, and almost no one back on October 30—when Culpepper was injured— would have bet that the team would finish with a 9–7 record and just miss the playoffs.

No one was surprised when coach Mike Tice was fired after the last game of the season, a 34–10 win over the NFC North champion Chicago Bears, who were more interested in preparing for the playoffs. Tice more than once told confidants during the season that he expected to be fired. In the end, Zygi Wilf made the decision not so much because of Tice's win–loss record, but because he felt that the team needed to change its public image—starting with a new coach.

What was surprising was the way the firing was handled—in a news release handed out to the media less than an hour after the Bears game. Tice had no opportunity to speak to his players and family before the news broke and was forced to call his wife on her cell phone to warn her before she heard about it on radio or television. When asked what he felt about the way it had been handled, Tice was gracious. "Is there a good way?" he asked.

Minneapolis Star Tribune, January 3, 2006

AT HANGOUT, TO KNOW TICE IS TO MISS HIM

Patrick Reusse

To the regulars at Bunny's Bar and Grill in St. Louis Park, the fired Vikings coach is a regular guy with plenty of football savvy.

On the night he was fired as the Minnesota Vikings head coach, Mike Tice was forced into hoity surroundings to find some liquid relaxation.

"Mike was on the way here last night," Bunny's bartender Steve (Crazy) Johnson said Monday. "Then, a camera crew from a local TV station showed up. I called Mike on his cell phone and he said, 'I don't need that tonight.'"

So, Crazy and a few other Tice pals left the usual hangout of Bunny's Bar and Grill in St. Louis Park and met Mike and his wife, Diane, at Kozy's Steak and Seafood, a new place in the Galleria in Edina.

Galleria? That's very uptown for Tice and a friend called Crazy, isn't it?

"Yeah, but it also tells you something about Mike Tice," Johnson said. "He wasn't looking for attention."

"He just wanted to have a couple of drinks with friends on a tough night," Johnson said.

There was more than Tice missing from Bunny's on Sunday night. During the evening, the sign that declared a prime parking spot as belonging to Tice was removed from its post.

"The post wasn't bent and there was no other damage, so it wasn't vandalism," Steve Koch said. "It must have been someone wanting a souvenir."

A REGULAR SINCE 1995

Koch is the co-owner of Bunny's with Gary Rackner. He became Rackner's partner in January 1999, when the old building was lost to urban renewal and Bunny's moved farther west on Excelsior Boulevard.

"The old Bunny's was a classic saloon," Johnson said. "A lot of regulars had a tough time adjusting to the move. They have gotten used to it, though. The spirit of Bunny's still is here."

Johnson said he picked up the "Crazy" nickname during a seven-year odyssey in earning a degree at St. Cloud State. "I was there from '65 to '72— and the nickname was well-earned," he said.

Johnson used his degree to carve out a career as a bartending legend. Crazy first encountered Tice when Mike was playing his final NFL season as a tight end for the Vikings in 1995.

"Mike was sitting in a corner at the old Bunny's, playing pulltabs," Johnson said. "He wanted to play a box and needed 100 bucks. I gave it to him. He didn't hit any winners and left, saying, 'I'll give you the $100 when I see you next time.'

"I figured the $100 was gone—that I would never see him again."

Tice came in a few days later and repaid the $100. Conversation followed. Johnson found out Tice's family was living at home in Seattle as he played his last NFL season.

"He came over to our house for Thanksgiving," Johnson said. "We became friends. Our families became friends. His wife, Diane, and the kids are great. Mike's a genuine nice guy. And I have news for people: He does know football.

"I was hoping that he would get one more year with Zygi [Wilf], to work for an owner committed to winning.

"Mike lost his offensive coordinator Scott Linehan because Miami was willing to pay him four times more than he was making with the Vikings. Then, [Red] McCombs wouldn't let him hire a replacement. He said, 'Give it to someone on the staff.' So, Steve Loney wound up with two jobs.

"What kind of a chance does a coach have working for an owner who was too cheap to let him hire an offensive coordinator?"

AN ALL-AROUND FONDNESS

Tice's Bunny's tradition has been to hang out at the front end of the bar. That's the locale of 20 to 25 regulars, several of whom were in attendance Monday afternoon and talking fondly of Tice.

"You should have been here earlier this morning," Dave Braun told a visitor. "Most of Mike's gang was here—at the Rabbit, as we call it—for breakfast. We aren't surprised by Zygi's decision, I guess, just disappointed."

At that moment, a gentleman walked past and leaned toward the table. "Buzzy, what do you think?" Braun said.

Buzzy shook his head and said: "How can we get a good Minnesotan like Glen Taylor to own the Vikings, rather than some East Coasters who don't appreciate someone like Mike Tice?"

The events of the previous 36 hours were not all gloom for the Bunny's crew. Crazy did receive an important reassurance from Tice as they shared a cocktail Sunday night.

"Mike says the golf tournament in Seattle is still on," Johnson said. "This will be the tenth year that seven or eight of us have been going out there around Memorial Day. We spend a week with Mike and his family. Three or four great golf courses, the casino, the racetrack—definitely the racetrack with Mike. You can't have a better time."

Jack Moore was sitting in Sherm's, the small back bar at Bunny's. He was eating lunch and watching Iowa play Florida in the Outback Bowl.

"Bunny's is a place where you can find someone with $30 million sitting next to a guy with 30 bucks," he said. "And the guy with 30 bucks probably is going to buy the first round."

If Bunny's had a slogan, it could be, "Where Meadowbrook meets Minikahda." And Mike Tice has fit in that atmosphere for over a decade.

"What I've appreciated the most about Mike is that he has the time of day for everybody," Moore said.

●

Wilf wasted no time hiring Brad Childress, the offensive coordinator for the Philadelphia Eagles, to replace Tice. Many wondered if Wilf had acted too hastily—the Vikings were the first of eight teams to fill coaching vacancies. Childress was not well known—he had been coaching since 1978, but had never been a head coach. However, he was given credit for helping Donovan McNabb succeed as quarterback with Philadelphia, and Eagles players were positive he would be a great head coach. Childress impressed Vikings' officials, including Bud Grant, with his football knowledge during several interview sessions.

One of the first items on Childress's agenda was to forestall a potential quarterback controversy. Brad Johnson's quiet leadership and 7–2 record had improved locker room morale and helped restore the team's public image, but he made it clear he would like to be a starting quarterback in 2006. Childress, however, believed a player should not lose a starting position because of an injury, and said Culpepper would be his number one if he were physically able to play.

In a bizarre scenario, though, Wilf and Childress were unable to come to terms with the team's former franchise player. Culpepper was still smarting over the lack of guaranteed money in the 10-year, $102 million contract he signed in 2003—a contract since eclipsed by several other quarterbacks in the league. Wilf had given him an $8 million bonus just before the 2005 training camp, but Culpepper was now reportedly demanding another $10 million increase.

When the quarterback persisted in these demands, refused to rehab from his surgery under team guidance in Minnesota, and refused to meet with Childress to study the new West Coast offense the coach was planning to install, Wilf finally gave up and traded Culpepper to Miami.

South Florida Sun-Sentinel, April 11, 2006

CULPEPPER WENT FROM ICON TO OUTCAST IN MINNESOTA

Alex Marvez

The player touted as the next great Dolphins quarterback is well aware of the expectations that await.

Just like the association between Dan Marino and the Dolphins, Daunte Culpepper's name was synonymous with the Minnesota Vikings. For seven seasons, "Pep" was the franchise's cornerstone player and one of the community's sports icons.

Culpepper, though, won't enjoy the lifelong affection from the Twin Cities that Marino enjoys in South Florida. Not after a six-month stretch that included a sex scandal and a falling-out with team management that ultimately led to Culpepper's departure.

"It really just got to the point where it just wasn't beneficial for him to be in Minnesota," said Seattle wide receiver Nate Burleson, a Vikings teammate of Culpepper's from 2003 to 2005.

In the aftermath of last month's trade to the Dolphins, Vikings fans have given Culpepper a cold shoulder befitting the state's winter weather. One Minneapolis-area sports retailer began a clearance sale promoted as "Daunte's Inferno," with Culpepper jerseys marked down to half price.

"It's related to the whole Daunte burning in Minnesota," Pro Image America President Tim Moulton said. "He had the number one–selling jersey across the board easily for the past five years. When he got injured and the boat thing happened, everything stopped."

Culpepper already was having a rough 2005 campaign when he tore three knee ligaments in an October 30 loss to Carolina. He had thrown just six touchdowns and 12 interceptions, and the Vikings were 2–5.

But things took a turn for the worse when Culpepper and three team-mates were levied with three misdemeanor charges related to lewd conduct stemming from a charter boat cruise on Lake Minnetonka earlier in October. The charges against Culpepper were dismissed last week, but stand against his former teammates.

Though Culpepper had maintained his innocence, the damage had been done. He had lost the public's respect, as well as an endorsement deal with Federal Express.

"It's Midwest values and Midwest culture," Moulton said. "That kind of behavior isn't acceptable here no matter how innocent or not innocent it might have been. It was probably overblown, but any small thing like that is going to expand to something big."

The incident struck a nerve in the state and especially in the communities around Lake Minnetonka, which is 20 minutes outside Minneapolis. Some locals said players showed a lack of respect with their behavior on the cruise and by reportedly urinating in front of houses near Al and Alma's, where the charter originated.

Aaron Mielke, a 24-year-old painter from nearby Tonka Bay, said race might have contributed to the outrage. All four players charged, as well as most of those identified as being on the boat, are black. Hennepin County, where Lake Minnetonka and the Twin Cities are located, is 80.5 percent white, according to the 2000 census. Minnesota is 89.4 percent white.

"A bunch of black guys out on a boat with strippers is perceived as being lowbrow and whatnot, but who knows what these executives [who live on the lake] do on their boats?" Mielke said.

"It's a very hypocritical state that acts like it's offended," said Earl Gray, Culpepper's St. Paul-based defense attorney. "If Daunte had not hurt his knee and had thrown for 50 touchdowns, he'd still be playing here."

Maybe.

Culpepper's commitment to the Vikings was questioned after he had knee surgery and decided to rehabilitate near his home in Orlando rather than under the supervision of team trainers in Minnesota. New head coach Brad Childress asked Culpepper to reconsider, but he refused.

Culpepper also approached the Vikings about an increase in guaranteed money in January, which didn't go over well considering the serious nature of his injury and his play before it.

Plus, there was a feeling inside the organization that Culpepper was taking advantage of special treatment he was given.

According to a source, Culpepper didn't have to follow curfews during the regular season and was allowed to arrange his own lodging during training camp when Mike Tice was head coach. New Vikings owner Zygi

Wilf had given Culpepper use of the team's charter airplanes following his injury to commute to Minnesota. Wilf even made sure one of the team's minority owners was in the waiting room after Culpepper's knee surgery in mid-November.

All along, the Vikings seemed willing to accommodate. Culpepper even remained popular among his teammates.

Then, last month, Culpepper, who had fired his agent and was representing himself, sent an e-mail to the media, stating his request for a trade or release. That set off a wave of negative reaction.

"At that point," Burleson said, "people had a reason to dislike a very popular man."

Since joining the Dolphins' off-season workout program two weeks ago, Culpepper has allowed the team to oversee his rehabilitation. However, he has declined local interview requests since being traded, though he's expected to address the media for the first time today.

Whether a change of scenery aids Culpepper in repairing his image—or if his difficulties in Minnesota are a harbinger of his future—should be apparent by November 19 when the Dolphins host the Vikings.

●

This clash never occurred, as Culpepper was put on the injured reserve list after four ineffective games with the Dolphins. The 2006 season was no picnic for the Vikings, either. They were 4–2 at one point, but lost eight of their last 10 games to finish with a 6–10 record. Quarterback Brad Johnson had a tough year—his quarterback rating fell from 88.9 to 72.0, the lowest in his career as a starter, and he threw an interception for every 29 pass attempts, compared to one in every 74 in 2005.

Coach Childress pulled Johnson in the third quarter—after he had thrown four interceptions—in a loss to the Chicago Bears on December 3. Backup quarterback Brooks Bollinger suffered a sprained left shoulder, and Tarvaris Jackson saw his first action of the season. Jackson, from Alabama State, a small Division I-AA school, had been a surprise second-round draft choice in 2006.

Johnson started the next week at Detroit, but faced a growing crescendo of "We want Jackson" chants in a 26–13 loss to the New York Jets at the Metrodome on December 17. Jackson replaced Johnson in the third quarter and was named the starting quarterback for the remaining two games of the season. His first NFL start was against Green Bay quarterback Bret Favre, who was making his two hundred and thirty-sixth start.

In contrast to the Vikings' season, the 2006 "stadium season" had been a remarkable one. After years of struggles, planning, and re-planning, in April and May the Minnesota House and Senate had approved new stadiums for the University of Minnesota Gophers football team and the Minnesota Twins. The Gophers had always been the number one priority for the legislators. The Twins, who could vacate their lease after 2006, had priority over the Vikings, whose lease was effective through the 2011 season.

Shortly after he bought the Vikings, Zygi Wilf had expanded on Red McCombs's plans for a new stadium in Blaine. He pitched a proposal to state legislators that called for the stadium as part of a $1.5 billion complex, including retail stores and business offices in addition to the team headquarters, practice facility, and a Vikings Hall of Fame attraction. When they were not included in the legislature's 2006 bills, the Vikings regrouped to develop a new pitch for the 2007 legislative session. Anoka County began to cool to the rising price tag for the Blaine stadium, and Wilf's focus switched to a new downtown stadium.

On April 20, 2007, the Metropolitan Stadium Facilities Commission presented a plan for a $954 million, 65,000-seat, domed stadium on the Metrodome site. The MSFC said it was needed to keep the Vikings in Minnesota. Despite the team's pledge to contribute "hundreds of millions," the public was weary of the stadium battles, and many wondered what was wrong with the Metrodome that couldn't be fixed for football. The legislature adjourned with no action on a Vikings stadium bill. Subsequently, the I-35 bridge collapse, the credit crunch, and the recession have pushed the Vikings farther back on the list of state priorities.

Coach Childress had made a gutsy decision at the end of February by releasing Brad Johnson and naming Tarvaris Jackson his starting quarterback for 2007. No one doubted Jackson's physical skills, but he had looked overmatched in his only two starts in 2006—he managed only three first downs and 50 yards passing in the 9–7 loss to Green Bay, and in the 41–21 loss to the St. Louis Rams picked up most of his 213 yards passing only after the Rams had a 41–7 lead and went into a soft, prevent defense to run out the clock.

The Vikings traded a sixth-round draft choice to Philadelphia in August to obtain veteran Kelly Holcomb to back up Jackson. Holcomb was an 11-year veteran who had spent most of his career as a backup, but had started eight games for Cleveland in 2003 and eight for Buffalo in 2005.

USA Today, August 28, 2007

VIKINGS READY TO SEE THEIR FUTURE

JACKSON HAS EARNED RESPECT WITH ATTITUDE, THOUGH NOT YET PLAY

Larry Weisman

Tarvaris Jackson knows how important footwork is to a quarterback.

Most of it concerns successfully putting one foot in front of the other.

The second-year pro finished his initial season as the Minnesota Vikings starter and goes into this one as the immediate future of the franchise. When the struggling club promoted him last December, he became the third rookie quarterback in its history (Fran Tarkenton and Tommy Kramer were the others) to start.

He could dream of tight spirals thrown 60 yards for touchdowns, visualize playoff wins and a Super Bowl, but he's just too realistic to lose himself in flights of fantasy, despite his rapid ascent.

The job isn't easy under any circumstance, no less so after coming from Division I-AA Alabama State. While Jackson aims high, his practical side inclines him to hit the reachable goals first.

He's honest. Training camp and his preseason performances have been "up and down," he willingly acknowledges. So he just tries to be "consistent, take care of the football, do the little things right."

And that's what the job is—a series of small steps carefully planned and taken. The Vikings finished 6–10 in 2006 in Brad Childress' first season as coach.

Jackson, a second-round pick, replaced Brad Johnson in a couple of games and took over as the starter for the final two, both losses. Johnson, 38 and in his sixteenth season, is now a backup with the Dallas Cowboys. The Vikings have gone from a veteran who won a Super Bowl (with the Tampa Bay Buccaneers) to the 24-year-old Jackson, who threw 81 passes last year.

Expect growing pains. Hope that something measurable accompanies them. "Anytime a guy is a first-year starter, I just want to see that incremental growth and progress within the system," Childress says.

The Vikings on Monday acquired Kelly Holcomb from the Philadelphia Eagles to back up Jackson, who was named the starter. With 12 years in the NFL, Holcomb should be more of a resource than threat to Jackson.

Think it's easy to line up and take the snap? Some quarterbacks struggle to get the play across while huddled up. In the West Coast offense the Vikings run, play calls can match the Gettysburg Address. Veterans may roll their eyes when kiddie QBs can't spit out the lingo, but Jackson already shows command.

"His poise in the huddle is very strong, especially for a young guy," says wide receiver Bobby Wade, a five-year veteran who has played for two other teams. "We only call the play once in the huddle, and that's a big deal. Every huddle I've been in we were calling the play twice. He does an exceptional job with that. He enunciates well."

Jackson coupled his off-season training regimen in Montgomery, Alabama, with many hours of watching tape and absorbing the nuances of the playbook. Now he's trying to get that to translate into results on the field and to understand that progress can be halting.

"It's complex, but you've got to study your craft, you've got to try to be good at what you do. You can't just do it at practice and then go home and not open your book," he says. "The mental part is the hardest part. When you have a bad day, you have to block it out. When you have a good day, you have to move on."

His teammates like his approach. "The way he conducts himself, it doesn't seem as if he's overwhelmed or nervous," says center Matt Birk. "First-year guy or tenth-year guy, you're going to make mistakes, and you have to learn from all of it. He's comfortable, whether it's with himself or the situation, and that's the right attitude."

Jackson, at 6'2" and 232 pounds, combines mobility and a strong arm in a compact package. His willingness to work and a lack of ego make him an eager student.

"He's a quick study, he's a bright-eyed guy, he can put things into play that you tell him on the next snap, which is rare," says Childress. "He can take volumes of information—and this is a wordy offense—and spit it out. He can paint a picture with words. But he can't get enough reps in terms of training camp. Everything is a new thing, whether it's a blitz period or the red area, and things happen quicker."

Experience only comes the hard way. It is probably not an asset to Jackson that the receiver corps is undergoing a continuous makeover.

Two of the three leading receivers last year, Travis Taylor and tight end Jermaine Wiggins, are gone. Wade was signed as a free agent, and the Vikings drafted the promising Sidney Rice in the second round. Troy Williamson, a number one pick in 2005, still drops too many passes.

Jackson wants to try to build on last year's first steps and then measure out the coming strides.

"Guys have a year under their belt in this offense, and we put a lot of work in. We'll just try to be more detailed on things we do and scheme it down a little bit, just be good at what we do," he says. "We don't have to have a whole bunch of plays, just be good at the plays we do."

●

The Vikings made another gutsy call in the college draft when they selected Oklahoma running back Adrian Peterson with their number seven overall pick. Peterson was an amazing physical specimen, but seemed injury prone—there were questions during the draft whether surgery might be needed to repair the broken collarbone that had limited him to seven games in the 2006 college season. He probably would have been a number one or two selection without the collarbone injury. Some draft experts also wondered whether his upright running style might limit his durability.

The six teams who passed on Peterson soon regretted their timidity. The Vikings had decided to play him behind Chester Taylor, the six-year veteran who had rushed for 1,216 yards in 2006. Peterson came in when Taylor suffered a bruised hip in the first quarter of the opening game against Atlanta, and gained 103 yards in 19 carries. He was held to 66 yards the following week against Detroit, but then gained 102 and 112 yards in games three and four—and ignited a fan frenzy that only intensified when he broke a Vikings rushing record at Chicago after a bye week on October 14, with 224 yards and three touchdowns in 20 carries.

Meanwhile, Tarvaris Jackson was having a difficult time. He was ineffective in the win over Atlanta in the season opener, and was replaced by Brooks Bollinger in the second game after he had thrown four interceptions. Coming into the November 4 home game against San Diego, the Vikings were 2–5 for the season. Jackson had won two games as a starter, but Kelly Holcomb was 0–3 in three starts. Then Adrian Peterson put on an amazing display of speed and power.

Minneapolis Star Tribune, November 5, 2007
ALL DAY LONG
WINNING FORMULA IS SIMPLE: GIVE THE BALL TO PETERSON
Kevin Seifert
Adrian (All Day) Peterson had a day for the ages, rushing for an NFL-record 296 yards to go with three TDs.

Whew! The magic elixir has finally arrived. It came not from Bora Bora or Morocco or any other exotic locale, just a small town near Dallas that produces men who singlehandedly can win football games.

After a global search, the Vikings have found the secret to winning: Hand the ball to Adrian Peterson and wait for him to reach 200 yards. Sunday, they rode Peterson's NFL-record 296-yard performance to a 35–17 victory over San Diego.

The Vikings are 2–0 this season when Peterson crashes that heavenly barrier and 1–5 when he does not; he amassed 224 yards in a 34–31 victory last

Adrian Peterson (28) electrified Vikings fans in 2007 by rushing for 224 yards against the Bears, and then for an NFL-record 296 yards against the Chargers. He was NFL's leading rusher in 2008 despite facing defenses specifically designed to try to stop him, and he was voted NFL Bert Bell Player of the Year—only the third Viking to receive the award. Fran Tarkenton (1975) and Randall Cunningham (1998) were the others. PHOTOGRAPH BY RICK A. KOLODZIEJ. COURTESY OF THE MINNESOTA VIKINGS.

month at Chicago. Who would have thought winning could be so straight-forward?

The Vikings again played musical quarterbacks Sunday, replacing injured Tarvaris Jackson (concussion) with Brooks Bollinger, but fortunately they have thrust aside their tortured tailback rotation.

With Peterson starting and Chester Taylor working in relief, the Vikings finished with their best offensive performance—528 total yards, including a team-record 378 on the ground—in their past 51 games.

"That's the way I like to play football," coach Brad Childress said. "I do have a healthy respect for being able to run it and taking somebody's will from them, and then playing off of that with play-action. If you're looking for a benchmark [this is it]."

All it took was for Peterson to accumulate 253 yards in the second half alone, transforming a 14–7 halftime deficit into a rout midway through the fourth quarter. He accounted for three touchdowns himself and was par-tially responsible for a fourth; Bollinger' play-action fake to Peterson left receiver Sidney Rice wide open for a 40-yard score.

Peterson sealed the game on a 46-yard touchdown run with 7 minutes, 44 seconds remaining and broke Jamal Lewis's four-year-old rushing record with his final carry of the game. Peterson's season total of 1,036 yards rep-resents the best eight-game performance by a rookie in NFL history and is tied for fifth-best among all players.

Just as important, however, the Vikings have finally unleashed their pri-mary offensive weapon in its full fury. Peterson established a career high with 30 carries, touching the ball on 47 percent of the Vikings' offensive plays.

Their commitment to Peterson finally secure, the Vikings were carrying themselves early Sunday evening like a team far better than its 3–5 record indicates.

"The guys in the locker room and in this organization know what we have," Peterson said. "Other guys have tapped out on us. We know what we have. It's all on us. We have stayed positive and kept taking it one game at a time."

During a team meeting Sunday, in fact, Childress reminded players of the 2005 Vikings team that started 2–5 before winning six consecutive games. Twenty players remain from that team, and Childress said, "Some of those guys understand what it takes."

It didn't appear that way at halftime Sunday. Childress' decision to attempt a 57-yard field goal on the half's final play had ended in disaster: Ryan Longwell's kick was short, and San Diego's Antonio Cromartie returned it 109 yards for a touchdown, the longest play in NFL history.

Childress hurled his headset 15 yards toward the bench, knowing the Chargers shouldn't have the lead on a day his defense would hold tailback LaDainian Tomlinson to 2.5 yards per carry and harass quarterback Philip Rivers into a 19-for-42 afternoon.

The Vikings spent only a few minutes in the locker room before storming back onto the field. "It doesn't do any good to rant and rave," Childress said. "[The first half] was in the past . . . We were playing pretty good football, so if you want to come in and rant and rave, it's going to be a turnoff."

The Vikings scored touchdowns on four of their first six possessions in the second half and could have had more were it not for red-zone fumbles by Taylor in the third quarter and Peterson in the fourth.

"I think [the second half] determined the rest of our season right there," receiver Robert Ferguson said. "We could have folded, and if we folded today, the season would have been down the drain."

Instead, it entered historic territory when the Vikings regained possession at their 10-yard line with 1:58 remaining. The game was well in hand—Peterson already had crossed the 200-yard barrier, after all—and Lewis' NFL record still stood 37 yards away.

Peterson, however, dashed for 35 yards on the Vikings' first play—nearly scampering past Chargers cornerback Marlon McCree for what would have been a 90-yard score. Instead, he took one play off and then re-entered to break the record with a 3-yard run.

"Anything is possible, you know," Peterson said afterwards.

Sure. Just keeping churning out those 200-yard games.

Brooks Bollinger started the next week against Green Bay, a 34–0 loss that threatened to be even more disastrous when Peterson strained his right knee and had to leave the game. He missed two games, but returned to action with 116 yards in 15 carries against Detroit. It was his last 100-yard game of the season, as opponents stacked the line with defenders to stop him, daring the Vikings to pass.

Tarvaris Jackson sat out the Green Bay game with the concussion but returned to action in game 10 against Oakland. The Vikings won five straight games before losing the last two to finish with an 8–8 record. Jackson showed some improvement from his early-season performance. His passing percentage in the last seven games, for example, was 65.2 percent, compared to 46.4 percent in the first five. He was still inconsistent, however, and for the season threw more interceptions than touchdown passes.

For the second straight year the team led the league in rushing defense—and was last in passing defense. Thanks to Peterson's great rookie year—1,341 yards on 238 carries—the Vikings led the league in rushing yards. Peterson was selected the Associated Press Offensive Rookie of the Year, and was voted the Most Valuable Player in the Pro Bowl, where he ran for 129 yards and scored two touchdowns. Guard Steve Hutchinson, center Matt Birk, defensive tackles Pat and Kevin Williams, and safety Darren Sharper were also Pro Bowl selections. Hutchinson and Kevin Williams were repeat picks for the All Pro team.

The Vikings had shown solid improvement, thanks in large part to Wilf's willingness to sign free agents—Hutchinson, linebacker Ben Leber, and running back Chester Taylor in 2006, and receiver Bobby Wade in 2007.

Wilf loosened the purse strings even more in 2008, signing free-agent receiver Bernard Berrian and safety Madieu Williams, and trading for pass-rushing end Jared Allen, to whom he gave a contract with over $30 million in guaranteed money.

Expectations were high, and the star of the team—after only one year—was definitely Adrian Peterson. He drew crowds wherever he went, and he endeared himself to fans with his humble demeanor.

ESPN The Magazine, September 23, 2008

PLEASE DON'T REMAIN CALM

Allison Glock

Adrian Peterson just wants his ice cream.

A scoop of cake-batter flavor, in a cup, with pecans and caramel and maybe some crumbled Snickers. It is the wane of summer, and he practiced twice today at the Vikings training facility in Mankato, and he will practice twice tomorrow and again most every day until the three-week-long camp ends. It is "drudgery," explains coach Brad Childress, leavened not by nights out (there's a curfew) or female company (strictly prohibited) but only by the smooth, soothing deliciousness of a frozen treat.

Peterson, 23, has been thinking about his ice cream since the morning, fantasizing about it the way one would a Kardashian, his mouth curling up at the thought, a low, growly "Mmmmm" escaping from deep in his throat.

But first he must sign autographs. Because he is that guy. The fan favorite. Warm and generous. A hale young man, with white teeth and short, doll-like lashes, who runs with the elegance and intention of a wolf. A player who makes anything feel possible—even a Super Bowl. He knows that many of the people outside the gates are waiting just for him, that they have perched on a grassy bank or sidewalk for seven hours in 90-degree heat just to touch his forearm, get a signature on their number 28 jersey. So Peterson lingers longer than any other player. He signs and chats and hugs until finally hunger overtakes him. "I'm sorry, y'all, I really need to get going," Peterson says, ducking his head into his neck. "Next time. Tomorrow? Okay?"

The crowd begins to whine, frantically flapping notebooks and programs in his face. "Adrian!" they bellow desperately, a swarm of would-be Rockys. Peterson smiles, extracts himself from the rows of outstretched hands, some shaking at his very nearness. "Come on, man," one teenager pleads, tugging at his shirt. "I'm black! I'm like you. I'm black!"

Peterson yanks himself loose, backs away. The teen's face crumples, tears sliding down his cheeks.

"Dang," Peterson says, walking to the golf cart that will drive him away. "I wasn't expecting that."

Expectations are something Adrian Peterson knows a little about. He is only a few weeks into his second season as a pro but is already legendary. Not because of his records (rushing for an NFL all-time single-game-best 296 yards against the Chargers last November) or résumé (Pro Bowl MVP, Rookie of the Year, Heisman runner-up at 19) or even his supernatural physicality (able to race 100 meters in 10.3 seconds! Able to leap 38 inches in a single bound!). No, Peterson is a legend for that most modern of reasons, because he is being talked about. By his fans, of course, but also by his colleagues, awed into hagiography by his talent. "When he's not around we tell stories about the things he's done," says Vikings wide receiver Sidney Rice, Peterson's roommate on the road. "Like the time I saw him after a hard practice, in full pads, running full speed, trying to get somebody to run gases with him." Rice shakes his head incredulously. "You don't see anybody like that."

The Vikings started the season with big expectations of their own. In the overhauled NFC North, they were the ones to watch, largely because of the one to watch. Peterson is delivering, logging yardage and thrills, but the W's have been slow to materialize. For this, fans have mostly blamed third-year QB Tarvaris Jackson, who completed barely 50% of his passes in the Vikings' 0–2 start and was eventually replaced by Gus Frerotte. The 37-year-old journeyman promptly led the team to a home win over Carolina on Sept. 21, but the sense that all isn't quite right in Minnesota remains.

No one is more full of angst than Peterson. Moments after rushing for 160 yards in his team's heartbreaking 18-15 loss to the Colts on Sept. 14, he doesn't fixate on the team's QB struggles or its vulnerable secondary. He blames only himself. "Without the win, 160 yards doesn't mean anything," he says, tossing a towel into his locker. "I left plays out there. I left a touchdown out there."

Peterson blows air through his teeth, yanks his carefully pressed dress pants off a hanger, snapping the fabric. "I take it personally. I feel responsible. I do. I got tripped up. I need to do a better job picking my feet out of the hole. I can't make mistakes like that." His voice fades as he shakes his head. His body is tense, vibrating with disappointment. He rams his hands into his hips. "It's just," he grinds his teeth, "really, really frustrating."

The rest of the locker room is quiet, humid. Large purple duffel bags litter the floor like carapaces. Offensive guard Steve Hutchinson despondently swallows a sandwich from a cradle of tinfoil. Defensive end Jared Allen answers questions in his underwear, saying the team "needs to find a way to win"; he's one of the few Vikes talking. Peterson takes a seat, burying his face deep in his hands.

His despair surprises no one. His teammates have come to know this side of Peterson well.

"Adrian's never happy with himself," says receiver Aundrae Allison. "He doesn't understand his accomplishments." Of course, from this humility flow his greatest strengths. "Adrian is different," Childress explains. "He's 100 mph every day. He's never looking for the break. He's not looking to hide. We're always asking him to slow down. Because frankly, the other players can't go that hard."

Rice remembers the first time he spied Peterson. "Adrian was alone in the gym doing pull-ups. I just stood there and watched him, lifting himself up over and over. Everyone else had gone home. But he was still there." Since that day, Rice has witnessed more miracles. Players dragged 15 yards, defensive clusters blown out like confetti, speed that blurs the eyes. "We call him A-Robot," Rice says. "I can't remember ever seeing him exhausted. He'll tell us not to bend down when we're tired. He'll say, 'There's no air down there. Stand up. Lean on me.'"

During the Colts game, Peterson was true to form. As players tumbled, he nimbly leaped over their fallen bodies. Defenders tried to drag him down, but he shook them off like a grizzly shuddering off snow. Waiting for his go on the sideline, his legs jerked and lifted like sewing needles. He pranced, swung his hips, watched his teammates, cheered when they executed, fist-bumped as they jogged off the field. When his turn came, he raced back to the line, every play a Christmas morning. So astonishing was his effort, onlooking Colts president Bill Polian vociferously swore after each Peterson play.

None of this mattered to Peterson in the end.

"I feel like I didn't do enough," he says softly.

What more could you have done?

"I could have come up with the big play," he says flatly. "I could have done my job."

Before the season started, when all was promise and optimism, Peterson explained how his own expectations came to be. "When I was young, I had the dream of the NFL," he says, plopping down on a massage table after a camp practice. "My mom put it into my head: Don't settle for less. That mind-set has stayed with me."

Growing up in rural Palestine, Texas, with his mother, Bonita, he made a list of goals and posted it on his door.

Get on top of my grades

Get in my Bible more

Stay out of trouble

Be the best that I can be

"Believe it or not," he says, "some of the same things I did last year on the field I've been doing since middle school. I push myself harder. I do extra drills. No matter how tired I am, I make sure I'm first. I got a long way to go, but I figure if I just keep doing the things I have been doing, I should be all right."

Peterson tells a story about winning Offensive Rookie of the Year. How, after he broke his collarbone in 2006 during his final season at Oklahoma, some scouts saw him as damaged goods. How, before the season, he and some other rookies were asked to pose with the ROY trophy for an NFL promotion. How, when it was his turn to hold it, he cradled it like his baby girl, and thought, See you at the end of the season.

"I'm pretty sure other players said the same thing to themselves," he says, raising his eyebrows. "But I doubt they took it as seriously as I did. When I held it, it was like it was already mine."

For all his physical dominance, Peterson plays a head game. "You can tell yourself anything," he explains. "If mentally you don't cave in, if you push yourself beyond where you thought your body could go, you can do almost anything. A lot of people lack that ambition. I figured that out pretty early."

"I've been full speed since I was little," Peterson adds, shrugging. "I'm a spaz."

We all know what it looks like when promise fails. (Tony Mandarich.) When potential evaporates. (Lawrence Phillips.) When our chosen one descends into common humanity. (Ryan Leaf.) Which is why, when we see promise exceeded, when someone comes along who takes the job seriously—we can all be forgiven if we go a bit wobbly in the knees.

Even if he doesn't.

This, like everything else, is a result of perspective. When Peterson was seven, he watched as his eight-year-old brother, Brian, was struck by a drunk driver while riding his bike on the sidewalk. Brian was thrown into the air, landing on his head. A week later, the family decided to discontinue life support. "That was a lot of hurt," says Adrian's father, Nelson, who had split from Adrian's mom years earlier and worked in town as a forklift operator. "To have that taken away from him. They were like twins."

It was shortly after the accident when Nelson phoned Adrian and told him he was going to start playing organized football. Nelson would coach his son every day. Order another kid to hit him, four, five, six times in a row. Show Adrian how to meet the contact, stop bracing for the impact. Tell him to make his own daylight. "I made it mandatory that he be the first one to come across the line during sprints," says Nelson. "Then I'd make a side bet with the other kids: If they beat him, they'd get out of running. But he never lost."

Then, with Peterson entering middle school, Nelson went away to prison, sentenced to 10 years for drug-related money laundering (he served eight). "When he left," Adrian says, "all I could think about was how many games he was going to miss."

Peterson's drive began to slack. He played, but his appetite diminished. He made some questionable friends. Let his grades slip. Acted out in class. His mother propped him up, told him, "If no one believes in you, I believe in you." But there were money troubles, family troubles. Somebody threw a rock through the school window, and Peterson was blamed. People he believed were his friends weren't. As he started high school, nothing was solid. Nothing made sense. He felt, he says, "crazy." Then one day after Peterson's sophomore season, his father called him. The two had spoken weekly since Nelson was sent to prison, but this conversation wasn't the typical how-you-doing. "He said, 'I know. I know you are the best running back in Texas. But you got to show the world that you are the best.'"

Peterson closes his eyes for a moment.

"My next year, my junior year, I blew up. I worked my way up to being the number one recruit in the nation. That phone call was the defining moment of my life."

Peterson says he was never angry with his father. That he worked to understand. "The things that he was doing, they were bad, but he was also a coach in the community, helping kids who didn't have much try to do something with their lives. People say, Oh, he was messing with drugs, so he's got to be this bad person, this gangster. People judge him. But me? I have nothing but love for him."

When Nelson hears this, his voice cracks. "We share a bond like no other. I tell him every day, Don't waste your opportunities, your life is good. But like a light switch, it can cut off on you. Bam. Just like that."

Back in the day, Peterson was a big rabbit hunter. Pop them, skin them, eat them. He'd walk to the woods near his house and fire his BB gun at will. Nobody worried he'd put his eye out. "I was a good shot," he says. "It's funny. At my house now, in Eden Prairie, you see a lot of rabbits. My cousin and I joke, Man, these rabbits wouldn't stand a chance if we was in Palestine."

The town where Peterson grew up is the sort of place where roads start off gravel and end up dirt. The top two employers are the Texas Department of Criminal Justice and Wal-Mart. Still, Peterson misses home. "If I could live anywhere, I'd live in Texas."

Come winter, he often finds himself looking out his windows, the landscape an unfamiliar, deadening white. "Sometimes it seems like it doesn't get dark at night," he says forlornly. "And I'm like, Damn, my family, all my friends are back South."

Peterson is next in line at Cold Stone Creamery. Behind him, several people snap pictures with their camera phones. He takes his ice cream and sits outside, the iron chair buckling a little as he sits down. "I lost my first toenail today," he says proudly, pointing down with his tiny plastic spoon. Then he talks about having his four-year-old daughter, Adeja, "the smartest decision I ever made." Peterson was 19 when he became a father and remains close friends with Adeja's mother, who is raising their daughter in another state. "People tried to steer me away from having a child," he says, "but I wanted her. Bringing my daughter into this world is the best thing I've ever done. I'm happiest when I'm with her."

Happier than on the field? Peterson smiles the smile. "A man should take care of his family. That's the most important thing."

His thoughts return, as they often do, to his parents. His mother ran track at the University of Houston, went to the Junior Olympics. "Then she got pregnant with my brother. And right after him, she got pregnant with me. So her track career was done for good." His dad, a star hoops player at Idaho State, had his NBA dreams derailed when his brother accidentally shot him in the leg. "For a full year, they were talking about cutting his leg off."

Peterson has stopped eating, ice cream oozing to liquid in its cup. "I feel a responsibility to carry their dreams," he says softly. "I don't just do this for myself." He leans back in his chair, the cameras of fans clicking behind his head. He doesn't hear them. He is someplace else. Earlier that morning, Peterson was signing balls—before the first few games and inadvertent lessons about what he could and could not control—and he pondered his blessings.

"I sometimes wonder, Why me?" he said. "But no answer comes."

He clutched his pen for a moment to wave at a little boy. The boy, overcome, clutched his father's leg to steady himself.

"I figure," Peterson continued, "I should stop wondering. Sometimes there just isn't an explanation. Sometimes," he said, tossing a football into the air, then catching it, "you just get lucky."

Defensive end Jared Allen (69) was signed as a free agent from Kansas City prior to the 2008 season. His enthusiasm and tough play provided inspirational leadership for the Vikings defense. PHOTOGRAPH COURTESY OF THE MINNESOTA VIKINGS.

The Vikings lost their first two games, and quarterback Tarvaris Jackson was benched in favor of 37-year-old journeyman Gus Frerotte, who had been a backup quarterback for Daunte Culpepper in 2003 and 2004. He had made 82 starts in his 14-year career. His best year had been in 1996, when he started 16 games for the Washington Redskins and was selected to play in the Pro Bowl. Frerotte was not a very mobile quarterback, but he still had a strong arm and his veteran leadership steadied the team and got them back on the winning track. He was 8–3 as a starter before suffering a slight fracture in his lower back in the December 7 win at Detroit. Jackson stepped in and threw a fourth-quarter touchdown pass to Viasanthe Shiancoe to seal the 20–16 victory.

Minneapolis Star Tribune, December 7, 2008
LARGER THAN LIFE
THE VIKINGS MADE A BIG INVESTMENT IN JARED ALLEN, BUT THE DEFENSIVE END HAS BEEN WORTH EVERY PENNY
Chip Scoggins
The conversation lasted only about 10 minutes, but it clearly touched Jared Allen.

Former Vikings great Jim Marshall pulled Allen aside after a recent practice, and the two chatted about football, money, the pursuit of championships and their mutual admiration. It wasn't heart-to-heart; it was old school to old school.

"It was kind of nostalgic to sit there and talk to a man who is a legend in this league," Allen said. Marshall concluded by giving Allen some advice: Don't change your approach.

"He's just one hell of a football player," Marshall said. "I really admire him."

The Vikings knew they were getting one of the NFL's premier pass rushers when they traded for Allen last winter, then made him the highest-paid defensive player in league history with a six-year, $74.5 million contract. But the impact he has had on the field, in the locker room and on the entire organization has exceeded expectations.

Allen has a chance to repeat as the NFL's sack leader, the Vikings defense is ranked in the top 10 and, more important, the team is in first place in the NFC North.

"Anybody who gets a lucrative contract like that kind of feels the weight of the world on their shoulders and a lot of pressure," linebacker Ben Leber said. "But just knowing him and his personality, he kind of let that go by the wayside and let his instincts and talent take over. Look where he's at right now."

Allen leads the team in sacks (10½) and quarterback hurries (41) and is the reigning NFC Defensive Player of the Week, despite playing the past four games with a serious shoulder injury. He ranks ninth in the NFL in sacks (4½ behind the leader, Miami's Joey Porter) and has tied the NFL record with two safeties.

Since entering the NFL in 2004, Allen's 53½ sacks rank first in the league. His pass-rushing prowess has made more than one left tackle turn jelly-legged and forced offenses to get creative with protection.

"I think I can beat anybody on any play," Allen said. "I know that's not true. But when I go on the field, I think I'm the best player there is. I have to have that mindset.

"Are you tougher mentally than the guy across from you? To outwork him and just beat him snap after snap after snap. If he beats me, I'll get back up and go back at him."

HE'S EARNING HIS MONEY

Allen's live-wire personality, goofball antics and willingness to play through a shoulder injury that typically sidelines players two to four weeks have brought a certain energy to the defense and team. His tachometer is always red-lining, and he has refused to alter his approach even in the face of $90,000 in fines and a summons to the NFL offices.

"He's definitely a guy that leads by example on the field," said Vikings long snapper Cullen Loeffler, one of Allen's closest friends on the team. "He has just an unforgiving attitude. He's going full-bore every play. When he says he's going to do something, he usually does it."

That mindset has allowed Allen to avoid a common pitfall in professional sports. He signed a massive contract, but his play has not slipped. His contract calls for the fourth-highest total of guaranteed money ($31,000,069) in NFL history. That alone brings its own set of expectations, but he isn't burdened.

"It's not pressure, but it's a perception that people have," he said. "You can have bad years for any given reason. But if you get paid, people look at it like, 'Well, this guy shut it down.' But my motivations aren't contract-driven. Some people's motivation is to get paid. Once they get paid, they don't know how to reevaluate themselves.

"It's just like when I came into the NFL. My only goal in life since I was eight was to get drafted in the NFL. I got drafted in the NFL, and that was a scary day because I reached a life goal. Now what do I do? Do I want to be a guy that says, 'Hey, I'm in the NFL?' Or do I want to be a dominant player and hopefully one day be enshrined next to the guys who are the best to ever play this game? To me, that's what it is.

"Hopefully when I'm done, people will look back and say, 'That was one of the best defensive players to play the game.' And that he did it right. He played tough, he played hard, he played hurt, when things weren't going his way he didn't pout. I want that to be my legacy, not that he was the highest-paid defensive player in the league."

Allen's impact is easily measured. His presence has enabled defensive tackle Kevin Williams to face fewer double teams inside. Williams has responded with 8½ sacks, tied for first among NFL defensive tackles.

Allen's ability to get consistent pressure on the quarterback also has helped the secondary and Vikings pass defense, which ranked last in the NFL in 2007 but has moved up to number 21 this season.

"We thought we would get the sacks and that type of production," defensive coordinator Leslie Frazier said. "But he just brings so much energy. Along with the fact that he is a very hard-working football player. When your highest-paid player is maybe your hardest-working player, that bodes well for us as coaches when we're trying to talk to guys about the things that we think are important. He epitomizes what a coach looks for in a football player."

A FREE SPIRIT . . . AND A SOBER ONE

Teammates appreciate Allen's talent and work ethic and seemed amused by his daredevil personality and '80s mullet. Allen once showed up in the Kansas City Chiefs' locker room wearing a Borat mankini, according to his agent Ken Harris, who has a running argument with his client about whether Allen can defeat a bear in "hand-to-paw combat." Allen has run with the bulls in Pamplona, Spain, and gone swimming with sharks in Hawaii, although he was inside a cage for that one.

"His life is one long Bill and Ted adventure," Harris said.

Allen doesn't do anything halfway, but he has shaped up after getting two drunken-driving arrests while playing for Kansas City. He has embraced sobriety with the same enthusiasm that caused him to once purchase a drum set and guitar even though he had no clue how to play them. He also bought a smoke machine for effects.

"He just has a big personality," linebacker Chad Greenway said. "He's loud, he's funny, always cracking jokes. He's a good teammate. He makes a lot of people better in different ways."

Allen admitted it took time for him to adjust to a new team, new scheme and new city. He's also had to compensate for his shoulder injury, which was diagnosed as a third-degree sprain of the AC joint.

"I'm not going to let something stupid keep me out," he said. "I get something out of a hard day's work. You come off the football field and you got blood all over your pants and you're beat up and you're like, 'Damn, how I am going to get back out there and take this next snap?'"

That mindset is partly why Frazier described Allen as a "coach's dream."

"You don't always find great players being team players," he said.

Allen said his approach was reinforced during his talk with Marshall, the NFL record holder for consecutive games started. Marshall pointed to a wall inside the practice facility where banners representing the team's division championships hang.

"He was telling me that those plastic banners were the only thing they played for," Allen said. "That's what football is. Sports in general are bragging rights. At the end of the year my team was better than your team. That's what these banners represent. For me, whatever my personal stats are will never [equal] a Super Bowl or a division champion. A championship will outweigh any personal stats I have."

●

Jackson led the team to a 35–14 win over the Super Bowl–bound Arizona Cardinals on December 14. He completed 11 out of 17 passes for 163 yards and four touchdown passes, and was selected the NFC Offensive Player of the Week.

The Vikings clinched their first divisional championship since 2000 with a 20–19 victory over the New York Giants on December 28—on a 50-yard field goal by Ryan Longwell as time expired. This made possible the first home playoff game since 2000.

Since only half of the 55,000 season-ticket holders bought playoff tickets, team officials had to scramble to avoid a television blackout. Per NFL rules, the game could not be televised locally if not sold out—defined as 62,000 tickets for the Metrodome—72 hours before kickoff time. Perhaps because of the bad economy, ticket sales were slow—or maybe fans hadn't recovered from the heartbreak of 1998. Whatever the reason, there were 8,000 tickets left at the blackout deadline.

Fortunately, the NFL twice granted 24-hour extensions, and the game was finally sold out on Saturday, January 3, one day before kickoff. Unfortunately, the Vikings lost to the Philadelphia Eagles 26–14.

The prospects for the future look bright, however. The team has shown strong improvement in 2007 and 2008, and has many star players on the roster ready to take the team back into the playoffs again in 2009.

Adrian Peterson did not suffer a sophomore jinx. He led the league in rushing with 1,760 yards—going over 100 yards in 10 games despite having defenses set up to stop him. The offensive line, anchored on the left by tackle Bryant McKinnie, guard Steve Hutchinson, and center Matt Birk, looks strong, and the defense led the league in fewest yards rushing for the third consecutive year—an NFL record. Passing defense, ranked thirty-second—out of 32 teams—in yards allowed in 2006 and 2007, improved to eighteenth in 2008.

Hopefully, we will be reading many more stories about this new Vikings dynasty in the next few years.

PUBLICATION HISTORY

CHAPTER 1: THE DUTCHMAN AND 36 STIFFS

"Pro Grid Loops Battle Over Twin Cities Berth: Stadium Lease Is Issue," Reidar Lund, *St. Paul Pioneer Press*, November 23, 1959. Reprinted with permission from *St. Paul Pioneer Press*.

"Marshall, Brown Helped NFL Bid," from "Sid Hartman's Roundup," *Minneapolis Tribune*, January 29, 1960. Reprinted with permission of *Star Tribune*, Minneapolis, MN.

"Twin Cities Unite in NFL Entry," Halsey Hall, *Sporting News*, February 10, 1960.

"Vikings Sit Down at NFL's Table—Munch Leftovers: Each Old-Line Club Offers 8 Names on Available List; Number Includes Fringe Players Scheduled for Release," Joe King, *Sporting News*, February 1, 1961.

"A Dutchman and 36 Stiffs," Jim Klobuchar, from chapter 2 in *Purple Hearts and Golden Memories: 35 Years with the Minnesota Vikings* (Coal Valley, Ill.: Quality Sports Publications, 1995).

"Vikings Blast Bears 37–13 in Debut: Tarkenton Hurls Four TD Passes," Jim Klobuchar, *Minneapolis Tribune*, September 18, 1961. Reprinted with permission of *Star Tribune*, Minneapolis, MN.

"Zamberletti Strong after 40-Hour Vigil," Roger Rosenblum, *St. Paul Pioneer Press*, August 2, 1964. Reprinted with permission from *St. Paul Pioneer Press*.

Excerpt from chapter 10 in Jim Klobuchar, *True Hearts and Purple Heads: An Unauthorized Biography of a Football Team* (Minneapolis: Ross and Haines, Inc., 1970). Reprinted with permission of Ross and Haines, Hudson, Wisconsin.

"Tark Planned Scramble on Crucial Pass Play," *St. Paul Pioneer Press*, October 5, 1964.

"Packer–Viking Tilt Was Last Word in Customer Football," Lloyd Larson, *Milwaukee Sentinel*, October 6, 1964.

"Marshall Loses Sleep But Not Friends," Roger Rosenblum, *St. Paul Pioneer Press*, October 27, 1964. Reprinted with permission from *St. Paul Pioneer Press*.

"A Woman's Guide to the Vikings," Barbara Flanagan, *Minneapolis Tribune*, August 15, 1965. Reprinted with permission of *Star Tribune*, Minneapolis, MN.

CHAPTER 2: 40 FOR 60

"Building a Viking Powerhouse," Bill McGrane, from chapter 7 in *Bud: The Other Side of the Glacier* (New York: Harper and Row Publishers, 1986).

"Writing Out Loud" column, Bill Boni, *St. Paul Dispatch*, October 6, 1969. Reprinted with permission from *St. Paul Pioneer Press*.

"'69 Vikings Have No MVP Since Kapp Refuses Trophy," Ralph Reeve, *St. Paul Pioneer Press*, December 18, 1969. Reprinted with permission from *St. Paul Pioneer Press*.

"The Worse They Look, the Better Vikes Are," Wells Twombly, *Sporting News*, January 17, 1970.

"Wham, Bam, Stram!" Tex Maule, *Sports Illustrated*, January 19, 1970.

"Vikings Refuse to Meet Kapp Demands," Merrill Swanson, *Minneapolis Tribune*, August 6, 1970. Reprinted with permission of *Star Tribune*, Minneapolis, MN.

"Viking Spectators Felt the Cold, But TV Viewers Saw the Snow," Brian Anderson, *Minneapolis Tribune*, November 23, 1970. Reprinted with permission of *Star Tribune*, Minneapolis, MN.

"Cold? Not Vikings: Play Best in Chill; But Bears Need Heat," Dick Gordon, *Minneapolis Star*, December 7, 1970. Reprinted with permission of *Star Tribune*, Minneapolis, MN.

"Message from Minnesota: Three Dots and a Dash," Pat Putnam, *Sports Illustrated*, December 14, 1970.

"Pigskins preceded by pâté on asphalt," Jerry Kirshenbaum, *Sports Illustrated*, December 6, 1971.

"Trucking Keeps Fans in High Gear," *Minnesota Truck Merchandiser*, Fall 1978.

CHAPTER 3: SUPER LOSERS

"Two Stars, Two Orbits," Jim Klobuchar and Fran Tarkenton, from chapter 2 of *Tarkenton* (New York: Harper and Row, 1976).

"From Worlds Apart, They Joined Together," Skip Myslenski, *Philadelphia Inquirer*, October 19, 1973.

"Eye Opener" column, Don Riley, *St. Paul Pioneer Press*, January 14, 1974. Reprinted with permission from *St. Paul Pioneer Press*.

"An afternoon of disappointment: Former Viking Karl Kassulke," Dick Gordon, *Minneapolis Star*, January 13, 1975. Reprinted with permission of *Star Tribune*, Minneapolis, MN.

"Vikes lose in final 24 seconds: Cowboys pull out 17–14 upset on 50-yard bomb," Ralph Reeve, *St. Paul Pioneer Press*, December 29, 1975. Reprinted with permission from *St. Paul Pioneer Press*.

Excerpt from chapter 1 in Thomas Gifford, *Benchwarmer Bob: The Story of Bob Lurtsema* (Blue Earth, Minn.: Piper Publishing, Inc., 1974).

"Nobody Sends in His Plays," Bob Oates, *Los Angeles Times*, December 23, 1976.

"Vikings: Super Losers," Jim Murray, *Los Angeles Times*, January 4, 1977.

Excerpt from chapter 14 of Jim Klobuchar and Jeff Siemon, *Will the Vikings Ever Win the Super Bowl?* (New York: HarperCollins Publishers, 1977). Copyright 1977 by Jim Klobuchar. Reprinted by permission of HarperCollins Publishers.

"Page put on irrevocable waivers," Ralph Reeve, *St. Paul Pioneer Press*, October 11, 1978. Reprinted with permission from *St. Paul Pioneer Press*.

CHAPTER 4: THE MAGIC BOUNCES AWAY

Robert T. Smith column from *Minneapolis Tribune*, November 5, 1979. Reprinted with permission of *Star Tribune*, Minneapolis, MN.

"Vikings win title again, but . . . it was no less than astonishing," Joe Soucheray, *Minneapolis Tribune*, December 15, 1980. Reprinted with permission of *Star Tribune*, Minneapolis, MN.

"Ahmad Rashad: Viking's 'good life' matches his elegance, savvy on the field," Joe Logan, *Minneapolis Star*, July 27, 1981. Reprinted with permission of *Star Tribune*, Minneapolis, MN.

"Where the Sun Don't Shine," Jay Weiner, from chapter 3 in *Stadium Games: Fifty Years of Big League Greed and Bush League Boondoggles* (Minneapolis: University of Minnesota Press, 2000).

"Party's over: Vike gourmands hold tail-end tailgate party; Met tailgaters wonder whether parties will be same at bus stop," Ozzie St. George, *St. Paul Pioneer Press*, December 21, 1981. Reprinted with permission from *St. Paul Pioneer Press*.

"Vikings begin search for dance line," Theresa Monsour, *St. Paul Pioneer Press*, May 11, 1984. Reprinted with permission from *St. Paul Pioneer Press*.

"Ironman test leaves Vikings aching," Bob Sansevere, *Minneapolis Star and Tribune*, July 22, 1984. Reprinted with permission of *Star Tribune*, Minneapolis, MN.

"A Most Enjoyable Year," Bill McGrane, from chapter 15 in *Bud: The Other Side of the Glacier* (New York: Harper and Row Publishers, 1986).

"Union workers join football players on picket lines: The boredom/13,000 watch replacement Vikings lose to Packers 23–16," M. L. Smith, *Minneapolis Star Tribune*, October 5, 1987. Reprinted with permission of *Star Tribune*, Minneapolis, MN.

"Magic bounces away: Vikings' hopes disappear," Doug Grow, *Minneapolis Star Tribune*, January 18, 1988. Reprinted with permission of *Star Tribune*, Minneapolis, MN.

"It's Never Worse Than He Expected," Jim Murray, *Los Angeles Times*, September 7, 1989.

"Sudden Impact: A megadeal sent Herschel Walker to Minnesota, where he ran wild," Peter King, *Sports Illustrated*, October 23, 1989.

"Attempt to Foster Unity Puts Vikings on High Wire: G.M. Takes Novel Approach to Solving Team's Problems," Gregg Wong, *Sporting News*, June 18, 1990.

CHAPTER 5: A NEW SHERIFF IN TOWN

"Vikings to buy out Pohlad, Jacobs," Ray Richardson, Bob Sansevere, and Charley Walters, *St. Paul Pioneer Press*, December 17, 1991. Reprinted with permission from *St. Paul Pioneer Press*.

"Going to War," Dennis Green with Gene McGivern, from chapter 11 of *Dennis Green: No Room for Crybabies* (Champaign, Ill.: Sports Publishing, Inc., 1997). Reprinted by permission of Sports Publishing, LLC.

"Most fans enjoy Vikings' get-tough ads: Only 30 percent say they're too harsh," Dennis Bracken, *Minneapolis Star Tribune*, July 10, 1992. Reprinted with permission of *Star Tribune*, Minneapolis, MN.

"Is It Easy Being Green? A rookie coach puts the Vikings back on top," Frank Deford, *Newsweek*, November 23, 1992. Copyright 1992 Newsweek, Inc. All rights reserved. Used by permission and protected by the Copyright Laws of the United States. The printing, copying, redistribution, or retransmission of the material without express written permission is prohibited.

"Vikings send message: Pack it in. A 27–7 romp ends Packers' playoff run," Jim Souhan, *Minneapolis Star Tribune*, December 28, 1992. Reprinted with permission of *Star Tribune*, Minneapolis, MN.

"Ahead for Vikings: blackouts. General Mills fund will soon run dry," Jerry Zgoda, *Minneapolis Star Tribune*, December 17, 1993. Reprinted with permission of *Star Tribune*, Minneapolis, MN.

"Walsh savors playoff success," Mike Augustin, *St. Paul Pioneer Press*, January 2, 1995. Reprinted with permission from *St. Paul Pioneer Press*.

"Blame for team's problems lies with Green, Headrick: Discontent among the players is rampant," Patrick Reusse, *Minneapolis Star Tribune*, January 31, 1995. Reprinted with permission of *Star Tribune*, Minneapolis, MN.

"Vikings fans will pony up for Johnson," Bob Sansevere, *St. Paul Pioneer Press*, December 22, 1996. Reprinted with permission from *St. Paul Pioneer Press*.

"If it lasts until tomorrow," Dennis Green with Gene McGivern, from chapter 19 in *Dennis Green: No Room for Crybabies* (Champaign, Ill.: Sports Publishing, Inc., 1997). Reprinted by permission of Sports Publishing, LLC.

"Warnings: Can Green, the embattled underdog, weather controversy from his book?" Paula Parrish, *Pro Football Weekly*, November 30, 1997.

"Embattled Green Laughs Last," Bob Glauber, *Newsday*, December 28, 1977.

"If a paper's going to have sports columnists, it can't tell them what to think," Lou Gelfand, *Minneapolis Star Tribune*, January 4, 1998. Reprinted with permission of *Star Tribune*, Minneapolis, MN.

"Vikings won't produce lead owner until NFL cements deadline," Tom Powers, *St. Paul Pioneer Press*, August 1, 1997. Reprinted with permission from *St. Paul Pioneer Press*.

"I Gotta Get Me One of These," Jay Weiner, from chapter 6 of *Stadium Games: Fifty Years of Big League Greed and Bush League Boondoggles* (Minneapolis: University of Minnesota Press, 2000).

"Vikings stadium? Our perspective: One sports palace at a time, please," editorial, *Minneapolis Star Tribune*, October 16, 1996. Reprinted with permission of *Star Tribune*, Minneapolis, MN.

CHAPTER 6: PURPLE PRIDE

"With Red in saddle, Vikings sitting pretty," Mickey Herskowitz, *Houston Chronicle*, July 6, 1998.

"Second Coming: Rejuvenated after a year in retirement, Randall Cunningham is setting the league on its ear and leading the Vikings to new heights," Austin Murphy, *Sports Illustrated*, December 7, 1998.

"Purple Wide: The last leg of the Vikings' season will be remembered for missed opportunities and an overtime loss to Atlanta," Jeff Seidel, *St. Paul Pioneer Press*, January 18, 1999. Reprinted with permission from *St. Paul Pioneer Press*.

"Facing the unfortunate truth: We're Minnesotans, so we lose," Nick Coleman, *St. Paul Pioneer Press*, January 19, 1999. Reprinted with permission from *St. Paul Pioneer Press*.

"Rampage: St. Louis blitzes Vikings with 35-point second half," Jim Souhan, *Minneapolis Star Tribune*, January 17, 2000. Reprinted with permission of *Star Tribune*, Minneapolis, MN.

"Leaving with class: Randall McDaniel was a man of few words, but he will leave an impact in the community, especially at a Plymouth grade school," Patrick Reusse, *Minneapolis Star Tribune*, February 12, 2000. Reprinted with permission of *Star Tribune*, Minneapolis, MN.

"Scouting Report: Coach Dennis Green is putting all his eggs in the basket of young, strong-armed quarterback Daunte Culpepper," Josh Elliott, *Sports Illustrated*, August 28, 2000.

"Viking Fever on the rise: Minnesota gets the home-field advantage for the playoffs if it wins Sunday," Randy Furst, *Minneapolis Star Tribune*, December 4, 2000. Reprinted with permission of *Star Tribune*, Minneapolis, MN.

"Vikings' Green Rewards McCombs, Who Stood by Coach Against All Advice," Bill Plaschke, *Los Angeles Times*, December 10, 2000.

"NFC Championship: Ugly playoff loss, not season, will stay with fans," Sid Hartman, *Minneapolis Star Tribune*, January 15, 2001. Reprinted with permission of *Star Tribune*, Minneapolis, MN.

"Goodbye, Mr. Smith," Dave Kindred, *Sporting News*, February 19, 2001.

"Vikings star Carter saving best for last: Receiver working harder than ever for final season," Jarrett Bell, *USA Today*, July 3, 2001. From USA TODAY, a division of Gannett Co., Inc. Reprinted with permission.

"Requiem for a Viking: It took his untimely death for the world to learn about Korey Stringer," Steve Rushin, *Sports Illustrated*, August 13, 2001.

"Play–don't play debate means very, very little," Dan Barreiro, *Minneapolis Star Tribune*, September 14, 2001. Reprinted with permission of *Star Tribune*, Minneapolis, MN.

"The mouth that roared: We've had it up to here with Randy Moss, who needs to get his act together immediately," Tom Powers, *St. Paul Pioneer Press*, December 10, 2001. Reprinted with permission from *St. Paul Pioneer Press*.

"Green is out as Vikings coach," Brandt Williams, Minnesota Public Radio, January 4, 2002. Copyright 2002 Minnesota Public Radio. Used by permission of Minnesota Public Radio and MPR News (mpr.org). All rights reserved.

CHAPTER 7: ALL DAY LONG

"Give the ball to Moss: How does a rookie head coach revive a once-potent offense and reinvigorate a sulking superstar? To the Vikings' Mike Tice, the answer is simple," Kevin Seifert, *Minneapolis Star Tribune*, April 26, 2002. Reprinted with permission of *Star Tribune*, Minneapolis, MN.

"Gone in a Flash: The full-of-surprises Vikings take a last-second fall from playoff contention and could lose their coach," Bill Williamson, *St. Paul Pioneer Press*, December 29, 2003. Reprinted with permission from *St. Paul Pioneer Press*.

"More to Birk than meets the eye," Bob Sansevere, *St. Paul Pioneer Press*, July 18, 2004. Reprinted with permission from *St. Paul Pioneer Press*.

"Thanks to football, a really silent night," Rev. Peter Geisendorfer-Lindgren, *Minneapolis Star Tribune*, December 24, 2004. Reprinted with permission of *Star Tribune*, Minneapolis, MN.

"Freak show," Kevin Seifert, *Minneapolis Star Tribune*, January 10, 2005. Reprinted with permission of *Star Tribune*, Minneapolis, MN.

"Moss arrives, but he won't be unpacking his baggage," Monty Poole, *Oakland Tribune*, May 1, 2005. Reprinted with permission from the *Oakland Tribune*.

"Wilf is ready to bring Vikings into the family," Jay Weiner and Randy Furst, *Minneapolis Star Tribune*, May 22, 2005. Reprinted with permission of *Star Tribune*, Minneapolis, MN.

"Mr. Big's shot," Paul Attner, *Sporting News*, August 26, 2005.

"Vikings show disrespect to state: After 20 years on the police blotter, it's time for reform," editorial, *Minneapolis Star Tribune*, October 14, 2005. Reprinted with permission of *Star Tribune*, Minneapolis, MN.

"At hangout, to know Tice is to miss him," Patrick Reusse, *Minneapolis Star Tribune*, January 3, 2006. Reprinted with permission of *Star Tribune*, Minneapolis, MN.

"Culpepper went from icon to outcast in Minnesota," Alex Marvez, *South Florida Sun–Sentinel*, April 11, 2006. Reprinted with permission from the *South Florida Sun-Sentinel*.

"Vikings ready to see their future: Jackson has earned respect with attitude, though not yet play," Larry Weisman, *USA Today*, August 28, 2007. From USA TODAY, a division of Gannett Co., Inc. Reprinted with permission.

"All Day Long: Winning formula is simple: Give the ball to Peterson," Kevin Seifert, *Minneapolis Star Tribune*, November 5, 2007. Reprinted with permission of *Star Tribune*, Minneapolis, MN.

"Please don't remain calm," Allison Glock, *ESPN The Magazine*, September 23, 2008.

"Larger than life: The Vikings made a big investment in Jared Allen, but the defensive end has been worth every penny," Chip Scoggins, *Minneapolis Star Tribune*, December 7, 2008. Reprinted with permission of *Star Tribune*, Minneapolis, MN.

ARMAND PETERSON is a retired engineer and manager and a lifelong sports enthusiast who had Vikings season tickets at the old Met. He is coauthor of *Town Ball: The Glory Days of Minnesota Amateur Baseball* (Minnesota, 2006).